# MODERN BUSINESS GEOGRAPHY

By Ellsworth Huntington
*Research Associate in Geography, Yale University*
AND Sumner W. Cushing
*Late Head of the Department of Geography in the
State Normal School, Salem, Massachusetts*

Introduction by Frank M. McMurry
*Teachers College, Columbia University*

REVISED EDITION

WORLD BOOK COMPANY
Yonkers-on-Hudson, New York

WORLD BOOK COMPANY
THE HOUSE OF APPLIED KNOWLEDGE

*Established 1905 by Caspar W. Hodgson*

YONKERS-ON-HUDSON, NEW YORK
2126 PRAIRIE AVENUE, CHICAGO
Also BOSTON : ATLANTA : DALLAS
SAN FRANCISCO : PORTLAND : MANILA

IN *Modern Business Geography*, the young student is called upon to consider problems for which the text has given the necessary background and to make use of geographical facts in thinking for himself. Such a textbook may well prove itself a worthy addition to the list of "books that apply the world's knowledge to the world's needs."

HCMBG-11

Copyright 1925, 1930, 1932, by World Book Company
Copyright in Great Britain
*All rights reserved*

PRINTED IN U.S.A.

# PREFACE

This book is designed for students at any stage during the five years or so after they have finished the usual course in elementary geography.

The book has two marked characteristics: First, it is grounded on the economic basis expressed in the four terms *Primary Production*, *Transportation*, *Manufacturing*, and *Consumption*. Second, it combines a large number of stimulating problems with an interesting text that guides the pupils and helps them to work out the problems.

The use of the economic basis is peculiarly effective in reawakening the interest of pupils who think that they have already had enough geography. Experience shows that it makes them realize the existence of great realms which their previous work has not touched. By the time the average child has finished the sixth or seventh grade he has studied each of the continents twice. Further regional study is likely to be irksome, and a really new turn to the subject is needed. The study of commercial geography according to the common plan of treating one commodity after another gives a new approach, it is true. Unfortunately, after a few commodities have been discussed the mode of treatment almost inevitably becomes stereotyped; since no new principles are brought forward, the pupils lose interest at the most critical period.

The method here employed attacks this difficulty by beginning with a geographical treatment of commodities in connection with the principles of primary production. Before this has time to become tiresome the field of transportation is taken up and a wholly new set of principles is introduced. A little later the field of manufacturing is introduced, giving a fresh point of view. Finally, the study of the field of consumption opens up another field, which maintains the student's interest to the end of the course.

Interest is also awakened and renewed by means of frequent questions, exercises, and problems. These are the result of prolonged experiments with normal school students and with classes of children. The United States is treated extensively in the problems of every chapter, as well as in special chapters. The rest of the world is treated more briefly, but each continent receives a special exercise in one of the four problem chapters which form the final parts of the four sections of the book. Thus material is provided whereby the pupils review the regional geography of the whole world, but in such a way that it seems to them like a new study, which in fact it is.

The highly developed form of the problems and exercises has also the effect of making the book elastic. By omitting a number of them, or by assigning some of the problems to individuals for report to the class, the whole subject can be covered in half a year. If all parts are carefully studied, the book provides material for a well-rounded course of a year.

The original draft of this book was to a large extent the work of the junior author, whose lamented death occurred before the book had received its final revision. Mr. Cushing was responsible for the general plan of the book, and for its development along the lines of the four great economic fields. To him also is due the pedagogical method illustrated in the text and problems, and especially in the problem chapters at the ends of the four sections. It should be added, however, that since Mr. Cushing's death the book has been completely rewritten to bring it up to date.

The death of Mr. Cushing makes it impossible to acknowledge all the various sources from which help was received. Therefore, rather than acknowledge the kindness of some and omit others, it has seemed wise merely to express deep appreciation for the services of all who have had a part in the book, and to omit personal acknowledgments. The work of Miss Lenox E. Chase of the Mount Vernon High School of Commerce, however, must be mentioned, for Miss Chase has had an important share in the preparation of the exercises and tables. As a student of Mr. Cushing's she knew and practiced his methods, and her assistance has been most valuable throughout.

ACKNOWLEDGMENTS

THE authors regret that it is impossible in the space available to acknowledge every source that has been drawn upon for information in the preparation of this book, in both the original and the revised editions. Particular acknowledgment must be made, however, for the statistical maps or drawings which have been reproduced directly from various publications:

To the Department of Agriculture for the following maps published in the latest issue of *A Graphic Summary of American Agriculture*: Figures 5, Cotton; 31, Corn; 33, Rice; 44, Barley; 50, Vegetables; 52, Sugar Crops; 57, Citrus Fruits; 60, Peaches; 70, Sheep and Lambs; 77, Swine; 78, Chickens; 79, Horses, Mules, and Colts.

To the Forest Service, United States Department of Agriculture, for Figure 109, showing the United States National Forests.

To Finch and Baker's *Geography of the World's Agriculture*, published by the United States Department of Agriculture, for the production maps of Europe: Figures 23, Rye; 24, Barley; 25, Grapes; 26, Cattle.

Likewise to Finch and Baker's *Geography of the World's Agriculture* for these maps: Figures 7, Cotton; 35, Rice; 38, Wheat; 39, Corn; 40, Oats; 48, Potatoes; 54, Sugar; 68, Cattle; 71, Sheep; 72, Swine.

To O. E. Baker for Figure 43, showing wheat acreage in the United States and Canada, reproduced from Dr. Baker's series of articles on Agricultural Regions of North America, published in *Economic Geography*.

For Figure 73, showing the milk supply for New York City, to M. P. Catherwood's *Statistical Study of Milk Production for the New York Market*, published by the Cornell University Experiment Station.

For data embodied in a number of the maps which have been redrawn for the revised edition, acknowledgment is due to a number of sources.

Figure 19, showing Federal Irrigation Projects, was based on a map furnished by the Bureau of Reclamation, United States Department of the Interior.

The Bureau of Agricultural Economics of the United States Department of Agriculture gave special information for Figure 22, Arid and Wet Lands of the United States.

To the Bureau of Mines, United States Department of the Interior, we are indebted for the information embodied in the series of maps showing mineral resources of the United States: Figures 87, 88, 89, 90, 98, 102, 160.

For Figure 129, showing the Railway Lines of South America, the latest available information was supplied by the Foreign Railway Service, Transportation Division, United States Department of Commerce.

The various maps showing cities of the United States, Figures 145, 146, 147, 148, and 150, are based on maps of the Geological Survey, United States Department of the Interior. The Geological Survey also furnished the data for Figure 160, showing waterpower resources of the United States.

The National Development Bureau of the Department of the Interior for the Dominion of Canada examined the drawing for Figure 153 and made valuable suggestions for bringing it up to date.

# LIST OF REFERENCES

In every good course in Business Geography some reference books are needed. The most important are a few standard books devoted largely to statistics. Nothing is more valuable to a student, or to a teacher, than to learn to make frequent and easy use of the books in Section *A* below. The first four cost very little, and the current copies should be kept at hand in every school. As a brief compendium of statistics outside the United States, *The League of Nations Statistical Yearbook* is by far the best. It should be renewed annually. *The Statesman's Year-Book* is extremely valuable, but its cost is relatively high, and a new copy need be purchased not oftener than every four years or so.

The remaining books comprise a very small selection of some of the best. Many other highly valuable volumes could be added, but it is believed that the teacher will be most helped by a short list of books, every one of which ought to be in every school.

### (*A*) Annuals to be Renewed Frequently

(1) *The World Almanac and Book of Facts.* The New York World-Telegram, New York.
(2) *Statistical Abstract of the United States.* Superintendent of Documents, Washington, D. C.
(3) *Commerce Yearbook.* Superintendent of Documents, Washington, D. C.
(4) *Agriculture Yearbook.* Superintendent of Documents, Washington, D. C.
(5) *League of Nations Statistical Yearbook.* World Peace Foundation, Boston.
(6) Epstein, M. *The Statesman's Year-Book.* The Macmillan Company, New York and London.

### (*B*) Atlases

(7) Bartholomew, J. G. *Atlas of Economic Geography.* Oxford University Press, London and New York.
(8) Philip, G. T., and Sheldrake, T. S. *Putnam's Economic Atlas.* G. P. Putnam's Sons, New York.
(9) Finch, V. C., and Baker, O. E. *Geography of the World's Agriculture.* Superintendent of Documents, Washington, D. C.
(10) Goode, J. Paul. *School Atlas.* Rand, McNally and Company, Chicago.
(11) *A Graphic Summary of American Agriculture.* Superintendent of Documents, Washington, D. C.

### (*C*) Encyclopedias

(12) Any good encyclopedia. Some reference work of this sort is highly important, and the habit of using it is still more important.

### (*D*) Elementary Textbooks

(13) It is always wise to have the class review the previous work. For this purpose copies of the textbook used in earlier years are needed, also copies of several other good elementary texts.

### (*E*) Textbooks on Business Geography

(14) Bishop, Alvard L. *Outlines of American Foreign Commerce.* Ginn and Company, New York.
(15) Chisholm, George G. *Handbook of Commercial Geography.* Longmans, Green and Company, London and New York. This is a highly reliable and valuable book.

# List of References

(16) HUNTINGTON, ELLSWORTH, and WILLIAMS, F. E. *Business Geography*. John Wiley and Sons, Inc., New York. This book contains an extensive series of up-to-date tables devised especially for use by classes in geography.
(17) SMITH, J. RUSSELL. *Industrial and Commercial Geography*. Henry Holt and Company, New York.
(18) WHITBECK, R. H., and FINCH, V. C. *Economic Geography*. McGraw-Hill Book Company, New York.
(19) BLANCHARD, W. O., and VISHER, E. S. *Economic Geography of Europe*. McGraw-Hill Book Company, New York.

## (F) OTHER BOOKS

(20) BOWMAN, ISAIAH. *The New World: Problems in Political Geography: Fourth Edition*. World Book Company, Yonkers, New York. The fullest and most authoritative discussion of the relation of geography to political conditions.
(21) COLBY, CHARLES C. *Source Book for the Economic Geography of North America*. University of Chicago Press, Chicago.
(22) CRISSEY, F. *The Story of Foods*. Rand McNally Company, Chicago.
(23) HUNTINGTON, ELLSWORTH, and CUSHING, S. C. *Principles of Human Geography*, 3d edition. John Wiley and Sons, Inc., New York.
(24) HUNTINGTON, ELLSWORTH. *Civilization and Climate*, 3d edition. Yale University Press, New Haven.
(25) JONES, C. F. *South America*. Henry Holt and Company, New York.
(26) MILL, HUGH R. (ed.). *The International Geography*. 70 authors. D. Appleton and Company, London and New York. Although not recent, this book contains admirable descriptions of all parts of the world.
(27) MILLER, G. J., and PARKINS, A. E. *Geography of North America*. John Wiley and Sons, Inc., New York.
(28) SMITH, J. RUSSELL. *The World's Food Resources*. Henry Holt and Company, New York.
(29) VON ENGELN, O. D. *Inheriting the Earth*. The Macmillan Company, New York.
(30) WHITBECK, R. H. *Economic Geography of South America*. McGraw-Hill Book Company, New York.

# INTRODUCTION

AFTER the principal facts of location, physiography, climatic differences, and their combined effect on human life have been taught, in what direction should boys' and girls' further study in geography be directed? The tendency in recent years has been away from physical geography and toward economic geography and the relations between nations. There can be little doubt but that this movement is sound.

The present volume opens with a study of "Primary Production." This heading should give renewed interest to children who have been used to the regional headings of the earlier work in geography. Heretofore the child has studied countries or groups of countries as independent units. He has also, as a rule, studied only those steps in an industrial process which happened to take place in the region concerned. Now he is to get the entire picture of a process from beginning to end. He is to learn more definitely how various groups of workmen in many different regions are mutually interdependent. He is to learn also how the fact that certain groups specialize in the production of raw materials of manufacturing, like cotton and minerals, forces other groups to specialize in the production of food.

The essential need for transportation is next brought to the child's attention. Primary production must begin where physical and climatic conditions make certain kinds of agriculture profitable or where Nature has hidden her minerals. Consumption is likely to take place at distant places. True, the student has learned this before. But now he faces the problem in a new way, again getting an entire picture of a great occupation. He learns that in spite of the great advances in mechanical transport, human muscles are still among the most important means of moving goods.

The great complexity of manufacturing makes the next picture. Now the effects of physical and climatic differences are studied from a new point of view. The influence of physical features such as transportation routes and power and raw material resources is reëmphasized, and the importance of the distribution of population is stressed. The climatic influence on manufacturing presented in this section is a new idea to many persons, yet its significance can hardly be questioned.

The volume concludes with a study of world markets which summarizes the principles that have gone before. Very stimulating problems are proposed and their solutions outlined.

## Introduction

One of the striking features of this book is the constant use of statistics. The growing use of statistics is probably the most outstanding development among modern geographers. It seems especially fitting that children should be thus encouraged to approach many social questions from a quantitative point of view. Such a habit will be of immense value in adult life. When the question of cancellation of war debts is faced from the point of view of the cold numerical relation between the annual payments and the total value of world trade, a good deal of the hysteria of recent years can be eliminated. Looking up the quantitative facts will often give unusual clearness to tariff questions. Statistical study of the growth of industry in foreign countries will suggest a careful consideration of whether we should continue to depend for our prosperity upon the export of surpluses. Children who form the habit of getting at such statistical facts should make more valuable citizens.

FRANK M. McMURRY

# CONTENTS

## INTRODUCTION

| CHAPTER | | PAGE |
|---|---|---|
| I. | Cotton: An Example in Industrial and Commercial Geography | 1 |

## PART ONE: THE FIELD OF PRIMARY PRODUCTION

| | | |
|---|---|---|
| II. | The United States as a Farming Country | 27 |
| III. | Cereal Farming | 40 |
| IV. | The Vegetable Farm and the Truck Garden | 61 |
| V. | Sugar Beets and Sugar Cane | 68 |
| VI. | Where Fruit is Produced | 74 |
| VII. | The Sources of Animal Products | 83 |
| VIII. | Fisheries | 102 |
| IX. | The Mining Industry | 110 |
| X. | The Fuel Products | 123 |
| XI. | Lumbering and Forest Products | 132 |
| XII. | Problems in Primary Production | 145 |
| | (A) South America | 145 |
| | (B) Mexico, Central America, and the West Indies | 154 |
| | (C) The United States | 156 |

## PART TWO: THE FIELD OF TRANSPORTATION

| | | |
|---|---|---|
| XIII. | Means of Transportation | 159 |
| XIV. | Railroads | 175 |
| XV. | The Use of Ships | 189 |
| XVI. | Transportation and the Location of Cities in the United States | 207 |
| XVII. | Special Problems in Transportation | 225 |
| | (A) British North America | 225 |
| | (B) Africa | 228 |

## PART THREE: THE FIELD OF MANUFACTURING

| | | |
|---|---|---|
| XVIII. | The Geographical Conditions of Manufacture | 235 |
| XIX. | Manufacturing Regions of the United States | 247 |
| XX. | Manufacturing Outside the United States | 264 |
| XXI. | What Europe Does for a Living | 278 |
| | (A) An Exercise in Primary Production, Manufacturing, and Transportation | 278 |
| | (B) A Study of a European Country | 283 |

## PART FOUR: THE FIELD OF CONSUMPTION

| | | |
|---|---|---|
| XXII. | The United States as a Market | 285 |
| XXIII. | Foreign Countries and World Markets | 298 |
| XXIV. | The Contrast between Asia and Australia | 311 |
| Appendix | | 325 |
| Index | | 337 |

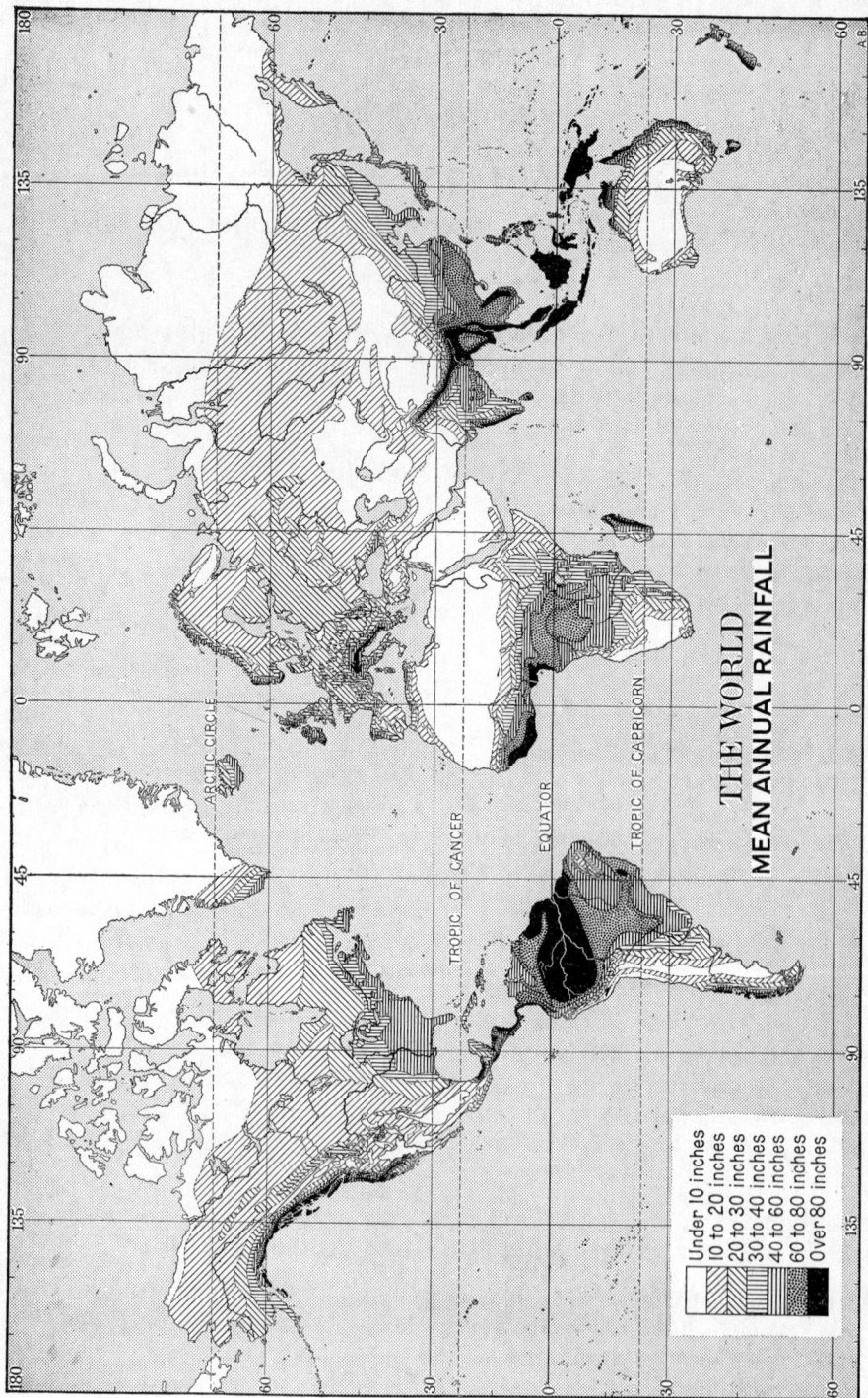

FIG. 1. Rainfall is among the most influential of the factors that determine where people can live and work efficiently, and where agriculture can be carried on. (Adapted from Finch and Baker's *Geography of the World's Agriculture*.)

# MODERN BUSINESS GEOGRAPHY

## INTRODUCTION

### CHAPTER ONE

#### COTTON: AN EXAMPLE IN COMMERCIAL AND INDUSTRIAL GEOGRAPHY

The world's main business is getting a living. To do this, man must first obtain the food, clothing, and shelter that he needs to keep himself alive, and then must satisfy his other needs. As he works at his business of getting a living, man finds himself constantly helped or hindered by his geographical surroundings; they affect his daily work in a thousand ways.

Business geography is the study of the relation between man's daily work and the geographical conditions upon which his work depends. It explains what these conditions are and what is their effect; it shows what man can do to utilize the benefits that they bestow upon him or to overcome the obstacles that they put in his way. We study this branch of geography in order to learn what man's working capital is and what use he makes of it.

When we look into the history of the things that we use in our daily life, we find that every one of them was originally produced directly from nature; that is, from field, forest, ocean, or mine. In order to get a living, then, the first thing people must do is to *produce* something — food, or wool, or lumber, or iron, or any one of a thousand other things that we use daily. This first step in the work of providing the things that we need is called *production*.

Few things can be used in the exact place where they are produced. Berries may be picked from the bush and transferred to the mouth with no intervening stages, but most products must be transported to the place where they are to be used. This second step in the business of supplying the needs of the world is called *transportation*.

Although a few commodities can be used in the raw state, the great majority must be prepared in some way. Wheat must be ground, copper smelted, leather tanned. Or perhaps many materials are combined, as glass, metals, jewels, and enamels are combined in a beautiful clock. This work of preparation is called *manufacturing*, or secondary production, in contrast to the original, or primary, production.

Finally, the materials or articles that have been produced, transported, and manufactured are consumed. This fourth step is *consumption*. Things may be consumed in the sense of being eaten, as in the case of food, or of being worn out, as happens to shoes, chairs, or machines. Some things are consumed in the manufacturing stage, as are the materials used in making a clock; although the clock itself is then consumed by being worn out.

We find, then, that business geography concerns itself with four great fields of man's work: (1) primary production, (2) transportation, (3) manufacturing, or secondary production, and (4) consumption. It will help us to understand these four fields, to find their limits and to know what is done in each of them, if a single commodity is followed through the four stages of its progress, beginning with its growth as a natural product and ending with its use in the field of consumption. Cotton is the commodity with which we shall begin our study; we shall trace its history from the seed on a southern plantation to the cloth purchased in a store.

### PRIMARY PRODUCTION OF COTTON

**The care of the growing crop.** The cotton farmer wishes the fiber to grow in great abundance and of good length. To insure the growth of such fiber he fertilizes the soil; he selects the seeds carefully and plants them in rows about three feet apart; later he thins the rows with a hoe, and destroys the weeds, so that each plant may have ample room to draw nourishment. He likewise fights the cutworm, the small gray beetle called the boll weevil, and the cotton flea.

When the cotton plant is about four months old, some of the bolls have reached the size of an English walnut; these now burst, showing a snowy mass of fibers. Soon the field is invaded by groups of cotton pickers—negro men, women, and children,—with bags hung from their shoulders to hold the cotton. The same field must be picked many times, for the bolls are ripening and bursting from the first part of August until the frost comes, sometimes as late as December. Each plant yields on the average about twenty bolls. The cotton must be picked as it appears, else the wind may carry it away or soil it with dust, or the rain may injure the quality of the fiber.

**How machinery helps in cotton production.** To pick cotton by hand is a slow and costly process, and the difficulty of getting enough labor at the proper season is great. Many machines have been invented to do the work; but none has proved entirely satisfactory.

*United States Department of Agriculture*

FIG. 2. The entire cotton crop of the United States, which now averages about 14,000,000 bales a year, must be picked by hand. A picker can pick enough for one bale of ginned cotton in about six days. The harvest lasts between three and four months.

The most successful of these machines can be used only in fields where the ground is hard enough to support its weight. It resembles a small gasoline automobile, and it travels over the cotton plants about as fast as a man can walk, plucking the fiber with steel fingers so deftly that it injures neither the plant nor the unopened bolls. If a machine meeting all requirements were to be invented, it would speedily lower the price of cotton goods; for then a farmer would be able to grow as much cotton as his land would allow, whereas now he is limited by the number of pickers he can secure. If more cotton were grown, the price of the fiber might come down, and the price of cotton goods might be lower.

After the cotton is gathered, the next step is to separate the fiber from the small, dark seeds, to which it clings closely. In the early days, when this was done by hand, it was a slow and difficult task, and one person could separate scarcely two pounds of fiber a day. Then cotton cloth was more expensive than woolen or linen, and even more costly than silk is now. In 1792 Eli Whitney changed all this by inventing the cotton gin. Many improvements have been made in the gin since 1792, and now a single machine is able to separate from

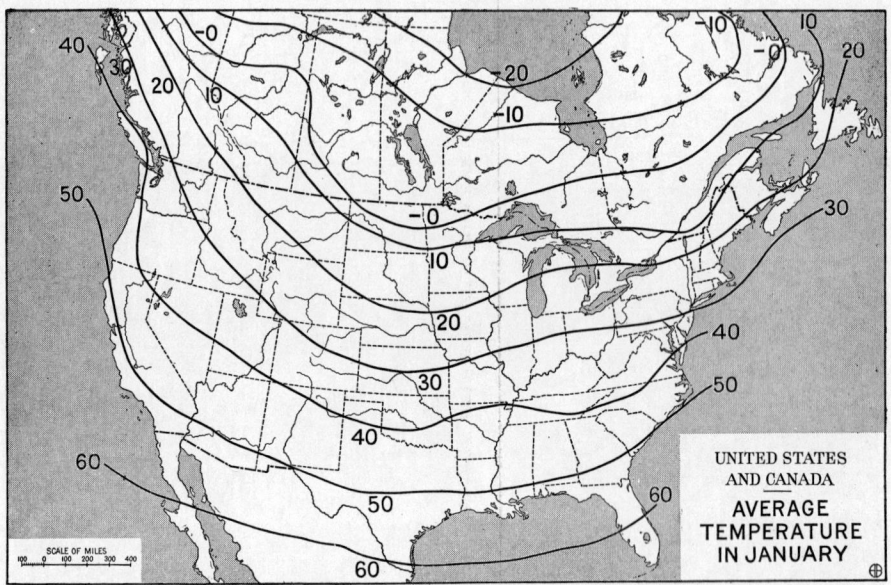

Fig. 3. The lines for 40° and 60° average temperature in January mark the general limits of the cotton-growing region in the United States. North of 40° to 42° farmers are never certain of a growing season of seven months free from frost. The southern boundary of the cotton belt is set at 60° by the character of the soil rather than the temperature, for the cotton plant is a native of the tropics.

25,000 to 100,000 pounds of fiber from the seed in a day. The gin consists of a revolving cylinder set with rows of saw teeth about half an inch apart. These catch the fiber and draw it through a comb so fine that the seeds cannot follow.

It is amazing to see how speedily and handily the work of separating the fiber is carried on. When the farmer draws up to the community cotton gin with his open wagon filled with freshly picked cotton, suction tubes unload the fluffy mass and drop it upon a carrying belt, which conveys it to the revolving cylinders. It takes only a few minutes for the saw teeth to draw the wagonload of fiber through the combs. Then the seeds are taken back to the wagon, while the cotton fiber is carried to the press to be pressed and bound into a bale weighing nearly five hundred pounds. A few minutes later the bale also is placed on the wagon, and both fiber and seed are soon on their way toward home or toward the railroad. Often the cotton gin is located at the railroad station to make transportation easy.

With the invention of the cotton gin the price of the cleaned cotton fell greatly. As cotton cloth became cheaper, more people used it, and the people who had formerly used it wanted still more.

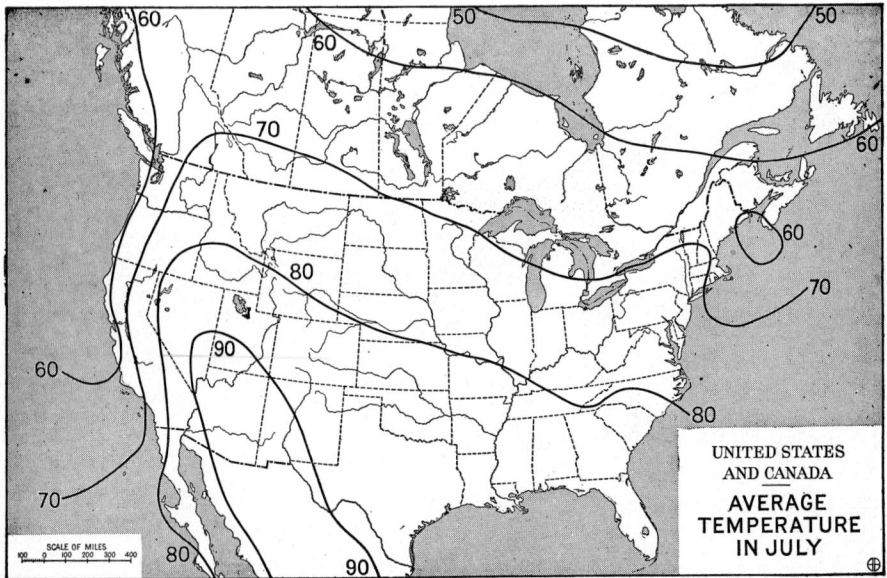

Fig. 4. Being tropical in its origin, the cotton plant requires a higher temperature than do the cereal crops, as well as a longer growing season. It grows best where the summer temperature averages at least 77°. Comparison of Figure 4 with Figure 5 shows that the bulk of the cotton crop is raised south of the line which marks an average temperature of 80° in July.

Farmers found cotton a more profitable crop than before and grew more of it. Since the invention of the gin, cotton has become the clothing of almost all the world. The story of cotton shows how the invention of even a single machine may affect the occupations and habits of many people in all parts of the world.

**Why cotton growing is limited to certain parts of the United States.** In order to produce abundant fiber the cotton plant requires

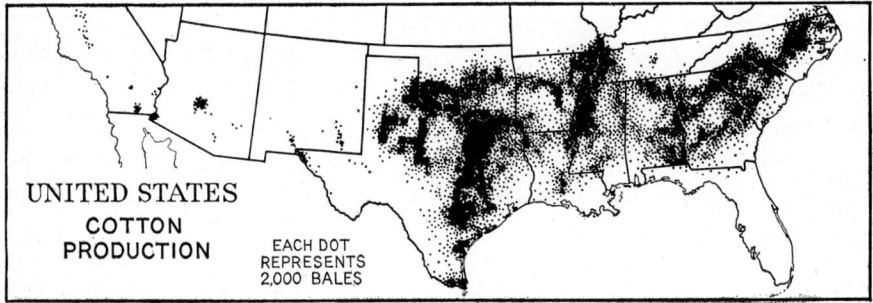

Fig. 5. The eastern and western boundaries of the cotton region are determined largely by the rainfall (Fig. 6). Notice the three areas of especially heavy production: (1) the uplands bordering the Atlantic coastal plains; (2) the level river lands along the Mississippi in Tennessee, Mississippi, and Arkansas; (3) the plains of east central Texas. Some cotton is now grown in the irrigated areas of southern California, Arizona, and New Mexico, where soil and climate are suitable but rainfall is lacking. Cotton is the second crop in the country in money value, corn standing first in this respect.

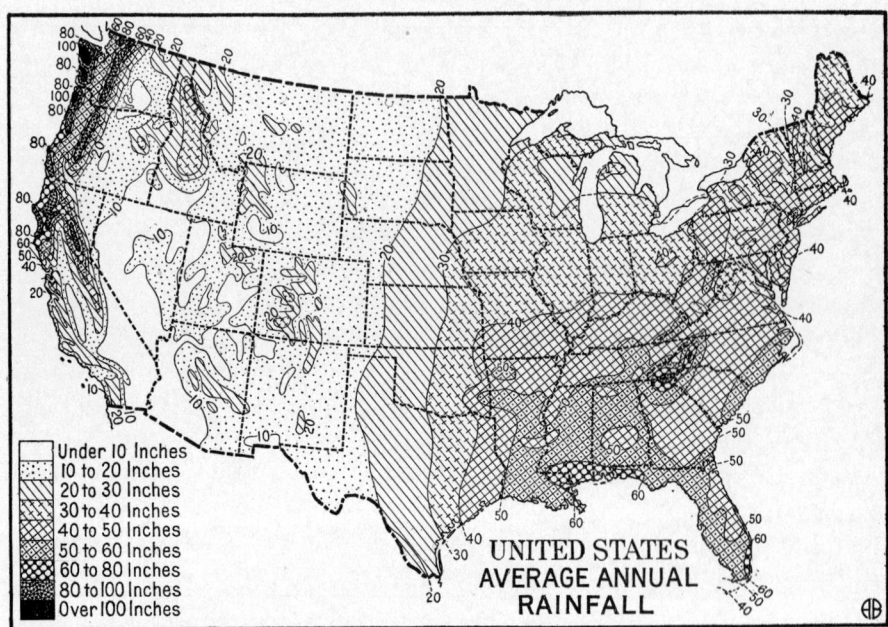

Fig. 6. By comparing Figures 5 and 6, we see that the heaviest production of cotton comes in regions that have an average annual rainfall of 30 to 50 inches. Without irrigation cotton production is not possible at all in regions of less than 20 inches of rainfall. More than 50 inches means too many cloudy days for the plants to produce large, firm bolls.

seven months of weather free from frost. This limits cotton raising in the United States to the part south of a line drawn from Norfolk, Virginia, to Cairo, Illinois (Fig. 5). The plant also needs ample water in the summer. Hence it cannot be grown in the region of light rains in Texas, New Mexico, and Arizona, except where irrigation is practiced. Since the cotton plant must have much bright sunshine, it does not grow well in the coastal region of North and South Carolina, Georgia, and Florida, where there is a great deal of rain and of cloudy weather. If the rainfall is too heavy, the plant produces luxuriant leaves rather than cotton. An exception is a variety of the plant called sea-island cotton, which produces a valuable long fiber in spite of the moisture that prevents the best results with other varieties. This variety gets its name from the low, sandy islands near the coast of Georgia and South Carolina, where it was first grown in this country.

Another important condition in cotton growing is the character of the soil. The plant grows best in limy soils or in the deep, rich soils in the valley floors along rivers.

Other conditions also help to determine where cotton shall be grown. Until the picking machine is perfected, cotton growing must be confined to regions where there is plenty of cheap, unskilled labor, the kind of labor that is supplied by the negroes of the southern states or the felaheen of Egypt. There must also be easy means of transportation to take the fiber to the factories where it is made into cloth; otherwise the marketing of the product may cost so much that it does not pay the farmers to grow it.

Hence we see that profitable cotton growing is limited by conditions of temperature, rainfall, sunshine, soil, labor, and transportation. Almost every other crop has similar limitations.

**Where cotton is grown in other countries.** Now that we know the conditions required for the growing of cotton, let us examine the world outside the United States to see where else it is grown, and why it is grown there.

*India.* Figure 7 shows that next to the United States, which raises from a half to two thirds of the world's supply of cotton, stands India. In India, cotton is grown principally in the western part of the southern plateau. There the temperature, rainfall, and sunshine are favorable and the so-called "black-cotton soil," formed by the decay of dark volcanic rock, is exceptionally good. There, too, labor is cheap; and as the British have built many railway lines, the crop is readily transported to market.

*China.* As a producer of cotton China probably comes next to India. The Hoang Ho valley is the region of greatest production. While southeastern China has favorable climatic conditions resembling those of our southern states, it has not so much level land covered with fertile soil, and it lacks adequate means of transportation. To offset these disadvantages, China has an almost unlimited supply of cheap labor.

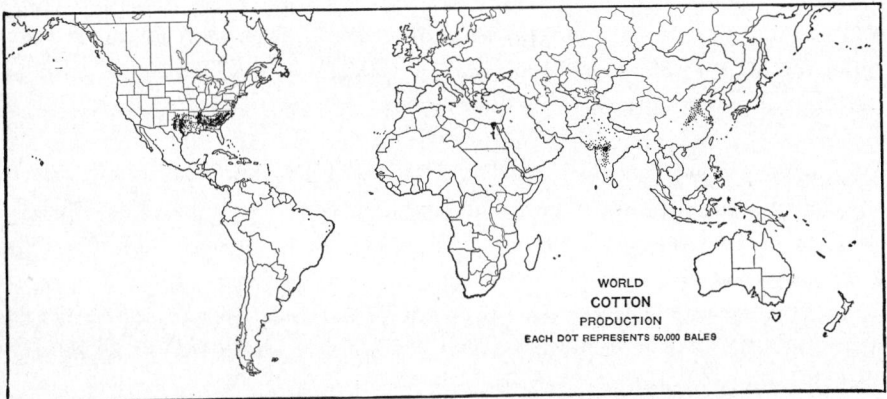

Fig. 7. Fully seven eighths of the world's cotton comes from the United States, India, Asiatic Russia, China, and Egypt. The remainder comes mainly from the southern hemisphere, especially Brazil and Peru; but Turkey, Persia, Uganda, and Sudan are also fair producers.

*Russia.* The southern part of Russia at the foot of the mountains east of the Caspian Sea in Uzbekistan and the neighboring regions has long been a cotton-growing region. In recent years the Russians have greatly increased the production here until now it rivals or surpasses that of China. The crop here is grown by means of irrigation, as is the case in Egypt, Sudan, and Peru.

*Egypt.* In Egypt, the fifth cotton-growing region of the world, almost ideal conditions for cotton are found. It is true that the rainfall is very light; but better than a good rainfall is the abundant water of the Nile River, which in times of flood overflows the low lands on either side. Part of the supply is stored in reservoirs made by damming the river, and can be fed to the plants as it is needed. To make sure of plenty of water for irrigation, the great Aswan Dam was built at a cost of $125,000,000. When the land is irrigated, much silt settles out of the muddy river and enriches the soil. Egypt produces twice as much cotton to the acre as the United States, and five times as much as India. Her cotton fiber is longer, silkier, and stronger than any other except sea-island cotton.

**The meaning of primary production.** Thus far we have considered, first, the conditions required for the satisfactory growth of the cotton plant and, second, the places where cotton is produced; that is, we have been considering the *primary production* of cotton. The first great step in any industry is to draw upon nature to produce a commodity. Nature is drawn upon when coal, for example, is taken from the mine, when logs are cut from the forest, when wheat plants are grown for the grains in the wheat-ear, when cattle are fed and tended so that their hides may be used for leather. All industry depends on primary production, as we find out if we trace to their origin the materials used in any of the industries. Primary production is one phase of business geography, or of commercial and industrial geography, as it is also called.

## TRANSPORTATION OF THE RAW COTTON

The second important step, as we have seen, is to move the commodity from where it is produced to where it is needed. Sometimes such *transportation* is easy, as when the farmer drives to the creamery near by with a few cans of milk; sometimes it requires weeks of time and the work of many persons, as when crude rubber from the South American forests is brought to factories in North America.

With cotton the problem of transportation is serious because the cotton mills, in the main, are far away from the plantations.

*United States Bureau of Public Roads*

FIG. 8. Cotton bales on the way to the railroad for shipment. Motor transport and good roads have been a great help to cotton growers. When the old-time grower moved his crop, three bales were a fair load for a pair of horses to draw over the country roads. When North Carolina has 800,000 or 900,000 bales of cotton to deliver to railroads or mills, motor trucks and hard-surfaced roads are a great help.

Some of the cotton of the South is used by the mills of North and South Carolina and Georgia, but the greater part goes to the mills of the northeastern states of the United States, western Europe (especially England), and even Japan.

**Transportation to the shipping point.** The transportation of the fiber from the fields to the factories begins at the ginnery. There the five-hundred-pound bales of ginned fiber are loaded on mule wagons or motor trucks, to be delivered at the nearest railway station or a river port a few miles away. This part of the journey, although short, is expensive. Away from the hard main roads which connect the larger towns it often costs 80 cents or a dollar to bring a single bale to the railroad.

**From seaport to mill town.** From the local shipping point the bales go direct to their destination. If they are to be used in Southern mills, they go all the way by railroad. If they are to be used in New England, the bales are usually carried to the nearest seaport by railroad or by the picturesque flat-bottomed river steamboats. The cotton of Texas goes to Galveston. The cotton of the region drained by the Mississippi and its navigable tributaries goes to New Orleans. That of the Atlantic states goes to such ports as Savannah and Charleston. For this part of the journey the average cost for each bale is one twentieth to one tenth of a cent a mile by water, and a quarter to a half cent a mile by railroad, not including the cost of loading and unloading. This shows how much cheaper it is, in general, to transport by water than by land. With water transportation there is no track to be built and kept in repair and there are no heavy grades to climb.

At the seaports huge storage warehouses line the water front; one such warehouse has been built by the city of New Orleans at a cost of $3,500,000. Here the cotton may remain for months, waiting for the call from the mills. When the call comes, stevedores load the bales on trucks and take them to the wharves, whence they are lifted by powerful derricks and deposited in the holds of the waiting ocean steamships. Then begins the longest part of the journey. It is not the most costly part, however, if we consider the rate per mile. From the Gulf ports to Liverpool, for instance, cotton is carried nearly five thousand miles for not much more than two dollars a bale. So cheaply can vessels be propelled on the free level highway of the sea, that even at so low a rate the steamship companies make good profits.

**Delivery to the factory.** Let us imagine that the particular bales of cotton that we have been following are carried by water from Galveston, the port that ships most of the cotton crop, to Fall River, our leading cotton manufacturing city. The steamship delivers the cotton at a wharf in the city, and from the wharf it is taken to the mill by motor truck. On the well-paved city streets a truck speedily transfers a score of bales at a load. Hundreds upon hundreds of bales are carried daily to the numerous mills, where they are put into storehouses.

When the time comes for the cotton to be used, each bale is taken out of storage and carried to the cleaning room of the factory on a hand truck, similar to that used for trunks at railway stations. Thus there is transportation by man during the later stages as well as at the beginning, when the fiber is carried in baskets by cotton pickers.

**Why methods of transportation differ.** The movement of cotton from field to factory is an example of the complicated journey that most commodities take in reaching the place where they are needed. Think of the different means of transportation used in the journey and consider why each was used. Take, for instance, the mule team. In many places mules are used in the first part of the journey, instead of horses or motor trucks. The mule is better than the horse for the heavy work of the South because he is better fitted for the southern climate and can thrive on coarse kinds of grass that are not good for horses. Moreover, many of the less used roads are difficult for automobiles in wet weather because of the mud. Then, too, many farmers of the

*Illinois Central Railroad*

FIG. 9. Loading cotton on a Mississippi packet boat. One of these broad, flat-bottomed river boats, with the barges that it can tow, will transport thousands of bales of cotton.

South cannot afford to own so expensive a conveyance as a motor truck, especially since it is little needed except for the few months in the year when cotton is being transported. During much of the remainder of the time the truck would be idle, while the mule can then be used for plowing, drawing the planting machine, and cultivating.

In the city, on the other hand, the motor truck is used economically to carry the bales to the factory, since the factory needs a constant supply at all seasons, and since the truck may be used also to take away cloth or even to bring coal and other supplies. Moreover, the truck is used far more economically on the paved city streets than on the dirt roads of country districts.

### COTTON MANUFACTURING

We have followed cotton through two of the great fields with which commercial and industrial geography deals — primary production and transportation. Now we are ready to see what happens to it in the third great field — *manufacturing*.

### Manufacturing Processes

**How cotton is cleaned.** In the cleaning room of the factory a workman swings an ax, the iron bands of the cotton bale are broken, and the cotton springs to double the size of the bale. At once it is thrown into a great bin where men loosen the large wads, and later

*Ewing Galloway*
Fig. 10. The weaving room in a modern cotton factory at Lowell, Massachusetts.

it is cast into the mouth of a machine to be cleaned. In the cleaning machine the fibers are thoroughly picked apart, so that all the dirt collected in the field or on the journey to the mill may drop out.

**How cotton is spun.** Let us follow our cotton hastily through the many processes of the mill. There are more than forty steps to be taken before it becomes finished cloth, but we shall observe only the main ones.

Spinning is one of the chief steps. To prepare the cotton for spinning, a great machine brushes it, straightening out tangles and carefully arranging the fibers in parallel order. The machine delivers the cotton in the form of a thick, porous ribbon called a "sliver." The sliver is passed through set after set of rollers which gradually pull it into a soft, fuzzy thread. Many threads are then twisted together by a spinning machine. The twisting makes strong, compact, smooth "yarn," such as the thread we buy for sewing.

We can get a good notion of how thread is spun by pulling a bit of cotton batting or absorbent cotton from a roll and twisting it between the thumb and forefinger. We should have difficulty in making a smooth thread of uniform firmness. Yet in ancient times spinning was carried on in almost this way. Even now, in backward regions such as the interior of China, central Brazil, and remote parts of India, people employ this crude method of spinning cotton for their simple clothing. Progressive peoples early began to invent better methods. The British were the first to succeed, but recently Americans have surpassed them in the invention of improvements.

The spinning machine of today spins more than a thousand threads at a time and winds each on a spindle. One man running two such machines can make more than three hundred pounds of thread each day. We may be certain that we have not come to the end of improvements; every few years new devices are invented to make thread faster, better, and cheaper.

**How cotton is woven into cloth.** When the thread is spun, the next step is to weave it into cloth. In ancient times this was done by placing two sticks in parallel positions a few feet apart and stretching a great many threads — the warp — from one stick to the other in such a way that they would lie side by side. Then a single thread — the woof — was passed across the other threads, running over the first, under the second, over the third, under the fourth, and so on until it reached the other side. It was then passed back again, but this time it went over the threads that it had previously gone under, and under those that it had previously gone over. Later, the hand

*Ellsworth Huntington*

FIG. 11. Primitive cotton manufacturing as carried on in northern India today. The man at the left is spinning; the man at the right is weaving.

loom lifted or lowered all the warp threads at once. Even today in the cotton-growing parts of Asia, Africa, and South America, much cotton is laboriously woven on hand looms. In our great factories the process of weaving is the same, except that it is done rapidly by machinery, with a fly-shuttle, instead of slowly by hand.

As England was the first to give the world high-speed machinery for spinning, so was she the first to invent a machine for weaving. The spinning machine made necessary the weaving machine. Before these two machines had been invented, a weaver could use the thread of six spinners; often he had to go from house to house among the spinners in the morning to get enough thread to weave during the afternoon. But the spinning machine produced such great quantities of thread that the weavers could not use it all. Then Arkwright invented the power loom, which could weave all the thread obtainable.

In weaving machines, as in spinning machines, there has been constant improvement, and now the mill operative has merely to tie up occasional breaks in the threads and at intervals to refill the automatic shuttle supply. One weaver can tend ten to twenty of the latest automatic looms, making in all two hundred or more square yards of cloth a day.

**How cotton cloth is bleached.** After the cloth is woven it may be bleached or dyed, or both, according to the use to which it is to be put. Most of the undyed cloth that we use is bleached. About half of all the cloth made of cotton is dyed.

Bleaching is necessary because the white cotton becomes discolored, chiefly with oil from the machinery and with the "sizing," or starch, which is put on the warp thread just before weaving to hold the fibers together and thus make the thread strong and smooth. In the process of bleaching, the cloth is boiled with lime, washed, soaked in sulphuric acid, washed again, boiled with lime and ash and resin, washed a third time, soaked in chlorid of lime, placed again in acid, and then given a fourth and last washing. Each treatment is to remove either some special impurity or the surplus of the previous chemical.

This part of the cotton industry shows how thoroughly dependent one industry is on many others. As modern spinning and weaving depend upon the industries that make machines, so bleaching depends upon the manufacture of chemicals.

**How cotton is dyed.** The dyeing of cotton, even more than the bleaching, illustrates the dependence of one industry on another.

The dyes or coloring materials come from both the vegetable and the mineral kingdom, and are obtained from nearly every part of the world. Most of the dyes come from coal tar, which is given off when coke is made from coal, but certain special colors are derived from other sources. As you read this sentence, many chemists are busy experimenting with coal-tar products and other chemicals, inventing cheaper ways of making old colors or producing new colors that they think people will like. In the forests of many distant regions men are now gathering bark, roots, flowers, and berries of various plants and trees for dyeing the cotton cloths that you will be wearing or using after a year or so. Others are growing plants in their fields for the same purpose.

Whatever the color of your cotton clothes may be, the greatest probability is that the dye came from a coal mine. Before the World War, Germany led the world in chemical industries, and her coal mines supplied most of the world with dyestuffs. So skillfully had German chemists worked upon coal-tar products that they were able to produce nearly seventy thousand different tones of color.

When the United States was cut off from Germany during the World War, our own manufacturers of dyestuffs increased their output enormously and made nearly all the colors formerly imported from Germany. The United States was in time able to supply other countries with dyes not only for cotton, but also for woolens, linen, paper, and leather.

### *How Geographical Conditions Affect Cotton Manufacturing*

**New England the center for cotton manufacturing in the United States.** We are now ready to consider the geographical conditions which cause cotton manufacturing to be concentrated in certain places. We have seen that in the United States, Fall River is the leading center of this industry. Figure 12 shows that many of the neighboring cities also manufacture cotton goods; for instance, New Bedford, Pawtucket, Lowell, Manchester, and numerous smaller centers. In fact, New England rivals the South as the leading cotton-manufacturing region of the country. Let us see why this is so.

**How water power and glaciation help cotton manufacturing.** A study of Fall River will help to solve the problem. In the first place, this city, as its name implies, is located on a river which, although small, has numerous falls and rapids. The falls were early used for power; today, however, they supply only a little of the power used, compared with that furnished by coal brought from Pennsylvania.

Many other New England cities are located where they can take advantage of the cheap power furnished by the numerous waterfalls and rapids due to the uneven surface of New England. The huge ice-sheet that swept over this region thousands of years ago filled many of the old river channels, and after it melted away the rivers had to seek new channels. Thus glaciation — that is, the work of the ice-sheet — has given rise to many waterfalls.

These waterfalls are all the more helpful to industries because above many of them are lakes, natural reservoirs that keep the volume of water in the river nearly constant from season to season. Consequently the amount of water power varies only a little, which is a great convenience for factories. We have to thank the ancient ice-sheet for these lakes of New England as well as for the falls, because they, too, result from the uneven surface of the land left by the ice.

**Why the clear water of lakes is valuable to the cotton industry.** Lakes not only steady the volume of the rivers; they also filter their waters. A river may be filled with muddy sediment as it enters a lake, but as it flows out it is clear as crystal; this is because all the mud has been deposited in the bed of the quiet lake. Hence the process of bleaching, which requires a great amount of clean water, can easily be carried on in New England. In the unglaciated region south of northern Pennsylvania and the Ohio River, the rivers are exceedingly muddy, and have no lakes to filter them. Accordingly, when cloth is made in the South, it is usually carried to New England to be bleached.

**The advantage of good harbors to the cotton manufacturer.** In addition to its supply of water for power and for bleaching, Fall River possesses a harbor that can accommodate ocean steamships. This means that it has good transportation facilities, which give it decided advantages in manufacturing. By means of the cheapest kind of transportation, the factories can receive not only raw cotton but coal for fuel to supplement water power, and also such raw materials as lumber and cement for building. They can also use the cheapest means of transportation to ship away their finished products.

Many other cotton cities in New England are located either on or near good harbors, for harbors are numerous in this region. This is because the coast has been submerged; the ocean has flowed over the edge of the land so that the lower parts of the river valleys have been drowned, thus being converted into bays. Water power and good harbors favor the manufacturing of other products as well as cotton.

Fig. 12. There are three points of concentration for cotton manufacturing in the United States: (1) New England, where the finest cloth is woven and where cloth woven elsewhere is dyed and finished; (2) the region about Philadelphia, where knitting mills are most numerous; (3) the piedmont section at the base of the mountains of the South, where factories are near the source of raw material and can utilize the power from the mountain streams.

**How a favorable climate causes the cotton industry to prosper.** Fall River is further fortunate in being so located that the prevailing southwest wind brings damp air from a broad expanse of ocean. This is of great help in spinning cotton, for the dampness prevents the fibers from becoming brittle and breaking constantly. In good cotton mills the air is usually dampened by steam jets or fine sprays of water; but in dry regions it is hard to keep the air in the right condition by artificial means, and consequently the thread often breaks, so that it is difficult to make good cloth.

Climate is favorable or unfavorable in another way — it has a marked effect on people's capacity to work. Fall River, like the rest of New England, has a climate that tends to make vigorous work a pleasure; therefore the workers are far more efficient than they would be in regions of monotonous cold or heat. A weaver in Mexico rarely tends more than two looms, while in Massachusetts it is common to tend six or eight.

**Why cotton factories are located near a labor supply.** Its location in the part of the country where labor is abundant gives Fall River still another advantage. Under present conditions a cotton manufacturing plant needs every class of labor, from the highly skilled to the unskilled, from the expert mechanic who cares for the machinery or the chemist who directs the bleaching and dyeing to the operative who simply watches a group of looms and stops them to tie the broken threads. New England lies nearer to Europe than does any other part of the United States, and it became settled earlier than other regions. Hence, when factories began to spring up, there were more people in New England from whom to obtain high-grade workers. Some of the descendants of the first mill-workers are now owners, superintendents, managers, and foremen of the mills.

Also because of its location, Fall River is able to draw labor from among the European immigrants who enter America through the neighboring ports of New York and Boston. Thus among the people of Fall River are many of English, Scotch, or Irish descent whose ancestors for generations have been engaged in manufacturing cotton either in the Old World or the New. Much of the unskilled labor is done by French Canadians from the province of Quebec. Recently machinery has become more and more automatic, and a kind of labor even less skilled is employed; for example, that furnished by newly arrived Poles, Finns, and Greeks. The employment of labor of this kind carries with it a disadvantage; for the unskilled laborers of the factory towns often lower the whole standard of the community.

Fall River is not alone in benefiting from the advantages of a position near the eastern seacoast. The large supply of labor helps the cotton business of neighboring towns too, and in fact the whole manufacturing business of New England.

**Geographical conditions that influence manufacturing.** Thus New England shows us how manufacturing in general, and cotton manufacturing in particular, may be influenced by geographical conditions, — glaciation, harbors, climate, and location. Due to glaciation, there are waterfalls and rapids that can be used for power, and lakes for filters and reservoirs. The harbors render transportation easy. The climate is good for manufacturing and is stimulating to man, and the location causes the labor supply to be abundant.

**Where cotton goods are manufactured.** Some of the cotton used in your home or in your clothes was probably imported. The United States normally makes only a little more than a fifth of the world's supply of cotton goods and consumes many varieties that she does not make. Great Britain and Japan each manufacture nearly one eighth; China, India, and Russia each one twelfth; Germany, France, and Italy about one twentieth. More than half of the remainder is manufactured in the other countries of Europe, and the rest in many minor countries (Fig. 13).

Figure 13 is based simply on *quantity*. If quality be taken into account, and if the *value* of cotton manufactures be made the basis of a table, the United States and the European countries stand higher than appears above; the Asiatic countries, being beginners, stand lower. In the United States the northeast, especially New England, which has long manufactured cotton, makes the best kinds of cotton cloth, while the South, where the industry is newer, turns out chiefly coarse varieties. This is partly because there is more efficient labor in Europe and New England, and partly because when the manufacture of cotton first begins it is easier to make the cheaper kinds which do not require such expensive machinery.

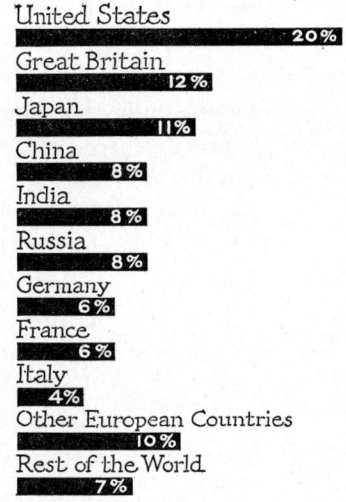

FIG. 13. The distribution of cotton manufacturing. Which of the nine leading manufacturing regions raise cotton? Which must import all their raw cotton?

**The making of cotton goods by hand.** Hand methods of making cotton goods, as we have seen, are still employed in many parts of the world; for example, in the interior of China and India and among the Japanese mountains. Most of the backward sections make no more than enough cloth for local use. In some regions, such as India and Japan, the thread is mostly spun in factories and is then sold to the weavers, who make the cloth by hand. Switzerland, central France, and Ireland, however, have a highly advanced cotton industry which produces hand-made goods of a quite different kind. These consist of laces, embroideries, and cloths of such delicate texture, graceful pattern, or lasting quality that they are much prized by people in distant regions. They have given rise to an important trade.

**Why England excels in cotton manufacturing.** The cotton imports of the United States come mainly from England. That country owes her leadership in the cotton industry to certain decided advantages:

(1) She was the first to manufacture cotton goods. Hence she early obtained a wide market, which she has largely retained, in spite of her rivals.

(2) She has a large supply of both skilled and unskilled labor.

(3) Her colonies have needed great quantities of cotton goods and have preferred to buy from the home country rather than elsewhere.

(4) England's shipping has been adequate to carry her goods everywhere. In this respect no other country has been so well provided.

(5) The cotton factories of Great Britain are located where the combined cost of transportation for raw material and fuel is lower than in any other part of Europe, and as low as in most parts of the United States. The mills are located largely in the county of Lancashire. As Lancashire lies just east and north of Liverpool, raw cotton is readily received from America through that port or through Manchester, which is connected with Liverpool by a ship canal.

(6) Coal of the best quality is mined close to the manufacturing district.

(7) The climate of Lancashire is uncommonly favorable. It is very healthful for the workers, and the prevailing southwest winds bring air that is damp enough for spinning.

Because of all these advantages, no other equally small region makes so much cotton cloth of all kinds as does the English manufacturing district.

**Our tariff on cotton goods.** The higher wages and higher prices of all commodities in this country give England and other countries of western Europe an advantage over the United States in the manufacture of cotton goods. They could undersell us if there were competition on equal terms. Accordingly, our government has long helped the home industry by imposing a tax, or tariff, upon nearly all imported cotton goods. Even when the duty established by a tariff law has ranged from 20 per cent of the value for cotton thread to 40 and even 75 per cent of the value for cotton gloves, hose, quilts, and laces, cotton goods have still been imported annually to values which sometimes exceed $100,000,000.

## THE FIELD OF CONSUMPTION

We have now followed the cotton through the intricate steps of manufacturing and are ready to trace it through the market to the store where it is purchased, ready to wear or to use in your home. You and the other users of the product use up, or consume, the goods made in the fields of production and manufacturing; hence the fourth field with which commercial and industrial geography deals may be called the field of *consumption*.

**Cotton goods consumed as clothing.** There are two principal markets for cotton cloth — people and industries. Certain cottons go directly to people, to be used by them in clothing or for various household purposes; others go to industries to be made into more complicated goods, usually in combination with several other materials.

A little thought will convince you that in your clothing cotton is used more than any other material. The fiber is so strong, so readily cleansed, so inexpensive, and so well adapted for many kinds of cloth that it has naturally become almost the universal clothing material. Gingham, percale, muslin, canvas, khaki, and denim are familiar as names of cotton fabrics adapted to special purposes. All the different kinds of weaves, patterns, weights, and colors are required to satisfy our need of comfort, long service, beauty, or style, or our desire for a change. Rayon and artificial silk are made of cotton fibers that have been made to look like silk.

We demand different cottons at different seasons. In summer we naturally incline toward white or light-colored goods and those of light weight, not only because they reflect the sun's rays and keep us cool, but also because they make us look more comfortable. For summer, cotton apparel has an advantage over other materials because it is at the same time the coolest and the cheapest. Woolen cloth prevents the heat of the body from escaping, while silk and linen are too expensive for most of us.

Most people prefer cotton underwear at all seasons, because the fibers do not irritate the skin as wool does. Moreover, cotton underwear, unlike woolen, shrinks but little in washing.

**The consumption of cotton for household use.** We have been thinking thus far of the cotton goods consumed in our clothing. Now let us consider those in use in our houses. A glance about your home will give you an idea of the large amount of cotton your family consumes directly. You may walk upon cotton rugs, pull down a cotton shade, wash with a cotton wash cloth, dry your face and hands with a cotton towel, eat your supper from a cotton tablecloth while using a cotton napkin, rest in a chair upholstered in cotton, read a book with extra good paper made of cotton rags, and in the end toss back a cotton bedspread, crawl in between cotton sheets, nestle under the warmth of a cotton quilt, and go to sleep on a cotton pillow. The chief reasons for the wide use of cotton articles in the home are their cheapness and durability, the ease with which they can be cleaned and kept fresh, and the adaptability of the cotton fiber to a great variety of uses.

**The consumption of cotton in occupations.** Nearly every occupation consumes cotton in one way or another. It is used in the fisherman's net and sail, the soldier's tent, the hunter's smokeless powder, the miller's flour bags, and the dairyman's strainer. Manufacturers use cotton in a great many things, such as shoes, automobile tires, books, and oilcloth. Often the manufacturer mixes some cotton with other fibers in making woolen, linen, and silk goods.

**Consumption of cotton in the tropics.** Although the greater part of the cotton produced is used by people who live in the temperate zone, those who live in warm regions also use it extensively. In fact, the people of the tropics use cotton goods almost to the exclusion of wool, linen, and silk. This is not only because cotton is cheaper, but because it is warm enough at all seasons. In this respect tropical people contrast strongly with those, like ourselves, who live in the temperate zone; we use a variety of clothing materials, partly because we can afford to do so and partly because of the variation of the seasons.

With many tropical people the question of clothing is not of great importance, because they wear so little. Many of them wear cloths instead of clothes. These they wrap gracefully about the body. Among some peoples, the clothing is merely an apron or loin cloth, which usually lasts a long time. Hence the tropical lands would make only a small market for cotton goods were it not for their vast populations. In India alone there are more than 350,000,000 people — almost as many as in Europe outside of Russia. Each of these millions of persons needs at least one garment. Many of them wear not only the body cloth, but a cotton turban of eight or ten square yards, and a cotton shawl about the same size, often embroidered with gold. Some, of course, use as much cotton as we do.

The annual import of cotton goods into India alone sometimes rises above $200,000,000, and this is in addition to the large amount made at home from cotton grown in India. China furnishes an even larger market than India for foreign cotton goods, but her foreign trade is not so well developed as India's.

**The by-products of cotton.** The consumption of the cotton fibers in clothing, homes, and industries does not tell the full story of the cotton farmers' contribution to the world's market. We have yet to consider the cotton seeds that were separated from the fibers in the gin (page 3). Their weight is twice as great as that of the fibers, and their bulk for the full crop is enormous.

*Cottonseed oil.* For many years the accumulation of the seeds was a great annoyance to the cotton farmer, who got rid of them by burning them or dumping them into the river. Now that the value of the oil they contain is known, they yield him an important part of his profit. The oil which is pressed out is an excellent food for man. It is like olive oil, and serves as a substitute for butter and lard. The oil is also manufactured into soap, candles, and plates for phonograph records.

*Oil cake.* The "cake" that is left when the oil is extracted is one of the best foods for dairy cows; moreover, the manure from cake-fed cows is a good fertilizer. Cotton farmers are learning that by keeping cows they can reap three profits, — a money profit from the fiber, a food profit from the cake-fed cows, and a soil profit from the manure. Dairymen are willing to pay such high prices for cottonseed cake that it is profitable to ship it to the northern states and Canada, and even to western Europe.

*The hulls.* Half the weight of the seed is the hull that is taken off before the rest is made into oil and cake. For a long time the hulls were burned to furnish power for the oil presses, and the ashes were used for fertilizing the soil, especially for tobacco and vegetables. Now the hulls are used instead of hay in fattening cattle for market.

### CONCLUSION

We have now traced the story of cotton through the field of primary production, along various transportation routes, through the complicated manufacturing field, into the field of consumption.

For almost every commodity a similar story can be written, with chapters on primary production, transportation, manufacturing, and consumption. Of course the chapters would vary in length and interest with different commodities. Thus the first chapter of the story of wood or marble would be very different from that of cotton. For some products the manufacturing chapter would be brief; or it might even be omitted altogether, as in the story of fresh vegetables. But these cases are exceptional. Almost everything that we eat, wear, or otherwise use in our daily life goes through a stage when its form is changed, even if the change is merely the difference between whole wheat and flour, or between fresh pears and canned pears. To bring about any such change is part of the work of manufacturing.

In studying commercial and industrial geography we need not trace the story of every commodity through each of its chapters. It is easier and more interesting to study primary production by itself, considering the most important commodities and finding out how they are taken from the farm, forest, ocean, or mine. The three other fields also need separate study.

Accordingly, in this book you will find (1) a section on **primary production**, (2) a section on **transportation**, (3) a section on **manufacturing**, and (4) a section on **consumption**.

### QUESTIONS, EXERCISES, AND PROBLEMS

*A.* **How climate influences the growth of cotton.**

1. If the farmers in your state tried to raise cotton, what conditions would they find favorable? What conditions would be unfavorable?
2. Why do not England and Germany raise cotton to supply their factories instead of importing it?

*B.* **Conditions that make cotton transportation expensive.**

1. Men carry the cotton from one conveyance to another for only the shortest distances; mules and motor trucks take the bales the next greatest distance; and railroads and steamboats are the long-distance carriers. Why is this so?
2. How would the cost of cotton cloth be affected if mules had to do the work of railroads, and if automobiles carried the cotton as far as the steamships do?
3. About how many times are the bales handled by men from the time the cotton is pressed into bales until the bales are opened in the mill? What effect does the amount of handling have on the cost of cotton cloth?
4. Sometimes bales of cotton are shot directly from the cars down a slide into the hold of a vessel. How else might handling by man be decreased?
5. Why is there more effort in the United States than in almost any other country to decrease the amount of transportation by man?
6. Describe the location of a cotton field and a factory so situated that the cost of transportation is as low as possible.
7. What is one advantage of the southern group of cotton mills shown in Figure 12? In which of the southern states are mills most numerous?

## Cotton

**C. How sections that raise cotton are related to those that manufacture it.**

1. Examine Figure 13, on page 19. Notice that the lines vary in length according to the percentage of the total amount of cotton that various countries manufacture. Make a similar diagram using straight lines to represent the following figures, which show the approximate percentage of the world's cotton crop grown by each of the most important cotton-growing countries:

   | | |
   |---|---|
   | United States 54 per cent | China .. 7 per cent |
   | India ...... 15 per cent | Egypt .. 6 per cent |
   | Russia ..... 8 per cent | Brazil .. 2 per cent |

2. Which of the countries specializing in cotton manufacture are obliged to import all the raw material?
3. Why do these countries find it profitable to import and manufacture cotton?
4. What countries are ready to sell them a surplus of raw cotton?
5. Why is the cotton cloth manufactured in India inferior in quality to that manufactured in England?
6. Name three countries included under the heading, "western Europe outside of Great Britain and Germany," in Figure 13.
7. Why would thousands of people in England go hungry if the cotton crop should fail in the United States? How does this question have a bearing on England's interest in our Civil War?
8. "Almost 70 per cent of the world's cotton is grown under two flags." Prove this statement by figures from the diagram that you have made.

**D. Conditions that affect the manufacturing of cotton.**

1. Which of the countries that manufacture cotton make enough to supply their own needs? (Assume that one per cent of the world's cotton manufacture is enough to supply the needs of 30,000,000 people in India, 12,000,000 people in Germany, 8,000,000 in England, and 4,000,000 in the United States. Use the table of population on pages 328, 329.)
2. Why does the use of cotton vary from country to country?
3. Why do we place a lower tariff on cotton thread than on cotton velvets and laces? Why do we call a high tariff "protective"?
4. Cotton from northern Peru can be mixed successfully with wool. How would you expect the price of such cotton to compare with that of ordinary cotton in a place like Boston? Why?
5. Look up rayon and other kinds of artificial silk. What is their effect on the demand for cotton?

**E. Use of machinery in the cotton industry.**

1. In a good encyclopedia look up the inventors James Hargreaves, Samuel Crompton, and Richard Arkwright. Explain what they had to do with the cotton industry.
2. Tell briefly the story of Eli Whitney's invention.
3. Find out what the Jacquard loom is, who invented it, and the effect of its invention on the cotton industry.

*International Harvester Company*

Figs. 14, 15. Fields were plowed a furrow at a time from before the dawn of history to the second half of the nineteenth century, when the gang plow was invented. In a few out-of-the-way corners of the earth the most primitive kind of plowing may still be seen, as in Turkestan, where a plow that is little more than a bent and sharpened stick is pulled by a pair of small, long-haired yaks.

# PART ONE

## The Field of Primary Production

### CHAPTER TWO

#### THE UNITED STATES AS A FARMING COUNTRY

When man obtains wild honey from a forest, gold from river gravels, grass from natural meadows, or fish from streams, he simply reaches out and takes what nature has produced. For such products, nature does nearly all the work. In most cases, however, man and nature enter into a more nearly equal partnership. They work together as producers. In agriculture, for instance, nature supplies soil, wind, rain, and sun; man furnishes seed and tools; and both partners work vigorously to make the crop profitable. In mining, nature furnishes deposits of rich ores that she has been storing up for ages, and it is man's work to discover and extract them. Forests are like mines in that they are nature's storehouses.

In the field of primary production we shall study the materials that are produced by man and nature together.

**The occupations of primary production.** Five occupations — farming, fishing, mining, lumbering, and hunting — represent the ways in which man obtains products directly from nature. Except for hunting, which is of little commercial importance, these primary occupations are all practiced extensively in every continent, most of them in every country, whereas manufacturing is highly developed in only a comparatively few advanced countries. The primary producers supply the world's pantry and the stock room for all manufacturing plants. Without them, the world's activities would come to a standstill. We shall study the four chief primary occupations separately, beginning with farming.

**The importance of farming.** Farming is the most important of all occupations. In the world as a whole the number of people engaged in it and the value of its products make it more important than all other occupations combined. In some countries, such as India, Hungary, and China, more than two thirds of the men are farmers. Even in the United States, where manufacturing, commerce, and mining are of great importance, a quarter of the men are farmers.

## GENERAL CONDITIONS OF FARMING IN THE UNITED STATES

**The position of the United States as a farming country.** Although in proportion to its population the United States has fewer farmers than many other countries, it is the leading farming country of the world. No other country grows such large crops of corn, cotton, tobacco, and wheat, and none has a greater variety of products. The United States excels Russia in the production of oats. It grows about three fifths of the world's corn crop, three fifths of the cotton, one third of the tobacco, one fourth of the oats, and one fifth of the wheat.

**Why the United States leads in farming.** The leadership of the United States in farming is due to many causes: (1) the great size of the country; (2) its favorable climate; (3) the energy of the farmers; (4) the intelligence and inventiveness of the American people; (5) the freshness of the soil; and (6) the transportation facilities for marketing the crops. In addition to these another cause may be mentioned: (7) the aid given by the government.

It must not be inferred that the United States is ahead of all other countries in every condition enumerated above. Russia, including Siberia, far exceeds it in size; France has a better climate; Holland has farmers who are equally energetic and intelligent; England has better roads and more convenient railroads; Australia has equally good soil; and Germany has given more governmental assistance to the farmers. It is doubtful, however, whether any other one country has so happy a combination of these fortunate conditions as the United States.

### SIZE OF THE COUNTRY

The leadership of the United States in farming rests to a large extent upon its size (Fig. 16). If it were not for its great size, the United States could not count its annual crop of corn, of wheat, and of oats in billions of bushels, of hay in scores of millions of tons, of tobacco in hundreds of millions of pounds, and of cotton in millions of bales. Other equal areas in Europe, India, and China do indeed produce much larger crops than the United States, because they have many more people; but no other region gets so much advantage from mere size. Europe is divided into many countries, which is a great hindrance to commerce and hence to production; while in India and China transportation is not so well developed as in the United States.

**Extent of the tillable area.** It is true that not all of our country can be used for farming. Some large areas, such as most of the Great

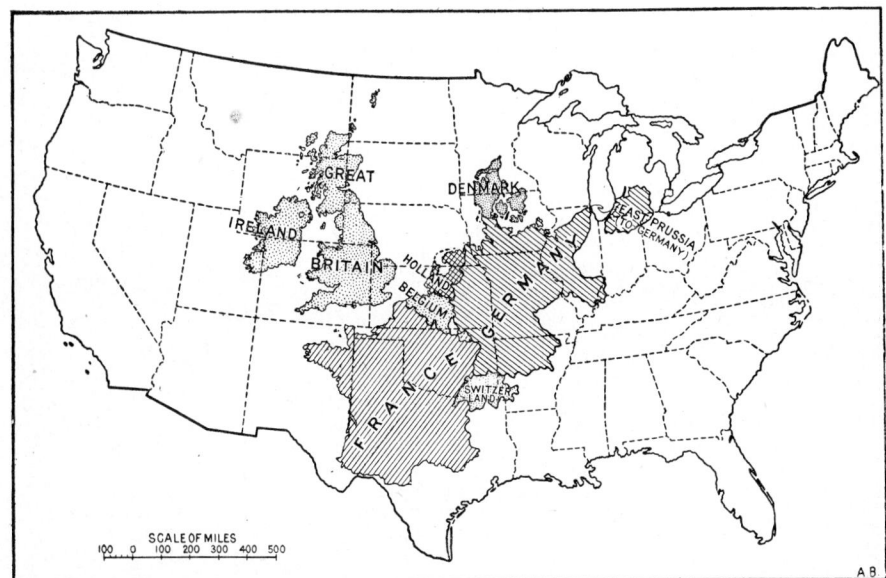

Fig. 16. Western Europe has about one fourth the land area of the United States, with about 50,000,000 more people to be supported by the land. Would you expect such a region to be mainly agricultural or mainly industrial?

Basin district which lies between the Rocky Mountains and the Coast Ranges, are too dry; others, like the Rocky Mountain district, are too rugged. Still, there remains nearly half of the area of the United States that can be successfully farmed.

**System of cultivation.** As yet, most of this favorable half has been farmed only by the method of *extensive* cultivation; that is, crops are planted once a year over broad areas, with little or no fertilizer, and are largely left to take care of themselves until harvest time. This method means a small yield per acre, but it allows one man, with the help of horses and machines, to cultivate many acres, so that large returns are possible.

Our crops might be doubled or even trebled if our lands were to be as *intensively* cultivated as most of western Europe, China, and Japan. In those regions, with the help of fertilizers and with proper care to remove the weeds, much of the land commonly yields two large crops a year. As our population increases, farming will presumably become less extensive and more intensive; for the area of new lands that can be occupied is fast diminishing. Under intensive cultivation the great size of our country will be a factor even more important than it is now in maintaining our agricultural leadership among the nations.

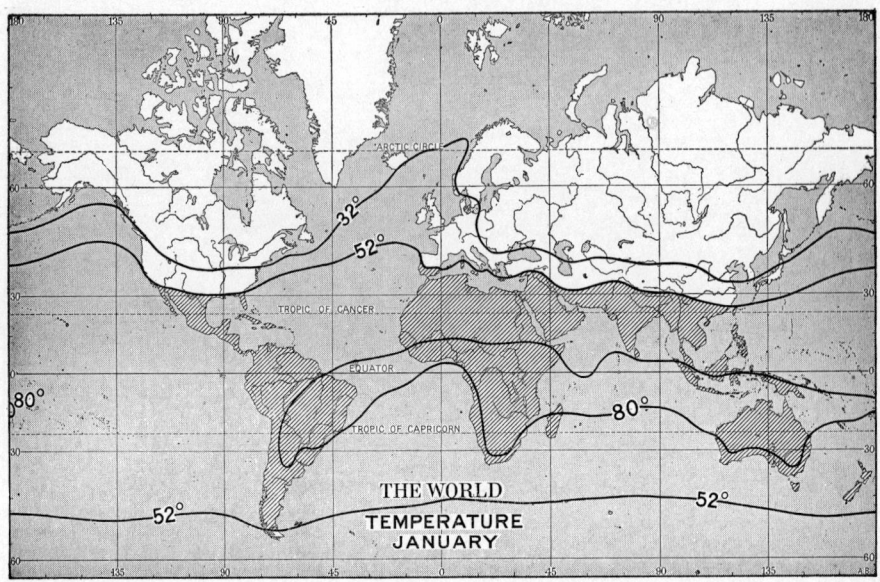

Fig. 17. Plants do not grow and produce crops in temperatures lower than 52°. The shaded belt in this map shows the area, north and south of the equator, in which agriculture goes on during our winter. South of the southern line of 52° agriculture cannot be carried on.

### CLIMATIC CONDITIONS

The temperature in the United States is highly favorable to farming. The country is not located far enough to the north to have the extremely long winters that prevent agriculture in most of Canada and thus keep that country from reaping the full advantage of its size. Neither is it so far south that it is unfit for raising such crops as barley and wheat. It is fortunately placed, being in the latitudes where many of the crops most desired by the world markets can grow under ideal conditions of temperature.

**Effect of the uneven rainfall.** In rainfall our country is not so fortunate as in temperature. The eastern half, to be sure, has as favorable a rainfall as any part of the world. Because it has frequent cyclonic storms and because no high mountains shut off the interior from the Atlantic Ocean and the Gulf of Mexico, this half receives rain in abundance. Most of the western half of the United States, on the contrary, gets too little rain for ordinary farming; the rain-bearing winds from the Pacific Ocean are unable to bring enough moisture over the high Sierra Nevada and Cascade Mountains. Nevertheless, cattle and sheep thrive on the dry grasslands to the east of these ranges. In the northern part of the Pacific slope, in several sections in California, and in the northern Rocky Mountain region, however, there is an abundant rainfall (Fig. 6).

## The United States as a Farming Country 31

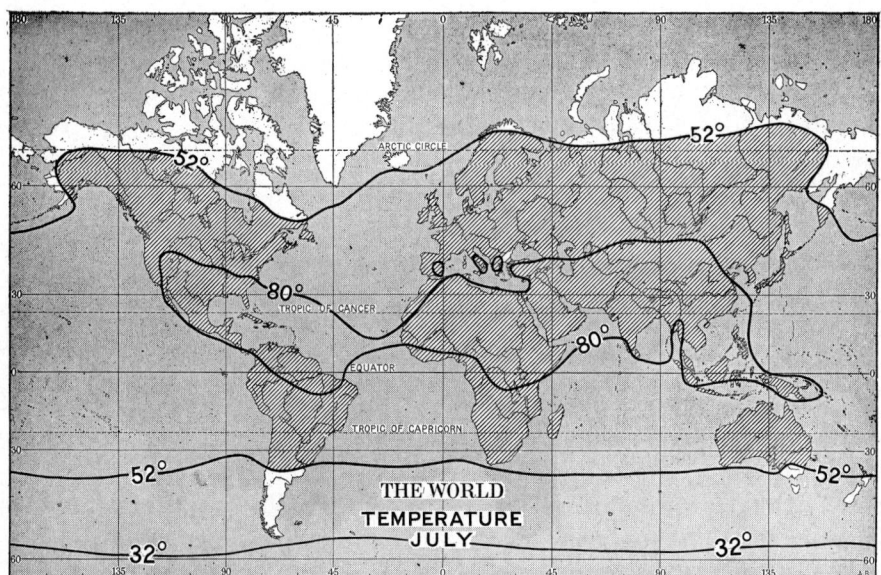

FIG. 18. Above the northern line marked 52° agriculture is not possible. A few crops may be grown, to a limited extent, in sheltered valleys opening toward the south; but in general people who live north of that line must depend on hunting, fishing, or mining for their living.

**Methods of farming used to offset unfavorable rainfall.** In some parts of the dry regions large crops are grown by *irrigation;* that is, water is taken from the rivers by means of canals and is then led into little ditches in the dry but rich soil. The regions irrigated under the control of the United States government are shown in Figure 19.

In other dry sections *winter farming* is practiced. Advantage is taken of the rains that come regularly in the winter, and a hardy winter crop is raised.

In still other regions, especially those just east of the Rocky Mountains, the farmers make the most of the light rainfall by means of what is called *dry farming*. Before the rainy season begins, they plow the ground to let the rain soak in as much as possible. After the soil is wet they keep the surface finely pulverized with a harrow so that the moisture will not evaporate. Then, too, they are careful in selecting crops that can thrive on light rainfall, such as wheat, Kafir corn, and alfalfa.

In these various ways the effect of unfavorable rainfall is partly overcome even in the dry West. Nevertheless, this section contains large deserts which cannot be used even for grazing, irrigation, winter farming, or dry farming. The driest and most barren of these deserts are in Nevada, southeastern California, Arizona, and Utah (Fig. 22).

**A great variety of crops due to variety of climate.** The size of the United States gives it another advantage besides that of an enormous total yield; for its great extent causes it to have a variety of climates, and this wide range of climates makes possible a great variety of products. They range from the semi-tropical fruits of Florida and California to the hardy grains of the cold temperate regions, and from the dates and ostrich feathers of our desert oases in the southwest to crops like potatoes, that require abundant rainfall.

### CHARACTER OF THE FARMING POPULATION

Another cause of the leadership of the United States in farming is the energy of the people. A large part of the country, especially the northern sections, possesses a climate that keeps people energetic. Only for a month or two is the winter cold benumbing, or the summer heat depressing. The invigorating character of the climate is due in part to the storms that cross the country with the prevailing westerly winds. They bring changes in temperature from day to day that spur the workers to vigorous exertion. People in no occupation feel the energy thus given by the climate more than farmers.

In addition to this, the people who settled the United States brought with them an inheritance of energy and intelligence. They had this inheritance partly, but by no means wholly, because they came from western Europe, a region that also has a stimulating climate. Had these same people migrated to tropical lands their vigor might gradually have diminished.

**How the farmer's energy is utilized.** The vigor of the American shows itself not so much in the number of hours of labor as in the speed with which he works and the quickness with which his mind turns from one thing to another. During the busy season the farmers in oriental countries from the Near East in Turkey to the Far East in China, and even in tropical countries, often begin their work as soon as it is light and end it only when darkness comes. But the Oriental works slowly, and when he has finished one piece of work he often sits down to rest and think it over before beginning another. The American does not merely work quickly: he wastes little time in going from one thing to another; he is competent to use complex machinery; and he is usually ambitious. The tropical farmer, on the other hand, is usually content if he raises just enough to feed and clothe his family, and he often seems averse to the use of machinery. If favorable weather gives him a double crop, he sometimes wastes it in feasting, or saves the surplus in order that he may do less work during the next farming season.

**Evidence of the farmer's intelligence.** The intelligence of the American farmer shows itself in his eagerness to improve his farming methods. He is continually seeking to make his own labor more effective by the use of improved machinery, which will enable him to farm more acres or to farm the same area in a better way. On many a farm machinery is at work plowing, planting, cultivating, or reaping a crop. A machine, instead of a team, may be used to haul the crop to the market. Machinery is often employed for much of the incidental work of the farm, such as separating the cream from the milk, sawing the winter's wood, and clipping the horses.

The American way of farming by machinery has been adopted to a large extent in such new countries as Canada, Argentina, and Australia, and to a less degree in the progressive parts of Europe. In tropical and oriental countries, farming is carried on chiefly with the hoe, with a simple plow drawn by horses or cattle, and with a sickle. It is no wonder that while the American farmer raises, on the average, more than two thousand dollars' worth of products a year, the farmer in India produces crops worth only about twenty dollars there and worth only four or five times that amount in our own country with its far higher prices.

## THE ADVANTAGE OF NEW SOIL

**How new soil has helped the United States.** In farming, new countries usually have an advantage over older countries. The advantage lies chiefly in the fact that the soil has not been robbed of its plant food. It has long been known that when the soil of almost any region is first cultivated, it yields large crops; but after a few years the crops decline, and in time the yield becomes very small unless the farmer devotes much time and energy to renewing the soil by means of fertilizers and the rotation of crops, and by allowing the land to lie fallow. The fact that the yield of wheat in North Dakota fell quite steadily from 14.5 bushels of wheat, between 1886 and 1895, to 10.4 bushels, between 1914 and 1920, illustrates how the wheat crop in some of our western states fell off after the first years of cultivation. The large crops in the early years are certainly an advantage to the farmer, yet in a sense they do harm, because they lead him to be careless of the soil and to think that he can gain wealth without much work.

## TRANSPORTATION FACILITIES

Still another important reason for our leadership as a farming country is the ease with which the crops are marketed.

**How our system of transportation aids farming.** Railways and sometimes waterways take the farm products quite cheaply to most parts of our country where they are needed either as food or as raw materials for manufacturing industries. For products to be exported, there are excellent harbors facing the east, south, and west; and Europe, the most important of the world's markets, is not far from our shores.

Our transportation facilities, however, are still far from perfect; for though the railroads are excellent, the building of good roads has only begun. Fortunately the farms in most sections rarely lie more than eight or ten miles from the railroads, and automobiles are rapidly becoming the farmer's means of taking his products to market.

In a new country one of the most difficult problems is to establish means of cheap transportation so that the surplus products can be marketed profitably. Millions of bushels of wheat were allowed to spoil in the early days of our western states and of the Canadian West, because the cost of hauling over the roadless prairies to the distant railroad was more than the wheat was worth.

## GOVERNMENT AID TO FARMING

In advanced countries the government tries to aid farming in every possible way. Credit must be given to the Department of Agriculture of our own government for its work in helping the country to a leading position in agriculture.

**Work of the Department of Agriculture.** Members of the Department are sent to foreign countries to seek new kinds of seeds, plants, and breeds of animals better suited to the climate and soil of the various parts of the country than those now grown here. Other members are scattered over the country at state and Federal stations, where they raise all kinds of useful plants and animals and try to improve them. Some investigators are working out ways of protecting crops from frost and of suppressing animal diseases and the ravages of insect pests. Still others study weather and soils in relation to crops.

**Educational work.** State governments as well as the national government take an active part in aiding the farmer. Most of them have departments of agriculture, and also agricultural colleges, which have long been partly supported by the Federal government. In many states the elements of agriculture are taught in the schools.

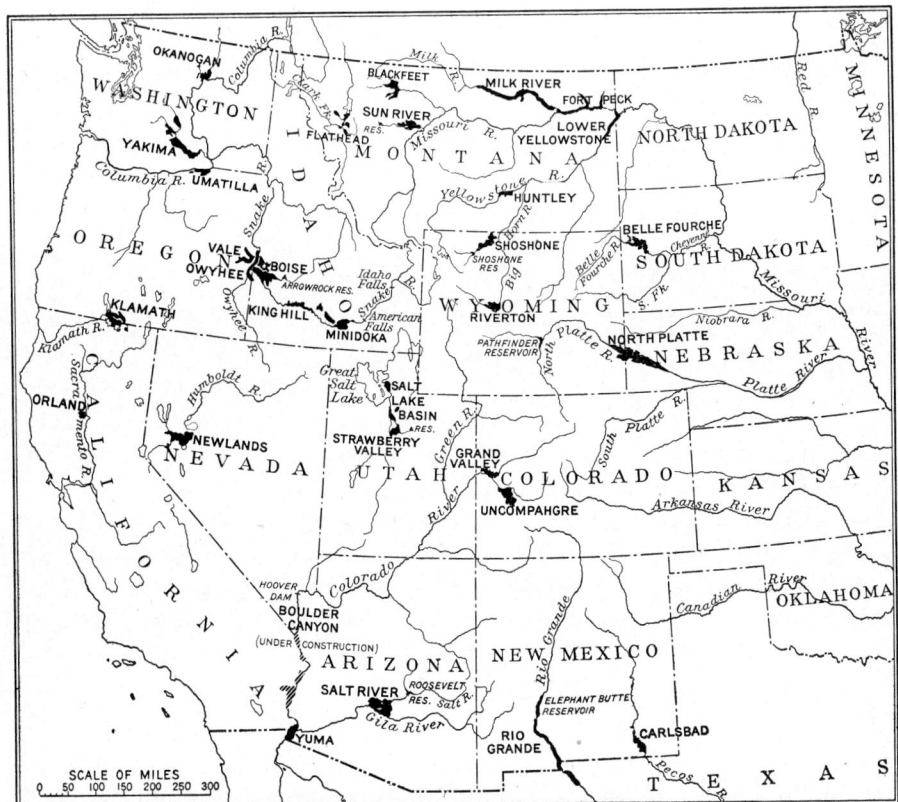

Fig. 19. Irrigation projects carried on by the United States Reclamation Service since 1902 have added more than 1,700,000 acres of farming land to the amount available in the United States. In the Salt River valley, irrigation makes it possible to grow Egyptian long-staple cotton, the finest kind of cotton, on more than 150,000 acres.

In 1914 the Federal and state governments combined in an effort to spread practical information relating to farming. As a result, in nearly every county of every state in the Union, government agents are showing farmers how to raise bigger crops, maintain the richness of the soil, and keep the domestic animals in the best condition. Some are showing farmers' wives the best way to can fruits and vegetables, to preserve eggs, to prepare farm products for the table, and to do economically the many other tasks that represent the women's share of farm work. Still other government agents are organizing boys' and girls' clubs whose object is to show the young people how to carry on farm work in such a way that it will be both interesting and profitable.

**Public works.** In addition to the huge sums spent directly on agricultural problems, the government of the United States has spent enormous sums in building dams and digging canals and even tunnels for the irrigation of parts of the dry West. It has also drained swamps and meadows to make them available for farming. Under the Reclamation Service of the Department of the Interior, more than thirty government projects have been started since 1902 for the reclamation of arid lands.

### QUESTIONS, EXERCISES, AND PROBLEMS

**A. The effect of rainfall on agriculture in the United States.**

1. On an outline map of the United States shade the areas of (*a*) heavy (over 50 inches), (*b*) medium (20 to 50 inches), and (*c*) light (under 20 inches) rainfall as shown in Figure 6. Pick out three localities and ask someone else in the class to tell why the rainfall is light, medium, or heavy there. Be ready to decide whether the answers are right or wrong.
2. Land receiving less than 20 inches of rainfall is considered arid or semi-arid. Make a list of fifteen states that are wholly or partly in the arid or semi-arid belt.
3. Name areas where the rainfall is 60 inches or more. Which of these are so level that the land is too swampy for farming? (See Figure 22.)
4. The total area of American farm land could be increased about one tenth if the 120,000 square miles of swampy lands were reclaimed by drainage. Compare the area of the swampy lands with the area of your state. Does Figure 22 show much waste land in your state? What kind?
5. On the irrigation projects of the United States the value of the crops per acre in a recent year was $63.60; the cropped area amounted to 1,100,000 acres. How much wealth was thus added to the country that year because of the irrigation work of the United States Reclamation Service? Locate three of the irrigation projects.

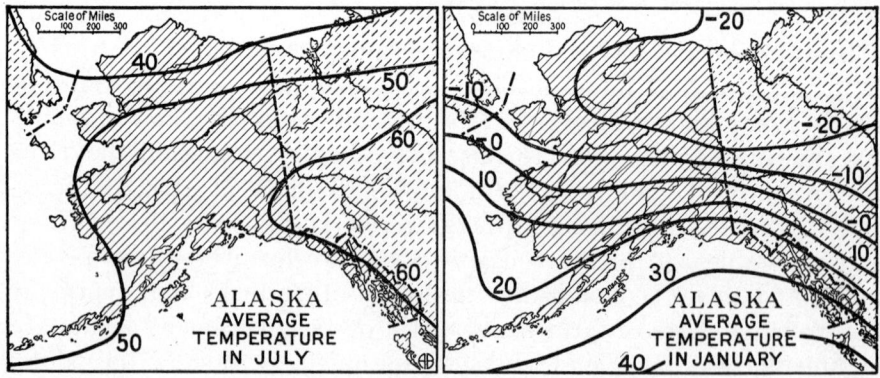

FIGS. 20, 21. Note the wide range of temperatures in Alaska. Note also the great difference between winter and summer temperatures in the Yukon valley; there the July temperature is high enough for agriculture, and the summer days are long and sunny. But the growing season is too short for many crops. The southern coast has about the same winter temperature as the North Atlantic states, and almost the same summer temperature as the coast of Washington and Oregon, and the growing season is long enough for any of the temperate-region crops; but heavy summer rainfall limits agriculture.

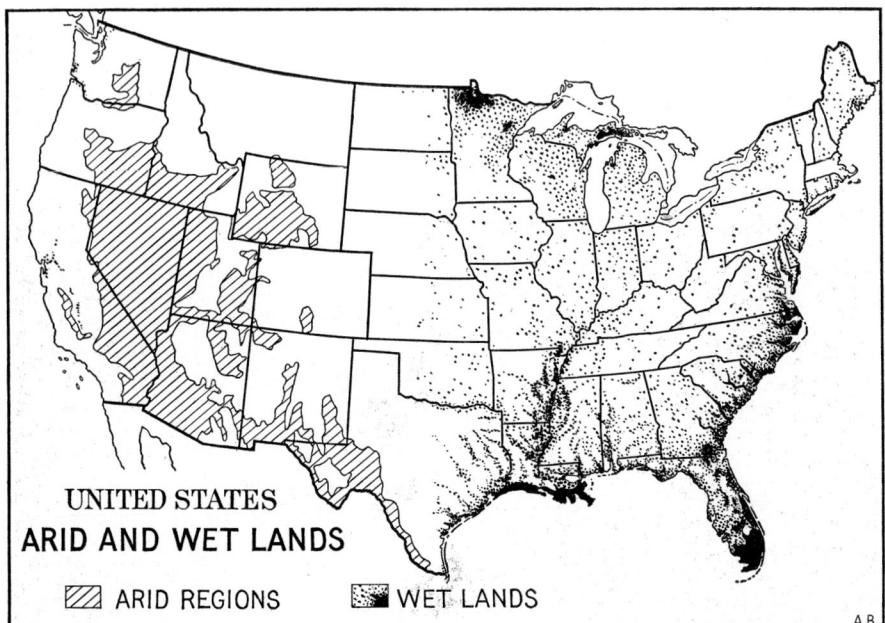

Fig. 22. Arid lands and swamp lands are not available for agriculture. Much of the arid region is mountain land that will never be productive. The swamps that need to be drained are small compared with the arid regions, and are located in a different part of the country. The draining of swamps is usually undertaken by the governments of the states concerned, not by the Federal government. Lovers of wild life tell us that some swamp areas should be left as refuges for birds and wild animals, for many species will become extinct when the last of the swamps are drained.

6. That same year the value of the crops per acre of improved land for the whole country averaged about $36.33. How do you account for the difference between this crop value and that mentioned in Question 5?
7. Explain how the reclamation of arid land benefits you.
8. Frame a brief statement to tell how these examples of reclaiming waste land by irrigation illustrate the importance of rainfall to agriculture.

**B. Alaska as a farming country.**

1. Compare Figures 3 and 4 with Figures 20 and 21. What parts of Alaska might we expect to be productive?
2. In what other parts of the United States are the summer temperatures like those of Alaska? the winter temperatures?

**C. Why some countries carry on intensive farming.**

1. A farmer in Shantung, China, had a wife and ten children. He supported them all on two and a half acres of land, where he kept one cow, one donkey, and two pigs, and grew millet, wheat, sweet potatoes, and beans. In the United States there are not far from three acres of cultivated land for each man, woman, and child. How many acres would an American farmer need, with his high standard of living, to support a family of the same size as the Chinese farmer's?

Fig. 23. The fertile fields along the Vetarrabia Canal, near Chiaravalle, in southern Italy. In many parts of Europe the most careful irrigation is practiced.

2. What methods of cultivation do the Chinese employ that enable them to support large families on such small tracts? (For information, consult King's *Farmers of Forty Centuries*, Huntington's *Asia — A Geography Reader*, Ross's *The Changing Chinese*, or an encyclopedia.)

D. **The relation of machinery to the number of farmers.**

1. Mention two ways in which the invention of farm machinery, such as the McCormick reaper, has aided in the growth of American cities.
2. During twenty years the number of farmers in Ohio increased only 10 per cent, but the production of crops increased about 40 per cent. Explain how this was possible.

E. **How the government assists agriculture.**

1. Explain how a Kansas wheat farmer, a Delaware peach grower, and a farmer near your home may be benefited by each of the following: (*a*) the United States Weather Bureau, (*b*) the Rural Free Delivery system, (*c*) an Agricultural Experiment Station, and (*d*) good roads built by the nation, state, county, or town.
2. The Department of Agriculture supports plant introduction stations which serve as little " Ellis Islands " for thousands of immigrant plants. To determine whether this service may be of value to the country, consider how many of our common fruits and vegetables were formerly natives of a foreign land. Make a list of fruits and vegetables that you commonly see in stores; cross off your list the names in the following list and see how many immigrant plants are left:

## The United States as a Farming Country

PLANTS NATIVE TO AMERICA WHEN THE COLONISTS ARRIVED

| sweet potato | squash | bean | peanut | pineapple |
|---|---|---|---|---|
| artichoke | red pepper | tobacco | cotton | tomato |
| | pumpkin | maize | potato | |

3. The *National Geographic Magazine* for August, 1921, contains a well-illustrated article on these "Ellis Islands." Let some one volunteer to bring in the magazine and give a short summary of the article.
4. The Year Books of the Department of Agriculture describe odd new varieties of plants that are being introduced. Find the names of at least two valuable food plants introduced during the last ten years.
5. Write to the Experiment Station connected with your State College of Agriculture for printed matter telling what can be done to improve the chief crop of the state. Write also to your Congressman at Washington and ask him to send your school a Year Book (free) from the Department of Agriculture.

**F. Why some countries excel in farming.**
1. The following countries are prominent or progressive in agriculture: France, Italy, Russia, Germany, Argentina, Japan, Australia, New Zealand. Select one, and from the maps and tables in the text and at the back of this book, get information with respect to the following points: (*a*) size, (*b*) relief, (*c*) temperature in January and July, (*d*) rainfall, (*e*) energy of people, (*f*) population, (*g*) density of population, (*h*) transportation facilities. Decide which of these conditions help to explain the prominence of the country in agriculture. From a geography or an encyclopedia learn something about the character of the people and about their government.
2. Compare the selected country with the United States in all the conditions listed above.
3. Are there any conditions unfavorable to agriculture in the country selected for study? If so, what are they?
4. Why is the country not so prominent in agriculture as the United States?
5. Make an oral report to the class upon the country that you select. Be sure to point out carefully on the wall map the parts of the country that are most important in farming.

**G. Why some countries are backward in farming.**
1. Select one of the following countries: Mexico, Spain, Bulgaria, Greece, Morocco, Siberia, Peru, Bolivia. Find out why it is backward in agriculture. Take notes under the same headings as in Problem *F*.
2. Has the country any conditions favorable for farming? Explain them.
3. Which parts of the United States does the country most resemble in relief? in temperature? in rainfall?
4. Make an oral report to the class upon the country studied.

*United States Department of Agriculture*

FIGS. 24, 25, 26. At the left are the two stalks of smooth, or beardless, wheat; in the center, two of bearded wheat; and at the right a stalk of rye. Rye looks like a poor kind of wheat. Barley also somewhat resembles wheat (Fig. 46, page 60). Wheat, rye, and barley are members of one division of the great grass family.

## CHAPTER THREE

### CEREAL FARMING

FARMING is the chief means of production, for through it we obtain all our cereals, vegetables, and fruits, as well as sugar, coffee, nuts, cotton, and many other products. The raising of animals is part of the work of farming, and this branch of the industry supplies not only food, but wool and fur for clothing, and hides to use in many ways.

Since farming is so large a field of production, we shall subdivide our study of it, taking up first the most important group of products, the cereals.

**The importance of cereals as food.** Most people look upon grasses as fit only for animals to eat, yet we get our chief food from them. According to the botanist, grasses include not only the vegetation that grows on our meadows and lawns, but also wheat, corn, oats, rye, barley, rice, and millet.

These grasses are called *cereals*, and their seeds are made into the " staff of life " for nearly all the peoples of the world. Wheat bread forms the chief food of the people of the United States, Great Britain,

France, and many other countries in both the northern and the southern temperate zone. Rye bread is a staple food in Germany and in northern and central Russia; oatmeal in Scotland; barley bread in Norway, Sweden, and northern Prussia; corn bread in Mexico, Central America, Rumania, and Egypt; and rice and millet for eight hundred million people in India, China, Japan, and the East Indies. As a rule the cereal most used in a country is the one which produces the largest crops with the least trouble.

**How great crops are raised.** Although the crops that are raised today are not nearly so large as the farmers wish, they are far larger than were once raised. Ever since the days when primitive man first began to cultivate the bearded wild wheat which still grows on the hills of Palestine, the farmers have been making improvements in the cereals themselves and in the methods of raising them. In the first place, the early farmers tried again and again to see what kind of crop

FIG. 27. Oats grow in loose panicles, instead of tight spikes, as do wheat, barley, and rye.

would grow best in their particular climate and soil, and what crop was the best for food. Some are still trying to solve this problem. The United States government coöperates with the farmers in trying to find wheat that will withstand drought, corn that can endure low temperature, and rice that will yield large crops with little or no irrigation.

Another problem was how to prevent the soil from losing its fertility. Early in the history of agriculture man found out about the use of animal fertilizers. Later he discovered that some crops, when plowed under, would benefit the soil. When it was learned that soil can be enriched by the use of substances known as commercial fertilizers, — such as guano, lime, and phosphate rock, — the problem was to discover the right kind and amount for each crop.

One of the chief ways of improving crops is to select the seed of those plants that produce the best and largest crops. So great have been the changes in the cereal plants that today a cornstalk, for example, may be five to ten times as tall as its remote ancestor and may produce ten to twenty times as much seed.

## WHEAT

In the four years of the World War, all the civilized people of the world were made to realize the importance of wheat. Because many millions of farmers had become soldiers, the production of all foodstuffs fell off greatly. But it was the falling off in the production of wheat that caused the greatest distress. The substitutes for wheat, such as corn, rye, barley, and potatoes, were not equally appetizing and satisfying. For a time it seemed that the side that could get the most wheat and make it go furthest would gain the victory. "Wheat will win the war," was a common assertion.

**Where our wheat is grown.** Although wheat is grown in every state in the Union, three regions are most important: (1) the central United States from Maryland and Pennsylvania westward to Kansas; (2) Minnesota, the Dakotas, and Montana; and (3) eastern Washington and Oregon (Fig. 28). The wheat belt, where production is greatest, extends northward across Nebraska, South Dakota, and North Dakota into Canada, and projects into Minnesota. In this region prosperity depends largely upon the wheat crop.

**Conditions for raising wheat in the wheat belt.** Let us see what conditions cause wheat to be so important in this belt. In the first place, a relief map of North America shows that the region where wheat is most abundant is part of the Great Plains. As in most plains, the soil here is fine and fertile. Furthermore, on rolling plains it is easy to use large machines for plowing, harrowing, and reaping.

Rainfall is even more important than relief. As Figure 6 shows, from 15 to 30 inches of rain fall annually in the wheat belt. Fortunately much of this comes in the fall and early spring, when the wheat most needs it. But the skies are usually cloudless for a few weeks before the harvest, and the resulting dry weather ripens the seeds.

Temperature is quite as important as rainfall. Wheat growing is restricted to the cool temperate zone; the southern states, for instance, have practically none. Even within the region favorable to wheat, extensive crops are obtained only by cultivating the particular kind of wheat suited to the temperature. There are two kinds: one, planted in the fall, is called *winter wheat*, while the other, planted in the spring, is called *spring wheat*.

In the region of winter wheat, — Kansas and Nebraska, — although the winters are cold, they do not kill the wheat, and it can grow in the late fall and early spring. Hence wheat is sown in the autumn, gets a good start before the winter sets in, is ready to grow vigorously in the early spring, and can be harvested in the late spring.

In South Dakota, Minnesota, North Dakota, and Canada, the cold winters would kill the wheat if it were planted in the fall. There the seed is sown in early spring and the crop is harvested at the end of summer. Accordingly these regions raise spring wheat.

**Conditions in other regions.** In the plains of south-central Canada, Argentina, southern Russia, Hungary, and northern and western France, relief, rainfall, and temperature are especially favorable for wheat (Figs. 28, 38). Regions other than those mentioned above may grow wheat, but at a disadvantage. This, however, may be balanced by the advantage of a position near a great market. In New York and Pennsylvania, for example, the land is hilly, and as a rule the farmers cannot use the best labor-saving machines in planting and harvesting wheat. Nearness to the great eastern markets, however, makes freight charges low, so that these farmers get more

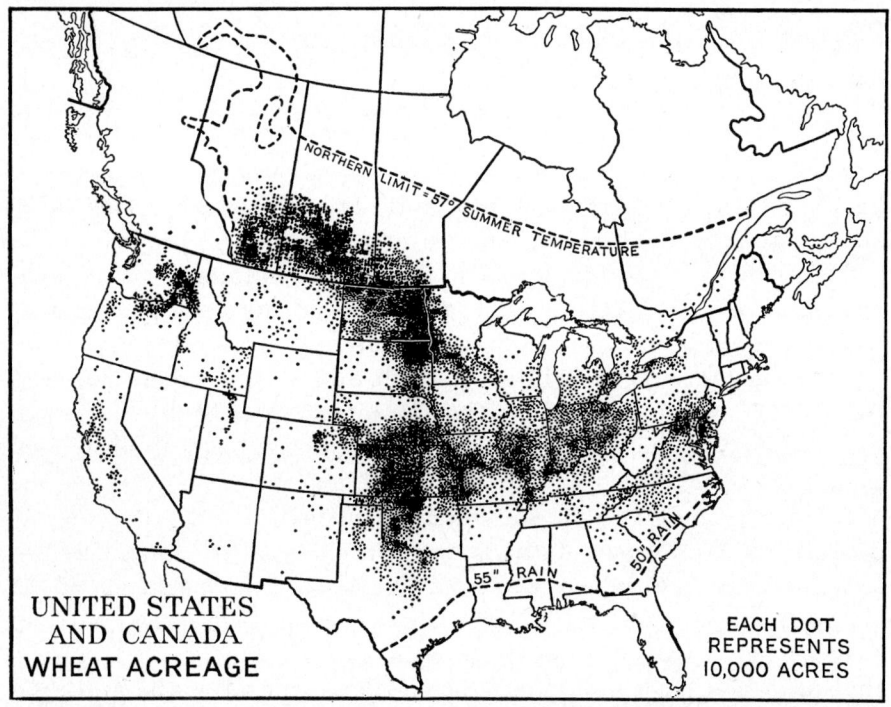

*Courtesy of O. E. Baker and Economic Geography*

FIG. 28. Wheat requires an average temperature of at least 55° for three or four months in the year. This requirement of a growing season lasting at least 90 days fixes the northern limit of wheat production. Wheat could be grown in the South Atlantic states, but cotton, being more profitable there, takes up the good land. Furthermore, fungi and insect enemies of the wheat are more active in a warm, moist climate than in the cooler, drier climate of the Great Plains.

*Ellsworth Huntington*

Fig. 29. Wheat harvesting in Turkestan. In Asiatic countries and in many parts of Europe wheat is still harvested with the sickle, as here, or with the scythe (Fig. 42). Behind the reaper follow the workers who tie the fallen stalks into sheaves, which are gathered into stacks that stand in the field until they can be carted to the threshing floor. There the grain is threshed by hand or by being trampled under the feet of animals and is then winnowed by hand. This is the way harvesting is shown on the Egyptian monuments, which record for us the wheat farming of forty centuries ago.

for their wheat than do those in Nebraska and Kansas. This helps to pay for extra hand labor, but does not lead to large production.

**Satisfactions and anxieties of the wheat farmer.** The wheat farmer, like every other farmer, has his special worries. If he plants winter wheat, he watches the weather carefully in the autumn to see whether the tiny plants will get enough rain to make them vigorous before the coming of winter. Then he looks for signs of the Hessian fly that attacks the wheat plant near the base, causing the leaves to turn yellow and die. He knows that if many flies appear in the autumn they may become so numerous in spring as to ruin the crop. Toward the end of winter the farmer watches his fields anxiously to see if there are many brown leaves, which would show that his wheat has been "winter killed." But with the opening of spring, warmer weather and good rains cause the fields to turn green. Yet even in the spring the farmer's troubles are not over, for after the grain has begun to grow rapidly, it may be injured by a severe storm.

When the crop should be having good rains and the weather continues fair, he watches every cloud as anxiously as does a boy on the morning of a championship baseball game; but the farmer hopes for rain, while the boy prays that it will be clear. When at last the hot winds stop blowing and the rain falls, the farmer's satisfaction is mingled with the fear that the rain may turn to hail.

If good fortune smiles on the wheat farmer, the stems grow rapidly, and in time the wheat " heads out"; that is, the seeds begin to form in the heads. Now if rust does not appear upon the stems or smut among the seed, the crop will be big — a " bumper crop," the farmer would say. Nearly all the dangers have been passed. Under the hot sun the field changes slowly from green to lighter hues until the golden yellow shows that it is ready to harvest.

The farmer enjoys one other scene even more than the field of ripened wheat. That he sees after the crop has been cut and the seed threshed out of the heads. He takes his way to the nearest railroad, driving a wagon loaded with wheat and leading a second wagon, while his sons and hired men may follow in the same way. The wheat procession is repeated many times, for the farmer has not enough wagons, horses, and men to take all the big harvest at once. This procession means the end of his worries and the reward for all his work, provided he is sure that he can sell at a good price.

**How machinery does the work on a wheat farm.** Methods of planting, harvesting, and threshing wheat are nowhere more ad-

FIG. 30. The use of power-driven machinery in farming is not yet a hundred years old. It has made possible the production of huge crops on wide stretches of new land. This combination harvester, run by eight men, cuts, threshes, winnows, and sacks 120 acres a day. By the old hand methods, the most expert reaper could cut only 3 to 4 acres a day, and often the grain was spoiled by rain before it could be gathered into stacks or carried to the barn for threshing.

vanced than in our five great wheat states. The land is often made ready for the seed by a gang of from eight to sixteen plows linked together and drawn by a steam or gasoline tractor. This is followed by a broad harrow drawn by four or five horses. Next comes a planting machine that scatters the seeds evenly and covers them to just the proper depth. One such machine can plant a hundred acres in a day.

The ripened wheat is usually harvested by a self-binder. This is a very ingenious machine that cuts the standing grain, collects it into a bunch, encircles it with twine, ties a knot, cuts the twine, and drops the bundle or sheaf. Usually four or five horses draw the machine. Sometimes four or five self-binders are drawn by one tractor.

After the wheat has been well dried, the grain is taken from the heads by another complicated machine, the thresher. This is even more wonderful than the self-binder. The sheaves made by the binder are brought from the field in wagonloads. The thresher takes a sheaf, cuts the binding twine, loosens the straw, and feeds it into a cylinder. There the seeds are knocked from the heads. Then the grain is separated from the straw by being dropped through a current of air, which blows away the light straw and chaff and stacks it at one side. Finally, the clean grain is automatically weighed and then dumped into a waiting wagon. As soon as one wagon is filled, another takes its place. Two or three thousand bushels of wheat a day can thus be handled by a single machine. What a change this is from the early days when the straw was spread on the barn floor and the wheat was pounded from the heads by a jointed stick, or flail, in the hands of the farmer!

In our most important wheat belt, machinery does nearly all the work. It can be used to advantage because the farms are level and large, often of several hundred acres. It is necessary because the population is scattered, and human labor is not only costly but also difficult to hire. Hence farm work consists of pulling the levers and opening the throttles of machinery rather than of wielding heavy tools.

**Wheat farming outside the wheat belt.** In Kansas, Nebraska, the Dakotas, and Minnesota we have seen that wheat farming is in its most advanced stages, and that machinery is there used most extensively. Elsewhere two factors largely determine the methods of wheat farming; namely, the relief of the land and the degree of progressiveness of the people.

In Oregon and Washington, where the wheat farms are large, the progressive farmers use machinery fully as much as in our chief wheat belt. The methods used in the Canadian wheat lands, which are the northward extension of those of the Dakotas, are the same.

Where the region is rugged, as in the Appalachian Mountains, wheat is raised only on the valley floors. Since the farms are small, the farmer cannot afford expensive machinery, and therefore human labor plays a large part in all farming operations.

### CORN

It is difficult for one who does not live in the great corn region to realize how important this cereal is to the United States. "King Corn" rules the land; he can bring prosperity or want. When he smiles upon the farmers with abundant crops, prosperity spreads far and wide. When he frowns with crop failures, business depression often follows and poverty knocks at many a door.

**Our greatest crop.** In a good corn year the United States raises more than three billion bushels. This would give twenty-five bushels to every man, woman, and child in the United States. What becomes of so many bushels? No matter how much a person may relish freshly cooked sweet corn, or corn that is canned, popped, or hulled,

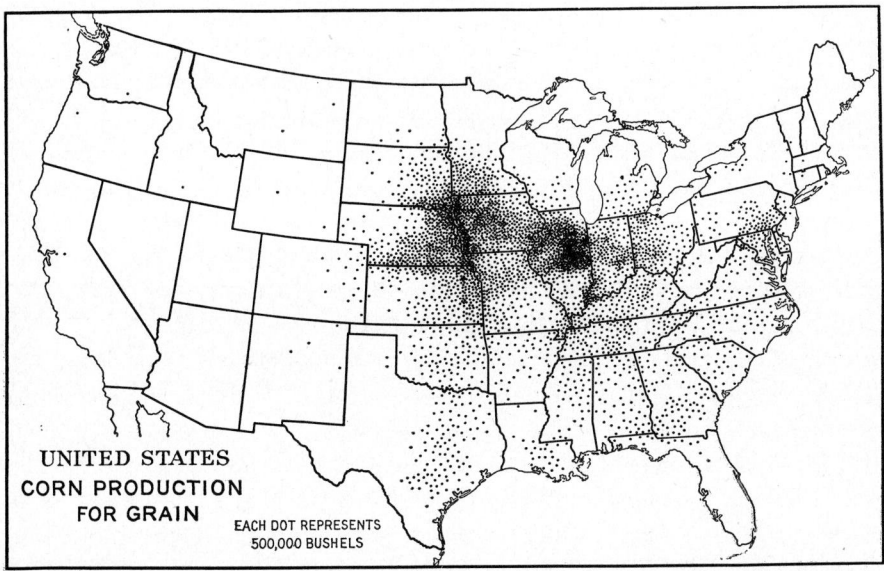

FIG. 31. Corn, or maize, was the only grain that Europeans found under cultivation in North America. The Six Nations had cornfields which they cultivated year after year. There are over 6,000,000 farms in this country, and some corn is grown on most of them. But corn growing on a large scale is not so widespread as wheat growing (Fig. 28). Corn demands a season of clear, warm sunshine and warm nights, with frequent light rains during the growing season. In the Corn Belt, which stretches across western Ohio, Indiana, Illinois, and eastern Nebraska, corn growers find the right conditions of soil, sunshine, and rainfall. Corn is our most valuable crop.

*United States Department of Agriculture*

FIG. 32. One of the members of a Boys' Corn Club in South Carolina and the corn that he grew. In an ordinary year the Corn Club members raise an average of 75 bushels to the acre in regions where 30 bushels to the acre is considered a good average crop, and some boys raise 200 bushels. Careful seed selection and intensive cultivation explain the high yield.

or corn flakes, corn cakes, or other corn dishes, it would be almost impossible for him to eat in a year the twenty-five bushels that represent his share. In a year each of us eats scarcely more than a bushel or two of corn. But we do consume much of the remainder of our share in the form of bacon, pork, lard, ham, beef, and other meat products; for hogs and cattle eat vast quantities of corn. It is the best cereal for fattening stock, partly because it contains more oil than any other. The rest of our share of the thirty bushels of corn is exported in the form of these same cattle products.

Corn is a truly American crop. It was king in America even before the coming of the white man. In those days Europeans had never heard of it. The early settlers soon learned about it from the Indians, who scratched the soil with a stick and put fish in the hills for fertilizer before dropping in the grain. Since then corn has been carried to many lands, but its most important production is still in America.

**Why corn thrives in our corn belt.** The United States, as we have seen, raises nearly three fifths of the world's crop of corn. As corn is grown in every state in the Union, it is easy for almost any American boy or girl to see just how it is planted, cultivated, and harvested. Not much, to be sure, is raised in the western half of the United States, where there is too little rainfall for it and the high plateaus are too cold, especially during the nights in summer. A good deal is raised in the Appalachian Mountain states, though the land is rugged and the soil coarse. But even there the crop is meager compared with the region of the greatest production, where the conditions for corn are so favorable that in summer it is difficult to get out of sight of growing corn. This region, as is seen in Figure 31, extends from eastern Nebraska across Iowa, Illinois, and Indiana to western Ohio. It is called the American corn belt.

On the rolling prairies of the corn belt it is possible to use machinery almost as freely as in raising wheat. The *relief* is so gentle that almost every acre can be planted. The *soil* is deep, fertile, and so free from stones that cultivators, which root out the weeds, can slide smoothly through it between the rows of corn. The *temperature* is such that there is a long growing season without frosts. Both the days and the nights are warm in summer, and the great heat of midsummer makes the corn grow wonderfully. Although a good amount of *rain* falls, it generally comes in brief thunder showers and the sun is little clouded.

**Corn in other lands.** Most of the conditions that favor corn growing prevail in Rumania, Hungary, Mexico, and Argentina, and in those regions corn is an important crop (Fig. 39). In Argentina, especially, corn has rapidly increased in importance, until now the crop is often larger than that of wheat. Corn cannot be grown in Canada — except in southern Ontario — or in northern Europe, because these northern regions do not have summers that are long enough or warm enough. They have less than five months free from frost.

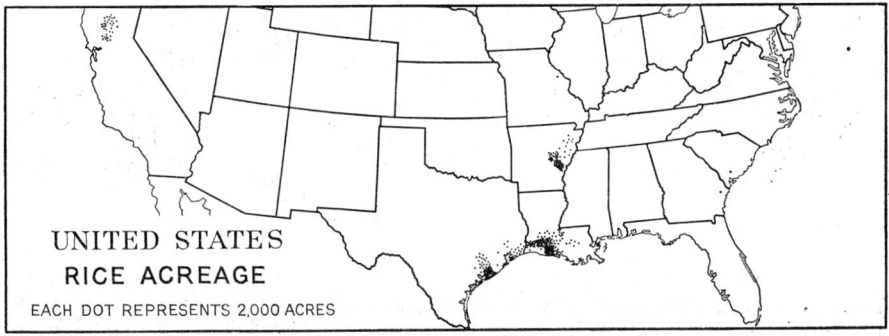

FIG. 33. In eastern Texas, along the Gulf coast, and in the Mississippi river lands of Arkansas are found level, swampy tracts of good soil within the belt of high temperature that rice needs. In the inland valleys of California, where soil, surface, and temperature are suitable for the upland varieties, rice is now cultivated successfully on irrigated land.

## RICE

FIG. 34. A head of rice has many short stems, each bearing a few grains, that lie close to the main stalk.

Rice feeds more people than any other cereal. In many parts of India, China, and Japan, the daily allowance of rice is as much a necessity as the loaf of bread is among the Western peoples.

It is most interesting to see the different ways in which rice is eaten in the Eastern countries. The native of India sits on his heels with a banana leaf spread on the ground before him, bearing a little pile of boiled rice. With his right hand he makes a small rice ball and skillfully tosses it into his mouth. Every meal is of rice if he can afford it; otherwise his main food is millet. Hot spices often add zest to the taste of the rice ball. The native of China or Japan pokes the rice into his mouth by means of chopsticks. He holds the rice bowl near his mouth, and with the chopsticks shoves in the contents as fast as he can. In some countries, as in Turkey and Persia, rice is cooked so that each grain is separate. Bits of meat, nuts, vegetables, or raisins are added, a heaping dish is set on a small, low table, and everyone eats from it with his hands.

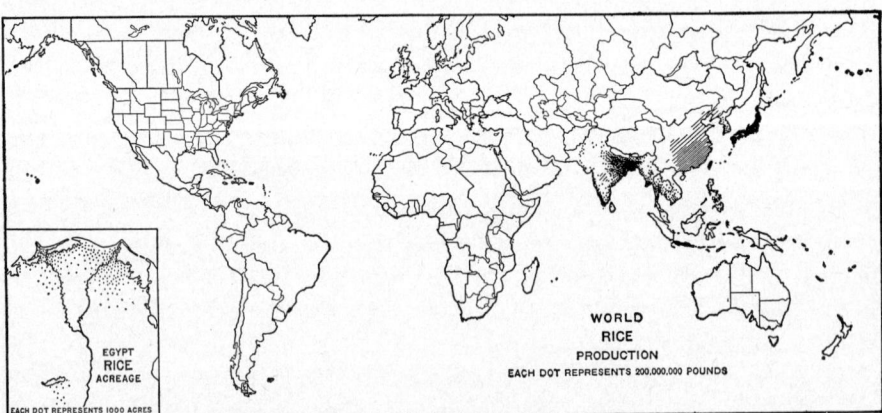

FIG. 35. Draw a line from the northern part of Japan to the eastern end of Java; then, going south of Java, to the Indus River in western India; then across Asia to northern Japan. In the triangular area thus marked off rice is the main food of perhaps two thirds of the 900 millions of people. More than 90 per cent of the world's rice crop is grown in this area. Here are found the conditions required for rice culture: high temperature; heavy rainfall; low-lying, level lands; a large supply of cheap labor. Egypt, Italy, Spain, Madagascar, Brazil, West Africa, and some districts in the southeastern United States (Fig. 33) are the main parts of the world outside this area where rice is grown on a commercial scale.

FIG. 36. Harrowing a rice field in the Philippines. The land is flooded to prepare it for planting; and the plow and the harrow are drawn by the carabao, or water buffalo.

**How rice is raised in the Orient.** The farmers of India and the Far East probably raise three or four billion bushels of rice each year. Some of this is exported, but most of it is eaten by the people. The most surprising thing about this huge crop is that it is grown with little or no help from farming machinery. Nearly all the work is done by hand.

A rice field is always nearly level. It is inclosed within low ridges of earth so that it can be flooded as the crop grows. If the rice is raised on terraces that are built on a steep slope, as it often is in these over-populated regions, the fields are small. The flat land of broad plains, valley floors, deltas, and swamps is ideal for rice farming, since there the level surfaces and the abundant supply of water make it easy to flood the crop.

It is interesting to watch the rice farmer of the tropics from the beginning of his labors, when the rains come, till the crop is stored away. In India, for example, after the fields have been soaked at the beginning of the rainy season, the earth is lightly plowed, or turned over by a large hoe. The plow is merely two pieces of wood fastened together, with a metal tip that goes through the earth. It is drawn by a pair of bullocks in dry land and by buffaloes

*United States Department of Agriculture*

FIG. 37. Millet is said to be the first grain that man gathered in its wild state and sowed in better ground to get a better yield; that is, it was the first grain cultivated.

in wet lands. The peasants then churn the soil into a creamy paste with their bare feet or with hoes, until the fields look like giant mud pies ready for baking.

Rice plants about eight inches tall are now brought from nursery beds in bundles of a hundred or so. A gang of women start from one side of the field and carefully push each plant into the mud, about ten inches from its neighbors. These women have transplanted rice ever since they were young girls, and they do it speedily and skillfully. Now the water is admitted to the fields and kept two to three inches deep for three to four months, or until the harvest time approaches. In the meantime the field is occasionally weeded.

The sight of hundreds of recently planted rice fields is one long to be remembered. The delicate green of the young plants suggests a rug of softest velvet. Equally interesting is the harvest scene, when women reap the rice with little hand sickles, while men with bullocks thresh and winnow it by the primitive methods described above for wheat.

### MILLET

While few people in the United States know much about millet, to the world at large it is almost as important as wheat. Its name comes from the Latin word *mille*, meaning a thousand. One seed may produce a plant yielding a thousand seeds.

**Why millet is an important cereal.** The number of people in India and China who depend almost entirely upon millet as their food is much greater than the whole population of the western hemisphere. In the Orient it is the daily food of the poor man's family and is eaten like corn, both in the form of bread and as porridge.

In the United States some millet is raised; but the crop is mainly cut for cattle feed before it ripens. The millet used for caged birds or for poultry is imported largely from Germany and Italy.

*Cereal Farming* 53

QUESTIONS, EXERCISES, AND PROBLEMS

**A. Where wheat is cultivated.**

1. Taken on an average the ten leading wheat states are Kansas, North Dakota, Montana, Nebraska, Oklahoma, Washington, Illinois, Ohio, Indiana, and South Dakota. Divide these states into four groups on the basis of climatic conditions. See Figures 3, 4, and 6.

2. Discuss each group with reference to (a) time when wheat is sown, (b) relief, (c) methods of cultivation, and (d) position in reference to markets.

3. Rearrange the states according to production of wheat. (See Agriculture Year Book.)

4. Wheat is so valuable that almost every country raises at least a little. The times of harvest in the wheat regions vary as follows:

| | |
|---|---|
| January | Australia, New Zealand, Chile |
| February, March | India, Upper Egypt |
| April | Lower Egypt, Persia, Mexico |
| May | Texas, China, Japan, Algeria |
| June | California, Kansas, Tennessee, Virginia, Spain, southern France, Italy, Greece, Turkey |
| July | Washington, Oregon, Nebraska, Iowa, Illinois, Indiana, Ohio, southern England, Germany, southern Russia |
| August | The Dakotas, Minnesota, southern Canada, Holland, Belgium, northern England |
| September, October | Parts of western Canada, Scotland, Norway, Sweden, northern Russia |
| November | Peru, South Africa |
| December | Argentina, Burma, New South Wales |

On a world map make a chart to show where wheat is harvested during each month.

5. Plan a journey lasting throughout the year so that all your time on land will be spent in a country where the wheat crop is being harvested. Write your plan in your notebook. Show the class, by means of a wall map of the world, where you would be during each month of the year and how you would get from one country to another. Be sure to make a reasonable estimate of the time required to travel from one place to another.

6. In Bolivia, Morocco, Spain, the Balkan states, and Turkey, wheat farming is carried on almost entirely by hand labor. What conditions may help to account for this fact? (Consult relief maps.)

7. Why is wheat grown in northern China, but not in southern China? Explain why there are no large wheat farms in eastern China (Fig. 176).

8. Compare Figure 38 with Figures 17 and 18. What do you find to be the general northern limit of wheat growing? the southern limit?

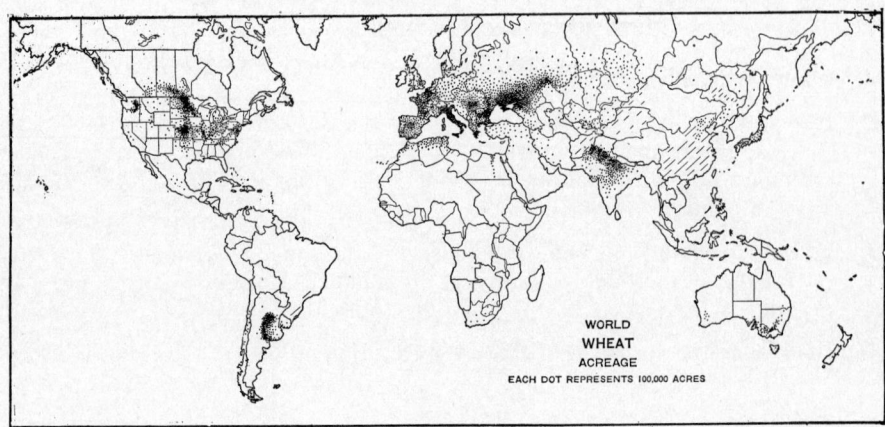

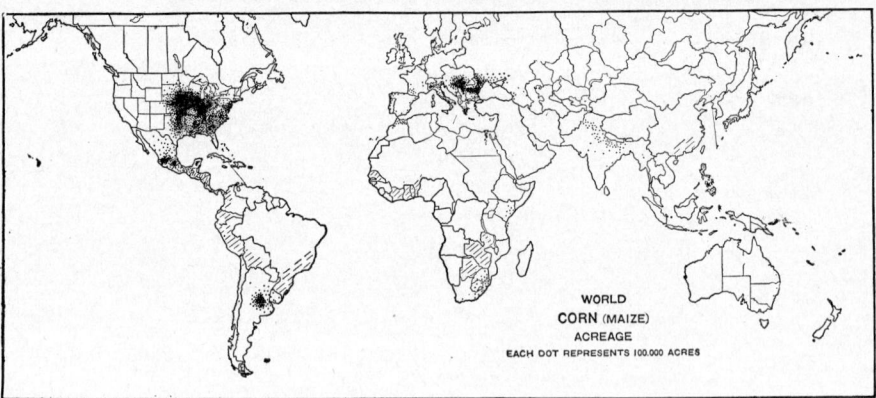

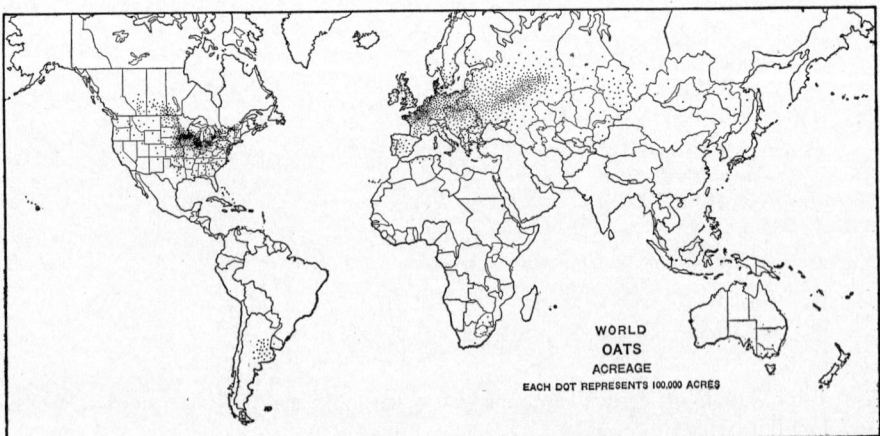

Figs. 38, 39, 40. Mankind depends on wheat, corn, oats, rice, barley, and millet for its chief foods. Comparing the maps of the production of these six grains with Figure 176 (page 284), we see that population tends to concentrate where grain can be grown.

## Cereal Farming

**B. Wheat as an important article of commerce.**

A Comparison of the World's Imports and Exports of Wheat

(I) Average Imports of Wheat in Bushels

|  | Total Imports | Imports per Capita | Yield per Acre |
|---|---|---|---|
| United Kingdom | 220,000,000 | 5.0 | 33 |
| Germany | 80,000,000 | 1.3 | 32 |
| Italy | 80,000,000 | 2.0 | 16 |
| France | 45,000,000 | 1.1 | 19 |
| Japan | 25,000,000 | 0.4 | 21 |

(II) Average Exports of Wheat in Bushels

|  | Total Exports | Per Cent of World's Total Production | Yield per Acre |
|---|---|---|---|
| Canada | 250,000,000 | 9 | 18 |
| United States | 175,000,000 | 18 | 15 |
| Argentina | 130,000,000 | 6 | 10 |
| Russia | 100,000,000 | 16 | 10 |
| Australia | 100,000,000 | 3 | 12 |
| Rumania | 60,000,000 | 3 | 14 |
| India | 25,000,000 | 8 | 12 |

1. Why do the United Kingdom, Germany, and Italy import so much wheat?
2. Why does Japan, with a third more people than the United Kingdom, import only a fraction as much wheat?
3. Compare the yield per acre in importing and exporting countries. Why do the importers need wheat when the yield from their own farms is so high? Why is it so high?
4. Rearrange all the countries in the wheat tables given above, according to the amount of wheat produced per acre. Be ready to ask a good question as to the position of each country in this new list.
5. How do you explain the fact that India exports far less wheat than Canada, though she raises almost as much?
6. Why does Australia export less than Canada and Argentina?
7. Although Russia raises much wheat, her people eat relatively little. In which part of Russia is wheat chiefly eaten? Why? (Fig. 43.)

**C. How the scientific farmer reaps his reward.**

1. The average yield of corn per acre among the farmers of the United States is about 26 bushels; among the Connecticut farmers, it is about 80 per cent greater; among the members of Boys' Corn Clubs, about 80 bushels. The prize winners among the boys often produce more than 160 bushels per acre. By what methods do the boys increase the yield?

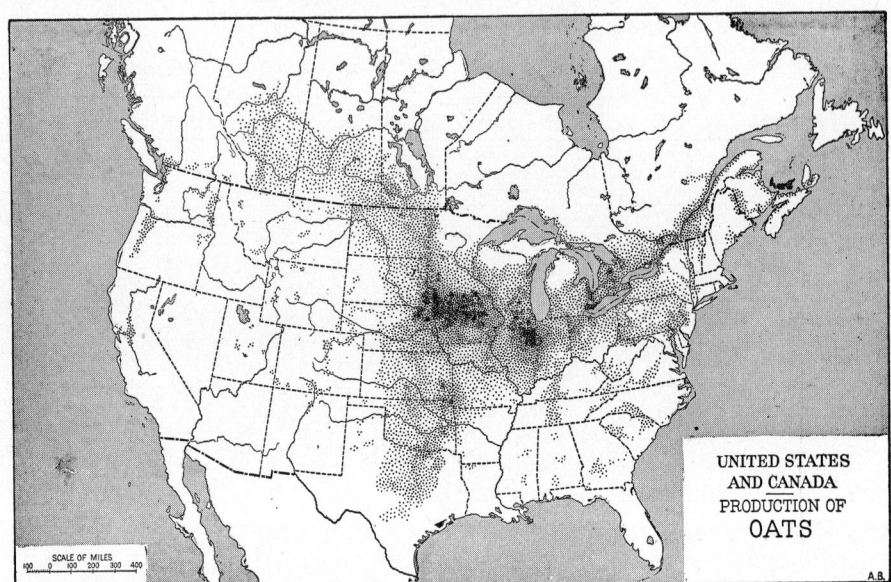

Fig. 41. The United States and Canada grow more than a third of the world's crop of oats (Fig. 40). Like rye, oats will grow in cooler climates than wheat; the crop will also stand more moisture. Notice the heavy production of oats along the lower St. Lawrence, where wheat production is relatively light (Fig. 28) and the summers are cool and humid.

2. The United States produces about 3,000,000,000 bushels of corn per year, practically all of which is consumed at home. If all the farmers in the country increased their yield to equal that of the Connecticut farmers, how many bushels would be produced each year? How could all the extra corn be used? What would happen to the price? Why does Connecticut excel in yield per acre?

3. Suppose a farmer in Illinois has 40 acres in corn and raises 40 bushels of corn to the acre, or a little more than the Illinois average. How much more money would he receive if he increased his yield to equal the average yield of the Boys' Corn Club members? of the prize winners?

4. What effect would such increased yields have on the prices of corn and of meat?

D. The consumption of corn.
1. What conclusion do you draw from the following figures as to the relation between the amount of meat and of cereals consumed by a country?

USUAL CONSUMPTION OF CEREALS AND MEAT PER CAPITA

| Country | Cereals | Meat |
|---|---|---|
| United States | 295 lbs. | 172 lbs. |
| England | 356 lbs. | 119 lbs. |
| Germany | 525 lbs. | 113 lbs. |
| France | 550 lbs. | 80 lbs. |

2. Farmers in Maine do not find it profitable to raise corn except for fodder or to sell as green corn to be eaten on the cob or to be canned. Why do they not deal in the ripe crop?
3. Make a list of the by-products of corn that might be useful in your home.

**E. Why oats are widely distributed.**

1. Oats stand third in acreage among the cereals grown in the United States. How do they compare in value with the two having larger acreage?
2. From Figure 41 name the eight states that are the greatest producers of oats.
3. In his dictionary, Samuel Johnson defined oats as a grain fed to horses in England and to men in Scotland. When this definition was quoted to a Scotchman he answered, " Yes, and that is why you have such good horses in England and we have such good men in Scotland." What geographical conditions account for the fact that oatmeal often takes the place of wheat flour in Scotland?
4. Compare the maps of oats and horses (Figs. 41 and 79) to see what relation can be found between the raising of horses in the United States

FIG. 42. On the hilly farms of Scotland, Norway, and Sweden, where oats and rye are the main cereal crops, harvesting is still done by hand.

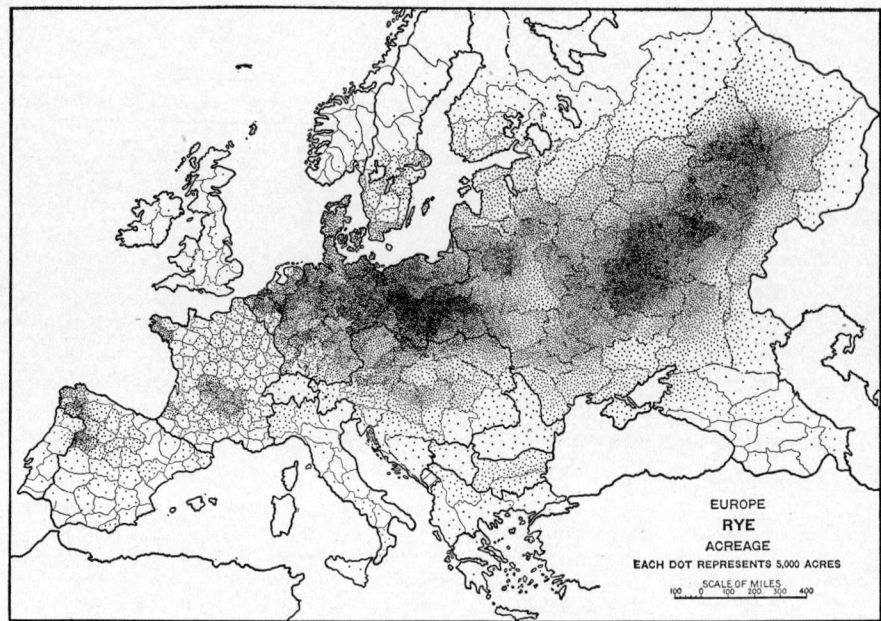

Fig. 43. Four fifths of the rye crop of the world is raised in Europe. The rye belt runs along the northern border of the wheat belt. Rye can grow where the land is too poor to produce wheat, and the growing season is too short and too cool.

and the raising of oats. Find two sections in which the two maps do not agree. Can you decide what cereals are fed to horses in these regions?

5. Oats are a favorite crop in the corn belt not only because they are needed to feed the many horses on corn farms, but also because the two crops do not interfere with each other in demanding attention from the farmers. Oats are sown in the early spring before it is safe to plant corn, and are harvested before the corn is ripe. Which states lie in both the corn and the oats belt?

6. What European country stands next to the United States in total production of oats? Why? (Fig. 40.)

F. **Why rye is the poor man's bread.**

1. In the north temperate zone rye is known as the poor man's crop, for it is made into the black bread which is eaten by the working people throughout Europe. It will grow in soil too poor and in regions too cold for most cereals. In what part of Europe is it grown most extensively?

2. Find out what black bread tastes and looks like. Ask a baker if he ever sells any bread made wholly of rye. Why do Americans use so little black bread?

3. Why does Russia raise more than half of the world's rye crop?

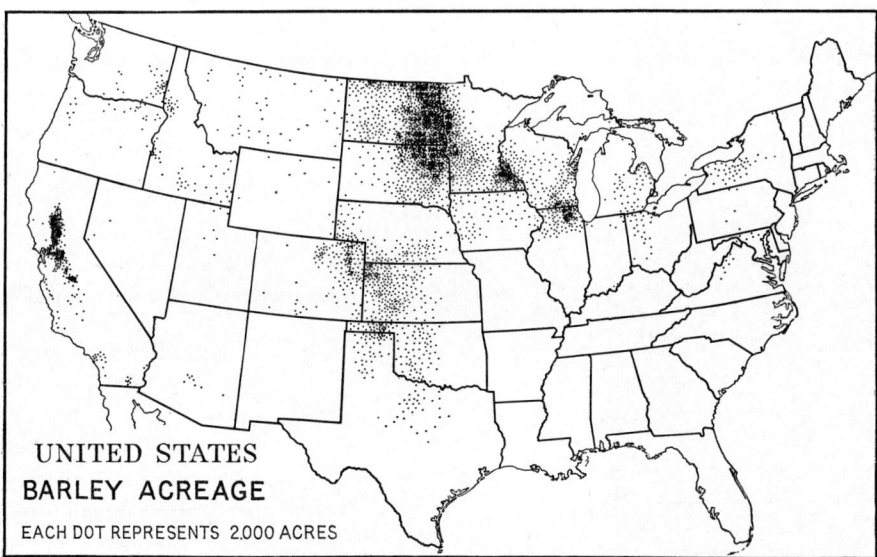

Fig. 44. Barley is grown in about the same parts of the United States as wheat. But it is a hardier crop, having a shorter growing season and being able to stand colder and drier weather.

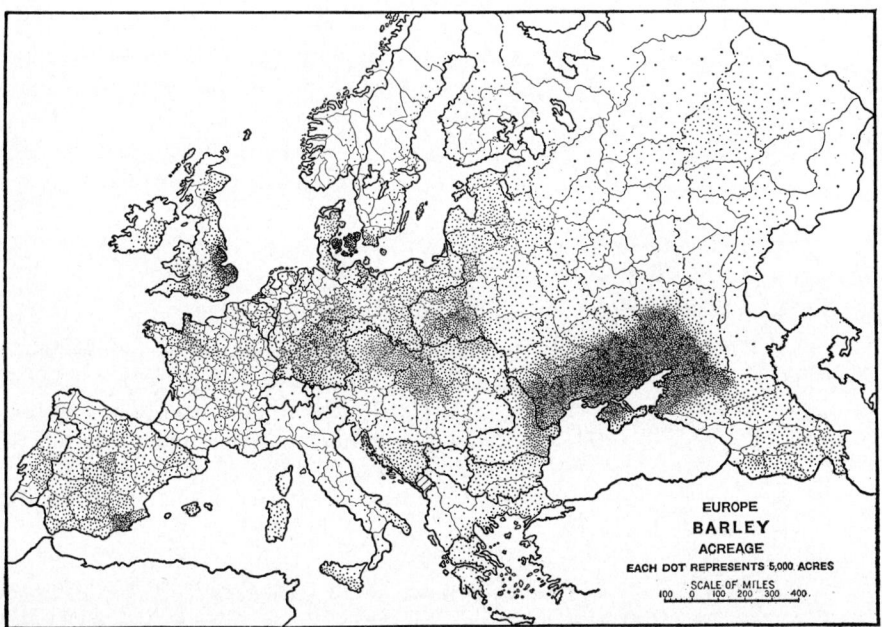

Fig. 45. In Europe also barley grows in the wheat belt, to the south of the rye belt. There it is much used for bread, as well as for feed for live stock and for malting. In the United States very little is used for bread; the crop is used almost entirely for feed and for malting.

Fig. 46. The barley stalk is stiffer than the wheat stalk and has fewer grains and longer straws. Like oats and rye, it lacks the gluten that makes wheat bread light, and is much used for bread only where wheat is too costly.

G. **The world's rice crop.**
1. What are the three greatest rice-producing countries? What conditions favor such heavy production?
2. How do you account for the fact that comparatively little rice is grown outside of southeastern Asia?

H. **Rice in the United States.**
1. Where is the rice belt of the United States? (Fig. 33.)
2. In this belt, what conditions of (a) relief, (b) rainfall, (c) temperature, and (d) soil favor the growing of rice?
3. Louisiana rice needs 45 inches of water during its growing season. The warm wet winds from the Gulf of Mexico bring enough rain to supply 20 inches of water. How is the rest obtained?
4. In the United States the rice fields are plowed and harrowed in the spring by big machines like those used in the wheat belt. After the water is drawn off in the fall, the fields are harvested and the rice is threshed with machines resembling those used in harvesting wheat. Why do we not sell such machines to Oriental rice growers?
5. The American rice grower is paid perhaps twenty times as much for his labor as is the Oriental laborer. But by the aid of machinery one American can take care of about 80 acres of rice, while one Oriental cares for 2 acres. What do you think as to the possibility of raising rice in the United States to export to Asia?

I. **The barley crop.**
1. Barley is so hardy that it is a winter crop in Mediterranean countries and a summer crop in regions that extend into the frigid zone. Barley and wheat dovetail like corn and oats, for they require attention from the farmers at different times. Hence we find much barley grown in the wheat lands, especially in the cooler and drier parts (Figs. 28, 44). Minnesota, North Dakota, South Dakota, California, and Wisconsin are generally the leading barley states. Which of these lie in the cooler parts of the wheat lands? the drier parts?
2. Compare the regions of heavy production of barley and of wheat shown in Europe (Figs. 38, 45).
3. Barley can be grown on poorer soil than wheat. In some parts of our wheat region, farmers who once specialized in wheat now grow barley. What may have happened to cause these farmers to change their crop?

FIG. 47. Truck gardening is a more intensive form of agriculture than cereal farming. It takes many acres of carefully cultivated land, as in this truck farm in the state of New York, to provide the great cities of the country with fresh vegetables and to supply the demands of the canneries.

# CHAPTER FOUR

## THE VEGETABLE FARM AND THE TRUCK GARDEN

VEGETABLE farming is an important industry in densely populated regions, like the plains of India and China, or western Europe and the northeastern United States. In Japan and China, except in the cities, nearly every family raises its own vegetables in tiny, well cultivated plots. Even in northern China three crops are often raised on the same land each year. One plot may produce early cabbages, followed by melons, and then by radishes; another may give a crop of winter wheat, then onions, and finally late cabbages.

In western Europe and the northeastern United States the number of gardens is relatively less than in Japan and China, for a smaller percentage of the people practice agriculture, even in the villages. For this reason, and because so many people live in great cities, it is profitable for the farmers to raise far more vegetables than they consume themselves.

**Truck gardening.** Raising vegetables for a city population is called *truck gardening*. From spring till fall the local truck gardeners send to the great cities a constant stream of fresh vegetables. Almost every kind of conveyance is used, from the leisurely farm wagon to the speedy motor truck and the fast express train. The vegetables are sold in the great city markets or at the corner grocery, or are peddled from house to house. Many of them lose their freshness and much of their value long before they reach the consumer.

**How the winter market of the United States is supplied with fresh vegetables.** Now that freight cars can be heated in cold weather and refrigerated in warm weather, all kinds of fresh vegetables can be carried long distances without spoiling. Accordingly, the southeastern quarter of the United States now ranks second only to the northeastern quarter in vegetable farming. The mild climate makes it profitable to raise vegetables in great quantities, even though the soil must be constantly fertilized and the northern markets are a thousand miles away. This is profitable because of the fancy prices obtained for southern vegetables from late fall to early spring, a period when the North produces only greenhouse products. Thus even in midwinter almost any vegetable can be obtained in the great cities of the northeastern quarter of the United States.

California competes with the South in supplying vegetables to northern markets in the late fall, winter, and early spring. Lettuce, celery, asparagus, and many other vegetables from California regularly appear in eastern markets as soon as fancy prices prevail. A careful study of methods of packing for long transportation has been made, and as a result the vegetable farms in the vicinity of San Francisco and Los Angeles have become remarkably profitable.

**Potatoes.** At the head of the list of our American vegetables stand potatoes. They are nearly twice as important as all the others combined. You can readily see why this is so when you recall that potatoes probably find a place on our dining tables more often than any other staple food except bread.

The states of Minnesota, New York, Michigan, Wisconsin, Pennsylvania, and Maine are the greatest potato producers. Certain parts of those states, where the climate is cool and moist and the soil sandy, are especially adapted to potatoes. Under such conditions they yield a profit even when transported long distances, whereas in most regions it does not pay to raise them for any except the local market. In the South potatoes require more fertilizer than in the North, and the crop is far less abundant; yet because of the high prices commanded by the first new potatoes in the spring, a good many are raised.

Aroostook County in the northern part of Maine is by far the best potato region in the whole United States. More than two hundred bushels per acre are produced, which is twice as much as in most of the other parts of the country.

In European regions having cool, moist climates, potatoes are often grown in sandy soil that is infertile for most crops. The potato

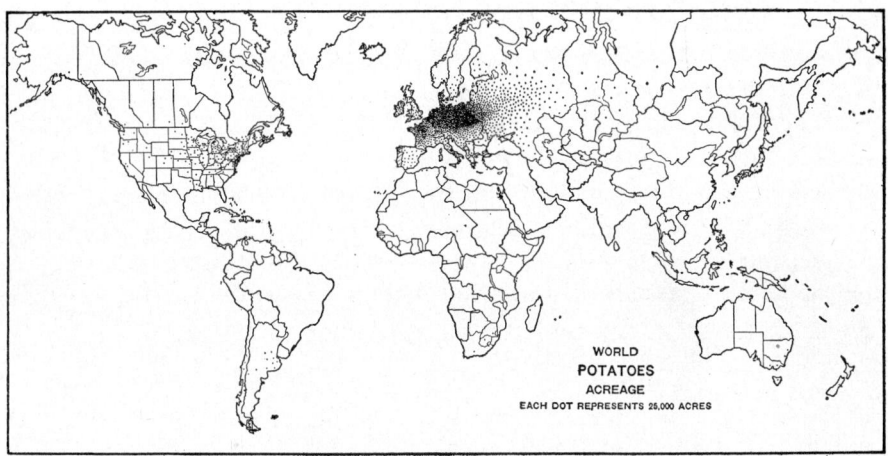

Fig. 48. Potatoes, like corn, are grown on nearly every farm in the United States; but only in a few parts are more grown than can be consumed locally. Although the potato is a native of the New World, nine tenths of the world's crop is now grown in Europe. Our hot, dry summers are not so favorable for potato growing as the cooler, moister summers of western Europe. In Europe, rye and potatoes are grown in much the same belt; they are the poor man's main crops. Outside of North America and Europe, practically no potatoes are grown.

belt extends from Ireland across northern Europe to eastern Russia. In the moist, cool climate of Ireland this vegetable is one of the crops that thrive best; hence it is sometimes called the Irish potato.

Throughout the whole of England, Belgium, and most of Germany, the production of potatoes per acre is as great as in Aroostook, our prize county. In proportion to her population, Germany, the greatest of potato countries, raises seven times as many potatoes as the United States. Of the twenty-four bushels per person which Germany raises each year on an average, about seven or eight are used on the table; ten or more are fed to the pigs, as we feed corn; about three are used for potato flakes, flour, and alcohol; while the rest are exported.

Although the potato is an American vegetable, first found by the white man more than four hundred years ago in Peru, 90 per cent of the world's crop is now grown in Europe.

**Sweet potatoes.** Among the vegetables of the world as a whole, the sweet potato stands next to the white potato in commercial importance. Like its northern companion it can thrive in a sandy soil, but it needs a warmer climate. Hence it is raised in all the southern states, especially in the coastal states from Texas to Virginia. The sandy plains of New Jersey, Delaware, and eastern Maryland are a little cool for sweet potatoes but raise a great many, being so near the great northeastern market. Throughout the tropics sweet potatoes and yams, their near relatives, are so easily raised that they are one of the chief food products, and are far more important than in the United States.

**Other vegetables.** The farmers of the United States are learning that nearness to large markets and climates that permit growth in the winter are the chief reasons for raising large quantities of fresh vegetables. The list below names the states that have stood first and second in each crop for several years. In which cases do you see the effect of nearness to market or of warm winters?

asparagus: California, New Jersey
string beans: New Jersey, Florida
cabbage: New York, Texas
cantaloupes: California, Colorado
carrots: California, Louisiana
cauliflower: California, New York
celery: California, Florida, New York

lettuce: California, Arizona
onions: California, New York
green peas: California, New York
peppers: New Jersey, Florida
spinach: Texas, Virginia
tomatoes: California, New Jersey
watermelons: Georgia, Florida

**Vegetable growing outside the United States and western Europe.** Outside of the highly civilized parts of the temperate zone vegetables are numerous, but are not to be compared in flavor with our own. In tropical countries, for instance, the native vegetables are tough and coarse, like the rest of the vegetation. They are like our beets and turnips when these grow too rank. The difficulty is that good native varieties have not been developed by continual selection of the

*Massachusetts Agricultural College*

FIG. 49. The cultivation of plants under glass represents the most intensive form of agriculture. It is profitable only where it supplies the demands of a large city that will pay high prices for early vegetables and cut flowers.

best types, while the good varieties developed in cooler countries will not produce good seed in the tropics. Europeans and Americans who live in the torrid zone find that they must import seed annually from the temperate zone in order to raise good vegetables.

In China and Japan vegetables are a particularly important source of food. The people are so numerous and land is so scarce that the farmers are forced to raise the plants that give the greatest possible amount of food. Vegetables serve this purpose admirably, since with great care and much fertilizing a very large yield can be obtained. A journey through an Oriental country shows an almost constant succession of gardens, with vegetables always prominent.

The soy bean is perhaps the most important vegetable of China and Japan, since, when combined with rice, it supplies almost all that is needed in the way of food. It takes the place of meat, which is too expensive for most Chinese and Japanese families.

### QUESTIONS, EXERCISES, AND PROBLEMS

A. **The importance of vegetables in man's diet.**
1. Let two members of the class list all the varieties of vegetables they can find in such books as J. Russell Smith's *Food Resources of the World* and Crissey's *The Story of Foods*. At the same time let every other member of the class make a list of all the kinds of vegetables he has ever tasted. Compare your list with the general list. Which of those that you have never tasted are grown in your state? Which are grown in an entirely different climate? Which can be obtained fresh in city markets, but at a high price? Which can be obtained only canned, dried, or preserved?
2. During how much of the year would you be able to have these vegetables if the science of canning were unknown and if there were no railroads, steamships, or motor trucks? What do you conclude about the diet of people who lived before 1800, when there were no steam or gasoline engines? During the winter, how did people then get the vitamins that are needed as part of every diet?

B. **Why vegetables come from many different sources.**
1. In a large vegetable market ask the market man about the region from which his different vegetables come. In your notebook make a list of the vegetables and opposite each write the name of the place where it was grown. If the market man is not sure of his answers, perhaps the names on his crates and boxes will help you; or you can probably find out what you wish to know from Crissey's *The Story of Foods*.
2. Select from the list those vegetables that were raised within a few miles of your town. Try to find out why these are produced locally. Perhaps a certain vegetable is produced locally because the soil is just the kind needed, or the climate is favorable, or your local market is willing

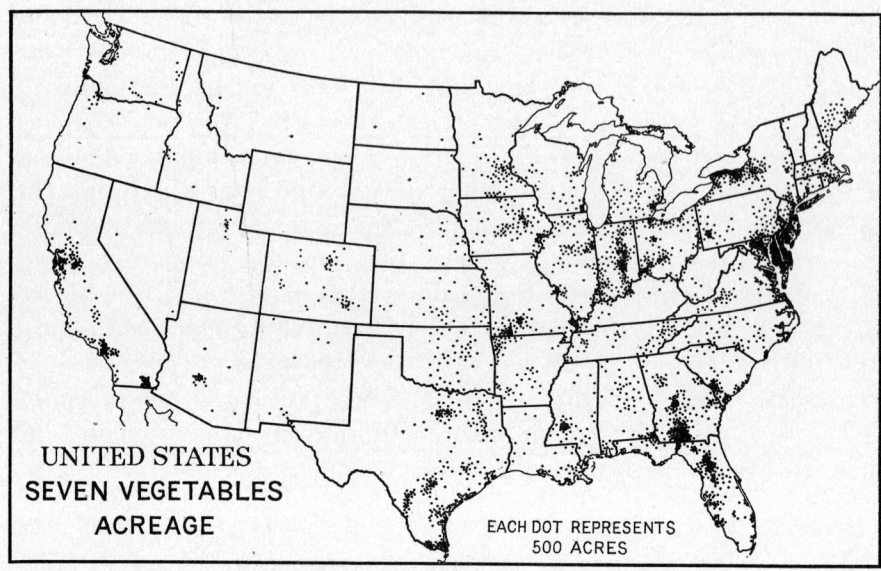

Fig. 50. This map shows where the chief vegetables are grown for sale. It does not include potatoes and home gardens. By far the most important areas are (1) from Long Island to Virginia, (2) south of Lake Erie, (3) around many large cities, (4) in the southern states from South Carolina to Texas, and (5) in three parts of California. Vegetable growing in the first area is helped not only by level land and a good climate, but by an abundant labor supply and huge markets. Explain this. What areas are helped by warm winters? How? Compare this map with the maps for large-scale crops, such as wheat and corn (Figs. 28, 31).

to pay high prices. Find out what vegetables are raised in your vicinity in sufficient quantities to supply other markets, and why this is possible.

3. From the list made at the market select the vegetables that were raised at a distance. Try to find out what special advantages make it profitable to raise them there.

4. Note the places named on the labels of canned vegetables in your mother's pantry or in the grocery store. These places are probably near the farms that raised the vegetables, for canning factories are usually located near farms. Can you see why? Explain why each vegetable can be grown successfully near the place indicated on the label.

C. **Vegetable growing in the United States.**

1. Figure 50 indicates the distribution of vegetable farms and truck gardens in the United States. Pick out ten localities where they are especially numerous. State the conditions that have attracted the vegetable farmers to these regions. Explain the relative importance of soil, transportation, relief, and climate in this matter.

2. Compare Figure 50 as a whole with Figure 176, which shows the distribution of population. What relation do you notice?

3. Write an account of Figure 48, showing the distribution of potatoes. What features impress you most and how do you explain them?

4. Make a list of the vegetables produced in your locality. What conditions make it profitable to raise them?

5. Find a short newspaper item about vegetables, perhaps a market report giving the prices and relative abundance of vegetables. Paste it at the top of a sheet of paper, and on the same paper write the name and date of the newspaper and your comment on what the clipping shows as to the relation of vegetables to climate, season, soil, markets, and transportation.

D. **How hungry populations depend on the potato.**
1. Potatoes produce a greater amount of food value per acre than almost any of the other main crops except corn. Explain how the introduction of the potato into Europe more than four hundred years ago helped to make possible a great increase in European population.
2. Few countries have increased in population more rapidly than Germany during the last one hundred years. How does her standing among potato-producing countries help to explain this fact?
3. In the seven principal potato-producing countries of the world, the total annual yield and the average yield per acre have recently been as follows:

| Country | Total Yield | Average per Acre |
| --- | --- | --- |
| Russia | 1,508,800,000 bu. | 132 bu. |
| Germany | 1,257,000,000 bu. | 190 bu. |
| Poland | 993,000,000 bu. | 157 bu. |
| France | 470,400,000 bu. | 129 bu. |
| United States | 391,000,000 bu. | 109 bu. |
| Czechoslovakia | 251,000,000 bu. | 120 bu. |
| United Kingdom | 165,000,000 bu. | 231 bu. |

Compare these countries in density of population. What effect will an increasingly dense population in the United States perhaps have upon the yield per acre? What feature of the climate of the United States is partly responsible for the low yield here? Why do not the densely populated countries of the Orient raise potatoes?

4. Explain how the bulk and weight of the potato cause it to be a widely distributed crop in the United States. Give another reason.

E. **An illustration of how a "new" vegetable enters commerce.**
1. The soy bean is a new vegetable to the people of the western hemisphere, but it has formed an important article of diet in China and Japan for centuries. The United States is rapidly increasing its purchases and production of soy beans. Why is the soy bean valuable? Find out what our Department of Agriculture says about it. (*Year Book of the Department of Agriculture*, 1917, 1923, and the January, 1919, issue of *Asia* give interesting information about soy beans.)
2. The recent demand of America and Europe is encouraging hundreds of Chinese families to move to new lands in Manchuria to take up the culture of the soy bean, even though the price the Manchurian farmers receive is as low as a cent or less a pound. Why is so low a price an inducement to a Chinese farmer and not to an American farmer?

Bruce Fink

Fig. 51. Seen from a short distance, a field of sugar cane looks like a field of corn. The tall canes are cut by hand with a large, straight knife.

## CHAPTER FIVE

### SUGAR BEETS AND SUGAR CANE

A few centuries ago most people satisfied their need for sugar by occasionally eating honey, by drinking the sap of such trees as the maple and the palm, or by chewing a stick of sugar cane. Now civilized people use pure sugar three times a day in various foods and drinks, and they use it in considerable quantities. Hence it pays thousands of farmers to raise plants for the sugar they contain.

**The sugar-yielding plants.** Sugar beets and sugar maples are raised in cold regions, sugar cane in warm regions, and sorghum cane in intermediate regions. By far the most important of these are sugar cane and sugar beets. In ordinary use no one can tell the difference between the sugar made from beets and that made from cane.

A sugar "cane," or stalk, looks like a cornstalk without the ears. It grows differently, however; for many canes spring from one root, and when these are cut new shoots begin to sprout from the old root. A sorghum cane also looks somewhat like a cornstalk; it grows like the sugar cane.

The sugar beet looks like a rutabaga turnip in color, size, and shape. It has been carefully developed for nearly a century by selecting year after year the seeds of the sweetest beets. Eighty years ago it took eighteen pounds of beets to yield one pound of sugar, while now only six to eight pounds are needed.

**Where the sugar plants grow in the United States.** The United States extends so far from north to south that all four sugar plants are grown within its limits — maple, beet, sorghum, and cane. Figure 52 shows where the three most important grow. Notice that the sugar beet is grown in the cool northern states, the cool plateau states of the West, and the cool Pacific coast states, while sugar cane is confined to the warmer southern states. Sorghum does well in the cooler parts of the South. Sugar maple trees grow in our northernmost states from Indiana eastward, and in southern Canada.

**Sugar beets.** Sugar beets could be grown much more extensively in the United States than they now are, but they are crowded out by more profitable crops, such as cereals. They are not well adapted to American methods of agriculture, because they require much hand labor. No machines have as yet been invented for weeding the young plants and thinning them out.

Because the better soil is used for more profitable crops, beets are often given only the sandy soil where little else will grow. This

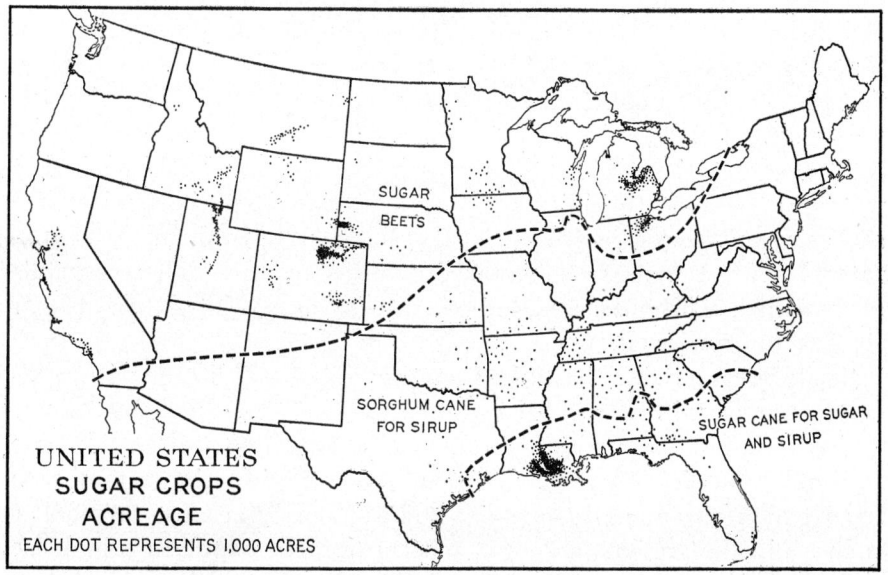

FIG. 52. Only 3 per cent of the sugar used commercially in the United States is produced in the cane region of the southern states (chiefly Louisiana), while 18 per cent comes from sugar beets. The rest is imported. This country takes almost the entire Cuban and Puerto Rican crop.

Fig. 53. Sugar beets growing on the irrigated land of the Salt River project, in Arizona.

fact helps to explain why eastern Michigan is prominent in the beet industry. But the best place for beets is in the irrigated lands of the dry West, where the cool but sunny weather of the long autumn causes the beets to grow large and sugary. That is one reason why Colorado, California, Utah, and Idaho are important producers of beet sugar. In those states, throughout the winter months, large factories receive a constant stream of wagons and trains, bearing the beet crop.

At the factories the beets are washed, sliced, and soaked in hot water to take out the juice. The juice is partly purified with lime and acid, and then is filtered. Next it is heated until the water evaporates, leaving the sugar as damp, brownish crystals. These crystals are purified, whitened, and broken into the granulated table sugar that we know so well.

**Sugar beets outside the United States.** The cool climate with moderate summer rainfall and fairly sunny autumns in which sugar beets thrive is found in much of northern Europe from northern France to central Russia (Fig. 54). Beets are an especially important crop in central Germany and Bohemia. This is partly because farm labor is cheap in that region, and partly because, with population so dense that there is not room for pasturage, the people find it profitable to feed their cattle on the pulp that is left after the sugar has been extracted from the beets. Moreover, there is a large market for sugar close at hand, and the great sugar-cane regions are far away. The summer traveler in northern Europe long remembers the great expanses of beet fields, and the peasant women and children on their knees pulling the weeds that would smother the young plants.

**The climate for sugar cane.** The coolest places where the sugar cane grows are our southern states, from eastern Texas to South Carolina, as appears in Figure 52. There the frost kills the cane each winter, but the difficulty is overcome by planting new canes every year early in the spring, after the last frost of the winter, and harvesting them late in the fall, before the first frost of the next winter. To follow this method successfully requires at least eight months without frost. Nearer to the equator, in such places as the great sugar-cane islands of the West Indies, Java, Hawaii, and Mauritius, the cane is allowed to grow from three to ten years before new plantings are made, and a heavy crop is cut from the plantation every year.

In the islands just mentioned and in sugar-cane regions of less importance, such as India, Egypt, Brazil, northern Argentina, and the Philippines, a high, uniform temperature prevails and the rainfall is abundant. Under these conditions not only is the cane full of sap, but the sap carries a high percentage of sugar. Sometimes as many as eight tons of sugar are made from the cane cut annually on one acre of land.

**Sugar cane on the Cuban plantations.** In Cuba, where sugar cane is king, the plantations are of great extent, — sometimes several thou-

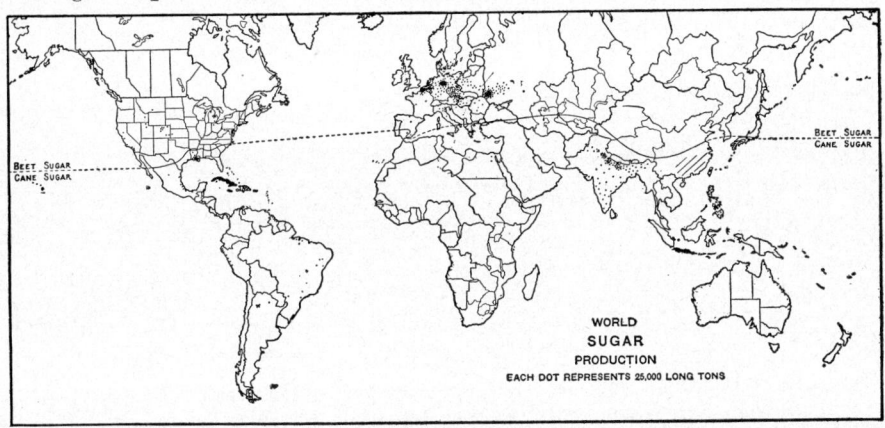

FIG. 54. Sugar cane grows only in regions that some time in the year have an average temperature of 80 degrees; that is, sugar cane is almost a purely tropical crop. (Compare with Figures 17 and 18, pages 30, 31.) India, Cuba, and Java produce the bulk of the world's supply. There are vast undeveloped regions in Africa and in Brazil that may sometime be used for sugar cane. Northwestern Europe is the greatest producer of beet sugar. About two fifths of the world's supply of sugar comes from beets and three fifths from sugar cane.

sand acres, — and the methods of cultivation and harvesting are relatively progressive. Gang plows are sometimes used to prepare the soil, and cultivators drawn by horses are used to keep down the weeds.

Very soon after the cane cuttings are set out they give off sprouts. When the cane stalks reach a height of from six to twelve feet, men with long, heavy knives pass through the rows and strike down a ripe cane at each blow. The crop, which is of enormous weight, is carried to the mill by means of many miles of light movable railways, made in short sections eight or ten feet long. As soon as one part of the plantation is harvested, the railway is quickly taken up and put down again elsewhere.

At the mill the juice is crushed out of the cane by rollers, and is then heated in huge boilers which thicken the syrup and crystallize the sugar. When sugar is first crystallized, it is brown. In this form it is sent to American coast cities, — Boston, New York, Philadelphia, Baltimore, New Orleans, San Francisco, — where it is refined, partly to please our sense of taste, and partly to please our eyes by its whiteness.

**Sorghum cane.** Sorghum is often called Chinese sugar cane because it resembles sugar cane and has long been grown in China. We hear little about it in this country unless we happen to live in the sorghum-cane belt, shown in Figure 52. It is grown chiefly to satisfy local needs. Most of it is made into molasses, which is often eaten on corn mush or corn pone. Sorghum is hardier than sugar cane and requires only five and one half months without frost. It is not so profitable as sugar cane, but its molasses, or sugar, is more easily extracted than the sugar of sugar beets.

### QUESTIONS, EXERCISES, AND PROBLEMS

*A.* The kind of sugar best produced in various parts of the United States.

1. From Figure 52, name the eight leading sugar-beet states of the United States. Tell in which of them the beets are raised by irrigation.
2. What special advantages have these states?
3. Why do some of the states bordering the Great Lakes raise sugar beets?
4. Look at the earlier product maps in this book and find what crop is more profitable than sugar beets in Ohio; in the Dakotas.
5. Name from west to east the states that produce the American cane crop.
6. Cane seems to grow best on the low flood plains and deltas of rivers, not far from the salt water. To what extent are these conditions found in the states that raise sugar cane?

7. Why can Cuba produce cane cheaper than Louisiana?
8. In what section of the country, and especially in what four states, does sorghum grow? Why do we not hear of it in other sections?

**B. The United States as an importer of sugar.**

1. The annual consumption of sugar in the United States is about 120 pounds per person. This country has ample land, good soil, and the proper climate for raising beets and cane in sufficient quantity to yield all the sugar we need. Why, then, do we raise less than a fifth of our total supply and import a much larger amount from the little islands of Puerto Rico and Hawaii?
2. Why does Cuba supply more than half of the sugar that we import from foreign countries?
3. Today the amount of sugar consumed per person in the United States is ten times as great as it was a century ago. Tell three ways in which the supply has been increased to meet this demand.

**C. How the United States ekes out its sugar crops.**

1. In addition to cane, beet, sorghum, and maple sugar, we use several other forms of sweetening. Each year these include about 200 million pounds of glucose extracted from corn and about 50 million pounds from grapes. Glucose is mostly consumed by bakeries and candy factories, which use it because it is relatively cheap. Judging by the production of corn, in what four states would you expect to find many glucose factories?
2. One effect of the legislation prohibiting the use of alcoholic drinks has been to increase the consumption of candy and other sweets. Mention two ways in which this legislation has affected the industry of extracting grape glucose.
3. Man can also satisfy his desire for sweets by eating honey. The supply produced in the United States could be increased perhaps ten times if beekeeping were to become more general. The flowers of alfalfa, buckwheat, and cotton furnish excellent food for bees. Name three states where honey might be produced extensively with the aid of these plants.

**D. How war affects sugar production.**

1. Napoleon I had much to do with the development of the beet sugar industry. When England's blockade cut off the cane-sugar supply, he ordered that thousands of acres of beets be planted and that French scientists perfect the methods of extracting sugar. Does Figure 54 show that France became a permanent sugar-producer? Compare Germany.
2. England was not blockaded in the World War, yet she suffered for lack of sugar. What former supplies was she unable to secure? Why?
3. What connection was there between England's inability to secure sugar from her regular sources and our own sugar shortage?

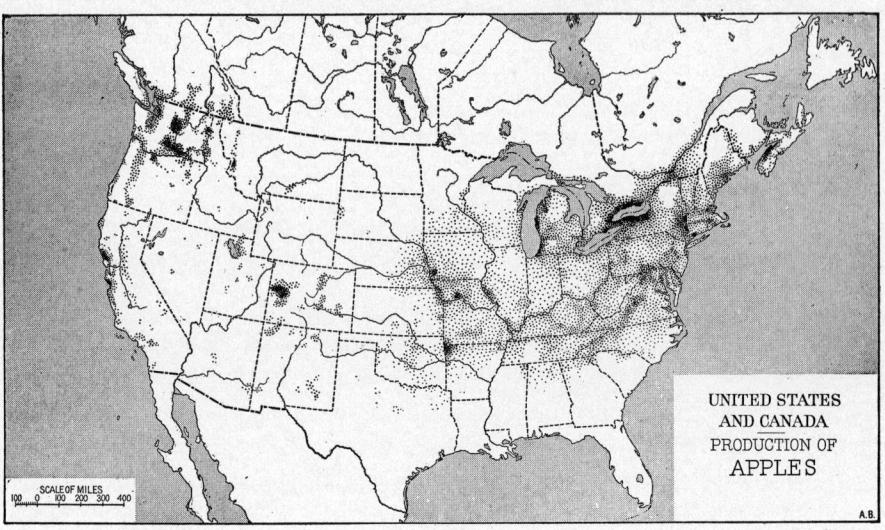

Fig. 55. The most important apple-growing regions of the eastern part of the continent are near bodies of water. In the West, apples are grown in the irrigated regions and along the coast. In Canada, apples are the only fruit crop of importance.

## CHAPTER SIX

### WHERE FRUIT IS PRODUCED

FRUIT is a product which was once supposed to be a luxury, but is now known to be a necessity. It is needed by everyone as a matter of health. Fruit farming or orcharding is much like vegetable farming in being a widely dispersed branch of agriculture, for nearly every farmer raises at least a little fruit for his own home supply. The two industries are also alike in that both are becoming highly specialized in favored localities of the United States.

Although there is a large variety of fruits in the plant kingdom, only a few are of great commercial importance. These few include, among others, *apples* and *peaches* in the temperate zone; *grapes* in temperate and subtropical regions; and *oranges* and *bananas* in semi-tropical regions.

#### APPLES

The leading fruit in the United States is the apple. The value of the crop equals that of all the other fruits combined, and is half as much as that of the potato.

**Where apples are grown in the United States.** Although the apple is grown in every state, it thrives chiefly in the cooler portions of the country, as appears in Figure 55. In three kinds of regions it prospers so well that a great supply can be shipped to distant cities, and even to Europe.

(1) The greatest apple regions are *northern districts where large bodies of water afford protection from the cold winter and from early spring frosts.* The frosts usually come with the northwest winds, and the orchards located on the south and east side of the lakes or bays are less likely to be nipped by the cold.

This is the case in the western part of New York near Lake Erie and Lake Ontario, and also in the part of Michigan which borders the eastern shore of Lake Michigan. In Canada, the peninsula of Ontario and the famous Annapolis Valley in Nova Scotia receive the same protection; hence these regions also raise great apple crops. Wisconsin and northern Illinois, on the contrary, get little protection against frost from Lake Michigan, since the prevailing wind is from the west. Their apple crop, therefore, is small.

(2) The second kind of region where apples are grown with marked success includes *cool places where there is much rough land with steep slopes and rather infertile soil.* This land is purchased at small cost, since it is worth little for most crops. Although not fertile, it is good for apples, because on frosty nights during the budding period the cooler air drains down the steep slopes away from the trees and settles in the valleys. The hills and ridges may also shelter the orchards from cold north winds.

Such an apple region is the Appalachian district from the western part of North Carolina to southern Maine. Southeastern New York, in the Appalachian district, with the added advantage of nearness to the metropolitan market, has an enormous number of apple orchards. The low Ozark Mountains in Arkansas furnish another illustration of a rugged apple region. Such regions are so abundant in the United States that there seems to be no good reason why there should ever be a shortage of our apple supply.

(3) The third kind of apple region is found in *the irrigated parts of the western states.* Here the special advantage is the brilliant sunshine from an almost unclouded sky. Such a condition gives the apples so much color that they are the most beautiful produced in America. Many persons think, however, that the apples of irrigated regions are more pleasing to look upon than to eat. Colorado, eastern Washington and Oregon, and California are important sections where apples are grown by irrigation.

Since apples do not grow well in warmer regions, they are of minor importance in the South.

**Apple growing outside the United States.** Elsewhere in the temperate zones apples are raised on a large scale in localities similar to

Fig. 56. The best markets for fruit are a long distance from some of the points of production; but care in packing and transportation by special freight cars that keep the fruit warm enough in cold weather and cool enough in hot weather make it possible for western and southern fruit to be shipped to the northeastern markets at any time in the year.

those described in the United States and Canada. For instance, the most important apple orchards of Europe are in the rugged lands of Switzerland, southern Germany, and western Austria, while the parts of southern England and northern France that are near the English Channel yield fine fruit. Nevertheless, Europe does not raise as many apples as she needs. Every year she imports thousands of barrels from the United States and Canada.

In the south temperate zone, rugged Tasmania and rugged New Zealand, both with ample water protection, are the leading apple producers.

### CITRUS FRUITS

Citrus fruits include the orange, lemon, lime, and grapefruit. By far the most important is the orange. Nearly all the citrus fruits are esteemed for their refreshing flavor and attractive appearance.

**Where the citrus fruits can be grown.** Citrus fruits are tropical, as the trees cannot thrive where there is frost. Fortunately for the United States, two sections of the country extend so far toward the equator or are so well protected from frosts by large bodies of water that they supply most of our needs for citrus fruits (Fig. 57). These are the southeastern and southwestern corners of the country.

**The Florida orange groves.** The peninsula of Florida is nearly always free from frost, not only because it lies far south, but because most of the winds come from the warm waters of the Atlantic Ocean or the Gulf of Mexico. Only the wind from a little west of north comes from the land, and this land breeze rarely blows vigorously in central and southern Florida. When it does come it may bring chilling wintry blasts from the interior of the continent. Then buds and blossoms are frozen, and even the trees themselves may be killed. Orange growers have learned to protect their orchards during the winter by placing pots of oil or charcoal where they can be lighted to warm the lower air should the wind blow from the north.

**Climatic conditions in the California citrus region.** Southern California is doubly protected from frost by the mild Pacific on the west and high mountains on the east. But even there winds sometimes creep across the mountains on the east, bearing the winter chill of the continent's interior, with the same results as in Florida. Thus there is occasionally a disastrous year for the orange growers in California. They, too, have learned to use the fire-pot to warm the threatened groves.

Although oranges are the most important citrus fruits in Florida and California, Florida specializes also in grapefruit, and California in lemons.

**Special problems of the California growers.** California must supply its groves with expensive irrigation water, whereas in Florida

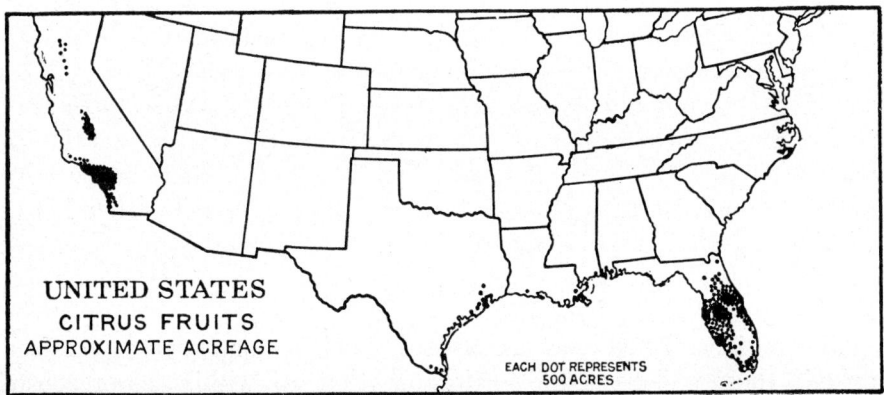

Fig. 57. Citrus fruits can be grown in the United States only where conditions approaching the tropical can be found; that is, (1) in Florida, (2) in a narrow belt along the Gulf coast, and (3) in southern California and Arizona. Puerto Rico, Hawaii, and the Philippines have the right climatic conditions; but only Puerto Rico has a well-developed citrus fruit industry; there grapefruit of excellent quality are grown for the New York market.

the rains are sufficient. California, too, is more than twice as far as Florida from the greatest citrus-fruit markets — St. Louis, Chicago, Detroit, New York, Philadelphia, and Boston. These handicaps have been largely overcome by an efficient coöperative organization of the growers, with the result that the fruit is picked, packed, shipped, and marketed to the best advantage. Florida growers are slowly following the California example of working together.

**Orange growing outside the United States.** Oranges and lemons are grown in many tropical and semi-tropical regions, but they enter into commerce only on the edges of these regions, near highly civilized countries of the temperate zone. Thus the Mediterranean countries, especially Portugal, Spain, Italy, and Algeria, raise oranges and lemons for the countries to the north and ship them thither by both rail and steamer. Although the California industry is rapidly expanding, the United States still receives one or two million dollars' worth of lemons annually from Italy.

### BANANAS

Among the fruits of the torrid zone the most important are bananas. In many tropical lands of abundant rainfall, bananas are as important to the people as are the cereals in the temperate zone. Some are as big as a man's arm; a single one of this kind makes a good meal for three men. Others are as small as one's finger, sweet and delicately flavored. Some are yellow and slender, others red and fat. Some are eaten raw, but many require cooking. Among the tropical people who really live on bananas, the cooking varieties are much the most important. The flower bud and the soft new shoots are eaten as salad. There are seventy kinds of bananas in the Philippines alone.

**How bananas are grown.** The people of many tropical regions use a great many bananas because it is easy to raise them. A sucker from an older tree is set into the ground. Within less than a year a great fat stem like a cornstalk fifteen feet high bends over under the weight of a huge bunch of bananas, which often hangs within easy reach from the ground. When the fruit is ripe the stalk dies; but as other stalks have sprung meanwhile from the same root, there is nearly always a supply of ripe bananas.

**The regions that export bananas.** Bananas for export are raised only in those regions of the torrid zone that are within easy reach of densely populated parts of the temperate zone. This is because the fruit is perishable. Thus the United States gets its supply from the West Indies and Central America, especially from Jamaica, Guate-

Figs. 58, 59. Coconuts and bananas are the most valuable of the tropical fruits, and both are grown throughout the tropics, except in regions of slight rainfall. Although coconuts are much used for food in tropical countries, their value to the rest of the world comes from the dried meat (called copra) and the oil pressed from it. Coconut products form one of the leading exports of the Philippine Islands. Bananas are an export crop chiefly in Central America and the West Indies.

mala, Honduras, Costa Rica, and Panama. From this region we import about 60,000,000 bunches of bananas annually, or about half a bunch for each person in the United States. Ask the fruit dealer how many bananas an ordinary bunch contains; then decide whether you eat your share.

Western Europe draws its banana supply largely from the small islands off the northwestern coast of Africa, such as Madeira, the Canary Islands, and the Cape Verde Islands. Recently it has drawn some from the West Indies.

Europeans do not eat nearly so many bananas and oranges as we do. On the other hand, they consume far more grapes, partly fresh and partly in the form of wine.

**Transportation costs.** It might be thought that because bananas are raised so easily they ought to be much cheaper than they are on our market. But when we consider the railroad system that must be built and maintained to collect the fruit from the great plantations and carry it to tropical ports, the fleet of ships to bring it north, and the express trains to distribute it, we see that by far the greater part of the cost of our bananas represents transportation.

### QUESTIONS, EXERCISES, AND PROBLEMS

A. **How peach regions compare with apple regions.**
1. Peaches grow especially well in the three kinds of regions described as best for the production of apples. From Figure 60 name three peach-growing localities that belong under the first kind of region; three under the second; and one extensive region and two small ones under the third.
2. Peaches can also be grown profitably in regions so far to the south that the crop ripens early enough to bring high prices in northern markets, because they arrive before those from other regions are ripe. Find two of these southern peach-growing regions.
3. Peach trees are even more sensitive to spring frosts and severe winters than apple trees. Moreover, peaches require more sunshine. How do these conditions influence the position of the main peach-growing sections in the United States, as compared with the apple-growing sections? (Figs. 55, 60.)
4. Peach growing in Europe is largely limited to southern France and to Italy. On the basis of the maps of rainfall and temperature (Figs. 1, 17, 18), explain why Great Britain, Holland, and Germany are not important peach-growing countries.

B. **The grape industry.**
1. In some countries long sections of the schoolbooks are devoted to grapes. From Figure 61 decide which countries these are. On your

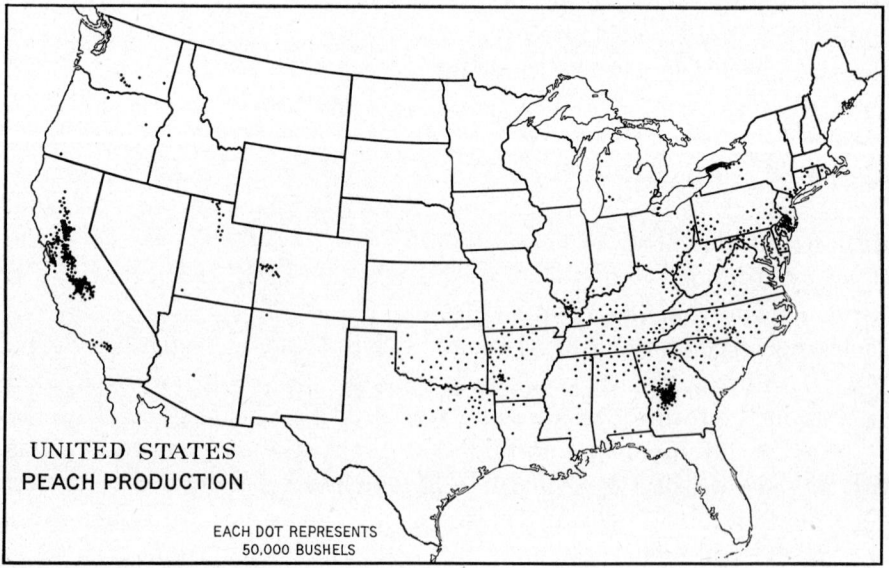

FIG. 60. One half of our peach crop is grown in California, and one tenth in Georgia.

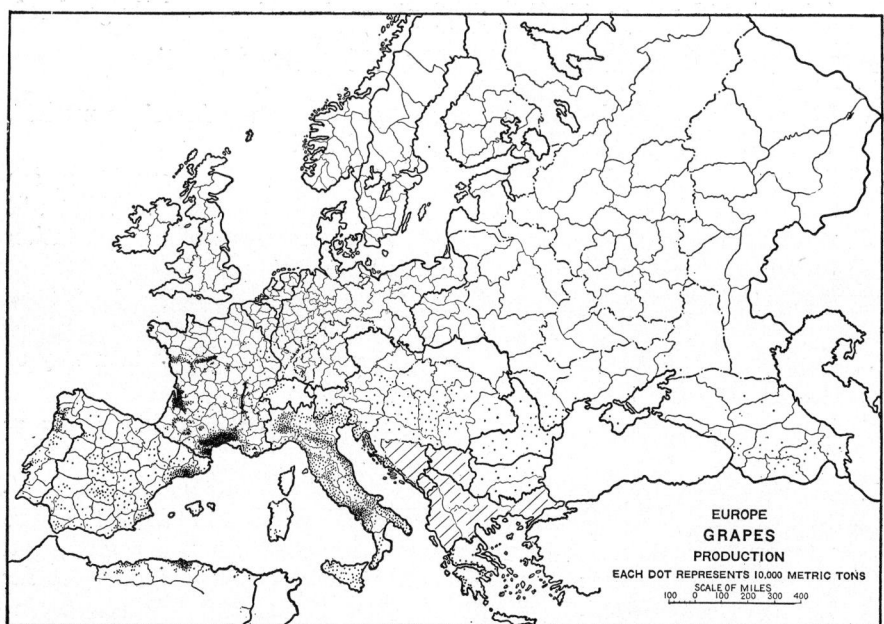

Fig. 61. About three fourths of the grapes grown in Europe are used for making wine. France leads in grape production, with Italy second. The drying of grapes for raisins is not important and is confined to Italy and the north coast of Africa.

table at home, how often do you have grapes compared with apples? oranges? bananas?

2. Name a dried product that comes from grapes. Find out how it is made.
3. From a study of Figure 61 decide what sort of climate and location in the United States is best for grapes.
4. From your own experience or from questioning other people find out the chief differences in appearance, quality, and use, between the grapes of California and those of New York or Michigan.
5. What geographic condition helps to cause raisins to be made in California and not in New York?
6. Judging by the climate, should you expect the grapes of Europe to be more like those of New York or those of California? Find out from a fruit dealer what kinds of grapes he has that come from Europe and from California.
7. Recently grapes from Argentina have appeared in the winter markets of our eastern cities. What conditions make grape culture possible in Argentina? Why are Boston, New York, Philadelphia, etc., good markets for these grapes?

C. Other fruits.
1. Let different individuals or different groups in the class take the following fruits for special study: (a) dates; (b) strawberries; (c) prunes

(plums); (*d*) pears; (*e*) olives; (*f*) pineapples. An especially good reference book for this problem is Crissey's *The Story of Foods*.

**D. How transportation influences the fruit industries.**

1. Fifty years ago the banana was a rare product in the American market. What has made possible its present general use?
2. Some of the most delicious tropical fruits, such as the mangosteen, are not known outside the tropics because they decay so easily. What will probably be the effect of increasingly speedy methods of transportation upon the regions producing these fruits?
3. Many bushels of apples sometimes rot beneath the New England trees because the individual farmers do not have means of marketing them readily. What does the experience of California suggest as to a way of saving this waste and turning it into a profit?

**E. What parts of the world are supplying your community with fruits or vegetables?**

1. Divide the class into two groups, one to work on fruits and one on vegetables. Watch your local stores for several days and make lists of the various kinds of fresh fruits and vegetables sold. See which group can get (*a*) the longer list; (*b*) the longer list of those grown in a place far from the local market.
2. Explain how and why the second list will vary from season to season.
3. How many of the fruits or vegetables on your lists are also sold in dried or canned form?

FIG. 62. Recent experiments have shown that the mango, one of the finest fruits known, can be grown successfully in Florida.

Fig. 63. Out on the range in the cattle country. *Ewing Galloway*

## CHAPTER SEVEN

### THE SOURCES OF ANIMAL PRODUCTS

ANIMALS stand second only to plants among the sources of the world's chief products. They also help man in his work. Some are used only as beasts of burden, a still larger number supply food, and all yield raw materials such as hides, wool, hair, or feathers. Moreover, cows and poultry yield not only meat, but still more valuable products in the form of milk and eggs. The products from animals are so important that they support numerous great manufacturing industries, such as slaughtering, meat canning, tanning, shoemaking, the wool industry, and the butter and cheese industry. In some countries — Uruguay, for instance — animal farming is even more important than all the other farming activities combined.

**Some difficulties of animal farming.** Although animals appear almost to take care of themselves, it is really very difficult to protect them from disease and injury, especially when young. It is difficult also to provide every animal with daily food of the proper quality and quantity. Even if pasture land is available during the warm part of the year, other food must be provided throughout the cold season. It must not be forgotten that great crops of hay, corn, and oats are raised primarily to feed domestic animals when they cannot be pastured. Moreover, the farmer must guard his domestic animals not only from disease and from pests, but from severe winter cold.

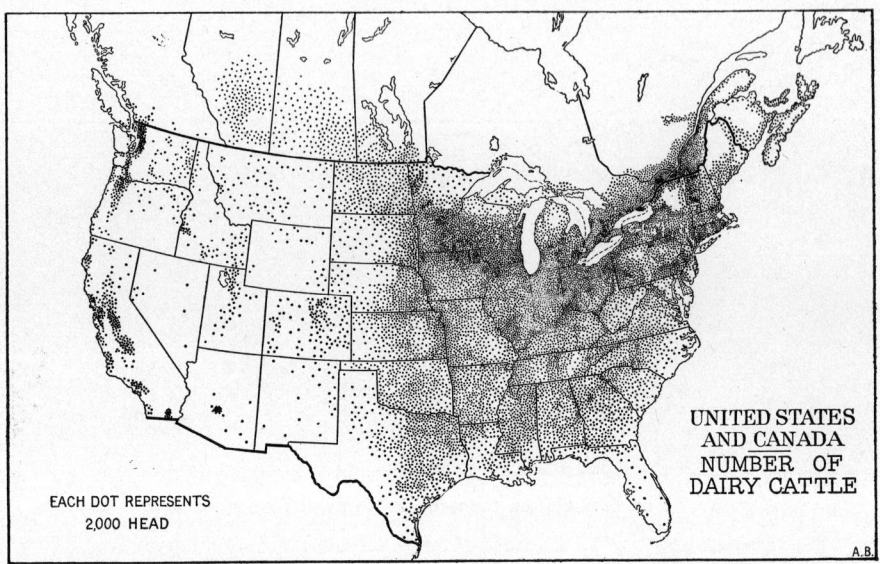

Fig. 64. Notice the general correspondence between this map and the map of hay and forage crops (Fig. 80, page 101). Compare it also with the map showing rainfall (Fig. 6, page 6). For pasturage in summer and hay in winter, dairy cattle need the kinds of grass that grow in cool, moist regions. They do not thrive in mountainous districts (except in fertile sheltered valleys), in tropical or subtropical places, or on semi-arid lands, all of which lack natural pasturage.

**Farm animals in the United States.** In the United States the typical farm has several horses, cows, and pigs, and a score or more of hens. Many farms specialize in raising animals. Some raise nothing but horses, others mules, still others beef cattle, dairy cows, pigs, sheep, or poultry.

**Cattle.** Because of the excellent quality of their flesh, the large amount of milk they yield, the tough but flexible quality of their hides, and their docility as beasts of burden, cattle are raised more than any other animals except sheep and hens. Near cities they are raised in great numbers to supply fresh milk, and thus support the industry of *dairying*. Dairying includes also the production of milk to be made into butter and cheese. On plains where the rainfall is sufficient to support natural grass, but insufficient for crops, cattle are raised for beef. This industry is called *cattle raising*.

### DAIRYING

Few persons who live in large cities realize the great amount of work required in order that the daily bottle of fresh milk may be left at the door. The supply for hundreds of thousands of families in a single great city means that farmers in many parts of several states labor hard to get the milk ready and start it on its journey.

Fig. 65. Dairy cattle in western Washington, where the long, cool summers, with light but frequent rains, are favorable to pasturage.

**How the city is supplied with milk.** Some of the milk comes from farms hundreds of miles from the city. Some comes from big farms that boast of scores of cows, and some from small farms that keep only two or three. On the first stage of the journey from producer to consumer a large can is carried to the nearest railroad station or electric car line. There the can is put into a milk car with many other cans of milk from other farms. At some central point milk cars from several routes are combined to form a milk-express train which speeds cityward. In the city the milk is bottled and distributed to the customers.

The collection and distribution of milk suggest a great river system. The widely scattered milk farms represent the innumerable sources of the system. The gathering of the milk in greater and greater quantities is like the joining of tiny rills to form brooks, brooks to form streams, and streams to form the main trunk river. Then the city is like the delta of a river; as the waters of a great river reach all parts of the delta by means of many distributaries, so the great milk supply reaches all parts of the city along the routes of the distributors.

**How dairy cows are cared for.** But these are matters that concern the transportation and consumption of milk. Let us go back

Fig. 66. Milking a camel. Primitive people who live largely on the milk of their flocks and herds make no attempt to keep it fresh. They find it both more palatable and more digestible when properly soured than when fresh. They convert much of it into a very hard, sour cheese.

to the dairy farm, where the primary production takes place. There we find that the mild-eyed cow is mistress of all she surveys. During cold weather, and usually at night during all seasons, she is kept in a clean barn where a bed of straw is spread for her comfort. She is provided with the food that is most to her liking — sweet hay, cotton-seed meal, wheat bran, or juicy cornstalks. In the best barns a stream of fresh water flows before her at all times. At the same hours, two or three times each day, a milker approaches her quietly with a clean pail and skillfully takes the milk from her udder. On some farms milking machines are used because they do the work at less cost and keep the milk cleaner than hand-milkers can.

All this care is designed to make the cow give a large amount of rich milk. The lack of it is one of the chief reasons why many cows give a small amount of milk or milk of poor quality.

**The care of milk.** As soon as the milk is taken from the cow it is strained through cloth and cooled. It is then kept cool until it is delivered to the refrigerated milk car at the railway station, or to the neighborhood creamery or cheese factory. Or the farmer may separate the cream from the rest of the milk by whirling it very rapidly in a machine called a "separator." He then takes the cream to the creamery, where it is made into butter, while the skim milk is kept at home and fed to the pigs.

The state governments care for the health of milk consumers by inspecting herds and requiring cleanliness on the farm and in handling the milk. Great improvements have also been brought about by large milk companies. These are equipped not only to handle enormous quantities of milk for delivery to customers, but to make butter and sometimes cheese. Many of them take great care to keep the milk clean, and sell " guaranteed " or " certified " milk.

**Other sources of milk.** Practically all the great cities of the United States, Canada, and Europe are supplied with milk in the manner described above. In other regions other animals besides the cow supply milk. For instance, many pastoral tribes live mainly on the milk of sheep; in some rugged regions goats are the milk producers; the desert Arab gets his milk supply from his camels, the Laplander from his reindeer, and many a dweller within the tropics from his water buffaloes.

In proportion to the amount of food and the care required, goats are the best producers of milk. The milk that they yield is as palatable as cows' milk, and one soon becomes used to it. It has the great advantage of never being infected with germs of tuberculosis, which sometimes are found in cows' milk that is not properly cared for. By keeping a goat or two, many families in America might have plenty of fresh milk with little trouble and expense.

### CATTLE RAISING

Beef has long been the principal meat used by the most progressive peoples. Before the days of the railroad almost every farmer kept a few cattle for his own supply of meat as well as for the milk, and the farms near the cities often kept large herds which were marketed by being driven into the city. Now the railroads and the steamships offer such cheap and convenient transportation that cattle can be profitably raised thousands of miles from the market. This makes it possible for the natural grasslands to be devoted especially to cattle raising.

**The cattle sections of the United States.** In two sections of the United States cattle raising forms the most important farming industry (Fig. 67). The first section is the plains at the eastern base of the Rocky Mountains from Texas northward, which are ideal for cattle, since the natural grass forms excellent food even when it is dried by the hot summer sun. The rains are sufficient to support the grass and to supply drinking water, but in the western part are not heavy enough to make unirrigated land valuable for crops.

The second section where the raising of beef cattle is the dominant industry includes the grasslands scattered throughout the mountains and plateaus farther west. There are not nearly so many cattle in this section, however, as on the Great Plains. Although the area is larger, the rainfall is less than in the plains, and grass is less abundant. In addition to this, much of the land is too rugged for cattle.

**Feeding cattle for market.** In both sections enormous quantities of alfalfa are raised in limited areas favored with irrigation (Fig. 19). This appetizing clover is fed to the cattle during the winter or when the natural pasture fails because of unusual dryness. Alfalfa is used also for fattening the cattle for the market.

Some of the cattle in the dry cattle-raising sections become fat on the natural pasture, but the majority are comparatively thin. When they are about three years old, those that are fat are collected into corrals in the fall and are driven into freight cars to be shipped directly to the meat-packing centers, such as Kansas City and Chicago. The thin animals are sent to the corn belt. They are purchased by the farmers, who feed them generously upon corn and hay during the winter, and pasture them on good grass for a few months in early spring. Then as sleek, fat cattle, they are sold to the slaughter houses for a sum that pays the farmer a good price not only for his corn and hay, but for his labor. Moreover, the manure from the cattle has enriched the soil of his farm.

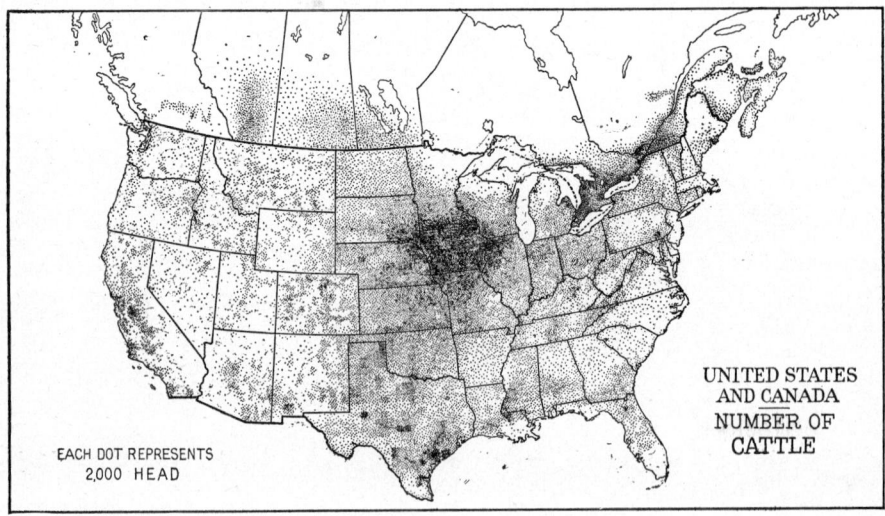

Fig. 67. Comparison with Figure 31, page 47, shows the close relation between corn growing and meat production. It also helps to explain why Chicago, Kansas City, and Omaha are the leading centers of the meat-packing industry. (Milch cows are not included on this map.)

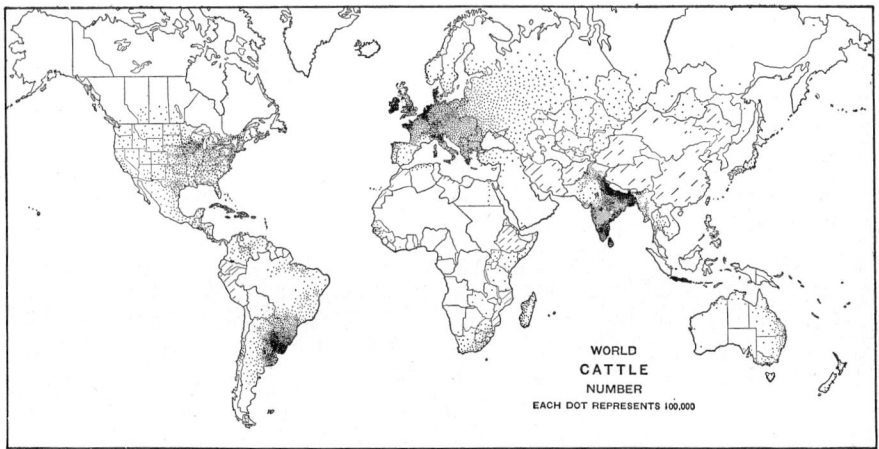

Fig. 68. There are four chief cattle regions in the world: (1) Europe, especially the northwestern part; (2) India; (3) the United States; (4) the Rio Plata region of South America, which centers in Argentina, Uruguay, Paraguay, and southeastern Brazil.

**The cattle ranch.** In the early days when settlers were few in the western United States, the cattle were allowed to wander from one range to another, wherever grazing was good. The cattle of many owners mingled in great herds, but each owner knew his own animals by the brand they bore. The brand was a mark burned on the flank of the animal with a red-hot iron. Once or twice a year the cowboys of a region mounted their wiry little ponies, or mustangs, and drove all the cattle to a place that had previously been agreed upon. Gathering the cattle in this manner was called a " roundup." The cattle that were ready for the market were sorted out and driven into corrals, while the calves that had been born since the last roundup were branded. Each calf was marked with the brand of the cow it followed.

This method of cattle raising had serious disadvantages. In the first place, it was easy for unprincipled men to steal cattle, especially unbranded calves, for the cattle wandered far and wide. Moreover, too many cattle were pastured in the same section, with the result that the grasslands became overstocked and great numbers of animals died in winter from cold and starvation. Still more died in summer, when both food and water were scarce. Most of the great ranges are now divided among the cattlemen and fenced with barbed wire. Winter shelters have been built on many of the ranches, especially in the cold north, and alfalfa is grown or purchased for winter foddering. Only in a few sections do the earlier conditions still prevail.

Fig. 69. A flock of sheep on a mountain slope in eastern Washington. Sheep crop the grass so close to the ground that the shepherd must keep his flock moving to new pastures. This gives the sheep better pasturage and preserves the old pastures.

**Cattle raising outside the United States.** Figure 68 shows that there are far more cattle in densely populated western Europe than in the whole of the United States. Many European cattle are raised in barns. They cannot be turned out to pasture, because practically all the land is needed for crops.

Argentina and Uruguay are the great cattle countries of the southern hemisphere (Fig. 68). From the vast grasslands of these countries enormous herds are driven amid clouds of dust to the cities, where they are slaughtered. The beef is frozen and sent to the seaports for shipment in great refrigerator steamships.

On the vast dry plains of southern Russia, the Hungarian plain, and the plains and plateaus of Australia and South Africa, cattle can be raised as easily as on our own western plains and plateaus. Many cities, like Buenos Aires and Sydney, owe part of their growth to the fact that they are convenient centers for the business of slaughtering animals and shipping the meat to western Europe.

**The increasing cost of meat.** Even before the World War the price of beef had been rising continually, because the population of the civilized world was increasing more rapidly than the number of cattle. This process is interrupted by hard times, but it still goes on, although farmers use tractors and raise cattle instead of horses. The faster our population grows the more necessary it becomes that the people of Europe and America, like those of the Orient, learn to use more of such foods as beans, fish, and milk. For a given amount of food, milk needs much less farm land than beef.

SHEEP AND WOOL

Sheep are, if anything, more generous to man than cattle or swine. They yield not only meat that is highly prized and leather that is especially useful for shoes and bookbindings, but wool that is converted into clothing, hats, and blankets. Moreover, sheep can thrive in a great variety of climates. It is not surprising, therefore, that sheep are raised throughout the inhabited world wherever grass can be found, or that they are the most numerous domestic animals, aside from hens.

**Sheep in the tropics.** Within the tropics, however, the warmth makes sheep become hairy, like goats, instead of woolly, and the poor and limited supply of grass makes them lean and lanky. There the skin is the most valuable part of a sheep, and it is not worth while to raise them for the sake of exporting this one product.

**In the temperate zones.** In the temperate zones sheep are covered with wool of good quality and are fat enough to yield large quantities of mutton. But the same sheep rarely produces both fine wool and

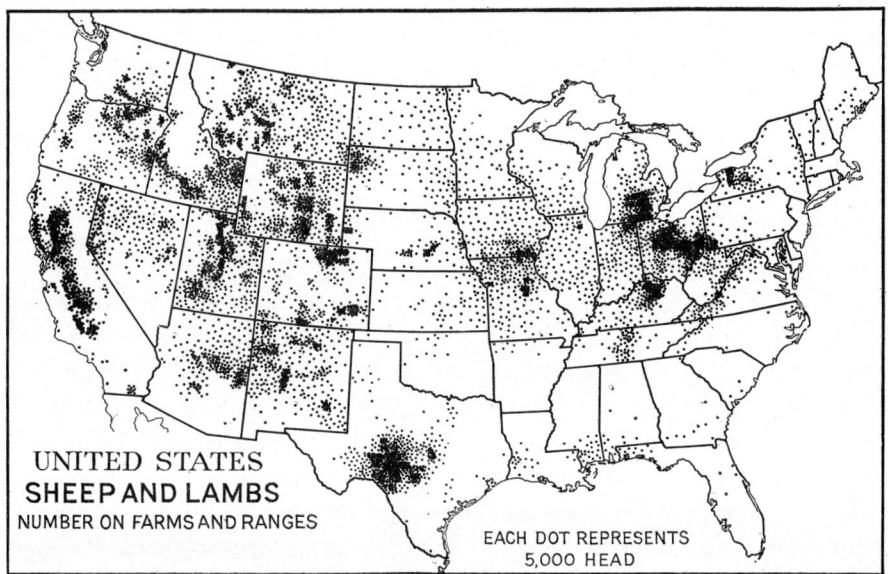

FIG. 70. In the West, sheep are raised chiefly in the Rocky Mountain states and on semi-arid lands. In the East, the industry tends to be concentrated in the hilly pasture sections of Ohio and southern Michigan.

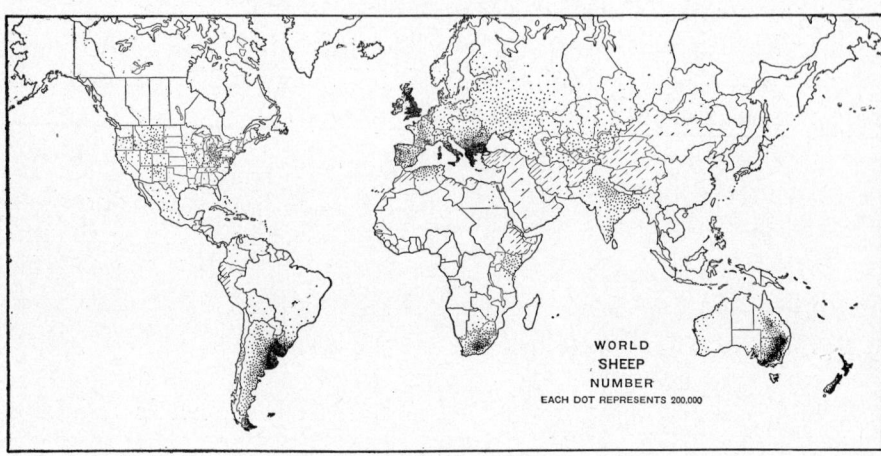

Fig. 71. Sheep raising is the only animal industry that is more important in the southern than in the northern hemisphere. Australia is the leading sheep-raising region of the world.

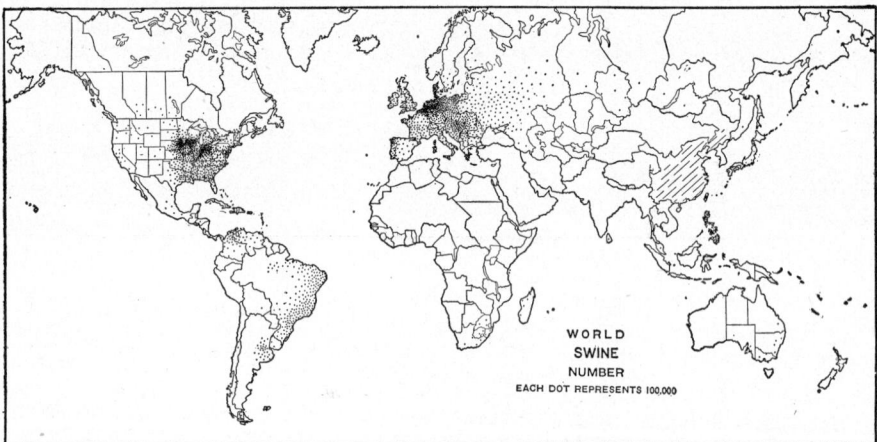

Fig. 72. Swine will thrive on the cheaper grains and on potatoes, and are found in settled farming regions where feed for them is cheap. Compare this map with Figures 39, 45, and 48.

abundant mutton. The small merino sheep produces the finest wool — sometimes 48,000 fibers to a square inch of skin. Other breeds have large bodies, but their wool is coarse. For decades sheep raisers have been trying to produce breeds that will yield both good wool and a large amount of mutton. They have partially succeeded by producing animals of a "general-purpose" type.

**Where sheep are raised.** Sheep are often more profitable to men than are cattle; for they thrive on lands almost worthless for other purposes. Thus they can live in rugged regions like our own Rocky Mountains, or Switzerland, Turkey, and New Zealand. Such rough lands are thought to be their natural homes.

Sheep live not only in rugged lands, but in dry lands; they are numerous in regions bordering deserts that are too dry for cattle, such as our western plateaus, the interior of Australia, Spain, and South Africa, and parts of Argentina. This is because they are able to go a long time without water, and their teeth enable them to nibble short grass which horses and cattle cannot possibly eat.

Then again, some varieties of sheep thrive in cold, wet regions like the Scotch Highlands and the Falkland Islands, since their thick, greasy wool protects them from both the cold and the rain.

Sheep are profitably grown in still another kind of region, — lands near the great meat markets of the northeastern United States and western Europe. Here sheep are grown primarily for meat. In the northeastern United States the farmer buys full-grown sheep that were raised on the ranges of the western states, and fattens them for a few months for the market; or he keeps them for several years in order to raise lambs, which are sold for high prices in the neighboring markets. On his small farm, the farmer of eastern Ohio, for instance, can give the lambs much more care than the Wyoming shepherd, and so can bring a greater proportion of his flock to maturity.

**The life of the shepherd.** The care of sheep is often one of the loneliest of occupations. One man with two dogs and a gun can care for several thousand animals; and for weeks the lonely shepherd may follow his charges without seeing anyone except his camptender. In the western United States many of the sheep graze upon the unfenced government lands. In summer they are driven to the mountains; but as the snows of autumn begin to cover the grasses and shrubs they are driven to the lower slopes and then out upon the plateaus.

Once a year the shepherd drives his sheep to the dipping pens. There they are thrown into great vats and washed. As soon as they are dry, a gang of shearers takes them in hand and skillfully clips the thick coat of wool from each member of the flock. The shepherd enjoys the shearing season, for it makes a break in the solitary monotony of his life.

### SWINE

Although the hog is found in all parts of the world, it is only a little more than a third as numerous as cattle and a quarter as numerous as sheep. In fact, horses and donkeys together are three fourths as numerous as hogs. Most of the hogs are raised in the United States and Europe, with a fair number in South America (Fig. 72). In

China, they provide the poor man's meat; it is seldom that the ordinary Chinese family has any other meat than pork. They are absent from large parts of Africa and Asia because the Mohammedan religion forbids its followers to eat the meat of swine in any form.

Hogs are valuable animals, because they will live on all sorts of food, are tame and hardy, and yield a large amount of nourishing meat. Many hogs weigh more than four hundred pounds when eleven months old. Moreover, they increase rapidly in number, for there are often ten or a dozen pigs in a litter.

Swine are important from the standpoint of commerce only where many are raised on a large scale and the dressed meat is sent elsewhere for consumption. This occurs in only a few places, where hog feed can be grown at low cost.

### QUESTIONS, EXERCISES, AND PROBLEMS

A. **Dairying in the United States.**

1. Compare the distribution of dairying with the distribution of population. From Figure 64 determine which quarter of the United States has the greatest number of dairy cows. Why?
2. Compare Wisconsin on the dairying map with the same state on the population map (Fig. 164). What two large cities draw upon southeastern Wisconsin for their milk supply? Name two products which are manufactured in that state from milk. How does the presence of many Dutch, Belgians, Swiss, Danes, Swedes, and Norwegians in Wisconsin help to account for the state's prominence in dairying? Why do so many "foreign-style" cheeses come from there?
3. From what parts of New York State is milk shipped to the City of New York? from what other states? How many miles from the city is the farthest point that ships milk to it? Find from what regions each of the following cities draws its milk supply: (a) Philadelphia, (b) Buffalo, (c) Pittsburgh. Which city is obliged to go farthest? Why? Explain how the location of these cities has influenced the location of the dairy farms.
4. The United States uses more than seven billion gallons of milk per year. About how many gallons is this per person? Where is your share produced? Is it more or less than the average? Can you explain why your proportion seems large?

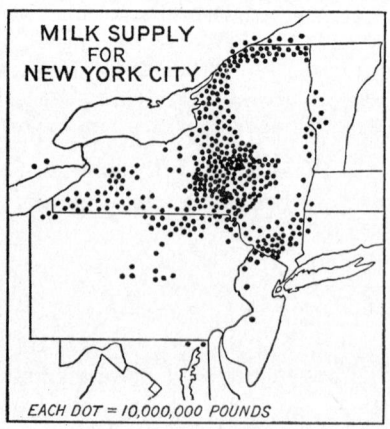

Fig. 73. This shows the territory from which milk is supplied to New York City.

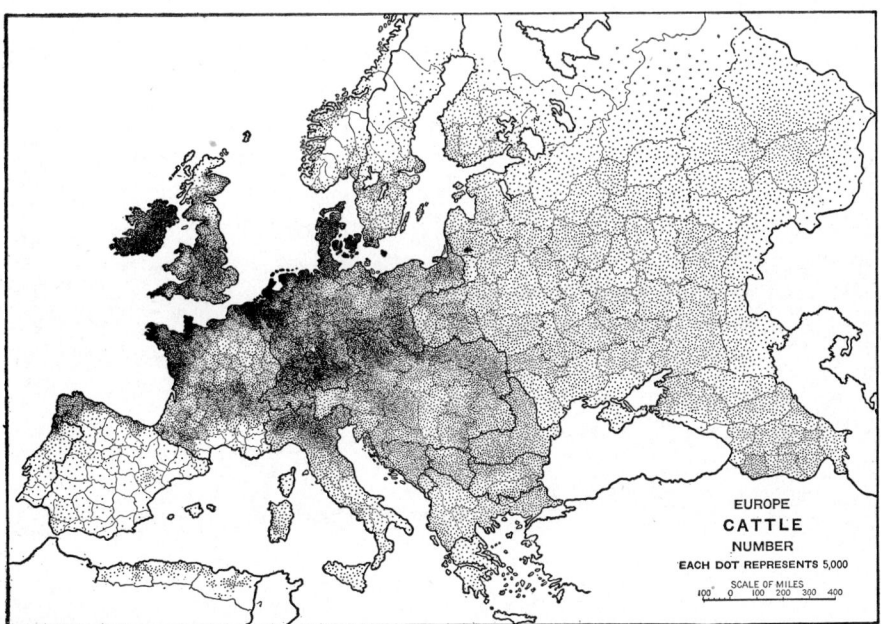

Fig. 74. Cattle production in Europe is concentrated toward the northwest, where climatic conditions are favorable for hay and pasturage. There the dairy products are especially important. On the Mediterranean side of Europe, the long, dry summers are unfavorable. In Russia, cattle production could be much greater than it is; there the limiting factors are the long, cold winters and poverty and lack of knowledge among the peasant farmers.

5. Some dairy cows are found in every state, for most farmers like to keep at least a few so that they may have an income all the year round. Explain this statement.
6. In the Rocky Mountain states compare the number of dairy cows with the total number of cattle. Give an explanation of what you find.

B. Dairying in Europe.
1. The conditions of transportation encourage specialization in the dairy industry. Using Figure 74, the map of cattle in Europe, make a general statement as to where the darkest shading occurs. Describe the climate. Compare it with that of the states most heavily shaded in Figure 64.
2. Compare the length of time that milk and cheese will keep. Compare the ease with which they can be transported. Then consider the transportation facilities of the main cattle-raising sections of Europe and decide which are more likely to specialize in cheese and which in milk. Can you find any relation between your answer and the following statement?

> Imports of cheese into the United States are derived approximately as follows: Italy 44%, France 7%, Switzerland 23%, Netherlands 4%, Canada 13%. (The remaining 9% comes from countries, mainly in Europe, that send us comparatively small quantities.)

3. Why does Europe export more cheese than butter to the United States?

Fig. 75. The vast stockyards of Chicago receive many thousands of cattle in a week.

4. The dairymen in Denmark specialize in making butter. Name two neighboring foreign markets to which they send it.
5. Denmark buys much of the cottonseed cake that is left after our factories in the South have crushed out the cottonseed oil. Why do her dairymen consider this cottonseed cake valuable?

C. **How different breeds of cattle suit different purposes.**

1. Two of the most popular breeds of milch cows are the Holstein and the Jersey. The first is a large animal that gives an abundance of milk containing a low per cent of butter fat. The Jersey cow is a smaller animal. She does not give so much milk, but her milk is very rich in butter fat. Which breed is preferred by farmers who sell milk to be used as a raw product, and which by those who sell to butter factories?
2. Would a cattleman in Wyoming purchase a large herd of either Holstein or Jersey cows? Why? Find out some other breeds of cattle that he might prefer.

D. **Distribution of beef cattle.**

1. How do you account for the fact that there are many beef cattle in the states from Texas northward, as shown in Figure 67? What conditions favor cattle raising in the western plateau and mountain states?
2. Why has Iowa more beef cattle for its size than any other state in the Union? Why is the position of Iowa an advantage?
3. Where does your own state stand as a raiser of beef cattle? Explain why.
4. Why are Argentina and Australia important cattle-raising regions? How is it possible to market the beef in Europe?

## The Sources of Animal Products

E. **The United States as a seller of meat.**

1. The United Kingdom and Germany are two great importers of meat. From what three countries do they purchase their chief supplies?
2. If it were not for the heavy exports of bacon, lard, and ham, our country would not rank high as an exporter of meat. Why does the United States specialize in exporting these three meat products?
3. Although there has been an increase at certain times, our exports of meat are on the whole decreasing. Why? Why are they likely to decrease still more?

F. **How transportation facilities affect meat-growing regions.**

1. The export of salted beef from Argentina is decreasing. What does this fact indicate as to the growth of railroad facilities?
2. What has the invention of the refrigerator car had to do with the exceedingly rapid growth of Chicago?
3. As a country increases in population, the sheep raisers are forced back to make way for the dairymen and beef-cattle raisers. Why are sheep raised in the places more remote from transportation?

G. **How the amount of meat consumed indicates the wealth of a people.**

1. Some nations are too poor to eat meat except as an occasional luxury. Even among nomads such as the Turkomans, Mongols, and Arabs the amount is far less than is usually supposed; for such people dare not eat many of their animals, lest they have too few to keep up the herds and flocks, or to exchange for flour and other necessities that must be bought.

Fig. 76. All meat animals and all meat products must be examined by government meat inspectors before they may be sold for food.

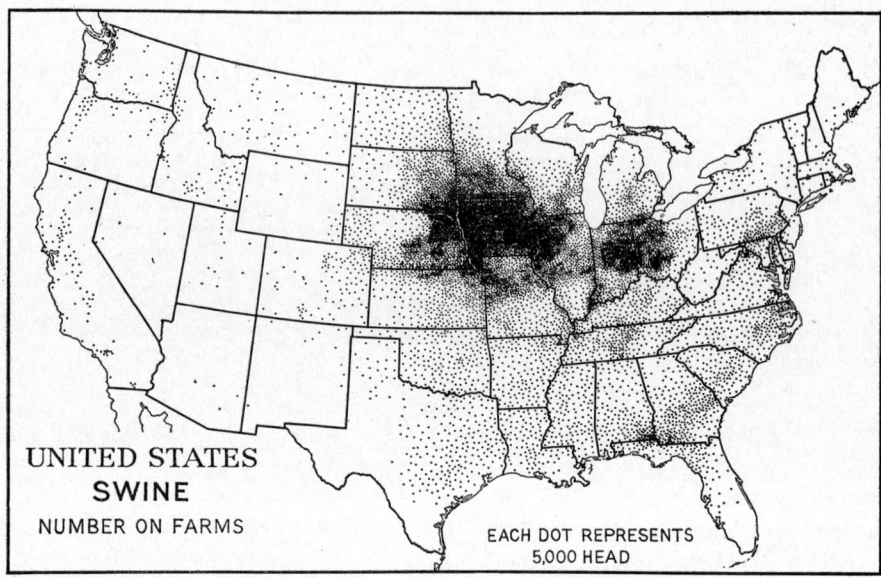

Fig. 77. Almost every farm in the country finds it profitable to raise some swine. But most of the swine are raised in districts where cheap food for them is available. (See Problem *J*, page 100.)

The average consumption of meat per person throughout the world is estimated at about 40 pounds a year. Name two countries that fall below this average; two that rise high above it. Why did you choose these? (See Problem *E*, page 97.)

2. From a study of the figures that follow, decide why densely populated countries like China and Germany raise more swine than cattle or sheep.

| Amount of Digestible Food Fed | Animal | Result in Dressed Meat |
|---|---|---|
| 100 lbs. | steer | 10 lbs. |
| 100 lbs. | sheep | 7 lbs. |
| 100 lbs. | hog | 20 lbs. |

3. The United States is now consuming meat at the rate of about 170 pounds per person each year. There is a steady tendency downward in the use of beef and mutton, and upward in the use of pork and of milk. What effect will this tendency have on the prosperity of the farmer of (*a*) southern Wisconsin; (*b*) the dry plains; (*c*) the Rocky Mountains? on the consumption of corn per capita?

4. Some governments discourage the eating of veal and lamb. Would this be a wise policy for our country to follow?

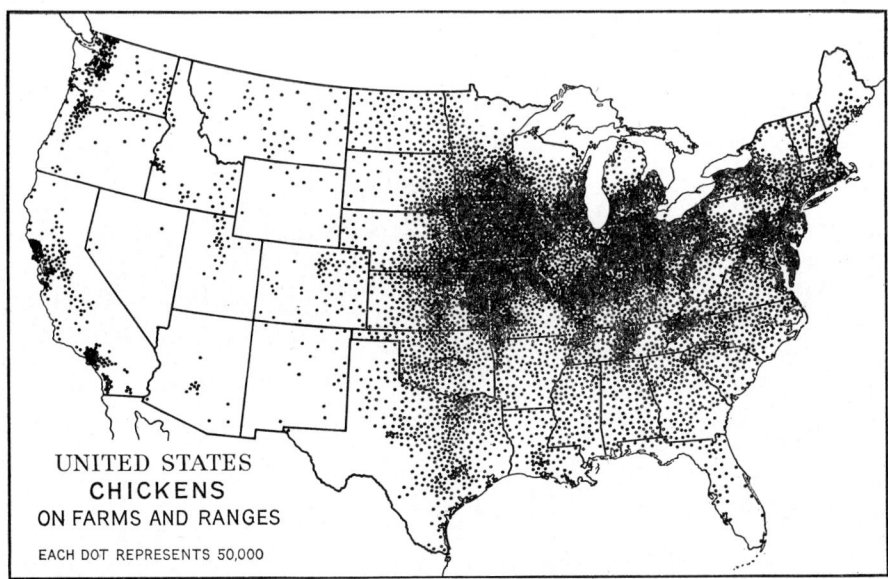

Fig. 78. Chickens, like swine, are very numerous where corn is raised abundantly. Why? Except in the South, they are numerous also in most places where many vegetables are grown for sale. Why?

**H. How the slaughtering industry makes use of its by-products.**

1. Only about 56 per cent of a beef carcass is sold as cuts of meat. Explain what would be the effect on the price of beef if the rest were not used as by-products.
2. A boy was asked to make a list of all the things in his room at home that contained some by-product of the packing house. Can you explain why he listed each of the following articles?

| Tennis racquet | Soap | Violin | Toothbrush | Plaster in wall |
| Jackknife | Shoes | Baseball | Mattress | Furniture |

**I. Sheep and wool.**

1. Where are the two main sheep-raising sections of the United States? Which section raises sheep primarily for meat? Why?
2. What conditions enable our western states to raise many sheep? Name the five leading sheep states in this section. Why are there practically no sheep in southeastern California, southern Nevada, and western Arizona?
3. What animal is more profitable than the sheep in North Dakota and the states to the south of it?
4. How does the climate in the southern states make sheep raising less profitable than in the North?
5. Where does your state stand as a sheep raiser? How do you explain its position?

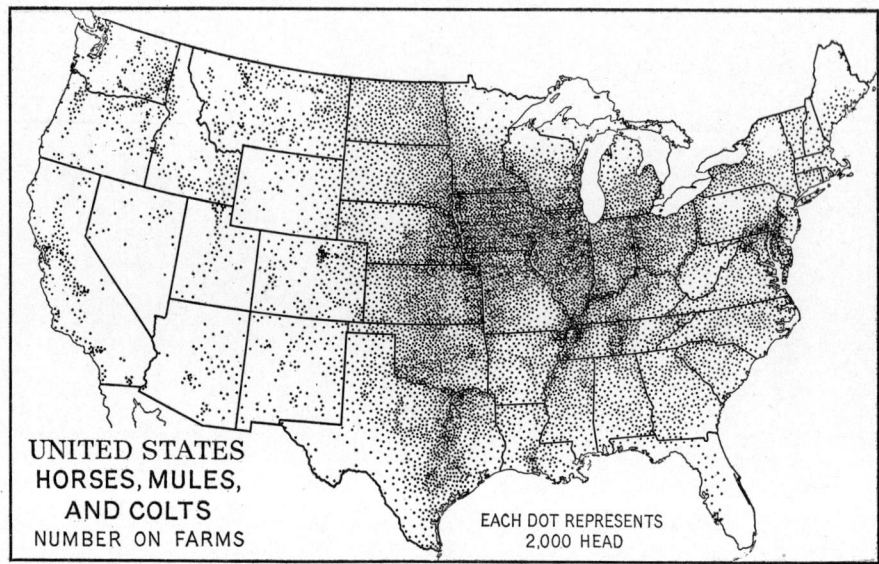

Fig. 79. Most of the horses and mules in the United States are on farms. In the greater part of the country there is one mature animal for about 19 acres of crops. Do you expect to find many or few horses or mules on plains and in river valleys where the land is mostly level? Why? Point out plains and river valleys on the map, to prove your point.

6. New England and the Appalachian region would probably have far more sheep if it were not for sheep-killing dogs. What are the conditions that favor sheep raising in these two sections? Discuss ways and means of lessening the damage done by sheep-killing dogs.

J. Why swine raising is carried on near cheap food crops.

1. The four chief foods used for fattening hogs are corn, barley, potatoes, and skimmed milk. Compare the swine map, Figure 77, with the corn map, Figure 31. To what extent do the two maps agree in the eastern two thirds of the United States?
2. What five states form the heart of the hog belt of the country? What five states form the heart of the corn belt?
3. Explain this saying: "More than one third of the American corn crop squeals as it goes to market."
4. Farmers feed corn to pigs because people prefer pork to cornmeal, and also because "pork can better bear the cost of transportation to market than can cornmeal." Prove the second statement from current market figures.
5. Change the word "pork" to "beef" and prove from the figures that the statement is still true.
6. What seems to control the distribution of swine, to a large extent, in the western third of the United States? See Figure 44.
7. Turn to the sections and exercises on barley in Chapter Three (page 60) and on potatoes in Chapter Four (page 62); study the maps of these

# The Sources of Animal Products

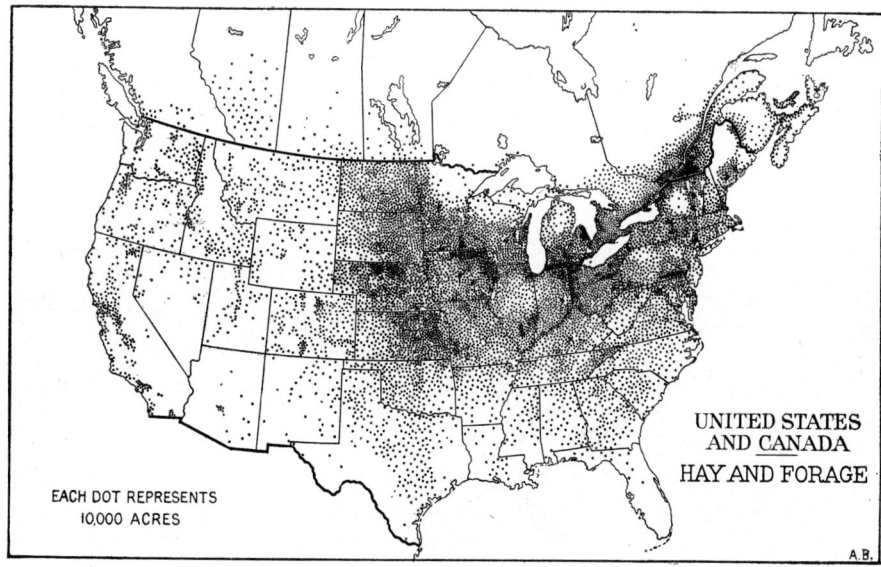

Fig. 80. Timothy grass, clover, and alfalfa are the main crops that are cut and dried for hay; a good deal of oat and barley straw is also used. These crops are bulky, and it does not pay to transport them far. Compare this map with Figures 64 and 67 (pages 84, 88).

products in order to see which of the two has a distribution more like that of hogs.

**K. Horses, farms, and hay.**

1. Most people think of the semi-arid plains or steppes as the main home of the horse. Does Figure 79 support this conclusion? On the basis of Figure 79 make a list of five foreign countries where you would expect to find many horses. Look up the map of horses in the *Atlas of the World's Agriculture* and see whether you are correct.

2. Figure 80 is a map of hay and forage in the United States. Compare it with Figures 64, 67, 70, 77, and 79, showing the distribution of cattle, sheep, swine, and horses. Which does Figure 80 most resemble? Why?

3. Explain why so little hay is raised in (*a*) Florida, (*b*) Nevada, (*c*) northern Maine.

**L. Poultry raising, a minor animal industry.**

1. Compare Figures 50 and 78. Point out similarities between the distribution of vegetables and that of poultry. Explain.

2. Make a similar comparison of Figures 31 and 78.

3. What kind of farm would you select, and where, if you wished to raise poultry at the least expense possible, and also to use all your time to the best advantage?

*A. Kupsinel*

Fig. 81. At the wharves in Gloucester, the former center of the fishing industry of the United States, thousands of tons of fish are landed yearly. As a fishing city Boston now outranks Gloucester.

## CHAPTER EIGHT

### FISHERIES

FISHING is the only form of primary production that takes men away from the land and out on the waters of seas, rivers, and lakes. Although fishing adds to the variety and abundance of man's food, the fishing industry is more interesting than important. In the United States in recent years 243 out of every thousand working people have been engaged in primary production. Of these, 214 were farmers, 24 were miners, 4 were lumbermen, and less than 2 were fishermen. In our country, therefore, fishermen are the least numerous of the primary producers. Moreover, the total yearly catch of fish is worth less than one of the minor crops, such as barley or tobacco. In countries like Norway, however, where the surface is rugged, the soil poor, and the coastline irregular, people turn to the sea for much of their food, and fishing is one of the chief industries.

**Fishing an industry of the north temperate zone.** Although food fish are found in all oceans, the kinds most highly prized thrive in the cool waters of the north temperate zone. Furthermore, the total amount of life in the oceans is actually much greater in high latitudes than in low. It follows naturally that fishing, as an industry, is of most importance in the north temperate zone. Additional reasons for the greater development of the industry in the cool regions are the less abundant supplies of food on land, and the fact that it is less difficult to preserve fish in cool weather.

In high latitudes the fish that are most prized live in shallow waters where food is abundant. Hence numerous bays, shoals, and banks along the northwestern and especially the northeastern coasts of the United States are the great fishing grounds of the country.

### ATLANTIC COAST FISHERIES

The greatest fishing region in the world is on the banks, or shallows, that extend from near the Massachusetts coast northeast to the Grand Banks of Newfoundland. Here the ships of many nations — the United States, Norway, England, France, Portugal, and other countries — share the rich harvest of the sea. Each country has exclusive fishing privileges within three miles of its own shores. Beyond this limit, fishing is free to all.

**Cod fishing on the Grand Banks.** A good way to understand the fisherman's life is to board a schooner at Boston or Gloucester, and go to the Grand Banks with the fishermen. Arriving at the Banks, about the middle of June, the crew of fifteen or twenty men lower into

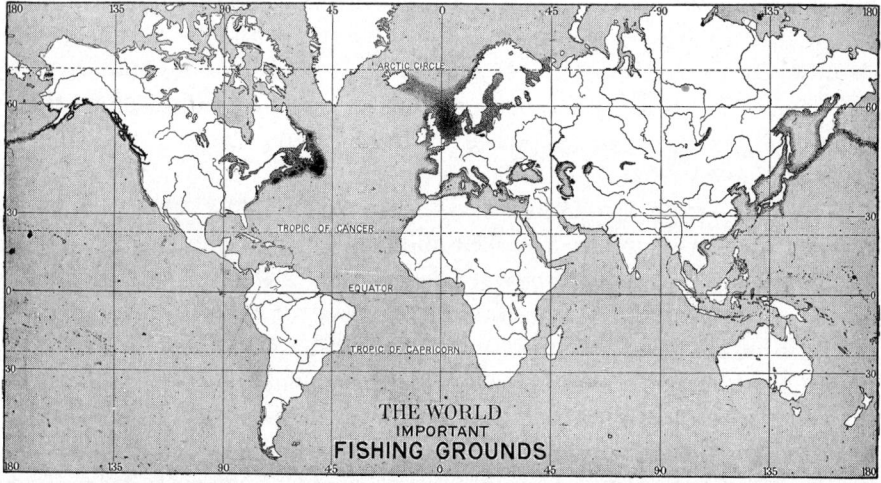

FIG. 82. The great commercial fishing areas of the world are: (1) the northeastern coast of North America; (2) the seas of northeastern Europe — the North Sea, the sea between Norway and Iceland, the Baltic Sea; (3) the northwestern coast of North America. Areas of secondary importance are (1) the Japanese coasts; (2) the Mediterranean Sea; (3) the Adriatic; (4) the Caspian; (5) the White Sea. Fishing is of great importance in many places where the product does not enter into commerce, as along the coast of China and throughout the tropical islands of the world; in these localities fish are sold in the local markets almost as soon as they are caught.

the water the dories that have been stacked like saucers on the deck. A crew of two in each dory throws out a buoy to which is fastened one end of a trawl. This is a rope perhaps a mile long, from which at intervals of about six feet hang lines three feet long, ending in hooks baited with bits of mackerel. The other end of each trawl is fastened to an anchored buoy.

At regular intervals the fishermen "under-run" the trawl by passing it over the dory, taking off the fish, rebaiting the hooks, and dropping it into the water again. If a snow squall or fog overtakes a dory while it is getting its load of cod, the men may lose sight of the ship, and become lost; or heavy seas may break over the boat and prevent it from regaining the schooner. The fishermen sometimes row for days before being rescued, and may be crazed by thirst, almost starved, or badly frozen even in relatively warm months. Hundreds of men are lost on the Grand Banks each year.

**How the fish are prepared.** When the laden dories return safely to the schooner, the fish must be dressed. One man in a group cuts off the fish's head and splits open the body. Another removes the organs, saves the liver for its oil, and throws the rest away. The third with two quick slashes of a long knife removes the backbone. The fish slide from one hand to another with almost incredible speed, and except when dulled knives are changed for sharper ones, no breathing spell is taken until the day's catch is dressed, washed, and salted down. Then the men drop into their bunks and sleep the sleep of physical exhaustion.

In spite of the dangers and hardships of the fisherman's life, there is no lack of fishermen. There are always men who love the life on the waves with its freedom and excitement.

**How cod from the Banks are disposed of.** When a schooner reaches port after a three or four months' trip it usually has a hold full of fish. These are graded according to size, salted again, and spread in the open air upon light frames, or "flakes," until they are thoroughly dried. Many thousands of tons are annually shredded, packed in small boxes, and sold widely as "boneless cod." Gloucester and Boston are the chief centers for the fishing fleets because their harbors face the fishing banks and are near the large markets of the northeastern United States. Gloucester packs great quantities of fish for distant markets and has large glue industries that use the refuse skins and bones of the fish. Cod are sometimes called "the bread of the sea," because of their abundance. Even those who live far from the codfishing grounds can use these fish, which are readily preserved by salting, smoking, or drying. Cod caught on the Labrador coast are marketed in Spain, in Italy, and even in Greece.

**The kinds of fish caught in the North Atlantic.** Haddock and halibut are caught with the codfish. Halibut are larger than cod and their flesh is more highly prized. Next to the cod and haddock in the Atlantic fisheries come the mackerel and herring. Mackerel swim near the surface of the water in schools and hence are caught in great nets, called seines. Seining mackerel is even more exciting than catching codfish, and the profits run higher if the schools are numerous.

**Oyster fishing.** Although the oyster is wholly different from a fish, it is called a shellfish, and oyster catching is included in fisheries. The oyster lives at the bottom of shallow bays, such as are found on the Atlantic coast between Cape Cod and Cape Hatteras. Chesapeake Bay, the largest of these, is the most important oyster region in the world, while Long Island Sound is second in importance. The oyster industry furnishes about one fourth of the total value of all the fisheries on the Atlantic and Gulf coasts of the United States.

### PACIFIC COAST FISHERIES

The salmon is the most important fish on the Pacific coast, with the cod and halibut next in order.

**Salmon fishing.** During the spring or summer, along the whole coast from the Columbia to western Alaska, the salmon ascend the rivers in order to lay their eggs in fresh water. At such times traps and rows of stakes and nets, called weirs, are set in the rivers; they often capture so many fish that the large canneries at the mouths of the rivers find it difficult to handle the catch even by working night and day. So great is the catch in Washington and Alaska that this country is able to satisfy its own needs and export five or ten million dollars' worth besides. Each year the salmon fisheries of Alaska alone yield products worth several times the $7,200,000 paid to Russia for that territory in 1867.

**Refrigeration of fish.** In most parts of the United States, the fish sold as "fresh" halibut come from our Pacific coast and especially from Alaska. Some years more than 40,000,000 pounds of halibut and 20,000,000 pounds of salmon are frozen as soon as they are taken from the waters of the Pacific and are kept in that condition till they reach thousands of markets scattered over the country. It is said that they are quite as nutritious and have quite as good a flavor as fish that have been caught only a few hours. When thawed, however, they spoil more rapidly than do fresh fish.

FIG. 83. Drying fish on the beach near Genoa. Because of the clear, hot sunshine fish are cured in this way in all the Mediterranean countries. On our North Atlantic coast, the handicap of foggy weather is being overcome by the use of artificial heat.

**The fur-seal.** The Pacific Ocean is noted also for its seal "fisheries," so-called, although the seal is no more a fish than is the oyster. The world's most famous herd of fur-seals raises its young on the cool, moist Pribilof Islands, an American possession in Bering Sea. So reckless was the killing of these seals that by 1911 the herd had been reduced to about 4 per cent of the number that it had when we purchased Alaska in 1867. Since 1911, however, our government, with the assistance of Canada, Russia, and Japan, has protected the herd by forbidding fishermen to kill the seals in the open sea and by restricting the killing on land.

### FRESH-WATER FISHERIES

Nearly every river in the United States yields many fish both for sport and for the fish market. The Mississippi River and its tributaries supply more than all the rest combined. The chief kinds are catfish, carp, and black bass. Although the Illinois and Wabash rivers and the White River of Missouri and Arkansas comprise only a small part of the Mississippi system, they supply about one third of the fish taken from the whole system.

The Great Lakes are well stocked with herring, trout, yellow perch, and whitefish. All that are caught find ready markets in the many large cities on the borders of the lakes. The greatest quantities of fish are taken from Lake Michigan and Lake Erie, which have many people living on their shores.

## FISHERIES OF OTHER COUNTRIES

Japan is the only country whose fisheries are more valuable than those of the United States. Great Britain comes next with a value about like ours excluding Alaska. Norway, Iceland, Korea, China, Canada, Germany, Russia, and Portugal also have important fisheries.

The cool shallow waters surrounding the British Isles, Norway, and Iceland, especially the North Sea, are ideal for the same kind of fish that are found along our Atlantic coast. The prominence of Russia and China in fishing depends partly on their many rivers, lakes, and inland seas. There, as in many other countries, fish are so cheap in some regions that they form an important part of the diet of the poor.

Japan has a favorable position similar to that of the British Isles in relation to shallow water. Fish are especially important to the people in Japan, where meat is very scarce.

### QUESTIONS, EXERCISES, AND PROBLEMS

**A. The fish harvest.**

1. The North Sea is one of the best fishing grounds in the world. From its waters Scotland alone takes 135 pounds of food annually for each of her citizens. What other countries in the list given below are well situated to share this ocean harvest?
2. It has been said that the fishermen of Brittany knew the Newfoundland coast long before Columbus discovered America. Do you think this possible? Why?
3. Why do countries with important fisheries usually have large merchant marines and large navies?
4. The *National Geographic Magazine* for July, 1921, contains a good article on the Grand Banks, with excellent pictures. Let some member of the class be appointed to bring in a copy and to give a short abstract of the article.

**B. The consumption of fish.**

Approximate Catch of Fish per Person

| | | | |
|---|---|---|---|
| Alaska | 12,000 pounds | England and Wales | 55 pounds |
| Newfoundland | 5,000 pounds | Netherlands | 37 pounds |
| Scotland | 135 pounds | Ireland | 22 pounds |
| Canada | 100 pounds | United States | 20 pounds |
| Japan | 85 pounds | Germany | 12 pounds |

1. The Faeroe Islands resemble Alaska and Newfoundland in producing vastly more fish than the people can possibly consume. Explain why this is so and what becomes of the fish.

2. Why does Scotland, even in normal times, catch many times as large a supply of fish as Germany? Compare the position, harbors, and coastline of the two countries.
3. Although the United States catches more fish than England and Wales, it stands relatively low in the preceding list. Explain this fact.
4. What becomes of the enormous catch of the United States?
5. "What grazing lands mean to the American, the sea means to the Japanese." Explain this statement.

C. **Conservation of fish.**
1. Why does the United States government each year place in rivers and lakes billions of little fish newly hatched from the eggs?
2. Uncle Sam hatches fish somewhat as a farmer hatches chickens. He maintains nearly one hundred widely distributed stations. In Washington 100,000,000 young salmon are sometimes hatched and planted in the streams in a year. Suppose that when these fish are well grown, one per cent are caught and canned. If the average fish results in about 5 pounds of meat when canned, how many pounds of food would the hatcheries of Washington supply in a year?

FIG. 84. A Japanese fisherman casting his net.

3. Find out at the stores in your neighborhood the price of canned salmon. At the average price, how many dollars' worth of food would result annually from the work of the Washington hatcheries?
4. Each state has game laws intended to protect the wild animal life of the state. How are the fish in the rivers and lakes of your state protected by law?
5. The state and Federal governments have passed laws to prevent oysters from becoming so scarce that only the richest people can afford to buy them. About half the oysters now produced in this country are grown on "farms" from 20 to 100 feet below the level of the ocean surface. Why are many of these oysters canned at Baltimore, Maryland?
6. Another variety of sea food which is conserved by the government is the lobster. Government inspectors check the lobster catch. What lobsters must the fishermen throw back into the water? The lobsters carrying eggs are placed in "nurseries," from which thousands of baby lobsters are turned into the sea.

D. **The world's unused ocean resources.**

1. The United States government spent a large sum to introduce a fish new to the market — the tile fish. As a result 12,000,000 were caught and sold in a recent year. Assuming that this fish averaged four pounds in dressed weight and brought twenty-five cents a pound, how many dollars' worth of food was thus added to the American table?
2. If one pound of tile fish is nearly equal in food value to one pound of steak selling at fifty cents, about how many dollars were saved in one year to the American housewives?
3. The fish supply of tropical waters is not well exploited. What hinders the transportation and marketing of fresh fish in the tropics?

E. **Fishing for other purposes than food.**

1. Why has the whaling industry declined? Whale meat is much like beef, and in Japan whales are caught for food. Why is not whale meat found in the markets in the United States?
2. Where do our sponges come from? How are they caught and prepared?
3. Where are the most important pearl fisheries?
4. Find out how and where coral is secured.

F. **A class project.**

1. Visit a local fish market and make a list of the fish that are on sale. Note after each kind whether it is fresh, frozen, dried, salted, smoked, or canned. Also find out if possible the source of each. (Labels will help you with the canned fish.)
2. Why is each prepared in the special way that you find in the store?
3. Let each member of the class make a special study of the fish he considers the best to eat and add his study as a chapter in the class book.

Fig. 85. Cutting away rock with a compressed-air drill in a Michigan copper mine. Note how beams are used to support the roof and sides of galleries in mines.

# CHAPTER NINE

## THE MINING INDUSTRY

Mining differs from other means of primary production in three ways:

(1) There is no way of increasing the original supply of the product.
(2) Production is restricted to a few localities.
(3) Until the rocks are actually examined in detail it is almost impossible to tell where it will be profitable to carry on operations.

**Why mining is the robber industry.** The mining industry takes from the rocks vast stores of wealth which nature has deposited, and which nature herself cannot renew for millions of years. For this reason mining is sometimes called the "robber industry." When man harvests a crop on a farm, the fertile soil still remains, and other crops can be raised; if a forest is cut down, another may grow in time; although many cattle are killed, the herd will increase in number; fish also multiply freely, even though great quantities are caught. But when once any form of mineral wealth is taken from the rocks it can never be replaced. It may indeed be used over and over, but nothing that man can do will cause a mine to furnish new ore when once the supply is exhausted, nor is there any known way of preventing the world's present store of metals from being gradually worn out and lost.

**Why mining is limited to a few small regions.** Mining can be carried on only in certain regions where minerals are stored. Coal must be mined where great quantities of dead trees and swampy reeds were buried long ago beneath thick layers of clay and sand. Gold can be mined only where it has been deposited in veins, or where the material from such veins has been carried away and laid down in gravel deposits. Man has no power to create new deposits or to transplant the old ones.

With the other forms of primary production the case is different. Man can make a million bushels of wheat grow where not a wheat stalk grew before, as in Canada. He can raise a flock of a hundred million sheep where no sheep grazed before, as in South America. He can cause a forest to grow in a region that was only grassland, as in many parts of our prairies. He can carry plants from one country to another, and he can stock a river or lake with fish that are strangers to its waters.

The possession of mineral deposits by a country is partly a matter of chance and partly a matter of political foresight. It is fortunate for the United States that its northern boundary was so run that it includes some of the richest of the world's iron deposits; but since at that time no one knew the value of the minerals near the head of Lake Superior, credit for giving the deposits to this country must go to mere luck. On the other hand, it was not luck that gave Alaska to the United States; it was the political foresight of Secretary Seward. For two cents an acre he bought a vast region which up to 1930 had yielded more than three dollars an acre, chiefly in gold. Today every advanced country is eager to obtain either political or commercial control of places that furnish any mineral wealth, but especially coal and petroleum. This eagerness has been a cause of political troubles in Mesopotamia, Manchuria, Mexico, Spitzbergen, and elsewhere.

**Why it is difficult to discover where minerals are located.** In mining we have almost no way of knowing where we may reasonably expect the product to be found. We know that certain conditions of climate and soil favor the growth of oranges and cotton or the raising of beef cattle. We know that forests require a good rainfall and will not grow where the cold is excessive. We even know under what conditions sea animals, such as codfish, thrive best.

With the products of the mines, however, the case is different. Since few surface conditions help to explain their distribution underground, the search for them must often be carried on with relatively little guidance from science. Nevertheless the geologist is often able to locate ore bodies. Metals are usually found in mountainous regions or where mountains previously existed. This is partly because most ores are formed far beneath the earth's surface, where intense heat and underground waters cause a concentration of metal-bearing compounds. Only when mountains are upheaved and worn away by rain and rivers are such ores exposed to our sight. But not all mountains contain metals. Because the distribution of metals is so irregular, it seems almost an accident that the Malay Peninsula and Bolivia produce most of the world's tin; the United States and northwestern Europe, most of the world's zinc; Mexico and the United States, the silver; and the United States and Chile, the copper.

### THE MINERAL PRODUCTS

The treasure that man digs out of the depths of the earth is of three kinds — metals, fuels, and stony products.

**The metals.** Even in prehistoric times industry and art used the chief metals, — iron, gold, silver, copper, tin, lead, and zinc. There are many other metals; but only a few are of large commercial importance; for example, aluminum, platinum, nickel, cobalt, iridium.

**The fuels.** Heat is needed not only for cooking and for warmth, but for power and to work the metals. For many centuries it was obtained by burning wood. It was not until modern times that Europeans discovered that coal can be mined and used for heat, light, and power. Still more recently, deposits of petroleum and natural gas have been found and utilized.

**Stony products.** In the earliest times man used stones as weapons and tools. Now he uses stone for buildings, pavements, and many other purposes, as well as vast amounts of clay, cement, sand, gravel, and other non-metallic minerals.

### HOW THE MINERAL PRODUCTS ARE OBTAINED

Metals and coal are mined in nearly the same way, by digging holes by which men can go down into the earth, get out what they seek, and bring it up to the surface. For petroleum and natural gas, deep wells are bored, and the oil or gas is carried off in pipe lines.

## The Mining Industry

RECENT VALUES OF CHIEF MINE AND QUARRY PRODUCTS IN THE UNITED STATES

| | | | |
|---|---|---|---|
| METALS | Iron (pig iron) | | $ 698,000,000 |
| | Copper | | 232,000,000 |
| | Lead | | 96,000,000 |
| | Zinc | | 83,000,000 |
| | Gold | | 47,000,000 |
| | Silver | | 37,000,000 |
| FUELS | Coal: | | |
| |   Bituminous | 1,106,000,000 | 1,554,000,000 |
| |   Anthracite | 448,000,000 | |
| | Petroleum | | 1,310,000,000 |
| | Natural gas | | 309,000,000 |
| STONY PRODUCTS | Cement | | 281,000,000 |
| | Stone | | 193,000,000 |
| | Sand | | 112,000,000 |

**What a typical mine is like.** In mining for metals and also for coal, vertical shafts are usually sunk. In some mines they extend a mile below the surface; practically always great elevators are needed to carry the workmen and the cars containing the ores up and down. From the shaft, nearly horizontal tunnels or galleries are dug at various levels to follow the veins that contain the mineral. In the great mines there are many shafts, and the galleries form a complicated network. Occasionally rooms or chambers are formed where large masses of ore have been mined. In galleries and chambers the roofs must be supported by strong beams to prevent the overlying rock from falling. The galleries contain railway tracks for the speedy transportation of both the ore and the miners.

Often electricity is used in lighting the galleries, in hauling the trains of cars, and in driving the drills. In many mines mules do the hauling; they thrive in their strange homes so long as they are well cared for, and many of them spend their lives under the ground.

Most mines must be drained and ventilated. Water is continually seeping out of the surrounding rock, and it would soon flood the mine if powerful pumps were not employed. The presence of large numbers of men and perhaps animals causes the air in the mine to become foul, and the smoke from the lamps in the miners' caps and the gases that are given off by the explosions when the rock is blasted make it still worse. The air, especially in coal mines, may also be contaminated by gases that come from the rocks themselves.

To make a mine more healthful, therefore, the foul air is sucked out by "blowers" located usually at the mouth of a small air shaft, which causes fresh air to rush in through the main shaft.

**A visit to a mine.** Perhaps the most interesting part of a mine is where the ore is being loosened, placed in cars, and started on its way to the upper world. The miner sometimes uses simply a hand drill and hammer to drill holes in the ores, but more often he is equipped with a machine drill operated by compressed air or steam. When the holes have reached the required depth, they are filled with explosives. Then a warning shout is given, and a fuse is lighted which burns slowly enough to let everyone get out of the way. Soon a muffled report is heard, and tons of the ore are hurled to the mine floor. The workmen return and pry down any loose fragments that might drop upon them. Then they shovel the ore into waiting cars, breaking with great hammers any fragments that are too large to be lifted readily. When full, the cars are pushed down to a main gallery, where they are soon picked up by a passing train and drawn to the foot of the shaft. There each car is placed in the elevator and lifted to the surface.

After the ore leaves the mine it must be crushed and melted in

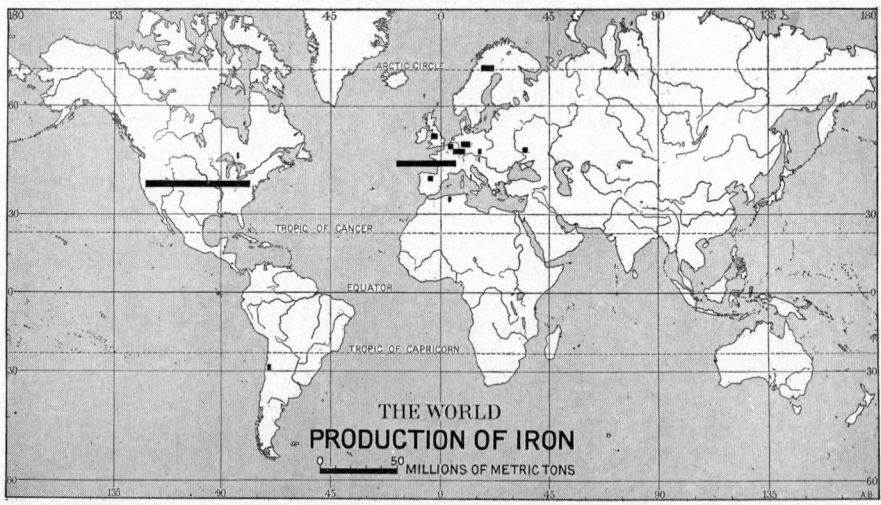

FIG. 86. From North America and Europe (especially western Europe) comes most of the iron used in commerce and industry. Six great regions of ore deposits are now known: (1) the Lake Superior district; (2) the Lorraine district, in France; (3) northern Sweden; (4) Cuba; (5) Newfoundland; (6) Brazil. Of these, the first three are now producing fields. The others have great reserves, but it is not at present profitable to work them extensively; none of the three is near to active manufacturing regions. As a rule the United States smelts two fifths or more of the world's output, Germany one eighth, and France and Great Britain somewhat less. The amount in Russia is steadily increasing.

great furnaces to separate the pure metal or other mineral from the slag or waste material. Often the slag rises to the top like froth, while the heavier liquid metal can be drained off below. Sometimes this work of smelting, as the melting is called, is done in mills near the head of the shaft; but usually it is cheaper to do it where there is an abundance of coal, and hence the ore is often carried great distances from the mine. This is done with the Lake Superior iron ores, which are smelted in Pittsburgh, Cleveland, and elsewhere.

**Why some mines are open pits.** Some deposits of minerals are so near the surface and cover areas so large that it is easier to reach them by removing all the overlying soil and rock than by digging shafts and tunnels. This is called the "open pit" method of mining. The Mesaba range of Minnesota, near Lake Superior, containing the greatest iron deposit yet known, is mined by the open pit method. One can stand on the edge of one of the great pits and watch a train of empty ore cars take its way along the sides, down into the pit, and draw up beside a great steam shovel. The iron ore is here so easily pulverized that mild blasts with dynamite serve to loosen great quantities, and therefore it is readily handled by the steam shovel.

### IRON

Iron, the most useful of metals, exists in great abundance. At present only the richest deposits are mined. That is why the iron-producing regions are not numerous. Iron can be procured so cheaply from the rich deposits that it does not pay to work the poorer ones.

**The consumption of iron.** The time will come, however, when man will eagerly turn to the deposits he now passes by. In 1820, the iron goods made in the United States averaged only forty pounds for each individual. The amount rose to 175 pounds in 1870, to 400 pounds in 1900, and is now about 700 pounds. During the World War the demand increased still further. It is fortunate that iron, unlike coal, can be used again and again. After iron has served its purpose in one form, as in a kitchen stove, it is collected as scrap iron and may be made into something else, like steel rails or nails. Hence, the iron deposits of the world will probably not be exhausted for thousands of years, whereas the coal deposits are likely to become seriously depleted within a few centuries.

**Where iron is mined in the United States.** Each year fifty to seventy million tons of iron ore are mined in the United States. This

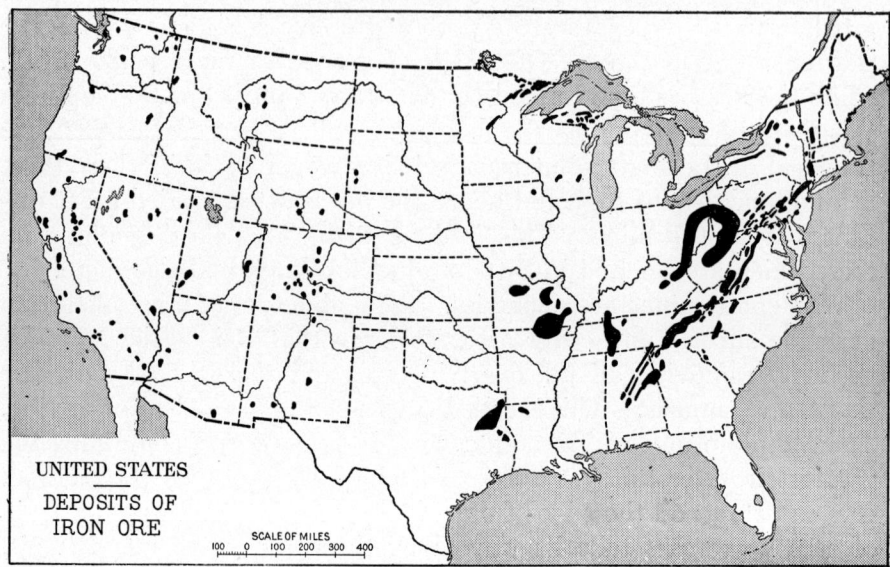

Fig. 87. Iron ore is widely distributed in the United States. But ore alone is not enough to make mining a profitable business. There are several other requirements: (1) the ore must be easy to get out; (2) it must have a good percentage of metallic iron; (3) it must be so situated that it can be smelted at low cost, that is, either near supplies of fuel and limestone (used in smelting) or near cheap transportation to such supplies.

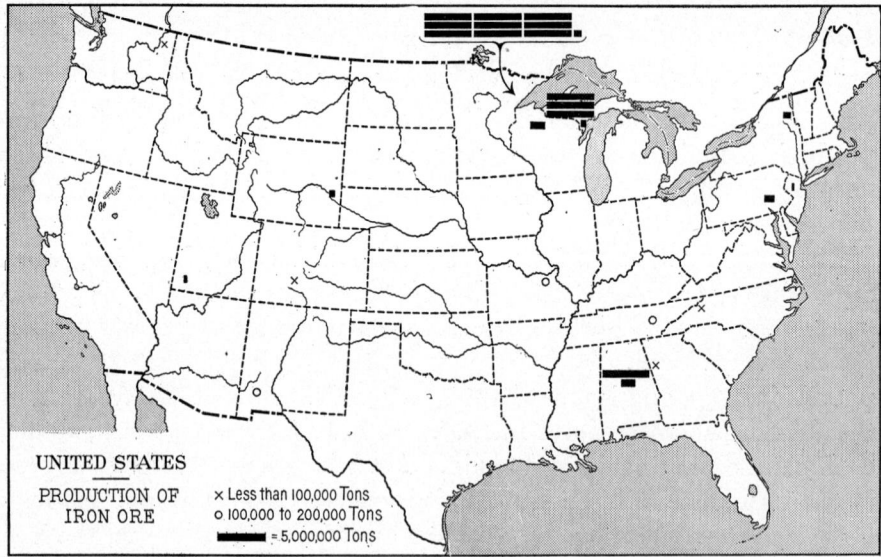

Fig. 88. This map shows in which states the three requirements for profitable iron mining (as given above) are most completely met. Minnesota produces more ore than any other state; Michigan comes second; Alabama is third. The Great Lakes offer cheap water transportation for the Minnesota-Michigan ore to the large industrial cities near the Pennsylvania-Ohio and Indiana-Illinois coal fields. Alabama has coal fields near the iron mines. Note the states that have deposits but do not produce ore enough to figure on a map showing commercial production.

is about two fifths of what is mined in the whole world. Six sevenths of the supply for the United States is taken from the deposits around the western end of Lake Superior, principally in Minnesota and Michigan (Fig. 88). One twelfth comes from mines near Birmingham, Alabama, and the rest is produced in New York, Pennsylvania, Tennessee, Virginia, and a dozen other states. No state west of the Mississippi River produces more than a few thousand tons. This is because the western states are distant from the great markets for iron goods. What they mine is for local uses.

**How iron and coal underlie civilization.** Our modern civilization is built upon iron and coal. The machinery, tools, and means of transportation used by civilized people are made almost entirely of iron, and iron is taken from its ore by means of coal. Practically everything used in our daily lives is produced with the help of iron and coal.

**The stony products.** The table on page 113 shows the importance of cement, stone, and sand. Besides their use in buildings, road construction, and street paving, they have many uses in industry, also; for example, limestone in smelting iron, and sand in making glass.

### QUESTIONS, EXERCISES, AND PROBLEMS

A. **Where iron is mined.**

1. Where are the world's two great iron-mining regions? State two facts that partly explain the concentration of iron mining in these two regions.
2. Good iron ores occur in many countries. Nevertheless Figure 86 shows that little iron is produced except where much coal is produced. What climatic condition has something to do with this?
3. Name the six leading iron-mining countries. Compare the iron-ore production of the United States with that of the others.
4. What continents mine practically no iron ore? Why? What is the only tropical country that mines iron ore in appreciable quantities?
5. England takes most of the iron ore mined in Spain and much of that mined in Sweden; this ore is smelted in the English foundries. The ore mined in Cuba is carried to the United States to be smelted. How can you account for these movements of the ore?

B. **The use of iron.**

1. About half a ton of iron and steel goods is made annually in this country for every inhabitant within our boundaries. Make a list of the iron and steel goods that account in a general way for your share. Put ten items under the following headings:

| Preserving or Preparing Food | Building a House | Housekeeping | Preparing Articles of Personal Use | Transportation |
|---|---|---|---|---|
| *Examples:* tin can | nails | flat iron | shoe machinery | iron rails |

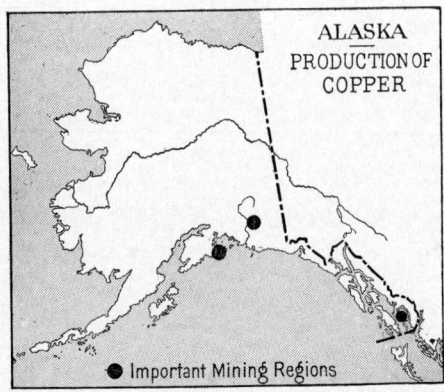

FIG. 89. In 1921 Alaska produced more copper than any of the states except Arizona and Michigan. The crude ore is shipped down the coast to smelters on Puget Sound.

C. **The story of copper.**
1. Choose a committee to present the story of copper to the class.
2. In an encyclopedia or some other book, find information on the topics of the following outline:
   (a) Uses of copper. (Remember that brass is chiefly copper.)
   (b) Countries that produce the two million tons now used annually.
   (c) States in the United States prominent in copper production (Fig. 90).
   (d) How copper is mined.
   (e) How copper is extracted (smelted) from the ore.
   (f) Why the United States smelts great quantities of imported copper ore.

D. **The story of aluminum.**
1. Let another committee study aluminum in the same way that copper was studied in Problem C.

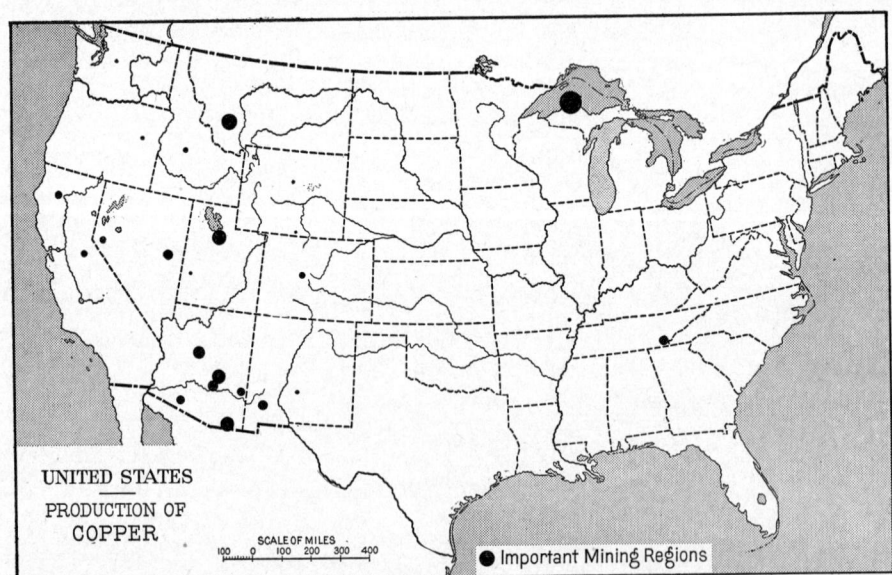

FIG. 90. The circles on this map are proportionate to the amounts of copper smelted in the districts indicated. Arizona, Michigan, Montana, and Utah are the leading states. Much of the copper is smelted near the mines. The United States supplies more than half the copper used in the world.

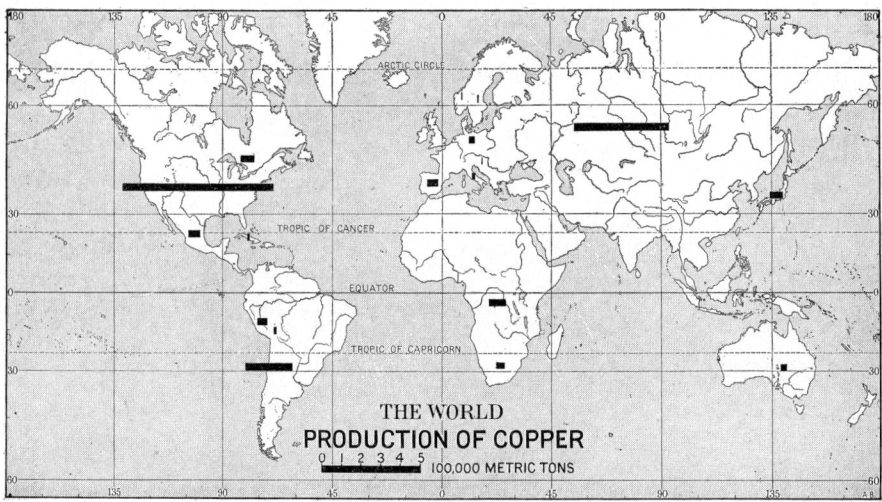

Fig. 91. Most of the copper mined in the world is found in the Americas, chiefly in the mountain chain that stretches along the western coast of both continents. Some copper is found also in eastern Canada, the eastern United States, and Cuba. Russia now stands next to the United States in production, with Chile third. Belgian Congo comes fourth, followed by Canada, Japan, Mexico, and Spain. South Africa, Australia, Peru, Germany, Italy, and Yugoslavia have productive copper mines.

*E.* **Metal mining in the United States.**

1. Compare the table of metal production on page 325 with a relief map of the United States. Name the mountain range with which you associate (*a*) the iron fields of Alabama; (*b*) the lead and zinc deposits of southern Missouri and adjacent states; (*c*) the gold of California; (*d*) the silver of Colorado; (*e*) the gold and silver deposits of South Dakota.

2. The metal deposits of the Lake Superior district are associated with low ranges that have been worn down from high mountains. Why may these ranges be called " mountain roots "?

3. Name the states in the interior of the country and on the Gulf of Mexico that have practically no metal deposits. Why should you expect these regions to contain few metal deposits?

4. Aside from the *quality* of the ore, what other two great advantages have the iron mines of the Lake Superior region?

5. What one metal is produced in every one of the western states?

6. What four western states mine important quantities of each of six chief metals?

7. What state leads in the mining of two of these metals? What is our leading gold state? silver state? copper state? iron state? Point out each of the leading metal states on the wall map and tell the class for what metal each is noted.

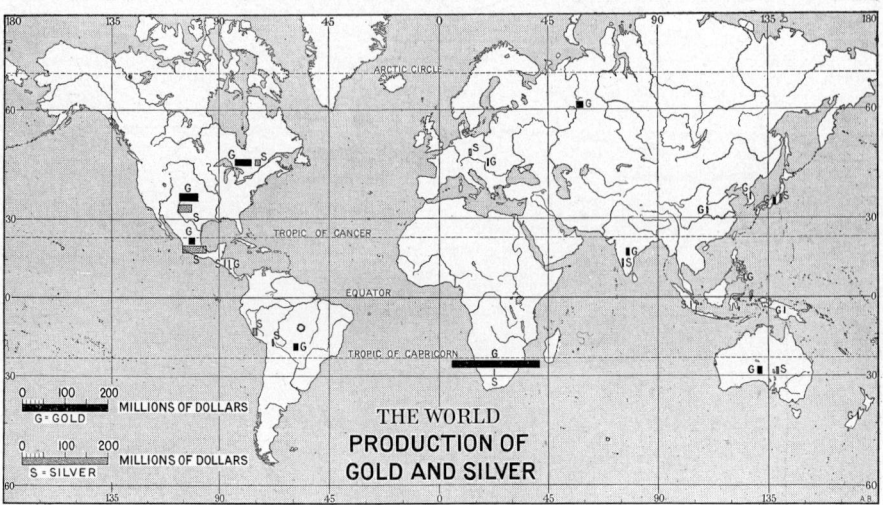

Fig. 92. In gold mining South Africa easily leads the world. The Transvaal produces about five times as much gold as the United States or Canada and fifteen to twenty times as much as Mexico, Russia, Rhodesia, or Australia.

In the production of silver, Mexico stands first and the United States second. Within the United States, Utah leads in silver and California in gold; almost all the silver, as well as the gold, comes from west of the Great Plains.

(Note that *values*, not *quantities*, are here represented. If quantities were represented and the gold bars remained as above, the bar for silver in Mexico would have to extend over the whole map.)

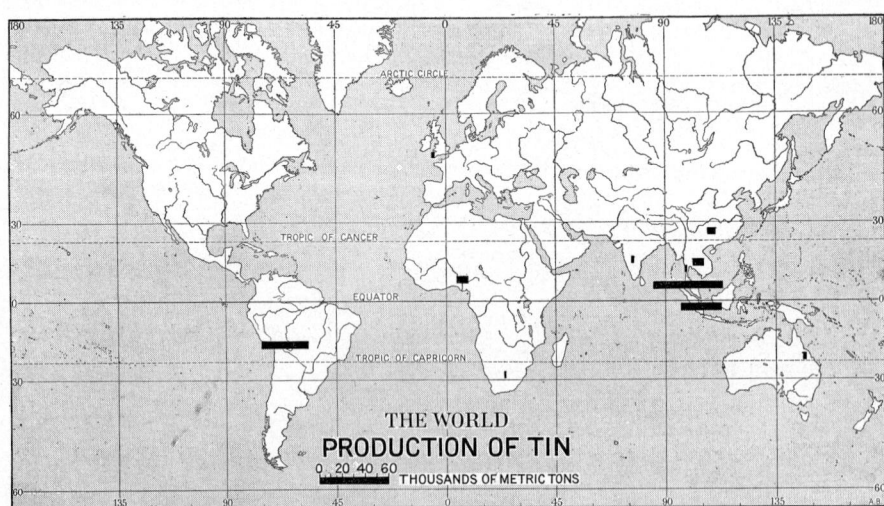

Fig. 93. Tin is the only one of the seven chief metals whose main centers of production are in southeastern Asia. The Malay Peninsula and the East Indies produce half the world's supply. North America has no tin, and Europe has only a little in Great Britain and Spain. In Africa, Nigeria and South Africa produce small amounts, as does Australia. The South American supply (about a fourth of the world's total) comes from Bolivia. In Asia, China and Siam together produce about a tenth.

## The Mining Industry

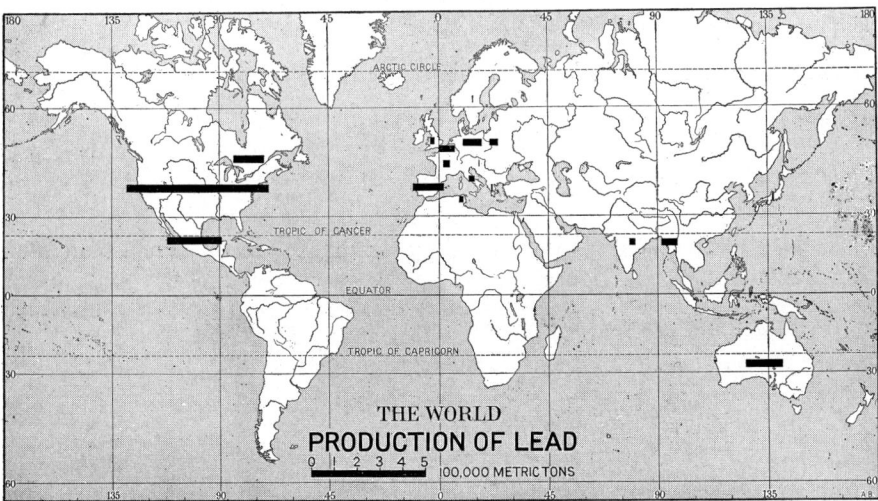

Fig. 94. Comparison of this map with Figure 95 shows that lead and zinc are usually found together. The United States and Mexico produce the greater part of the world's supply of lead.

8. Let different members of the class or different committees report on the mining of (a) zinc; (b) lead; (c) tin; (d) gold; (e) silver. Use the following outline:
   (a) Uses, especially in your own town and at home.
   (b) Where found in the United States.
   (c) The deposits nearest to your home.
   (d) How prepared for the market.
   (e) Increasing or decreasing in use and why.

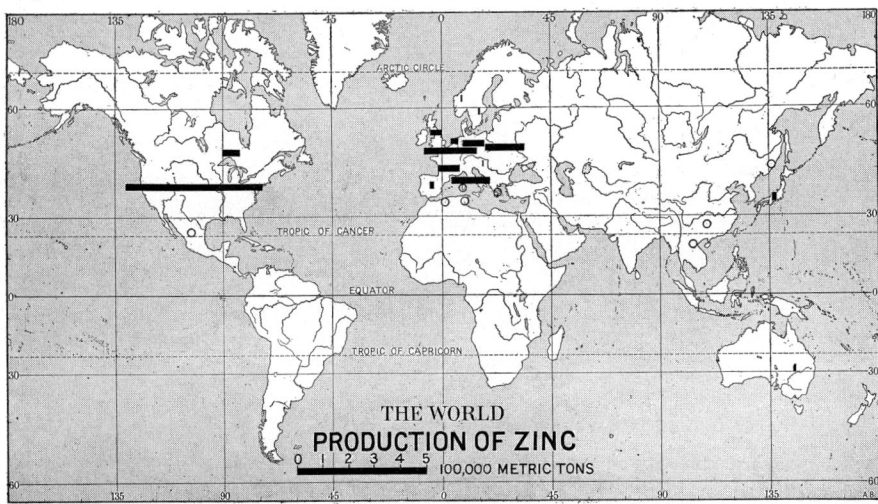

Fig. 95. Zinc, like lead, occurs chiefly in the United States and western Europe (especially Poland and Germany). The circles on this map indicate regions where zinc is mined in small quantities; ore is smelted in Japan, but the other minor production areas export their ore for smelting. Belgium smelts a great deal, but brings the ore from a distance.

122  Modern Business Geography

F. Quarrying.

1. Explain the difference between mining and quarrying.
2. Let different individuals or committees report on each of the following: (a) granite; (b) limestone, including marble and onyx; (c) slate; (d) sandstone; (e) clay. Use an outline similar to the one given on the preceding page.
3. Is cement a primary or a secondary product? Bring to class an oral report on its production and uses.

G. Mining countries of the world.

1. Why is the United States the leading mining country of the world?
2. Why do the following countries carry on relatively little mining?

    Switzerland    Italy    Ireland    Brazil
    China    Norway    Argentina    Egypt

3. Why do the following countries hold a fair position in mining?

    Mexico    Spain    Chile    Sweden    Japan

FIG. 96. One of the quarries at Carrara, in Italy, where the finest marble for statuary is obtained. The ancient Romans and the Italians of the Middle Ages worked the quarry, and marble is still being cut there.

*United States Bureau of Mines*
Fig. 97. Undercutting in a coal mine to make a borehole.

## CHAPTER TEN

### THE FUEL PRODUCTS

COAL furnishes the strong muscles of a country. Human and animal muscles by themselves can accomplish only the little tasks. Without coal a country is a weakling; with it, a giant that can easily do the heaviest sort of work, such as drawing long trains of heavy cars, propelling great steamships, driving the machinery of huge factories, and digging tunnels through mountains. Coal furnishes the power for the world's work, and man furnishes the brain to guide it.

The Chinese were perhaps the first to use coal. More than six centuries ago the famous traveler, Marco Polo, reported that in China he found people burning black stones which grew red and remained hot for a long time. England was the first country to use coal extensively in her industries. There this mineral has furnished heat for more than four centuries and has been used in smelting iron for nearly two centuries.

The United States was slow in mining coal even after deposits were found, because the forests furnished abundant cheap fuel. With

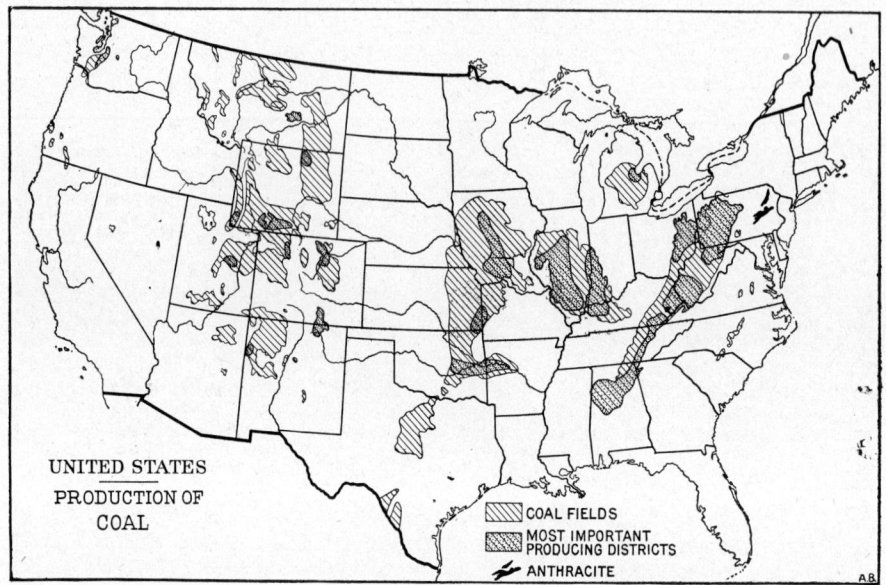

Fig. 98. Coal is mined most profitably (1) when it is where it can be easily reached from the surface, (2) when it is of good quality, and (3) when it is near a market or can be cheaply transported to market. In the United States, the Appalachian coal fields meet these requirements most nearly; the middle-western fields come next; while the Pacific fields are much the least important. The anthracite coal (in eastern Pennsylvania) is indeed buried deep and is hard to mine; but as it is the best kind of coal, and there is only one deposit of it, the fact that it cannot be reached easily does not prevent the field from being worked.

the extension of the railroads after 1850, however, the demand for coal grew steadily. Now our country mines two fifths of the world's coal; Great Britain mines about one fifth, and Germany one eighth.

**Coal fields in the United States.** As shown in Figure 98, coal fields are both extensive and numerous in the United States. No large section of the country is entirely without them.

The three most important coal fields of the United States are:

(1) The anthracite field of eastern Pennsylvania.
(2) The bituminous field in the western Appalachian Mountains from western Pennsylvania and West Virginia to Alabama.
(3) The bituminous field which centers in Illinois.

These three fields produce nearly nine tenths of the coal of the country. Besides containing rich deposits, they have the further advantage of nearness to populous regions. Since Pennsylvania contains the anthracite field and the best part of the Appalachian field, it stands supreme as our greatest coal state, turning out nearly 40 per cent of the country's supply. Pennsylvania mines nearly as much coal as the British Isles and more than Germany.

Outside of the three main coal fields, some of the deposits in the United States, such as those of the Pacific slope, are not large enough to satisfy local needs. Others, such as some of the Utah deposits, are so deep in the earth that for many years to come it will not pay to work them. In some regions, like parts of eastern Kentucky, the coal fields are rich and easy to work, but the rugged relief makes transportation so difficult that to carry the coal where it can be used costs more than it is worth. The quality of other deposits, such as those extending from Iowa to Texas, is inferior.

In the inferior deposits a great deal of rock, especially slate, is mixed with the coal. With good coal only a little slate is usually found, and an attempt is made to take this from the coal at the mine. After anthracite coal has been broken and graded according to size, it is shaken in such a way as to separate the shale from the coal, but a great deal reaches the consumer.

**Why cities grow up near coal mines.** Coal is so important for the manufacturing industries in general and for the smelting and manufacturing of iron in particular, that it is not surprising to find these industries clustering around the mines. Hence the great iron and steel city of Pittsburgh is located among the bituminous coal mines of western Pennsylvania. In the same way, Scranton, which also

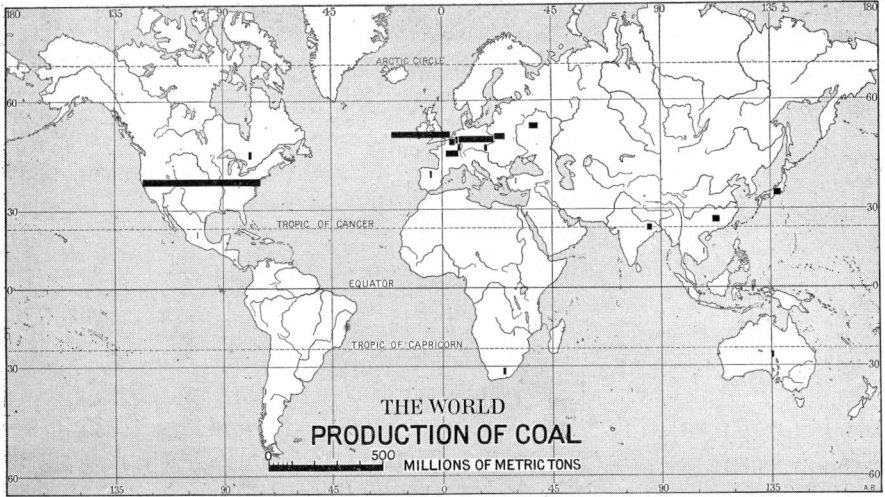

FIG. 99. The eastern half of the United States and northwestern Europe produce most of the coal used in the world. They are also the regions where the machine industries are most highly developed, and most of the steamships in the world are owned in their ports. What connection has the production of coal with industries and shipping? Why are Sweden, France, Spain, and Italy especially interested in methods of utilizing water power for industries? Remembering that coal and iron are the basis of modern industry, compare this map with Figure 86 (page 114) to find out one reason for Great Britain's leading position in commerce and industry.

*United States Bureau of Mines*

FIG. 100. The coal tipple is an instance of the way in which machinery works for man. The smaller building is the weighing house; the larger one is the breaker. Trace the route which the mine cars take. What two processes take place in the breaker? Where does the coal go next? How are all the cars propelled? Where are the empty cars going? Compare the amounts of man labor and machine labor employed in the work illustrated in this picture.

has extensive iron industries, is surrounded by the anthracite mines of eastern Pennsylvania. The growth of Birmingham, in Alabama, has been encouraged by both coal and iron deposits.

In Europe, "coal cities" are more numerous than in our country. The best known are Birmingham, Manchester, Newcastle, and Glasgow, in Great Britain; Essen in Germany; and Liége in Belgium.

### PETROLEUM

Petroleum has been much used for only about seventy years, yet in this short time the United States has consumed nearly half of its known supply. Petroleum has become so essential to modern man for lighting his home, lubricating his machinery, and feeding his motors that a French general is quoted as saying that the Allies' battles in the World War " could not have been won without that other blood of the earth which is called oil."

Perhaps the general who called petroleum " the blood of the earth " would think the name even more appropriate if he could look a few feet beneath the surface in some parts of the United States and see the net-

# The Fuel Products

work of pipe lines. Through these, by means of pumping stations, the oil is forced from the tank at the source of production to the refinery near the market (Fig. 104).

### QUESTIONS, EXERCISES, AND PROBLEMS

A. **Where the world's coal is mined.**
1. What are the two great coal-producing regions of the world? (Fig. 99.)
2. Make a list of the five countries that produce most coal, beginning with the chief producer.
3. China is thought to stand third among the world's coal fields. How do you explain her small coal production? What relation has this to political conditions?
4. What two possible explanations can you give for the absence of coal mining in equatorial regions?
5. Pennsylvania and England are of about the same size, and each produces more than two hundred million tons of coal annually. What advantages for coal production does each possess?

B. **How coal is formed.**
1. From a local coal dealer secure samples of the following kinds of coal: anthracite, bituminous, cannel, and lignite. If possible, get also a piece of peat. This may be found in almost any marsh.
2. In an encyclopedia or a general geography read about the formation, distribution, and uses of the different kinds of coal. Take notes and make a report to the class, using the samples you have gathered to illustrate your points.

C. **How coal is used.**
1. About six tons of coal are burned in the United States each year for every man, woman, and child in the country. Under the following headings, make lists of things that you use, to show in a general way how your share is consumed.
   (a) Buildings heated by coal.
   (b) Metals smelted with coal.
   (c) Manufactured goods made with machines driven by power obtained from coal.
   (d) Means of transportation for which the power is furnished by coal.

D. **How we may conserve our coal supply.**
1. Since coal is exceedingly important and our supply is limited, it is short-sighted to waste it thoughtlessly. It is estimated that for every ton of coal that we burn another has been wasted. Smoke consists of particles of unconsumed coal. In the United States at least twenty million tons of coal pass into the air yearly as soot in smoke. In what other ways is smoke a detriment? Is it a sign of progress that certain cities are famous for their smoke? What are the laws in your city in regard to the smoke nuisance? Consult some encyclopedia to find out the uses of soot.

Fig. 101. A "gusher" in the Sunset oil field of California. The drillers struck a deposit of oil and gas under great pressure, and a column of oil and gas shot up 150 feet. For several weeks the well flowed at the rate of 40,000 barrels of oil a day.

2. Near coal mines may be seen great piles of refuse material called culm. This refuse contains slate and bits of coal. The thrifty Europeans mix culm with coal tar and make small bricks, "briquettes," to burn. Cities having large manufacturing populations, if situated near enough to the culm piles to secure cheap transportation, would probably be glad to buy these briquettes. Name some such cities. Would your community furnish a good market for this cheap substitute for coal?

3. In their eagerness for profits many companies abandon a worked mine and seek a new one as soon as the most accessible coal seams are exhausted. After an abandoned mine has caved in, it usually does not pay to reopen it for the small amount of coal left there. How does more effective mining machinery help to remedy this waste?

4. Coke, the fuel necessary for iron smelting, is made by baking coal in great ovens. Two kinds of ovens are used, the "beehive" and the "retort." In the beehive oven, coke is the only product. In the retort oven the valuable gases are saved, and the following products are obtained in addition to the coke: coal tar, ammonia, benzol, illuminating gas, graphite, oils, dyestuffs, disinfectants, explosives, and substances used in medicine. Find out how many of these by-products are used in your home.

E. **How the civilized world depends upon petroleum.**

1. Is petroleum used in the crude state? Consult an encyclopedia or a book on petroleum.

2. Suppose that there were no more petroleum in the world. Consider in how many ways your life would be affected by lack of the following products made from petroleum: gasoline, naphtha, benzine, kerosene, lubricants, oils, vaselin, paraffin.

3. Each year the United States consumes about a billion barrels of petroleum. Some persons think that this is at least one twentieth of our untouched

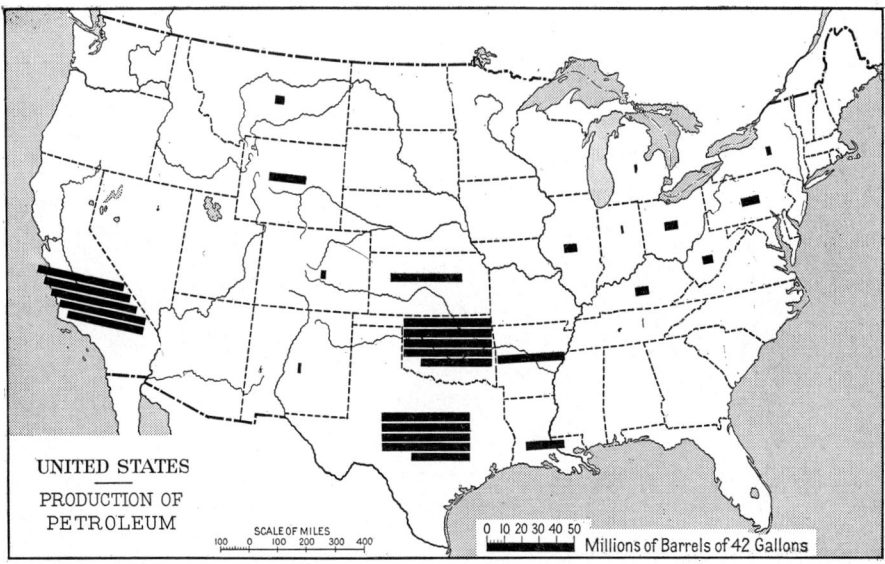

Fig. 102. The four areas of petroleum production in the United States, in order of productiveness, are: (1) the mid-continent area; (2) California; (3) the Middle-West and the Gulf; (4) the Rocky Mountain area.

supply. How do these figures explain the constant discussion, in newspapers and magazines, about our supplies of gasoline?

4. Many people think the conservation of petroleum so important that they are proposing government restriction of its use. How do the figures given above explain their attitude?

5. In 1909 President Taft, in his capacity as Commander-in-Chief of the Army and Navy, ordered that no government lands suspected of containing petroleum should be sold until Congress could pass a law to insure the government a sufficient supply for its future needs. What was his reason? What is the government's present policy in this respect?

6. Not far from 25,000,000 automobiles and trucks are registered in the United States. We have hundreds of oil-burning vessels in our navy, and our merchant marine contains one or two thousand additional oil-burners. What effect would a petroleum shortage have upon transportation in this country?

7. Name another kind of transportation that may in the future require a great deal of gasoline or of some good substitute. For what purpose may the up-to-date farmers also need a great deal?

8. Wood alcohol can be used as a substitute for gasoline. Learn what you can about this fuel. Will the sources of supply of it become exhausted? How can they be increased?

9. During the past seventy years the United States has produced about 60 per cent of the world's supply of petroleum. We have exported about one fifth of this production. How will our increasingly large automobile traffic probably affect the export figures?

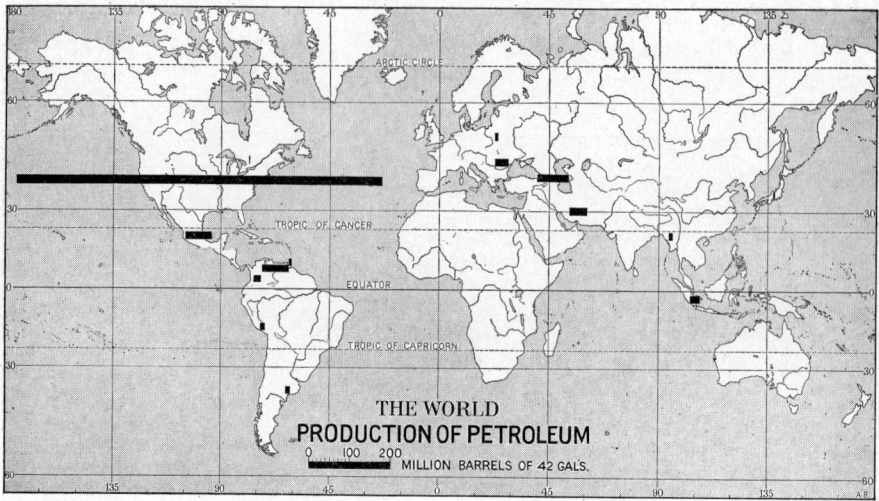

Fig. 103. Six or seven tenths of the world's petroleum comes from the United States. Another tenth comes from Venezuela and another from Russia. The remainder is supplied mainly by Persia, Rumania, Mexico, and the East Indies. A production map for 1950 may tell a very different story; for the oil supplies of the United States are being exhausted, while the oil fields of western Asia (Persia, Mesopotamia, Transcaucasia) have immense reserves. It is possible, also, that before 1950 oil will be discovered in regions that have not yet been explored for it, or that most will come from shale.

F. **Where petroleum may be obtained.**
1. *In the United States.* Examine the map showing the petroleum resources of the United States (Fig. 102). Which is our leading oil state? Explain why this state finds it cheaper to burn oil than coal in its locomotives. Try to find out what state has the most " oil shale." Report on such shales.
2. Which of the oil fields producing more than 4 per cent of the country's total are most advantageously situated to supply the greatest number of automobiles? Which are best situated for transportation (a) by pipe line (Fig. 104); (b) by tank steamer; (c) by tank car?
3. *In the rest of the world.* From Figure 103 list the six chief oil regions in the order of their production.
4. Explain why many of the Mexican wells are drilled with English and German capital.

G. **How the petroleum industry has developed its peculiar transportation facilities.**
1. *The pipe line.* Examine the map of pipe lines, Figure 104. Why do so many lines center in New Jersey? Give three reasons why they are located in this section of the country.
2. Why do no lines run to the southeastern states?
3. Where are the chief centers from which most of the oil is pumped? If we liken the pipe lines to arteries, what name may we apply to these regions?
4. What reasons are there for pumping Oklahoma oil to Chicago rather than to Baton-Rouge?

## The Fuel Products

5. *The tank steamer.* The oil which is pumped to the Gulf of Mexico is carried away in steamers built especially for this purpose. Name two companies that own most of these "tankers." Why does it cost much less to load one of the tank boats than to load an ordinary cargo boat?

6. Explain why you would (or would not) expect to see many tankers passing through the Panama Canal. In which direction would most of them be carrying oil?

7. *The tank car.* Before pipe lines were extensively used, — and even to-day where the demand for oil is not sufficiently heavy to pay for their installment, — a special type of railroad car carried the oil. On the map showing the pipe lines, name ten large cities that depend on the tank car to supply their petroleum.

8. Decide whether it is better for each of these cities to get its supply from some city on a pipe-line route or from some port at which tank steamers call.

9. *The tank automobile.* It was an easy task to adapt the motor truck to the special purpose of carrying oil. What advantages has a motor tank over the other methods of transporting petroleum?

**H. Natural gas.**

1. Usually when a reservoir of oil beneath the earth's surface is tapped by man, great quantities of natural gas rush out. No other resource has been so recklessly wasted as this rich and cheap natural fuel. The daily loss in the United States is estimated to have been equal to the heating value of one million bushels of coal. Since there are about 26 bushels in one short ton, approximately how many tons of coal have been wasted yearly?

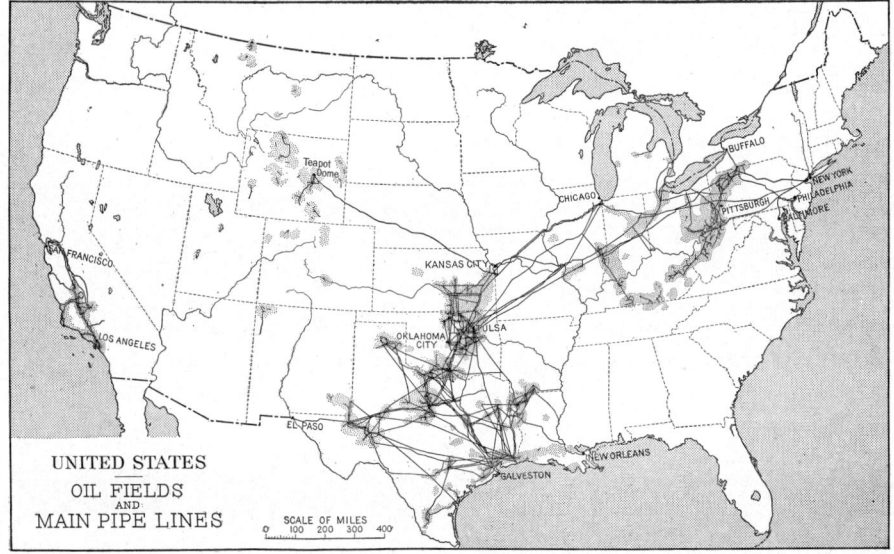

Based on map by International Map Co., Inc., New York

FIG. 104. This map shows only the main pipe lines in the United States. The total mileage of pipe lines would reach about twice around the earth.

*United States Forest Service*

Fig. 105. Compare this load of white pine logs, hauled out of the Minnesota forests over the snow, with the load shown in Figure 106. The difference helps to account for the fact that lumbering is a winter occupation in the northern states.

## CHAPTER ELEVEN

### LUMBERING AND FOREST PRODUCTS

Wood ranks with iron and coal as an aid to man in his attempts to rise in civilization. From the earliest times man has burned it to cook his food and to keep him warm. For thousands of years it has been the chief material for building his house. As time passes new uses are continually being found for this valuable substance. For instance, when railroads came into use wood was found to be the best material for the cross ties, and now a billion and a half cubic feet of wood are used annually for that purpose alone. Wood also furnishes good fiber for cheap, strong paper. A single newspaper firm in New York uses daily more than two hundred tons of paper, which means the product of more than three hundred cords of spruce wood.

### LUMBERING

In view of the many uses of lumber, it is not surprising that the forests of the world are attacked every year by thousands of workmen, armed with axes and saws and equipped with all sorts of machinery. Since we must have wood, even remote forests in rugged regions are made to give up their trees.

**How lumbering is carried on.** Before the trees of a forest can be used as lumber a great deal of preparatory work must be done. Roads are built into the woods. Buildings, usually made of logs, are erected at each camp for the men and the horses, and for a blacksmith's shop. A foreman marks the trees to be cut and directs all the work. Some men do nothing but fell the trees. They make a deep cut in one side of the trunk and then saw into the other side until they can insert a wedge and topple the tree over. Other men trim off the branches and saw the fallen trees into logs of the proper length. Some are employed to bring food and other supplies from the railroad. One man does the cooking, and one or two keep the axes and saws sharp and the harnesses in repair. Still others haul away the logs.

To get the logs out from among the trees and brush where they have fallen and haul them to a road of some kind, is usually the lumberman's most difficult task. In the northern United States, logs are "snaked" out by horses or oxen to the lumber roads, where they are put on sleds, which are easily drawn over the winter's snow. Sometimes the work is done by donkey engines. The engines are carted high into the mountains and long cables are carried from them into the woods. A log that is being snaked out moves along as if it were a living creature, for at even a short distance the cable is invisible and one cannot see how the log is pulled.

In many sections the logs are taken to the bank of a stream to wait for the time of the spring thaw, when the rising waters will float them down to the mill. On this journey the logs must be guided by skillful "river drivers," who prevent them from "jamming" or becoming stranded in rapids or elsewhere. As the stream broadens, the logs are often made into rafts on which several raftsmen make a shanty of rough boards for shelter. Occasionally several rafts are towed by a tug.

In very rugged regions, smooth, steep slopes are cleared and the logs are allowed to slide down. Sometimes rough troughs are made of logs to guide the sliding timber. An even better method in such a region is to use a flume, which is a large trough of boards. A flume often extends many miles from near a mountain crest to the valley or plains far below. A spring or mountain stream is diverted into the trough, and if there is plenty of water the logs float down the flume; but if there is only a little, they partly float and partly slip.

In the South the levelness of many logging regions and the openness of the forests make it easy to drive through the woods. Here the logs are suspended from the axles between large cart wheels and are drawn out by mules, or are transported on narrow-gauge railways. In such a region the lumbermen use light steam sawmills that can be moved as one part of the forest after another is cut. This is advantageous, for boards can be transported much more easily than heavy, awkward logs.

### FORESTS OF THE UNITED STATES

Before the early settlers cut many trees in the United States, forests covered practically all the land, with the exception of the drier parts that extend from eastern Washington, Oregon, and California to the Dakotas, Kansas, western Oklahoma, and western Texas. Even in the drier region many of the mountain ranges bore forest growth (Fig. 107). While the different parts of the country were being settled, enormous areas of the forests were cleared to make room for farming, and use of the forests as timber was only incidental. As time went on, a supply of lumber became the main purpose in cutting down the forests. Naturally the eastern forests were cut first. Then, as settlers moved westward, other forest regions heard the ring of the woodman's ax. If the rate at which our forests are being cut continues to increase as it has increased in the past, our lumber supply will last only fifty years more. Even with great care to conserve the present supply and replanting of as many forests as possible, lumber is likely to continue to rise in price. We shall be obliged to make increasing use of brick, stone, and plaster.

*United States Forest Service*

FIG. 106. A device used for hauling logs out of the pineries in the southern states.

## Lumbering and Forest Products

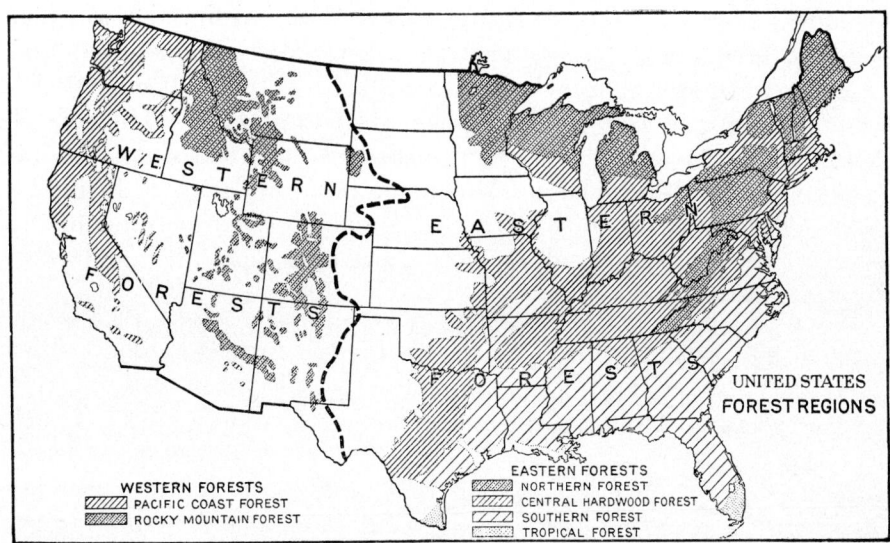

Fig. 107. Only about two fifths of the standing timber of the United States is now found in the eastern section; and only one twenty-fifth of this supply is in the forests northeast of the Ohio. The Rocky Mountain states have about a tenth of the total supply, and the Pacific forests have half of it. Washington, Oregon, and California, therefore, have the reserves of lumber for the whole country.

**The forest regions of the United States.** Figure 107 shows the five forest regions of the United States, aside from Alaska. They are as follows:

(1) *The northeastern forest* stretches from Maine westward to northern Minnesota, and southwestward along the Appalachian Mountains to northern Alabama. In Canada it broadens to include nearly a fourth of that country.

In the United States the most common tree in this northeastern forest was originally the white pine. But because this pine is so light, strong, durable, and easily worked, it is wanted for nearly everything, from houses to matches; no other wood is so generally useful. Hence the white pine has become very scarce, and its price is soaring higher and higher. Other trees in this forest are the spruce and the hemlock, whose lumber, although much poorer, is taking the place of the white pine. These trees thrive in the cold climate of the northern United States and the Appalachian heights. Many broad-leaved trees, such as maples, beeches, birches, and oaks, are scattered throughout the region. The northeastern forest now supplies less than one twentieth of our wood.

(2) *The central forest* in Ohio, Indiana, Illinois, Iowa, and southward is sometimes called the hardwood forest, because the chief trees

are oak, hickory, maple, chestnut, walnut, and tulip, the wood of which is hard in contrast to the soft wood of the pine, spruce, and hemlock. These hardwoods are used extensively for furniture, interior finishing, tools, farming implements, and wagons. The central forest still yields about one seventh of the total wood supply of the country. Grand Rapids, in Michigan, built up a great furniture business by using the local hardwood supply. Even now it remains a great furniture center, although it must draw upon distant forests for much of its wood.

(3) *The southern forest*, along the Atlantic coastal plains from the Carolinas to Texas, is the home of the yellow or long-leaf pine, the short-leaf pine, and the cypress. All these thrive in the mild climate of the southland. The southern pine seems to like best the sandy soil of the coastal plain, while the cypress prefers the swamps bordering the rivers. The wood of the yellow pine is often used in our houses for floors and inside finishings. It is used also for the frames of buildings and ships. This kind of pine supplies the country with nearly a third of its lumber. The short-leaf pine is rapidly coming into favor for a great variety of uses. Cypress is replacing the white pine as a cabinet wood and for many other purposes. Nearly every port from Galveston to Norfolk ships quantities of southern pine or of cypress.

The southern pines contain a resinous sap which is collected in large amounts. The sap is obtained by tapping the trees near the base. It is heated, and the vapors are collected and condensed into turpentine. The process is called distillation. The solid which remains is resin. Pitch and tar are distilled from the roots, trunk, and limbs of the pine trees. All four of these materials are used on shipboard for such purposes as caulking seams to keep out the water and coating the fibers of ropes to prevent them from rotting. These supplies as well as some others used on ships are called naval stores. Savannah, Georgia, and Fernandina, Florida, because of the neighboring pine forests, are the world's leading markets for naval stores.

At the southern end of Florida and of Texas we find two comparatively small regions of tropical forest. They are of slight commercial importance.

(4) *The Rocky Mountain forests* grow only where the mountains rise high enough to make the winds give up much of their moisture. Hence the forests lie in scattered patches, usually difficult of access. Because of the low temperature of the high regions, the only trees

*United States Forest Service*

Fig. 108. Riding a log-boom. When the ice breaks in the spring, the freshets carry down to the mills the logs that have been cut and hauled to the river during the winter. The lumberjacks run along the logs with their long steel-hooked poles to break up the log-jams that obstruct the progress of the stream of logs.

found there are those that can stand the cold, such as hardy pines, spruces, firs, and cedars. In this region less than a fourth of the trees have been cut.

(5) *The Pacific forest* is the finest in the world. Nowhere else are trees so large. The sequoias — that is, the " Big Trees " — and the redwoods are far the largest; but others, like the Douglas fir and red cedar, also reach great size. Here an average acre often supplies as much wood as ten acres in the eastern forests.

The largest of the sequoias are nearly three hundred feet high, twenty-five feet in diameter at the base, and more than three thousand years old. A single tree would yield lumber enough to build a little village. Fortunately the biggest of the trees are now included in the Sequoia National Park, and no ax will reach them.

The great size of the trees in the Pacific forest is in one way a disadvantage. Even after they are successfully felled and sawed into logs, it is difficult to get them to the sawmill. Sometimes they are split by blasting. Often they are dragged by donkey engines over a road paved with small logs. The most successful method is to use a giant derrick to lift and drag them to waiting flat cars.

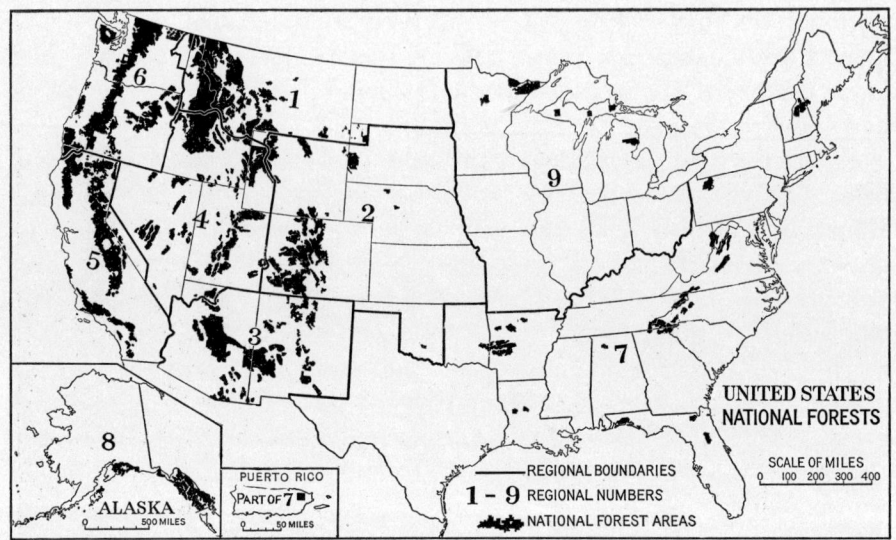

FIG. 109. The National Forests are cared for and managed by the Forest Service, which now controls about one fourth of the western forest lands.

Several kinds of wood from the Pacific forests almost rival the white pine in strength, durability, and smoothness, and excel it in beauty of color. Sailing vessels take great quantities of this lumber from Seattle, Tacoma, Portland, and San Francisco to the lands bordering the Pacific Ocean; they take it also through the Panama Canal to the eastern states, and even to Europe. It is not surprising that Oregon and Washington are the leading states in lumber production, and that the Douglas fir stands next to the yellow pine in importance as a source of lumber. The Pacific forest extends northward along the western border of Canada even into Alaska.

**The Alaskan forests.** The forests of Alaska are sure to play an important part in mining, railroad construction, and home building, when such activities are developed on a large scale in that region. The southeastern part contains excellent forests of spruce, hemlock, and cedar. In the colder climate farther to the northwest and north, the forests dwindle both in extent and in the size of trees. Yet even in the interior of Alaska, the trees are large enough to be suitable for the pulp used in paper making.

**Our National Forests.** Figure 109 shows the extent of forest lands that have been set apart by the government as National Forests. They are for the good of all the people. Sixty-five per cent of the money derived from the sale of trees, from rent for pasturage of animals, and from the rent of land for summer homes, goes into the national treasury. The rest is returned to the states in which the forests are located, for the benefit of their schools and roads. The lands most recently included in the National Forests are in the White and the Appalachian Mountains.

Forest rangers are employed to build trails and roads, to prevent fires, to fight fires, and to see that the forests are not abused. Effort is made to keep the forests in the best condition for tree growth. Underbrush is cut out regularly, and diseased and stunted trees are felled. The healthy trees are sold and cut only when they are full grown.

The Forest Service makes a special effort to preserve a forest growth on steep slopes in order to prevent the soil from being washed away. Thus the flow of the rivers is made steady, with the result that their water power is of increased value, and the danger of floods is diminished.

### FORESTS IN FOREIGN LANDS

**Other North American forests.** We have already noted that the forests along our northern border extend into Canada. There they expand into vast primeval wastes where Indians still hunt fur-bearing animals, and where the people of the United States and Canada find an enchanting summer playground. The parts of our northeastern forest that continue into Quebec and the parts of our Pacific forest that continue into British Columbia are especially valuable and extensive. Both support thriving lumber industries. Most of the Canadian forest growth, however, is fit only for paper making, since in high latitudes the trees dwindle, until in the far north they are mere shrubs. A cold, grassy, treeless waste extends throughout northern Canada.

To the south of the United States, in Mexico, there are almost no forests throughout the great area of the dry northern desert and central plateaus. The forest wealth of Mexico is in the tropical forests of the lowlands and the seaward slopes of the south.

**Conservation of European forests.** In most of Europe the climate is well suited for forests, and within historic times they flourished almost everywhere. As the population increased it was necessary to cut the forests in order to use the land for crops. In some places this was done unwisely; the soil was washed away and the growth of new forests was hampered. Some countries, like France and Germany, early recognized the foolishness of thus slashing away the country's forests. Now their policy is to plant many trees and to give them painstaking care. Fire losses are small, and waste in lumbering, at the sawmills, and in the wood-using industries is slight. Refuse wood that would be thrown away in our country is there made into small objects, such as clothespins and toys. Rarely are all the trees cut from an area at once, as with us. Since only the larger trees are cut, the forest lands always bear an abundance of valuable trees that are rapidly growing. Forest pests are fought successfully, and tree cutting is regulated by law.

The method of caring for trees so as to conserve the supply is called *scientific forestry* in distinction from *wasteful lumbering*, such as has been practiced in our country nearly up to the present. In America scientific forestry is as yet practiced only in our National Forests and in a few other forest regions; but people in general are coming to see its advantages. Great Britain is practicing excellent methods of forestry in many of her colonies, especially in India.

The more remote parts of Norway, Sweden, and north central Russia still contain a great deal of timber. Scotch pine and spruce predominate there. These are among the most valuable forests in the world today, chiefly because they are so near the great European markets. Some paper pulp from this region is exported to the United States, but this circumstance does not mean that Europe has a supply of wood sufficient for her own use. Even though lumber is very little used for house building — stone or brick being the material most used — a great deal of wood is imported from the United States and Canada. In the future Europe may use the vast forests of Siberia, although there the trees as a rule are rather small.

**Tropical forests.** Both Europe and the United States draw extensively upon tropical regions for certain woods, such as mahogany for expensive furniture, quebracho for its sap, which is used in tanning leather, teak for ship building, and bamboo for a multitude of purposes. But lumbering in the tropics is slow and expensive; the wood is usually so hard that it is difficult to fell the logs and cut them up, and transportation is difficult. Consequently only a few of the hardwoods of the tropics have been exploited. Nevertheless, the abundant forests in the well-watered tropical regions may soon be used to take the place of those that are now being exhausted in the temperate zone. But tropical wood, as a rule, is so hard that it cannot readily take the place of our convenient soft woods.

# Lumbering and Forest Products

*United States Forest Service*

Fig. 110. A mill plant with a capacity of 200,000 feet (board measure) of lumber a day.

## QUESTIONS, EXERCISES, AND PROBLEMS

A. **To illustrate the uses of wood.**

1. The following is a rough classification of wood according to its uses:
   - (a) Unworked wood (logs, etc.), as for posts.
   - (b) Worked wood (cut and prepared), as for buildings.
   - (c) Burnt wood, as for the ashes.
   - (d) Pulp wood, as for paper.
   - (e) Wood extracts, as for medicine.
   - (f) Waste wood, as for excelsior.

   Find from two to five illustrations of each use.

B. **The forest resources of the United States.**

1. The ten states that have recently led in lumber production are Washington, Oregon, Mississippi, Louisiana, California, Alabama, Texas, Arkansas, Georgia, North Carolina. In which of the five forest regions of the United States is each of the states?

2. Give three reasons why Washington is the leading state in lumber production. Why is Nevada the least productive?

3. In what part of the United States do you think wood for a house may be purchased cheapest? In what part do you think it would be most expensive? Explain.

4. Study the coal map of the United States (Fig. 98), in connection with the map of forest regions (Fig. 107), and decide whether coal or wood is probably the chief fuel for household use in (a) California, (b) Maine, (c) Florida, (d) Illinois, (e) Nebraska.

5. Alaska has been called the "Norway of the United States." What does this phrase suggest as to the character of the forests of Alaska? For what purpose do we now import wood from Norway? What quality

of wood is used for this purpose? Could wood for this same use be imported from Alaska?

6. Man's respect for trees is rising. The early settlers in the United States destroyed trees as if they were weeds. Explain why such destruction was not wrong then, but is wrong today.

7. Why is it unwise to place a high tax on land covered with standing timber and a low tax on the land from which trees have been cut?

C. **The protection of forests from fire.**

1. At the present rate of use our forests will be exhausted in the next fifty years. The best three fifths of our timber is now gone. Three fourths of what is left is privately owned, and of this only about four per cent is scientifically cared for. We cannot greatly increase our imports; therefore we must reduce our waste and increase our annual growth of timber. One of the great wastes of wood is in forest fires, which cause a yearly loss of more than fifty million dollars. It is estimated that the forest fires occurring during a period of six years were due to the following causes:

    (a) Sparks from locomotives . . . . . . . . . . 26.7 per cent
    (b) Lightning . . . . . . . . . . . . . . . . . 17.5 per cent
    (c) Carelessness of campers . . . . . . . . . . 16.9 per cent
    (d) Spontaneous combustion in brush piles . . . 4.8 per cent
    (e) Deliberate purpose . . . . . . . . . . . . 4.5 per cent
    (f) Sparks from sawmills . . . . . . . . . . . 1.1 per cent
    (g) Unknown causes . . . . . . . . . . . . . . 28.5 per cent

    Which of these causes could be eliminated by making and enforcing proper laws?

2. Suggest rules that might be made to check the loss from locomotive sparks.

3. What can we do to check the fire damage caused by careless campers? Explain the proper method of extinguishing a camp fire.

4. What uses might be made of the wasted brush piles?

5. Sawmills should be compelled to put "spark arresters" in their smoke stacks. Why is it a short-sighted policy for lumbermen to refuse to bear this extra expense?

6. Suppose that a man sets a forest fire. Explain at least four ways in which his action may cause damage to the country.

D. **The protection of forests from poor methods of cutting.**

1. Why is it unwise to cut all the trees in a wood lot at one time?

2. Why does it waste wood to cut it in winter at the snow level?

3. If stumps are left with level tops, standing rainwater soon causes decay, and decayed wood furnishes breeding places for insects. How may these insects cause damage?

4. New York City and Chicago together demand more than half a million of the straightest and best young trees each Christmas. From what kind of places should these trees be secured?

E. **Forestry lessons to be learned from other countries.**

1. Our forests could yield four times as much as they now do if we gave them scientific care. The rate of annual growth of trees per acre in the United States is about 12 cubic feet. In Germany, where care is scientific, the new growth averages 50 cubic feet. Explain what is meant by "scientific care."

2. Compare the rate at which the forests are being consumed in the following countries:

   (a) Great Britain . . . . . 14 cubic feet per capita per year
   (b) France . . . . . . . . 24      "         "         "
   (c) Germany . . . . . . . 36      "         "         "
   (d) Russia . . . . . . . . 63      "         "         "
   (e) Canada . . . . . . . 192     "         "         "
   (f) The United States . . . . 260     "         "         "

   The United States could reduce her 260 cubic feet to 150 without reducing the supply of wooden products. What becomes of the other 110 cubic feet?

F. **Conservation through treating wood with chemicals to prevent decay.**

1. Lumber used where decay is rapid, as in railroad ties, telegraph poles, paving blocks, and piers, should first be made waterproof by being soaked in creosote. Suppose a cedar pole 40 feet long costs $8 and will last about 10 years when exposed to the weather. A pine pole of the same length costs only $5, but decays sooner. However, if the pine pole be treated with creosote at a cost of about $1.60, it will last 20 years. How much money would a company save by using a thousand treated pine poles in place of an equal number made of untreated cedar? What other expense is saved besides the extra cost of the wood?

2. In what states does the cost of transportation make it especially profitable to use creosoted pine poles?

3. Choose some members of your class as a committee to find out and report how creosote is obtained.

G. **Topics for special study.**

1. The Southern turpentine industry.
2. Control of the browntailed moth and gypsy moth pests. (*Year Book*, Department of Agriculture, 1916.)
3. The Forestry Department of your state.
4. The National Parks.
5. The work of forest rangers.

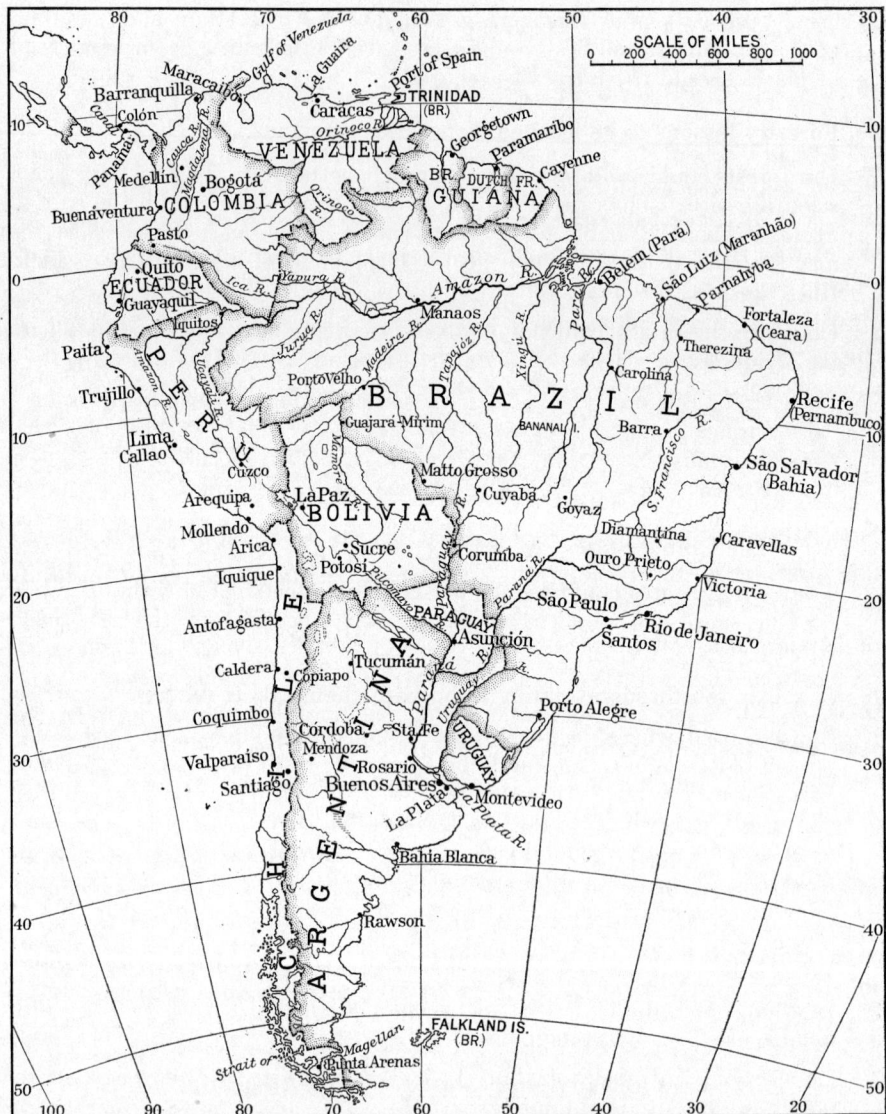

Fig. 111. In area South America, with about 7,242,000 square miles, is not much smaller than North America, which has 9,355,000 square miles. The difference between the two in population is much greater, South America having about 81,400,000 inhabitants and North America about 167,000,000. This gives South America a population of a little more than 11 to the square mile, while North America has nearly 18 to the square mile.

What part of the United States is in the belt of north latitude corresponding to the south latitude of Argentina, Uruguay, and Chile? About how much of South America is within the tropics? Why are large parts of Colombia, Ecuador, Peru, and Bolivia not tropical in climate?

Find a city in the United States that corresponds in latitude with Buenos Aires and Montevideo. What city in the northern hemisphere corresponds in latitude with Rio de Janeiro? Is Rio de Janeiro or Santiago more directly south of New York?

Where in South America is Spanish the official language? Portuguese? French? English? Dutch?

# CHAPTER TWELVE

## PROBLEMS IN PRIMARY PRODUCTION

In the preceding chapters the chief primary products of the United States have been studied. We have seen that in addition to fibers like cotton these fall into certain great classes which give rise to occupations such as cereal farming, truck farming, sugar raising, fruit raising, animal raising, fishing, mining, and lumbering. In this chapter the principles which have been learned in connection with these occupations will be applied to the study of the primary production of other parts of the Western Hemisphere.

### (A) South America

Because of its scanty population, its newness, and the debilitating climate in many portions, South America is prominent chiefly in the field of primary production. The continent has little manufacturing, and except in some of the great cities in the southern part, the people buy relatively little from outside; consequently their trade is of minor importance in the field of consumption. In the field of transportation also South America is backward, for except in the south its railway and steamship lines are relatively few in number and for the most part poorly equipped.

Let us see how the primary products, together with the geographical conditions, have influenced the growth of cities. Study of the maps of products and railways in this book, supplemented by reference to a good elementary geography and to a relief map, will explain why some South American cities have grown great and others have remained small.

#### (1) THE DEVELOPMENT OF SEAPORTS

**Where seaports have developed and why.** In studying the coast of South America to find out where the seaports have developed and what primary products have especially aided in their growth, we will start at Ecuador.

From the southern point of the coast of Ecuador to the Isthmus of Panama, then from the isthmus around to central Brazil, the coast of South America is almost everywhere bordered by a low plain, narrow on the west and wide on the east. It is hot, marshy, forest-clad, and infested with malaria.

1. What influence do you think these conditions have upon the abundance and nature of the primary products, and thus upon the growth of seaports? Explain.
2. What influence do they have upon trade with the interior?
3. Table 7 (page 336) gives the chief exports of South America in the order of their value and shows what countries export them. Which of these come from hot, tropical lowlands? How important are they?
4. Table 6 (page 335) gives the chief cities of South America. Arrange them in order of size. How many are found on the north and northeast coast? How do these stand as to size? How many and of what size are the cities south of latitude 20° S?

Because of the scantiness and relative inefficiency of their inhabitants, the tropical forests furnish few primary products for commerce, even though their possible resources are large.

5. What fraction of the entire South American seacoast is therefore unfavorable to the growth of seaports?

Returning to southern Ecuador, let us examine the coast from there to Valparaiso in Chile. This almost rainless coast is bordered by a desert, except where irrigation is carried on by means of streams from the Andes.

6. What fraction of the total western coastline is bordered by desert?
7. Explain why there is so little rain on the west coast.
8. What influence does this desert have on primary production? upon the growth of seaports?
9. How many of the products of Table 7 (page 336) come from deserts?
10. How many of the cities of Table 6 (page 335) are found on this coast?

Now examine the rest of the west coast of South America.

11. How many of the cities of Table 6 are found south of latitude 45°?
12. What does this lead you to infer as to the importance of the primary products of this far southern part of South America?

Turn next to the west coast between 30° and 45° south of the equator, and to the east coast from the coffee plateaus of Brazil in latitude 20° to latitude 45°.

13. Which of the chief primary products come from this section?
14. How many of the chief cities are located here?

Certain other conditions also help to make the southern region highly productive. One is the presence of Europeans; for this is the part of South America where people of European ancestry largely outnumber the colored races.

*Ewing Galloway*

Fig. 112. Rio de Janeiro, although second in size to Buenos Aires, has a larger and even better harbor. Few harbors can compare with it in size and safety combined. All the navies of the world could ride at anchor within it.

15. What climatic conditions make these parts attractive to Europeans? Study Figures 17 and 18 (pages 30, 31) to find one of the reasons why Argentina and Uruguay attract many Italian and Spanish immigrants.
16. Why does the presence of many Europeans increase the amount of primary production?

### (2) THE FIVE GREAT PORTS

There are five leading ports in South America. In the order of their importance they are: Buenos Aires, Santos, Rio de Janeiro, Montevideo, and Valparaiso.

**How primary production has made Buenos Aires great.** Buenos Aires, including La Plata, thirty-one miles to the southeast, where the largest ocean steamers discharge their cargoes, has a commerce whose value is equal to that of the other four chief cities combined.

17. What products have made it both possible and wise to spend millions of dollars upon harbor and dock improvements at Buenos Aires and La Plata?

The Plata river system is of great importance to Buenos Aires. Ocean steamers ascend to Rosario, 230 miles northwest of Buenos Aires, to bring out hides, meat, and wheat. River steamers ply to Asunción, while small vessels navigate 680 miles farther northward, well within the tropics, and bring out rubber and forest products.

18. What city on the Mississippi corresponds in position to Buenos Aires on La Plata?
19. What corresponding city lies on the Rhine?
20. What city on the Ganges?

Besides being a center of waterways, Buenos Aires is the leading railroad center of the southern hemisphere, as appears in Figure 129.

21. How many lines cross the Andes to Chile?
22. What advantage does this railroad connection give Buenos Aires?
23. What fractional part of South America can thus be regarded as tributary to Buenos Aires?

Buenos Aires exports great quantities of wheat, hides, wool, and quebracho wood.

24. Where does Buenos Aires get these goods?
25. Where does she find the largest market for them?
26. From what region, then, would she be likely to import manufactured goods?

**How one important luxury has caused the growth of two great cities.** The island-dotted harbor of Rio de Janeiro, with its mountain setting and its luxuriant tropical vegetation, is one of the most beautiful in the world. The high value of the commerce of Rio de Janeiro and of Santos results largely from their being the outlets of the plateau of Brazil, which produces nearly two thirds of the world's supply of coffee.

27. What difficulties have these ports had to meet in providing easy access to their up-country districts?
28. How could people afford to build an extensive railroad system there?
29. What primary product gives your family an interest in these ports?
30. Suppose the world's appetite for coffee should be lost; what would then happen to Santos and " Rio "?

**Effect of Montevideo's position with relation to South America's main primary products.** Montevideo has a better natural harbor than Buenos Aires. It is 125 miles nearer the open sea, and the country lying behind it receives a heavier rainfall. Yet the value of its commerce is less than one sixth that of Buenos Aires.

31. In Figures 38, 39, 68, and 71, study the distribution of wheat, corn, cattle, and sheep, and study also a relief map, to explain why Montevideo, although a great city, cannot rival Buenos Aires.

Fig. 113. The Brazilian cattle ranger grazes his herds on the plains of southeastern Brazil, where the high plateau gives the region a temperate climate, although within the tropical latitudes.

**The port of the west coast.** Valparaiso, the fifth of the great South American ports, is the chief port of the west coast. It lies on the narrow coastal plain between the high ranges of the Andes and the sea. Its distance from Buenos Aires by water is about the same as the distance from New York to England.

32. What does Figure 1 show about the climatic advantages of Valparaiso, as compared with the other ports of the west coast?
33. What causes its exports of primary products to be of far less value than those of the four ports on the east side?
34. How do the up-country regions of the five chief South American cities compare in (a) size, (b) relief, (c) general productions, and (d) nature of their primary products?

### (3) THE SOUTH AMERICAN PORTS GROUPED BY PRODUCTS

The South American ports may be grouped as: (a) mineral ports, (b) cocoa ports, (c) sugar ports, (d) rubber ports, (e) coffee ports, and (f) grain and animal ports.

**The mineral ports of the continent.** Scattered along the desert portion of the west coast from Valparaiso to Callao are the mineral ports. Every port shown in Figure 111, between these two cities, is a mineral port. Nitrates are their chief exports, although copper, tin, silver, and gold also are exported.

35. How do the mineral ports rank in size in Table 6 (page 335)?

There are numerous small mineral ports instead of one large one, because the minerals come from a long stretch of the Andes and are sent to the coast by the nearest route. Moreover, no one port has a harbor that much excels the others, and all have poor anchorages.

Iquique is the most important of the mineral ports, since the land behind it contains the best of the nitrate deposits. It is the greatest nitrate port in the world. More than a score of boats are usually to be seen riding at anchor in the outer harbor, waiting to take on a cargo of the precious nitrate. In more advanced countries this mineral is used for fertilizing the soil. It is used also for making explosives.

36. In the latitude of the mineral ports the prevailing winds blow from the east and strike the high wall of the Andes. What has the direction of the winds to do with the fact that the people of the mineral ports are dependent for food on supplies shipped from other cities farther south or farther north?

37. Does it seem likely that the nitrate ports will become great cities, like Rio de Janeiro and Buenos Aires? Give reasons for your opinion.

**The cocoa ports.** As we go northward from the mineral ports we come to the cocoa ports of South America. A good share of the world's supply of cocoa comes from Ecuador, Colombia, Venezuela, and Brazil; hence their ports are the cocoa ports. Guayaquil is the most important, but La Guaira also carries on a lively trade in the cacao bean from which we get our cocoa and chocolate.

38. Why are these ports so small?
39. How does cocoa compare with tea or coffee in importance as a product?

**The sugar ports.** Nature seems to have grouped the ports of South America appropriately, since the sugar ports come near the cocoa ports. Those which chiefly export sugar are Georgetown, Pernambuco, and Bahia. The plantations near Georgetown are particularly successful in raising sugar cane, partly because the British government has induced many people to go there from India. The Hindus, though not rapid workers, labor as steadily in South America as in their former homes. Western Europe takes this South American sugar surplus; little of it comes to us.

40. Why does not the South American sugar come to the United States?
41. What sort of climate favors the cultivation of sugar and cocoa?
42. How does the climate help explain the small size of the ports?

Fig. 114. Almost three quarters of the coffee used in the world is produced in Brazil.

**The rubber ports.** The United States is the greatest consumer of South American rubber, as well as coffee. Hence we have a special interest in the cities of Pará and Manaos, since they border on the great jungle of the Amazon in which wild rubber trees flourish.

With a huge area back of it abundantly producing so valuable a product, it would seem that Pará should have more than 200,000 inhabitants. But its development is slow because white men cannot stand its tropical diseases, great heat, and swarms of insects.

Manaos seems at first glance to be an inland city, but like Montreal it is a seaport a thousand miles up a broad river. Manaos is naturally the great rubber gatherer of interior Brazil, for three of the largest tributaries of the Amazon join the main river near this port.

43. Why does Pará fail to rank among the chief South American ports?

**The coffee ports.** We have already noticed that the coffee ports of Rio de Janeiro and Santos are among the five chief ports of the continent (page 147).

44. Explain what conditions have influenced the growth of these cities.

**The grain and animal ports.** The last group of ports is much the most important. It includes not only Montevideo, Buenos Aires, and La Plata, but Bahía Blanca and, far to the south, Punta Arenas. The chief grain exported is wheat, although corn is coming into prominence. Formerly animals were shipped alive in great numbers to western Europe, but now they are shipped in the form of beef, mutton, hides, and wool. Punta Arenas, the southernmost of the world's towns, is interesting rather than important. A very small place, it is included in this group only because it exports sheep.

45. Practice making a sketch map of South America. Show the location of every port mentioned in this section, and after the name of each seaport put in parentheses the name of its chief export. Underline the names of the important ports of the continent, and double-underline the name of the leading port. At first, have before you the map in the book while you sketch. After a few trials see if you can do all the work from memory in three minutes.

**The chief work of the ports.** All the ports of South America are engaged chiefly in sending raw materials to European nations and the United States. The returning steamers bring back manufactured products. During the World War, the European nations were so occupied with fighting that they could not keep up their former volume of trade with South America. Germany, which had been one of the chief South American customers, could do no trading whatever. Hence the United States in part took the place of the

FIG. 115. European settlers are responsible for a good deal of the development of the cattle-raising industry in the southeastern part of South America. Their experiences in many ways resemble those of the pioneer cattlemen in our own West.

European nations as a source of manufactured articles and a purchaser of raw materials.

46. Explain how it was possible for the United States partially to replace western Europe in South American trade.
47. What advantage is this trade to the United States?
48. How does the Panama Canal assist in this trade?
49. What section of South America has been most benefited by the canal?

### (4) INTERIOR CITIES OF SOUTH AMERICA

The interior of South America is so little developed and so sparsely populated that there is little need of centers for collecting primary products. In fact, an inland area as large as the United States and all its possessions is without a single important center.

50. What has most hindered the development of the interior?

The few important interior cities of South America lie only a short distance from the coast. In order of location, beginning at the north, they are: (a) Bogotá, (b) Caracas, (c) São Paulo, (d) Rosario, (e) Córdoba, (f) Santiago, (g) Lima, (h) La Paz, and (i) Quito.

51. Locate the interior cities on the map in the order given.
52. Referring to the population table in the Appendix (page 335), arrange these cities in the order of size.

Each of the interior centers, with the exception of São Paulo, Rosario, and Córdoba, is the capital of a republic. Each is also located away from the unhealthful coastal lowlands, but on a highway which keeps it in touch with a port that exists chiefly for its benefit.

53. Name for each of these centers (a) the country of which it is the capital, (b) the highland on which it is located, (c) its port, and (d) the chief primary product shipped from the port.

Of the three interior cities that are not capitals of republics, São Paulo and Córdoba are located on healthful highlands and are capitals of large states, while Rosario is a river town and might almost be called a seaport. Each of the three is a center for the collection of primary products.

54. Name the products and decide with which group of seaports these three interior cities should be placed.

Fig. 116. From the stiff leaves of the henequen plant comes the sisal fiber which is made into binder's twine and used to tie the many thousands of bundles of wheat harvested in the United States.

## (B) Mexico, Central America, and the West Indies

Our next problem is concerned with the countries and islands between the United States and South America. We shall study this region by taking an imaginary journey through it.

### A Journey to the Lands of Silver, Sisal, and Sugar

Although this section is headed "A Journey to the Lands of Silver, Sisal, and Sugar," we could truthfully substitute "The Lands of Oil, Rubber, and Fruit," or "The Lands of Copper, Mahogany, and Coffee." Each of these titles would include three great types of resources; namely, minerals, vegetable raw materials, and food. As you make your journey and as you hear the reports of the others, try to decide which name is best, or whether some other name would be better.

**A journey of exploration.** Choose four guides from your class, and let each guide take a group from the class to explore Mexico, Central America, and the West Indies, following the plan outlined below. Since you cannot take steamers and travel, you will have to explore by reading and by gathering all the pictures you can find. Geographical and travel magazines will help you in this, as will encyclopedias, school readers, and travel books from the library. When each group returns from its journey, let the leader report to the class the facts which the members of the group have given him as their discoveries on the journey.

*First Group.* Purpose of journey: To explore the West Indies, and to obtain information on the following topics:

(1) The location, climate, and natural vegetation of the four chief islands.
(2) Their chief products and whether these are raised on farms, on plantations, or in gardens; or whether they come from the forest, the mines, or the sea.
(3) The chief difficulties in procuring these products.
(4) The relative importance of the four islands to the United States, commercially and otherwise.
(5) How the islands are governed, by whom, and how well.

*Second Group.* Purpose of journey: To discover the mineral resources of Mexico.

(1) Their kind and the relative importance of each kind to Mexico and to the United States.
(2) Where each kind is found, the nature of the climate and relief, and whether these conditions help or hinder in the work of mining.
(3) Methods of mining, and extent to which the products are refined before being shipped.
(4) The people who carry on the mining, including both foreigners and natives, and the kind of work done by each.
(5) Foreign investors; their effect on the growth of the country.

*Third Group.* Purpose of journey: To examine the forest and plantation products of Mexico and Central America.

(1) Kinds of products and their uses.
(2) Location of the products; climate and relief of the sections where they are found.
(3) Methods of raising or of procuring them.
(4) Kind of people who raise them, whether foreign planters or native laborers.
(5) Methods of sending to the United States, and importance to this country.

*Fourth Group.* Purpose of journey: To study the principal cities of Central America and the West Indies. (Include among the cities the capitals of Mexico and Guatemala, the chief Canal city, the port and capital of Yucatán, the two main ports of the east coast of Mexico, Puebla and Guadalajara, and the two main cities of the West Indies.)

(1) The reasons for their location.
(2) Their transportation methods and routes.
(3) Their chief occupations and the chief products that enter or leave them.
(4) Their inhabitants, and their relations to commerce and industry.
(5) The chief railroads that connect them.

**A combination map.** An interesting combination map may be made by the four groups.

(1) Let some one in Group 1 make a large outline map of Mexico, Central America, and the West Indies, showing in heavy lines the outlines of the countries and of the four main islands.

(2) Let the members of Group 3, with the help of a commercial atlas, color with crayons on the same map the areas which raise important amounts of cotton, sisal, fruit, cocoa, coffee, sugar, and tobacco.

(3) Pass the map to Group 2. Let the members of that group place a piece of tracing paper over it, fastening the paper only at the two left-hand corners, and on the tracing paper write in small-sized letters G, S, C, P, and so forth, where the minerals are located.

(4) Now pass the combination map to Group 4, which will put on a second sheet of tracing paper above the first. On the second sheet will be shown the railroad lines and the cities whose growth has been especially favored by the products of the hinterlands for which they serve as centers of transportation.

### (C) A Review Problem in Primary Production of the United States

**A local study of primary production.** Let each member of the class choose one of the following sections, study its primary products, and make a booklet on the results of his research. (About three classroom periods and three hours of outside work will be needed for this study.)

1. New England
2. New York
3. Pennsylvania
4. New Jersey
   Delaware
   Maryland
5. West Virginia
6. Virginia
7. North Carolina
   South Carolina
   Georgia
8. Florida
9. Alabama
   Mississippi
   Louisiana
10. Texas
11. Wisconsin
    Michigan
12. Illinois
    Indiana
    Ohio
13. Kentucky
    Tennessee
14. Minnesota
15. Iowa
    Missouri
16. Oklahoma
    Arkansas
17. North Dakota
    South Dakota
18. Nebraska
    Kansas
19. Montana
    Idaho
    Wyoming
20. Colorado
    New Mexico
21. Nevada
    Utah
    Arizona
22. Washington
    Oregon
23. California
24. Alaska
25. Hawaiian Ter.
26. Philippine
    Islands
27. Puerto Rico

Information may be gathered from this volume and from general geographies, encyclopedias, magazines, and newspapers. If possible, illustrate the booklet with appropriate pictures, and give it an attractive cover. The following material should be included:

(1) A sketch map of the whole of the United States, showing the location of the particular section treated, which may be marked with heavy lines.

(2) A map of the section, as large as a page of the booklet will permit, showing cities, rivers, mountains, and other features mentioned in the text of the booklet.

(3) A brief statement of the conditions of (*a*) temperature, (*b*) rainfall, (*c*) relief, and (*d*) soil.

(4) A description of (*a*) the farming conditions, (*b*) the chief crops raised, (*c*) the manner of raising them.

(5) A description of lumbering conditions.

(6) A description of mining conditions.

(7) A description of fishing conditions.

(8) At the end, a list of the books used in preparing the material.

When the booklets are completed, have an exhibit of them, so that each member of the class may have an opportunity to learn from the work of the others.

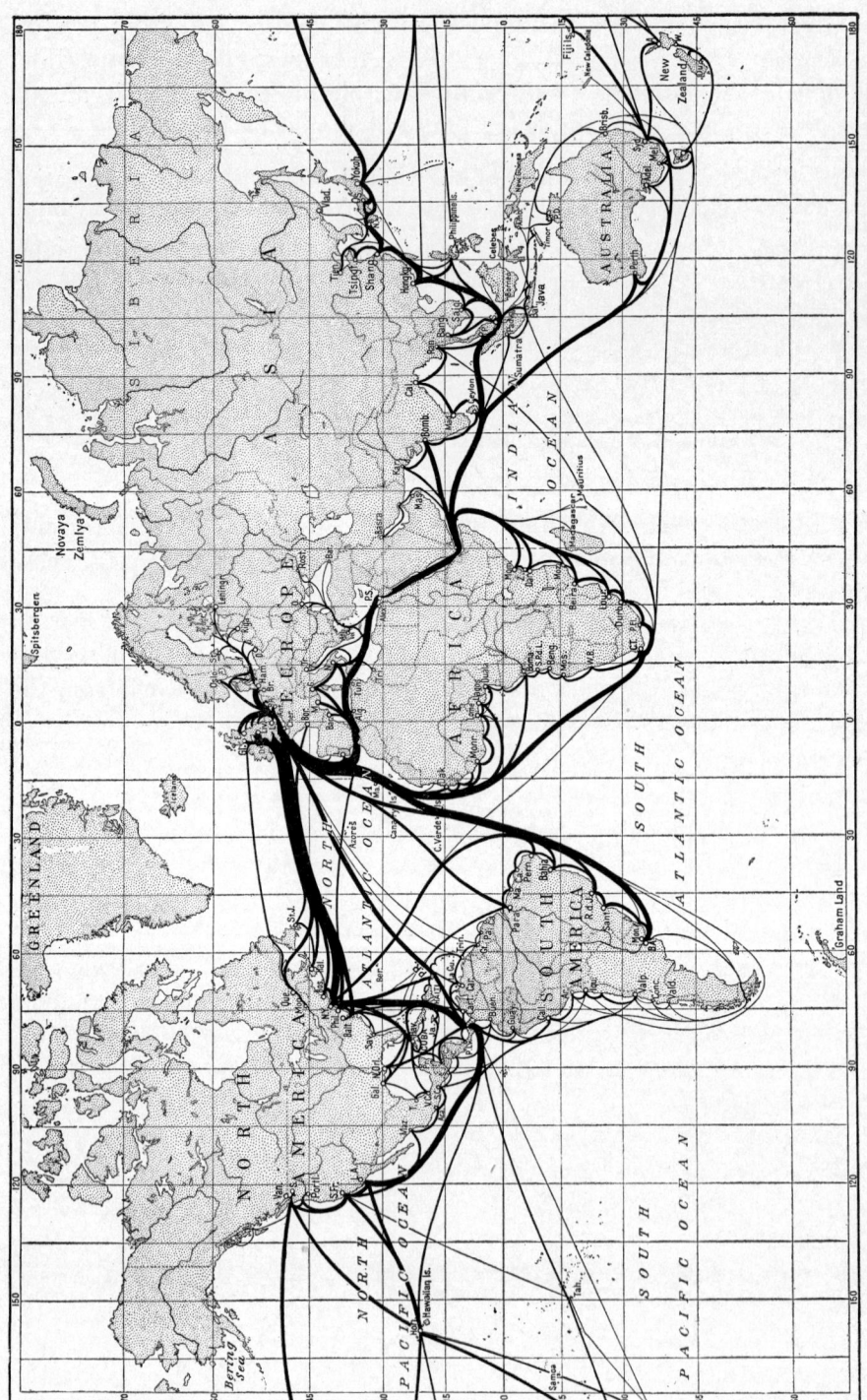

Fig. 117. Shipping routes of the world. The North Atlantic is the most traveled sea-road. (Based on Bowman's *The New World: Fourth Edition*.)

# PART TWO

## The Field of Transportation

### CHAPTER THIRTEEN

#### MEANS OF TRANSPORTATION

EVERYTHING that people need must be brought — that is, transported — from where it grows or is manufactured to where it is consumed. In different parts of the world the means of transportation vary greatly. The jungle tribes of Africa and India, for instance, carry practically everything in their hands or on their heads. In a civilized community conditions are far less simple. Probably groceries are brought to your house in an automobile or truck, while a man on foot brings the mail. A motor truck may bring furniture; the florist's messenger may come by electric car; coal may be hauled by a mule team. In most of these cases we see only the last part of the journey; earlier parts may have been made by railroad, or perhaps, for articles like tea and coffee, in steamships.

##### THE CHIEF MEANS OF TRANSPORTATION

In the order in which they came into use, the six most important means of transportation are: (1) man; (2) horses and other animals; (3) ships; (4) railways; (5) automobiles; (6) airplanes.

**How man is used for transportation in backward countries.** In primitive parts of the world, such as Africa, India, and China, men move the world's commerce long distances as well as short. In advanced countries, however, man power is used only for short distances. Such work is very expensive. For men to move a ton of goods a mile in one of our great cities would probably cost four or five dollars. Nevertheless, there is no part of the world where man power is not used extensively.

In central Africa a traveler who goes beyond the terminals of the railroads must often have his baggage transported on the heads of natives. In some places beasts of burden cannot be used because of disease-bearing insects that thrive in the hot, humid climate. Hence the ivory and the forest products of central Africa are carried on the heads of straggling lines of lightly clad natives. Among the Himalayas similar lines of carriers, clad in heavy quilted garments and straw sandals, tramp through the snow and slush with cloth, tea, and dates

*Caspar W. Hodgson*

Fig. 118. In the streets of Shanghai, as in all Chinese cities, man power is still used in the three ways here shown. Two men are pulling jinrikishas, another man is carrying two heavy baskets hung to the pole on his shoulder, and a fourth is pushing a well-laden wheelbarrow.

for Tibet and western China on their backs. In Syria, Persia, China, and Japan the peasants bring home great sheaves of wheat and barley on their heads. In China the wheelbarrow also is largely used for all sorts of transportation. Such use of human power is possible because labor is very cheap, so cheap that two or three men can be hired for what it would cost to support a horse.

**How man is used for transportation in advanced countries.** In spite of marvelous inventions there is still no substitute for man in transporting goods short distances. Even in the most advanced countries man power is used for at least four stages: (1) as products start on their journey; (2) as they are transferred from one means of transportation to another; (3) as they pass through a factory; and (4) as they finish their journey to the consumer.

**Transportation by man in mine, farm, and forest.** Deep down in mines, like those of Pennsylvania and the Rocky Mountains, human muscles are usually the means whereby the coal and ore are shoveled into cars. Even on farms where labor-saving machinery is most common, human muscles still lift most of the products from the ground to the wagon or truck. In the forests, whether in Maine, Louisiana, or Oregon, man's strength is still strained in starting the logs on their journey to the mills.

**Transportation by man at points of transshipment.** Along the waterfront and in the freight houses of cities like New York, Chicago, Philadelphia, St. Louis, and Seattle, thousands of longshoremen and freight handlers transship goods from one means of transportation to another. If a strike in New York causes them to cease pushing their slender trucks and lifting the countless boxes, barrels, bales, bags, crates, and kegs, freight may be held up all over the country and even in foreign ports, and factories may have to shut down for lack of raw material.

**Man power for transportation in factories.** In the factories new materials and parts of unfinished articles are continually being carried from workman to workman. In a shoe factory at Lynn or Brockton, for example, some men carry piles of leather on their shoulders, others push little trucks loaded with soles, and still others shove racks filled with shoes. The modern factory does as much of this work as possible by means of elevators, belts, endless chains of buckets, small motor trucks, and other devices, but even these have by no means done away with the necessity for man power.

**Man power for transportation to the consumer.** Lastly, man carries all sorts of products on the last lap of their journey and thus delivers them to the consumer. Whether we buy a piano, a new hat, or a squash, somebody's muscles are used to bring it into the house.

**Examples of cities where man power is used.** Although man depends upon his own strength for transportation everywhere, this use is particularly noticeable in certain regions. For instance, at the

FIG. 119. The "American coolie" is the small motor truck, which factories and warehouses use to great advantage for the work that formerly required a number of porters.

Fig. 120. An elephant piling teak logs at Rangoon. This "animal derrick" brings both strength and intelligence to the task.

docks in Yokohama crowds of jinrikisha men try to persuade the passengers to jump into their little two-wheeled carts and be carried to the hotel. At Foochow coolies with bare legs and arms come swinging down the narrow streets to leave at great warehouses the bales of tea which they have brought scores of miles on their backs.

At Madras, in India, although jinrikishas are fewer than in Japan and not so comfortable, rough carts for carrying freight are more numerous. In western Asia, one of the commonest sights is the *hamal* with a pad on his back. He may be carrying anything from a goatskin full of water to a load of melons or earthen water pots.

In the New World, in the highlands of Mexico and Guatemala, one sees hundreds of men and women running at a little jog trot with great baskets of fruit and vegetables on their heads, or with loads on their backs steadied by slings that pass over the forehead. Thus, in the backward parts of the world, there are almost countless ways in which man does the work of transportation.

**Animals in mountainous or backward countries.** In regions like Mexico, Peru, and Morocco, and even among some of our own mountains, horses or other pack animals transport goods almost everywhere. In advanced and well populated regions, however, horses are used only to carry goods short distances. They are an expensive means of transportation, for in cities it costs about fifty cents to haul a ton a mile by horse power. Horses or other beasts of burden are used somewhat in all parts of the world, but chiefly in the temperate zone and especially in western Europe and on the farms in the United States.

The traveler in the mountain regions of Utah, for instance, sometimes meets horse after horse winding up a narrow trail, each carrying on his back a load of provisions for a mine. In countries like Persia, Turkey, China, and Siberia, such pack trains or caravans are common in both mountains and plains. Often they consist wholly of horses; but in Turkestan, Arabia, and North Africa, many are composed of camels tied together by ropes running from the pack saddle or tail of one animal to the nose of the next. In Mexico and many other tropical countries, pack trains of mules are more numerous than those of horses; while in Greece, Spain, and other Mediterranean countries, trains of donkeys are common. In Siam and India the elephant is often used for such work; in the Himalayas the grunting yak with his sharp horns, and grinding teeth, and slow, steady tread is the safest and surest animal; in the Andes the llama, a little cousin of the camel, carries the commerce of the high, cold upland.

Even in the countries where pack animals are the main means of transportation, there are usually some roads where wagons can be used. In our own desert regions great mule teams of ten or even twenty animals haul supplies to mines and come back with a wagon and several trailers loaded with ore or borax. In Siberia each wagon usually has

*Ellsworth Huntington*

Fig. 121. In Central Asia transportation is still entirely dependent on animal power. The traveler has his choice of the ox, the camel, or the horse.

*Ellsworth Huntington*

FIG. 122. The sledge, the first form of vehicle devised by man, is still in use in many parts of Asia and in some backward farming districts in Europe.

three horses, one between the shafts, with a high arch above him, and the other two on either side. In Manchuria the carts have two big wheels, and two or three horses are driven tandem, with only a single rein attached to the front horse.

Crude as these methods are, a large part of the commerce of Asia, Africa, and South America, as well as of the mountainous or more remote sections of North America and Europe, is carried on by means of animals.

**Why the horse is still important in advanced countries.** Even in the most advanced countries, the horse still continues to help the farmer in plowing, seeding, cultivating, and harvesting. It also helps to carry the products of farm, forest, and factory to the barn, railroad, or steamship, and to distribute them to the store or the consumer when they are ready to be used. This is because: (1) among animals used for transportation the horse is superior in intelligence, alertness, strength, and endurance; (2) the horse costs less than an automobile and needs less repairing; (3) the horse can be used at all seasons and in almost all places, while the automobile is often useless in snow or mud, and requires special equipment for rough places or for plowing; and (4) the farmer can raise his own horses and also their food, while he cannot raise automobiles and gasoline.

*Ellsworth Huntington*

Fig. 123. The earliest form of cart had solid wheels, and the solid-wheeled cart is seen today in Turkey, Persia, China, and other parts of Asia.

The horse is largely limited to the temperate zone, not only because brisk commerce and active agriculture require him there, but because in tropical regions he readily contracts diseases, and his thin skin makes the insect pests especially annoying. Of the hundred and forty million horses and mules in the world, the United States has nearly an eighth and Europe nearly half. European Russia has almost ten times as many as Africa, although its area is much smaller and the population only a sixth as great. What few horses there are in Africa live largely in the more temperate regions of the Mediterranean coast and South Africa.

**Some cities where animals are important.** Although race horses bring the highest prices, some having been sold for much more than one hundred thousand dollars, the most useful animals are the heavier horses used for hauling loads and for farm work. Moscow was formerly noted for huge, sleek animals, which, though spirited, are also gentle. Equally fine horses are seen in Glasgow and in some of our own cities, like Chicago. In the northern United States the horse is the only animal commonly used for transportation in our cities; but in the South the mule team is common.

More interesting, because less familiar, are the caravans of donkeys or camels that crowd the narrow streets of oriental cities, like Damascus, Baghdad, Algiers, and Tashkent. When a caravan of camels from the desert with loads of dates, wool, or cheese, meets a caravan of donkeys, the camels usually stalk calmly along, while the donkeys crowd this way and that, turn about, and perhaps go in the wrong direction.

In some countries the ox is still in use. In Calcutta, for instance, from daybreak to sunset, long lines of two-wheeled bullock carts with white-clad Hindu drivers cross the bridge over one of the distributaries of the united Ganges and Brahmaputra to the railroad station at Howrah. They keep to the left, according to the British rule, which prevails in most British colonies. Where an animal so slow as the ox is used for transportation, man power also is likely to be used a good deal. In Calcutta, now and then, four men can be seen bearing on their shoulders a pole from which is slung a sort of box containing a reclining passenger.

**Steamships.** Steamships are the world's long distance carriers. The average journey of freight in steamers is more than a thousand miles, and ten thousand is not uncommon. Though steamships are not so rapid as railroad trains, they cover long distances almost as quickly because they make few stops. They are very cheap, for a ton can be carried a mile in a steamship for only about one fifth of a cent, and in some cases for less than one tenth.

Steamships sail on practically all the world's navigable oceans, lakes, and rivers. By far the larger number, however, are found (1) on the coast of Europe from Norway to Portugal; (2) on the American

Fig. 124. This Burmese junk of today is the type of vessel in which water-borne commerce of large parts of the world was carried for many centuries.

*Swiss Aviation Service*

Fig. 125. This photograph of Zurich illustrates three means of transportation: (1) man's easiest roadway, a river; (2) running alongside the river, a railway; (3) and following the course of the river, an airplane.

coast of the Atlantic from Newfoundland to Texas; (3) on the coasts of China and Japan; (4) in the Great Lakes; (5) in the Mediterranean; and (6) on the western coast of the United States.

Transportation by ship is so important that it will be studied separately, in Chapter Fifteen (page 189).

**Railroads.** Railroads carry goods rapidly for long distances on land. Although they are not so cheap as steamships, the cost of carrying a ton a mile is less than two cents. Most countries have some railroads, but in tropical and far northern countries and in most of Asia, they are scarce. In the United States, Europe, Japan, Java, parts of India, and northern Argentina, they are numerous.

Railroad transportation will be studied more in detail in the next chapter (page 175).

**Automobiles.** Automobiles transport goods longer distances than do horses, but not so far as railroads. The cost by motor truck is about thirty cents a ton per mile. Most of the world's automobiles are in the United States and western Europe.

**Why motor trucks are important in transportation.** Long hauls where the loads are heavy wear out horses quickly and make their use expensive. This kind of service is best performed by motor trucks. If there is work enough to keep them busy most of the time, the trucks are cheaper as well as more speedy. This is why very few large American companies that constantly handle heavy loads now use horse wagons. The companies that use horses are mainly small local companies with only a few customers, many milk companies whose wagons have to keep stopping, and a few large companies in cities where the congestion forces trucks to move slowly.

Although the automobile ordinarily works best on graded roads, it can also be used on bad roads. Tractors also enable motors to perform many kinds of farm work, such as plowing and reaping, especially if it can be done on a large scale. Nevertheless, even in our own country there are two thirds as many horses and mules as there are automobiles. In Great Britain there is about one motor car for every horse, in France one for two horses, in Germany one for about five, and in most other countries the proportion is still smaller.

**Motor vehicles in cities and on farms.** Motor trucks are preëminently vehicles of the cities. At such a shipping point as Jersey City, trucks in a seemingly endless line are backed up against scores of warehouses. No sooner does one rumble away from the docks of the great transatlantic steamship lines with its load of boxes, bales, machinery, bananas, or other products, than another takes its place.

At first used only in cities, motor trucks now carry goods hundreds of miles from one city to another or from farms to railroads. So heavy are they and so much do they wear out the roads that the upkeep of the highways where they are used is a most serious problem.

Ordinary passenger automobiles are about six times as numerous as motor trucks. On such a street as Fifth Avenue in New York, cars of every make, from morning to midnight, form a vast procession, two abreast on each side of the street. In certain cities, like Detroit and Akron, automobiles are important not only because great numbers are made there, but because the workers in the automobile factories are so highly paid that they can afford to own cars, while the surrounding country is level and a motor car can go almost anywhere. In the level prairie states, such as Iowa and Kansas, the number of automobiles in proportion to the population is even greater than in the cities, for almost every farmer has one.

**Airplanes.** Airplanes are so new that they have as yet had little effect on transportation. Their use is to carry passengers, mail, and light, expensive articles, like silk and precious stones, very rapidly for long distances.

**How geography influences air navigation.** At first thought it may seem that airplanes and dirigibles can go everywhere with **equal ease**.

Fig. 126. The Wright Flying Field at Fairfield, Ohio. On the left are the hangars, alongside the landing field. In the center and to the right are workshops and workmen's cottages.

This is not true; although it is almost equally easy to fly over land or sea, mountain or plain, it is not everywhere equally easy to land. Hydroplanes, since they are built especially for this purpose, can land anywhere in the water, but are not well adapted for use over the land. Dirigibles and especially airplanes, on the other hand, cannot land everywhere, even on the land. Dirigibles need mooring masts, and airplanes must have broad, level landing places, the standard size being at least one third of a mile by one sixth. Hence in mountainous regions they are always at a disadvantage; for such large level areas are rare, and it is still more rare to find them free from trees.

Air navigation is easiest in open plains where there are people enough to make it worth while to maintain regular landing places, and where there are many large, smooth fields that can be used in an emergency. Dayton, Ohio, where airplanes were first developed, is in this kind of region. Such a region, surrounded by mile after mile of large fields, is a good place for airplane factories.

### GOOD ROADS AS A FACTOR IN TRANSPORTATION

Good roads mean good service by horses, automobiles, and trucks. The motor vehicle and the good road, between them, put an end to the extreme isolation that was formerly the lot of many small communities off the main lines of travel.

**The qualities of a good road.** In the backward or very mountainous regions, most of the roads are merely trails worn by the feet of people and animals. In slightly more favored districts, the roads are rough tracks worn by the wheels of carts. Where the traffic is light and the soil firm, such a track may be sufficient in dry weather, but is likely to be difficult when wet. For heavy teams and automobiles, roads of gravel, broken stone, brick, cement, or the like are needed. It is also necessary to crown the road; that is, to make the surface slope gradually from the center so that rain water will drain away immediately rather than flow along the roadway and wear gullies. The ideal road must be as straight and level as possible, and therefore cuttings and embankments are needed, even in regions of low hills, while on steep slopes the roads must zigzag back and forth.

**Why it pays to build good roads.** Good roads cost from ten thousand to fifty thousand dollars a mile, even in regions of gentle relief, but it pays to build them. They are an advantage to both the country districts and the cities. A farmer who lives on a bad road only a mile or two from the railroad may find it as difficult to get his produce to market as one who lives on a good road twenty miles from a station. Good roads lower the price of food for city people. They also make it easy for those who dwell in the noisy, crowded city to have some share of the restfulness and beauty of the country.

Europe long ago appreciated the value of good roads, and England, France, Germany, Austria, and Italy have improved hundreds of thousands of miles of their roadways. In Russia and southeastern Europe, however, the roads are poor for the most part. This hampers those regions greatly. The thickly settled northeastern United States was the first part of this country to follow the example of western Europe. Now other sections are so rapidly improving their roads that soon automobiles will be able to go freely all over the United States.

**Difficulties of making good roads.** Everywhere in civilized countries people are beginning to realize that bad roads are a disgrace. Merely to keep the roads in repair, however, is difficult where no good road-making rocks are found within hundreds of miles, as in our prairie plains. It is even more difficult in thinly settled places where there are only a few persons for each mile of road, or where most of the people are poor and cannot afford to pay high taxes. It is most difficult of all in rugged regions where the farmers are poor and scattered, and the cost of construction is great.

## QUESTIONS, EXERCISES, AND PROBLEMS

**A. How the six common means of transportation compare in cost.**

1. Arrange the six means of transportation (page 159) in the order of (a) speed; (b) size of loads; (c) cost of carrying a ton a mile; (d) length of time that they have been in use; (e) extent of the earth's surface where they are common. Explain your reasons for each arrangement.

2. A horse and wagon may cost $500 and be able to carry a ton. A motor truck may cost $2000 and carry three tons; a train, $100,000 and carry 2000 tons; a steamship, $1,000,000 and carry 10,000 tons. Explain why the cost of transportation diminishes as the cost of the *means* of transportation increases.

**B. Examples of the different kinds of transportation.**

1. Be able to point out on the wall map the location of each of the examples in the table below.

EXAMPLES OF TRANSPORTATION CLASSIFIED BY KIND OF POWER

| KIND OF POWER | ILLUSTRATIONS OF USE |
|---|---|
| I. *Human Power* | |
| (a) On heads | Jars of sacred Ganges water at Benares |
| (b) On shoulders | Buckets of fish on poles in Yokohama |
| (c) On backs | Freight from steamers in Constantinople |
| (d) By wheeled vehicles | Passengers by jinrikisha in Hangchow |
| (e) On water | Cheese in rowboats on the canals of Holland |
| II. *Animal Power* | |
| (a) Horse | Farm products and the mail to Omsk |
| (b) Mule | Pack loads of chestnuts among the Pyrenees |
| (c) Donkey | Silver ore to elevators in mines near Mexico City |
| (d) Ox | Logs out of forests near Vancouver |
| (e) Elephant | Passengers through the jungle near Rangoon |
| (f) Yak | Pack loads at Lhassa |
| (g) Camel | Pack loads of dates to Bagdad |
| (h) Reindeer | Food supplies by sled to Point Barrow |
| (i) Dog | Milk to customers in Antwerp |
| (j) Llama | Tin ore from the Andes to La Paz |
| III. *Mechanical Power* | |
| (a) Gravity | |
|     Through flowing water | Bamboo rafts loaded with teak, Irrawadi River |
|     On land | Grain out of elevators, Liverpool |

| | | |
|---|---|---|
| (b) | Wind | |
| | On water | Sailing vessels with fish from the North Sea to Aberdeen |
| | On land | Water pumped for household use at Mérida in Yucatán |
| (c) | Steam | |
| | Locomotive engine | Wheat from the Black Earth region of Ukraine to Odessa |
| | Marine engine | A liner with wool from Sydney to London |
| | Pump | Petroleum through pipes from Baku to Batum |
| (d) | Gasoline | |
| | Automobile | Tourists over the battle fields around Lille |
| | Boat | Boats bringing milk to the doors in Venice |
| | Airplane | Mail and passengers from London to Paris |
| (e) | Electricity | |
| | Street car | Passengers in the streets of Damascus |
| | Railroad | Passengers and freight through the Simplon Tunnel |
| | Automobile truck | Freight over good roads between Manchester and Liverpool |
| | Crane | Loading freight and moving machinery on the docks at Hamburg |

2. Examine the pictures in this book. Classify the means of transportation shown in them under the preceding headings. Can you find pictures for all the headings?

3. Make a table as nearly as possible like the one given above, using examples from the United States. Be able to locate each of your examples on the wall map.

4. Make a list of all the means of transportation you observe during one week, numbering them according to the table given above. Explain the influence of each of the following conditions on the kind of transportation: (a) kind of goods; (b) weight of load; (c) distance transported; (d) cost of power; (e) condition of road.

*Example.* A woman, evidently a foreigner, is carrying a load of wood on her head. Number this I a, because in the table given above, No. I stands for human power, while a means that the load is carried on the head. The kind of load, its weight, etc., are described as follows:

I a. A woman carrying a load of wood on her head.

*Explanation.* (1) Kindling wood picked up to cook with at home. Easily tied up and balanced.

(2) Light load for a woman who in her foreign home carried many things on her head because too poor to hire other means.
(3) Distance short, perhaps half a mile; hence not exhausting.
(4) Very low cost of power, since the woman is an unskilled worker. The value of the wood, although slight, more than pays her for the labor.
(5) Road level, well paved, making transportation easy.

**C. Discussion of a transportation item or picture.**

1. In the upper left-hand corner of a sheet of paper mount a newspaper or magazine clipping or a picture dealing with transportation. On the rest of the paper discuss the item on the bases of this chapter and the table in Problem *B*, page 171.

**D. The condition of the roads near your home.**

1. Which are the best roads in your town? Why are these kept in the best repair?
2. Find out from your local street department the annual cost of keeping a mile of the best road in repair. Would it be wise to save this expense? Why, or why not?
3. Where have you seen an ideal road? Whose money built it and keeps it in repair?
4. Where is the worst road you know of? Why is it in bad condition?
5. Do you think it would be wise to improve (*a*) more of the roads in your state; (*b*) all the roads? Why?
6. Has the rural free delivery of mail helped to improve the roads near your home? Name a locality where the roads have been benefited by this system.

**E. How the quality of roads depends on geographic conditions.**

1. Why has Massachusetts about four thousand miles of hard-surfaced roads, while Mississippi has less than a thousand?
2. Much of the soil of Illinois is clayey. What are some of the difficulties of road building in that state?
3. Switzerland is noted for its good roads. What difficulties have had to be overcome? Why are the roads a good investment in spite of their great cost?
4. In three groups of states both mileage and expenditure per mile are high, in comparison with other parts of the country: (*a*) northeastern states; (*b*) states bordering the Great Lakes; (*c*) Pacific states. Explain the conditions of prosperity, density of population, relief, and material for road building which probably are most important in causing each group to stand high.
5. The expenditure per mile for roads is low in these five groups of states: (*a*) southern coastal plain; (*b*) Allegheny plateau; (*c*) western plains; (*d*) Rocky Mountains; (*e*) Basin plateau. What factors hinder each group from spending much money on its roads?

6. How does your state stand in road making? Explain its position.

**F. Comparative cost of automobile and horse transportation on bad roads and good.**

1. Suppose you had to deliver thirty tons of coal each day at an average distance of four miles, over roads so bad that two horses could pull only one ton, making only two trips a day; a two-ton truck, the largest that could safely be used, could make three trips a day. How many horses or trucks would be needed?

2. Suppose that a two-ton truck and chauffeur cost $20 per day, including maintenance, repairs, interest, and depreciation, while a two-horse team and driver cost $10. How would the expenses compare in the two cases?

3. Suppose that the roads were improved so that two horses could pull two tons, or a five-ton truck could be used, and that the larger truck cost $30 per day. Calculate the saving in each case on the supposition that the horses can now average two and a half trips a day and the trucks six.

**G. How transportation helps maintain our high standard of living.**

1. Make a list of articles that were on your breakfast table this morning. On an outline map of the world print the name of each article at its source. Draw lines showing the routes over which the various parts of the breakfast traveled to reach your table.

2. Choose the article which came farthest, and make a list of the various ways in which it was carried from its point of original production to your table.

3. If each man, woman, and child who helped to carry your breakfast were in the room to greet you when you entered, how large a crowd of guests would you have? If you said "Thank you" to each one, in about how many languages would you have to speak?

**H. The relation of governments to transportation by land.**

1. Who builds and cares for the street on which you live? Find out how much money your town or city, your state, and the United States government spend for roads. A table in the Statistical Abstract of the United States Census will help you.

2. In Italy, Japan, and Germany the government owns and operates the railroads. How does this system differ from ours? Explain how the Interstate Commerce Commission and the Railroad Labor Board attempt to provide the benefits of government ownership without its disadvantages.

3. Macaulay said, "Of all inventions, the alphabet and the printing press alone excepted, those inventions which abridge distance have done most for civilization." What reasons can you give for thinking this statement true?

Fig. 127. Where railroads and steamships meet. The terminal of a grain-carrying railroad at Jersey City.

## CHAPTER FOURTEEN

### RAILROADS

THE number of railroads varies greatly from country to country. For example, the United States has more than a third of all the railways in the world, while in northern Siberia an area as large as the whole United States contains not a single mile of railroad. Great Britain and Ireland have over three times as great a railway mileage as China; yet China has eight times as many people and is thirty times as large. Although New Jersey is only a twelfth as large as Wyoming, it has more miles of railroad. Such differences are accounted for by four main causes: (1) degree of progress in civilization; (2) density of population; (3) relief of the land; and (4) natural resources. Let us see how each of these conditions does its work.

**Why progressive countries have many railroads.** Most of the railroads are in highly progressive regions like the United States and western Europe. Japan, too, in proportion to its area, has far more railroads than any other country in Asia. On the other hand, backward countries like Siam, Persia, Abyssinia, and Paraguay have very few. There are many reasons for this difference.

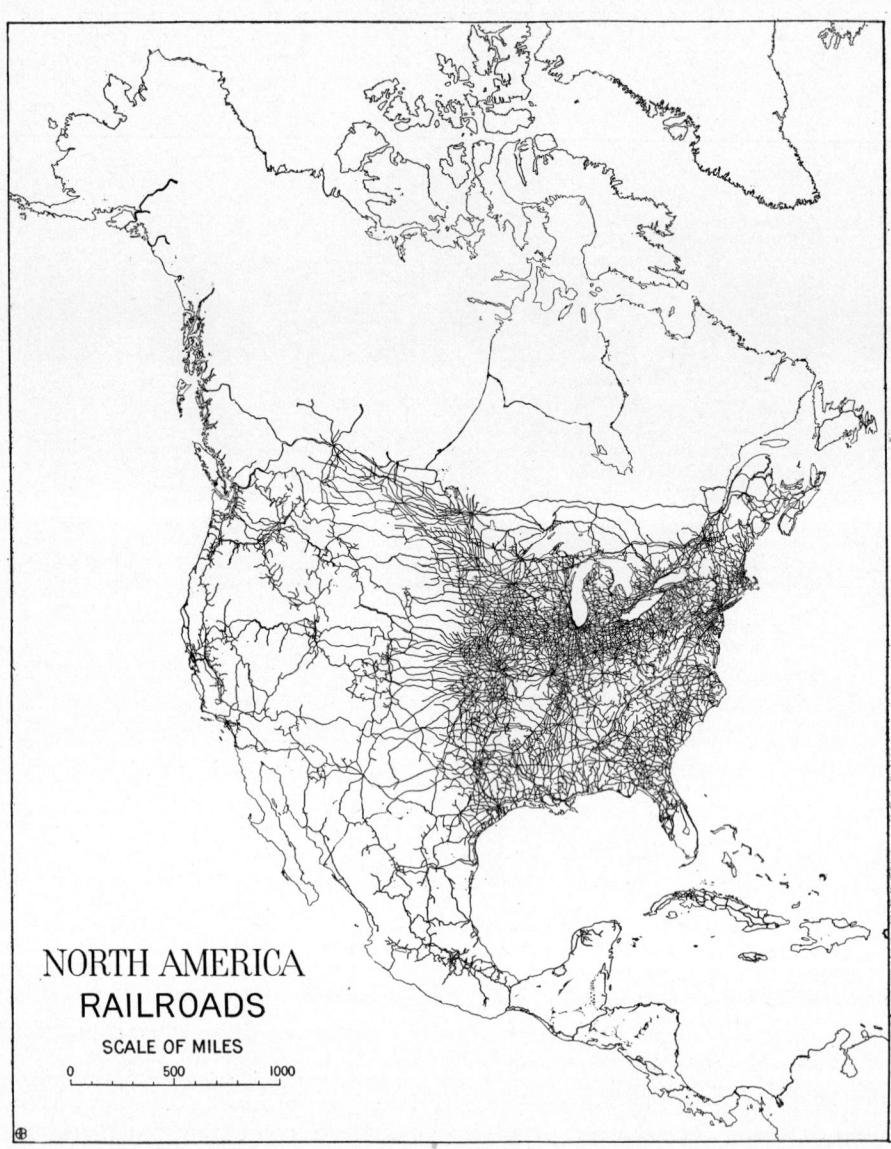

FIG. 128. This map shows all the railroads in North America. Notice the closeness of the network in the eastern half of the United States. Notice also the knot formed at Montreal, at Boston, New York, Philadelphia, Baltimore. Find Winnipeg, Minneapolis, Chicago, St. Louis, Kansas City, Omaha, Dallas, Galveston, New Orleans, Birmingham. Farther to the west, locate Denver, Salt Lake City; then Vancouver, Seattle, San Francisco, Los Angeles. Find the City of Mexico and Vera Cruz. Account for two comparatively open areas in the northeast; two in the south-central part of the eastern half of the continent. Compare this map with Figure 134 (page 186) and with Figures 164, 165 (pages 248, 249). What is the cause of the sharp contrast in the density of the railway net in the east and in the west? Is it due to relief (Fig. 134)? temperature (Figs. 3, 4)? rainfall (Fig. 6)? Trace the eastern base of the Rocky Mountains. What differences do you note between the railroads directly east and those west of this line? Can you explain the differences?

FIG. 129. Compare this map with Figure 128. Locate Buenos Aires, Rio de Janeiro, Santos. Where does a railroad cross the continent? Compare it in length with the North American transcontinental route from New York to Chicago, to Omaha, to Salt Lake City, to San Francisco. What special difficulty had to be overcome in constructing the South American transcontinental road? Compare Brazil and the United States (not counting Alaska) in size; compare them in railroad transportation. What serves interior Brazil as a transportation system? Account for the many short lines running inland from the Pacific coast. Locate Quito and Guayaquil; Lima and Callao; Santiago and Valparaiso. With what ports is La Paz connected? Are they Bolivian ports? How does Bogotá communicate with either coast? What effects of climate do you see in this map? Are they as clear as in North America? Compare the effects of relief in the same way.

(1) The people of highly progressive countries are energetic enough to carry out improvements. If a town in the United States grows up away from the railroad it tries to persuade the nearest railroad to build a branch line for it, and perhaps gives land for tracks, freight yard, and station. In Sweden many small railways are actually financed and managed by the local farmers. In backward countries, on the other hand, the people wait and wait, hoping perhaps that some one will build a railroad, but doing little to help get it.

(2) Progressive countries need many railroads because their people wish to move around a great deal and like to go rapidly. A business man in Chicago thinks little of a trip to Philadelphia, while most of the business men in Chungking rarely go outside their own city.

(3) In progressive countries, not only do people wish to travel rapidly, but they work rapidly, use much machinery, and produce large quantities of goods to be transported. One man's work in a cutlery factory in Leeds, for example, may produce as many knives and hence require as much freight business as the work of a hundred men in the old-fashioned shops of Damascus.

(4) Again, since the most progressive people generally work hardest and use the greatest intelligence in their work, they have far more money than those of other countries. Where a mechanic in Buffalo gets seven dollars a day, a man of corresponding position in Delhi may get only fifty cents. Such large earnings not only provide capital for railroad building, but enable people to buy a great many articles which must be transported by the railways. All the savings of a whole year in a city like Canton, China, would build only a few dozen miles of railways. But the savings of an equally large American city, such as Cleveland, would build hundreds of miles.

**Why densely populated countries have many railroads.** Suppose you were to motor around the city of Boston at a distance of twenty-five miles from the center. You would cross between twenty-five and thirty railroads, the number depending on which roads you took. On a similar ride around Chicago you would cross almost the same number of tracks, but you would see more freight trains and fewer passenger trains. On the same kind of ride around New York you would have to cross Long Island Sound and the broad Hudson River, but you would see an even larger number of railroads, more than thirty in all, and the trains would be even more numerous than around Boston and Chicago.

Suppose now that you were to take a similar ride in northern Maine, or the western part of South Dakota. Not a single railroad would you cross. The people there are as civilized as those in Massachusetts, Illinois, and New York, but they are so few in number that it does not pay to build railroads to carry their scanty freight.

**How plains and mountains influence the number of railroads.** On a relief map of California notice how largely the railroads are limited to the low, level regions of the coast and the great central valley or plain. In the first place, the mountains have too sparse a population to provide much railroad business, while the plain is thickly settled and productive. Second, railroads are extremely expensive among mountains. The grades, curves, bridges, cuttings, and tunnels make it cost ten, twenty, or even fifty times as much to build a mile of railroad in the mountains as in the plains. Moreover, the mountain railroad is relatively long because of the windings, and the expense of running trains is great not only because much coal is needed, but because of wear and tear, and low speed.

**How natural resources attract railroads.** Among the mountain railroads of the world a large number have been built to open up natural resources, such as minerals. For example, the Leadville road in Colorado is famous as the highest in the United States. The railroad would scarcely have been built if it had not been for the silver and lead ores that attracted large numbers of miners. Elsewhere mountain railroads have often been built to tap resources of lumber in rugged regions that would otherwise have no good lines of communication. The woods of northern Maine contain many such roads.

Another resource of rugged regions is the scenery. Many people will pay more than the ordinary rate of fare in order to enjoy it;

Fig. 130. Nine pairs of horses are hauling four wagon loads of wool to market, across the Wyoming sage-brush. Which would be the better substitute — a railroad train or a motor truck?

Fig. 131. Duluth, at the western end of Lake Superior, is a meeting point for the railroads ply to the industrial cities of Chicago, Detroit,

hence, it pays to build railroads among the rough Adirondacks, or even expensive cog-wheeled roads up mountains like Washington in New Hampshire, Pikes Peak in Colorado, and the Rigi in the Alps.

In plains quite as much as among mountains the presence of natural resources, especially the possibilities of agriculture, cause the building of railroads. On the map of the railroads of North America (Fig. 128), notice all the little railroads branching from the main lines in the Dakotas, for example. Their chief purpose is to collect wheat from the fertile farms of the Red River valley. Other railroads have been built to collect milk in northern New York, beets in Colorado and central Germany, and sugar in Cuba. In fact, more railroads are built to collect the products of regions of gentle relief than for any other single purpose.

**Why railroads are expensive.** People often wonder why it costs forty or fifty thousand dollars to build a mile of railroad even in a plain, and hundreds of thousands among the mountains. They also wonder why, when once a railroad is built, it constantly needs new capital. Let us consider some of the chief expenses.

(1) *Surveying.* When a railroad is planned, the route must be surveyed most carefully. This is easy in a plain, but among mountains or even hills it is a long, expensive process, and mistakes are frequent. For example, the Union Pacific Railroad — or, as it is now called, the Southern Pacific — from Cheyenne to Sacramento, is only one of many roads that have spent millions of dollars in relocating tracks because the first surveys were not sufficiently full and accurate.

bringing iron ore and wheat from the Minnesota mines and prairies and for the lake freighters that
and along the southern shore of Lake Erie.

(2) *Roadbed, cuts, and bridges.* To build a railroad is not merely a matter of laying down ties and rails. Although these are expensive, they usually cost much less than the roadbed itself. Even in a plain the roadbed should be raised a little above the general level, so that it will not become muddy in wet weather. Culverts must be provided to draw off the rain water where there are no regular streams; cuts are needed in almost every mile of road except in the most level regions; bridges are a most expensive item; and even the ballast — that is, the gravel or crushed rock which covers the roadbed — often costs a great deal, especially in regions like the prairies, where there is no good surface rock or gravel.

(3) *Special expenses of upkeep.* Under certain geographical circumstances special kinds of railroad equipment are required. For example, among the Sierra Nevada mountains the trains often run for miles through snowsheds. In sandy deserts, such as Transcaspia, the railroad must sometimes be protected from blowing sand by a special kind of desert bush which is planted in hedges and carefully tended until it gets a good start. In swamps the roadbed often sinks a little and must constantly be built up. For example, for several hundred miles the Amur Railway, in eastern Siberia, runs through swamps where the upper foot or two consists of peat which acts like a blanket and prevents the lower part of the swamp from melting. Thus most of the swamp remains frozen in summer as well as in winter. In order to build the railroad, the peat had to be taken off. The sun in summer warms the ballast which replaces the peat, and thus a little of the frozen swamp melts each summer and the railroad sinks a

*United States Bureau of Mines*
FIG. 132. Here mineral resources have attracted a railroad.

few inches. This makes the road very rough and dangerous, and also adds greatly to the expense of keeping it up.

(4) *Double tracks and sidings.* Some roads must have two tracks, and all must have frequent sidings where trains can pass one another. Among mountains it is often very expensive to blast out a space even for a siding. Nevertheless, the sidings must be frequent, for they determine how many trains can run per day on all single-track roads. If it takes an hour for a train to go from one siding to the next, only twelve trains per day can run in each direction.

(5) *Stations and freight yards.* Another great expense to railroads is the building and maintaining of stations and freight yards. As a town grows, it wants a new and better looking station; the manufacturers and merchants want more tracks and freight houses in the freight yard; and those who are not near the yards want spur tracks to their places of business. It is wise for the railroad to spend money for such purposes, but it costs a great deal.

(6) *New equipment.* Finally, not only does almost everything that is used on a railroad grow old and wear out, but new inventions and improvements demand large expenditures. For instance, when steel cars were invented people began to complain that wooden cars were not safe and to demand that the railroads replace them with steel cars. The invention of the block signal system led to another large item of expense, which will continue until all railroads are fully

"blocked." At present many railroads are substituting electric power for steam, and far more would do this if the change were less costly. On many roads the cost of operation would be diminished if electric power were used, but the expense of buying electric locomotives to replace steam locomotives and of installing wires and power stations makes the roads hesitate to change.

**Why the United States has the greatest railroad mileage.** The world has about 760,000 miles of railroads. The United States has about 33 per cent of this great length, Russia and Siberia 6, Germany 5, Canada 5, Australia 4, India 3, France 3, Great Britain 3, Argentina 3, Brazil 3, Mexico 2, Hungary 2, Italy 2, and South Africa, Sweden, Spain, Czechoslovakia, Japan, China, Chile, Belgium, Egypt, Austria, and Switzerland about one per cent each.

Although the United States is about three fourths the size of Europe, and has only a quarter as many people, its railroads are a little longer. There are four chief reasons for this fact:

(1) The United States is favored with great natural wealth. Rich mines, fertile fields, and valuable forests as well as active manufacturing industries furnish such abundant products that the internal commerce of the United States is estimated to be greater than the total international commerce of the world.

(2) While Europe has but one intensely active region, — the western part, — the United States has two, — the eastern half and the Pacific states. These two distant regions are connected by numerous long railroads.

(3) The coast of the United States is not so deeply indented as that of Europe, and is only about one fourth as long. Hence much of the commerce that would be carried by water in Europe must depend on railroads here.

(4) Europe has more than a hundred thousand miles of navigable rivers and canals to help carry her freight, while the United States has scarcely a tenth as much.

**Why the railroads of Europe differ from those in the United States.** A traveler from the United States is impressed by the small size of the European railway cars. Few of them have the size of our great coaches, pullmans, and dining cars. Instead of being arranged with the seats on the two sides of a corridor which extends from end to end, the European cars are divided into many little compartments entered by doors on the sides. Half of the passengers face forward and half backward. Often it is not possible to walk from end to end of the train except on an outside step which runs the whole length of each car.

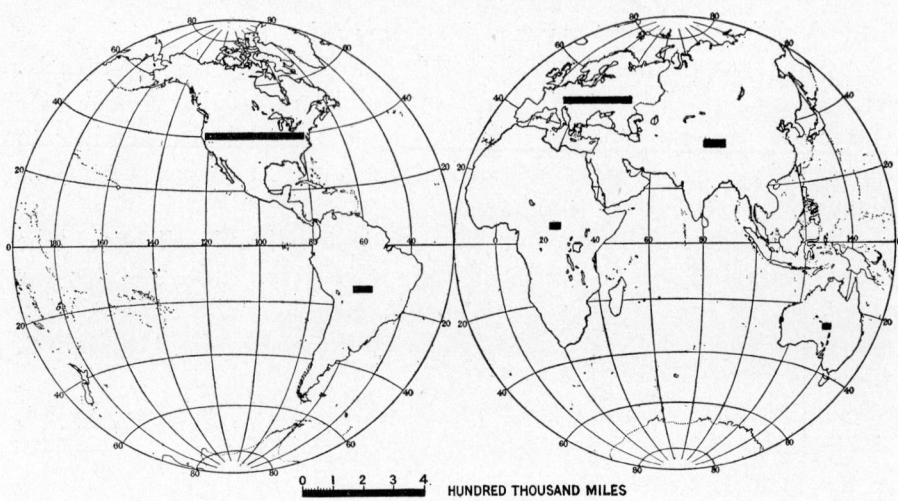

Fig. 133. The railroad mileage of the different continents from the latest figures available. North America has almost half of the total mileage. Compare this map with Figure 158 (page 236) and Figure 176 (page 284). With which of the two does it correspond more nearly?

One reason for the contrast between the United States and Europe is the size of the countries. Our own country is so large and the population so scattered that people take long journeys. The passengers need room to move around and to make themselves comfortable, and thus corridors are necessary. People must be provided with food, either in dining cars or at regular restaurant stations, and they must have places to sleep. In western Europe, on the other hand, trains rarely run beyond the limits of a single country. The countries are so small and the great cities are so close together that journeys of more than ten or twelve hours are rare, and therefore there is little need of so many conveniences to make people comfortable. In the larger countries, however, such as the former Austrian Empire and especially Russia, the distances are so great that people take long journeys, as they do in the United States, and there the trains are more like ours.

**How electric railways are useful.** Electric railways, or tramways, as they are called in Europe, are a type of railroad especially adapted to cities and their suburbs. There they transport passengers and freight for short distances much more easily and cheaply than can railroads. One reason is that their tracks cost much less than those of ordinary railroads. Moreover, their right of way — that is, the privilege of running in the street — costs little or nothing. Since the streets have already been graded and since the light cars can climb steep grades, little cutting, filling, and tunneling have to be done.

The special advantage of street railways is that they serve people almost from their own doors, and thus help many who are not reached by steam railroads. In some districts, such as the rich central plain of Ohio, Indiana, and Illinois, they not only take the suburban people to their work, but help the farmer get his products to market and his children to school. Electric railways can there be built and operated so cheaply and the population is so numerous and prosperous that interurban, as well as suburban, lines are common. With only an occasional change of cars one may travel hundreds of miles.

### QUESTIONS, EXERCISES, AND PROBLEMS

A. **Railroad mileage of the world.**
1. Let each pupil select one of the continents and explain why it has many or few railways (Fig. 133). Use the following outline:
    (a) Size of the continent
    (b) Number of people and their ability to pay for railborne goods
    (c) Recency of occupation by civilized people
    (d) Extent to which the resources have been developed
    (e) Extent to which oceanic and inland waterways make railroads unnecessary
    (f) Future prospects for railroad building
2. Explain this saying: "Railroad mileage is an index of civilization." How far does your study of railroads confirm it?
3. The growth of large cities has depended largely upon the inventions of such men as Watt, Stephenson, Bessemer, Pullman, and Westinghouse. Explain what this statement has to do with railways. Let members of the class report on what these men invented or discovered.
4. Make a diagram to illustrate the statement of railroad mileage given on page 183. Draw a line for each country mentioned, letting a quarter of an inch stand for one per cent.

B. **How relief and distribution of population have determined the location of the main railroads in the United States.**
1. Which do you consider more important in railroad building, the highest or lowest point in a mountain range? Why? Consider both business and pleasure. Point out places in New York, California, Colorado, and two foreign countries that prove your point.
2. Compare the map of the railroads in the United States (Fig. 134) with the map showing density of population (Fig. 164).
3. Explain the great difference in the railroad net in the eastern and western halves of the United States.
4. Which quarter of the country contains the densest network? Why?

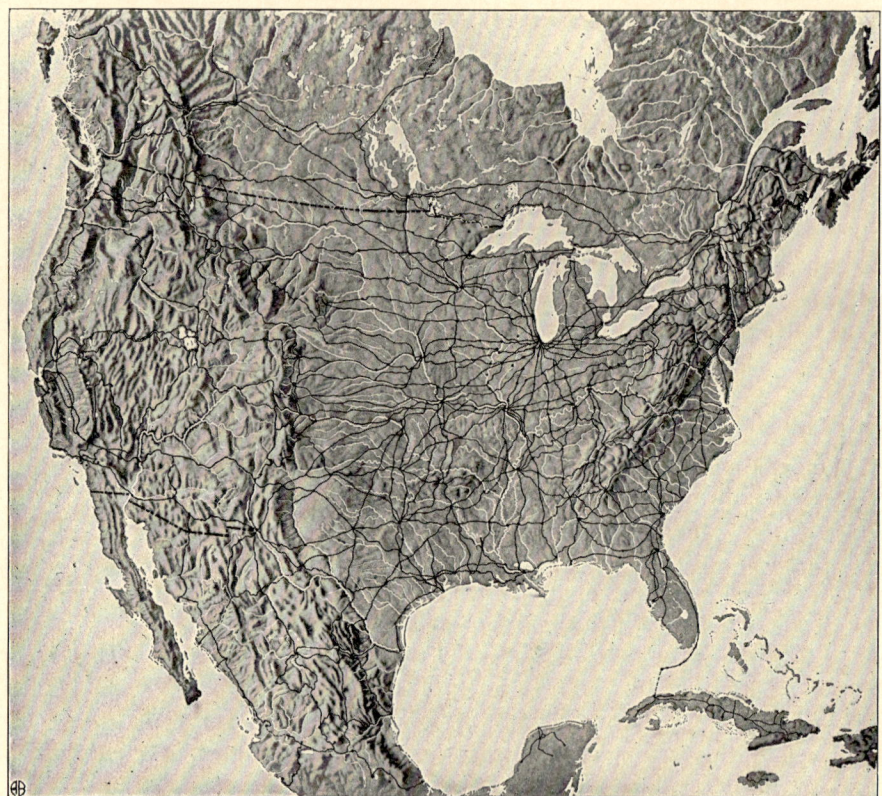

Fig. 134. Showing how the main railway lines of North America are related to the relief of the continent.

5. Name four transcontinental lines that connect the eastern half of the country with the cities on the western coast. In what cities does each line terminate? With what main eastern railroads does it connect?

6. Choose any one of the four lines and tell what states you would cross on your way to the Pacific coast. Describe the changes in scenery as you would view them from your car window. What differences would you notice in the occupations of the people from state to state?

7. Compare the routes of the two main lines that compete for the trade between our two largest cities. Which of these lines departs farther from a straight course? Why? What sort of relief is found along the shorter road? The shorter road has a local advantage that reduces its cost of operation and thus helps to make the expenses between New York and Chicago about the same as on the longer but more level route. What is it?

8. From time tables of the New York Central and Pennsylvania lines, list the large cities on each line between New York and Chicago, and find out how they compare in number and size.

## Railroads

C. **Railroad mileage by states.**

| | High Railroad Mileage | | | Low Railroad Mileage | |
|---|---|---|---|---|---|
| Rank | State | Mileage | Rank | State | Mileage |
| 1 | Texas | 16,085 | 37 | Arizona | 2,479 |
| 2 | Illinois | 12,126 | 38 | New Jersey | 2,352 |
| 3 | Pennsylvania | 11,657 | 39 | Maine | 2,269 |
| 4 | Iowa | 9,807 | 40 | Utah | 2,161 |
| 5 | Kansas | 9,386 | 41 | Massachusetts | 2,126 |
| 6 | Minnesota | 9,143 | 42 | Wyoming | 1,931 |
| 7 | Ohio | 9,012 | 43 | Maryland | 1,440 |
| 8 | Michigan | 8,888 | 44 | New Hampshire | 1,253 |
| 9 | New York | 8,389 | 45 | Vermont | 1,081 |
| 10 | California | 8,268 | 46 | Connecticut | 999 |
| 11 | Missouri | 8,193 | 47 | Delaware | 335 |
| 12 | Wisconsin | 7,609 | 48 | Rhode Island | 212 |

1. Let each pupil choose one state from each column and explain why the state holds a high or a low rank in railroad mileage. The following points, as well as others, should be considered:

   (a) Size of state  (d) Number of large cities  (g) Presence of transcontinental railways
   (b) Population  (e) Relief
   (c) Supply of freight  (f) Waterways  (h) Climate

D. **Regional railroads of the United States.**

1. How is the relief of the land indicated by the route taken by the Southern Pacific Railroad from the Puget Sound cities and Portland to San Francisco? Trace the course of the railroads in California and explain the routes they take from San Francisco.
2. Name three commodities which the states bordering the Gulf of Mexico supply to the Southern Railway Company.
3. Name five cities served by the Seaboard and Atlantic Coast lines.
4. What line carries New England's manufactured goods to the New York market?
5. Suppose all the railroad lines entering New York City were cut off. How soon would people be in distress for food? For what foods would they suffer first?

E. **Study of a local railroad.**

1. Visit a freight yard and observe a freight train. What railroads own the various cars? Where is each road located? From the location of the road and the kind of car, can you decide what commodity the car may have brought when it originally came to your vicinity?

2. Make a list of all the special types of railroad cars that you find. What are the reasons for each type of construction?

3. Note where the tracks are placed with reference to (a) waterways; (b) valleys or plains; (c) factories; (d) distributing houses; (e) retail stores; (f) residence districts.

4. What are the main cities through which the freight train observed by you has passed or will pass? Find out what a " division point " means on a railroad, and mark the division points on a map showing the line traversed by your freight train.

5. Find out how the number of freight trains on your railroad compares with the number of passenger trains. How many other kinds of trains traverse the line?

6. Look up the history of your railroad. When and why was it built? What were the chief difficulties in its construction?

7. What is the present financial condition of your railroad? Look up the values of its stocks and bonds in the financial pages of the newspaper.

8. Find out how many people the railroad employs in your town or city. List the different workers, as ticket agent, freight agent, etc., and explain briefly the work of each.

F. **How railroads are financed.**

1. Find out how the money is procured to build and equip railways. Try to ascertain how brokers and the stock market are connected with the matter. Study the lists of stocks and bonds in a newspaper and use them as the basis of a report on the degree of prosperity of various roads.

G. **The advantage of electrification of railways.**

1. In what way is the electrified railroad superior to the steam railroad for (a) city districts; (b) mountainous districts; (c) tourist and passenger traffic?

2. How does the use of the electric engine reduce the damage done by forest fires in the Rocky Mountain states?

3. What sections of the country can best use electric transportation developed from water power? How well are these sections supplied with coal?

4. New York does not permit the railroads to run steam locomotives into the city; electric engines are required. Why?

5. Investigate the electrification of some one railroad.

Fig. 135. Ships in the bay of Naples. In the background is Mt. Vesuvius.

## CHAPTER FIFTEEN

### THE USE OF SHIPS

Not many decades ago, wooden sailing vessels carried the whole of the world's commerce on the high seas, but now steel steamships carry the greater part of it. In almost every large harbor a few sailing vessels may indeed be seen; they are still extensively used to carry heavy, bulky goods, such as jute from Calcutta, grain and lumber from the west coast of North America, and nitrate of soda from Chile. But many of the sailing vessels now built have auxiliary steam power to take them through calms and into harbors. Only in small harbors or for the purposes of purely local trade is the wooden vessel still the principal carrier.

#### OCEAN TRAFFIC

No civilized country produces a sufficient variety of goods to satisfy all its own needs; every such country must draw upon other parts of the earth. Since three fourths of the earth's surface is water and the other fourth consists of detached land masses, the commodities from distant lands generally have to cross the water. If there is a choice between a land and a water route, the water route is generally chosen, because it is cheaper.

**How ocean liners differ from tramp steamers.** Just as express trains and locals, fast freights and slow freights, all run on the same railroad, so different kinds of steamships cross the ocean. One is known as the ocean "liner" because she keeps to the same line, or route, and plies on a regular schedule. Another is called the "tramp" steamer, or cargo boat, because she wanders from port to port wherever a cargo can be found.

We read about the liner in the newspapers because she carries the mails, advertises freely, and often brings well-known passengers. She makes a great impression when she arrives in a harbor, so huge, so stately, and so beautifully decorated; but the modest tramps carry a large part of the world's cargoes.

Some of the tramps are as large as small liners, although they do not look so because they lack the lofty decks amidships that accommodate passengers. Forward and aft the sides are high to meet the oncoming or pursuing waves. When heavily loaded, the tramps look dangerously low amidships; but they are completely "decked over" to prevent swamping in heavy seas. The deck is an almost continuous series of hatches, or trapdoors, leading to the hold. The great number of hatches and the low sides make it easy to load and unload quickly. Nine tenths of the interior of the latest type of tramp is cargo space.

**A year's voyage on a tramp.** How interesting it would be to live for a year on a tramp steamer! Suppose that we start from New York with wheat for Hamburg. At Hamburg our tramp takes on a half-million dollar cargo of beet sugar for Philadelphia. There it contracts to take railroad equipment to Yokohama via the Panama Canal. At Yokohama it stacks its hold full of bags of peanuts for Marseilles. In that port it secures a cargo of cans, kegs, and barrels of olive, coconut, and peanut oil for Buenos Aires. At Buenos Aires steamers are already engaged to take the available cargoes, so our tramp proceeds to Santos in ballast and there loads with coffee for New Orleans. At this busy port it is filled with bales of cotton for Manchester, England. It goes without cargo from that city to Glasgow, where it takes on structural steel and iron for Vancouver. Then it goes to Seattle for a cargo of lumber for Sydney, Australia, where it picks up a half-million dollar cargo of wool for Boston, proceeding via the Cape of Good Hope route and putting in at Cape Town to get coal for its engines.

Such is the year's work of our tramp. We have kept a record of only the chief cargo on each voyage. In addition to the chief cargo, our tramp loaded several hundred tons of miscellaneous cargo at nearly every port, and called at intermediate ports to leave or take on something else.

## The Use of Ships

**How the cargoes of tramps and liners differ.** During the next year our steamer may call at entirely different ports and handle entirely different cargoes, such as ores, coal, china clay, nitrate of soda, hemp, rice, and corn. Notice that these are all bulky raw commodities of low value in proportion to their weight. Hence they are likely to be shipped in great quantities, and a ship can often get a cargo composed of only a single product.

The liner, unlike the tramp, carries small quantities of a great variety of goods, besides passengers and mail. These are often manufactured goods, which are usually boxed for shipping and are of high value for their weight. They are collected from many different points and have many destinations. The principal routes for liners are between the chief ports of western Europe and (1) the northeastern ports of the United States, especially New York, (2) Buenos Aires and Rio de Janeiro, and (3) Asiatic ports and Australia via Suez. Less frequented liner routes run from (4) the Pacific ports of the United States to Japan and China, and (5) the eastern United States to eastern South America (Fig. 117).

Manufacturing countries, like England and Germany, need liners to carry away their finished products, and tramps to bring them food and raw materials. New countries, like Argentina, Australia, and South Africa, whose products are chiefly raw materials, need liners to bring them a variety of manufactured goods, and tramps to take away their exports.

*Canadian National Railways*

FIG. 136. At the lake ports the grain ships are loaded from the grain elevators by means of pipes through which the grain runs directly into the hold of the ship.

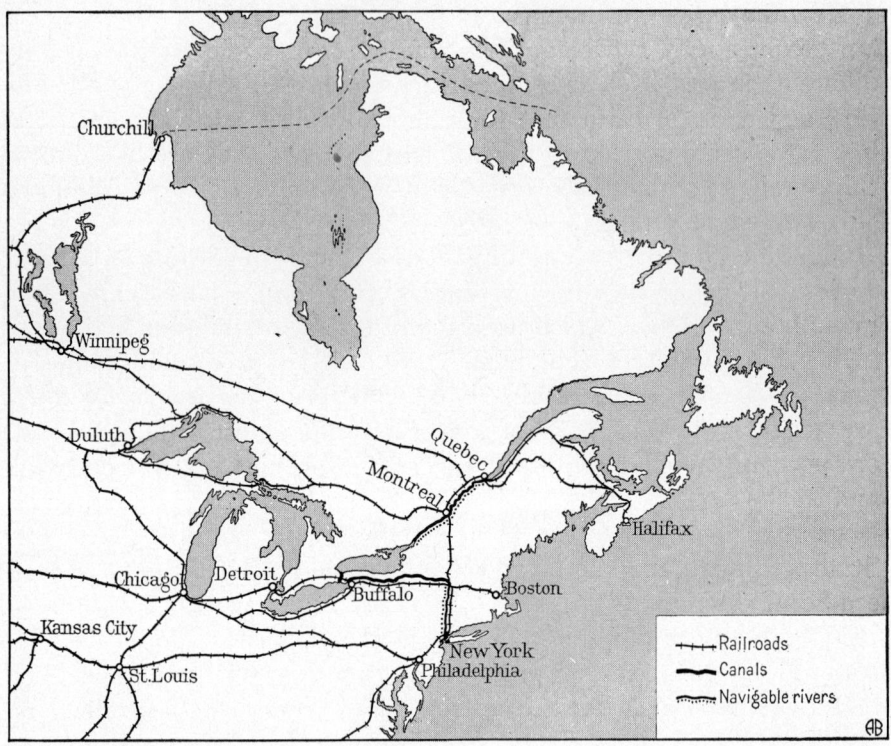

Fig. 137. This might be called the skeleton of the complex transportation system whereby the grain, ore, coal, and manufactured products of the northwest and middle west reach the Atlantic seaboard. The same region is given in greater detail in Figure 144 (page 204). How may iron ore from Duluth reach Buffalo? How may wheat from Winnipeg be shipped to Great Britain? meat from Chicago? motor cars from Detroit? How are imported goods transported from Boston to Detroit? from New York to Chicago?

### SHIPS ON THE GREAT LAKES

Among the chief natural blessings which the United States enjoys is its share of the Great Lakes. With a combined length of nearly 1500 miles and a shore line of about 4500 miles, they constitute the largest connected body of fresh water in the world.

The Great Lakes carry a greater tonnage of shipping than any other inland waterway. Their importance arises not only from their size but from their location and the direction of their longest dimensions. They lie in the heart of that part of the North American continent where the climate is most stimulating and where people are most active in farming, mining, and manufacturing. Their main axis extends east and west in the direction most convenient for trade.

**Why the Great Lakes are important for commerce.** Lock canals have been built around St. Mary's Falls between Lakes Superior and Huron, and around Niagara Falls between Lakes Erie and Ontario, and the limestone reefs of the Detroit River have been blasted out to form a deep ship channel. Hence the lakes can be navigated by large ships from Duluth at the head of Lake Superior, or from Chicago near the head of Lake Michigan, to the foot of Lake Ontario. From Buffalo the Erie Barge Canal makes connections with the Hudson River, while from the foot of Lake Ontario the St. Lawrence River connects with the Atlantic Ocean (Fig. 137).

The value of the Great Lakes as a waterway is increased by the fact that from their eastern end commerce finds an easy outlet through the Mohawk-Hudson valley to New York City. As far as the Hudson the valley contains the Erie Barge Canal, four tracks of the New York Central Railroad, two tracks of the West Shore Railroad, and two highways. These easy lines of communication have made the Great Lakes an important contributor to the growth of New York City.

**Why more freight moves east than west on the Great Lakes.** The movement of freight on the Great Lakes is largely from west to east. Not far west of Lake Superior, in Minnesota, Manitoba, and the Dakotas, lie some of the world's greatest wheat fields (Fig. 28). Around Lake Michigan are similar fields where corn as well as wheat is grown (Fig. 31). The grain raised on these western farms is carried eastward to be consumed in the Atlantic states or Europe. It forms a large part of the freight on the Great Lakes.

Iron ore also goes eastward. The richest and most extensive iron mines lie near Lake Superior, while vast beds of coal are found not far from Lake Erie in Pennsylvania and Ohio (Figs. 88, 98). Since about two tons of coal are needed to smelt a ton of iron ore, it is cheaper to carry the ore eastward to the coal than the coal westward to the ore. Moreover, the chief markets for the smelted pig iron and for the steel made from it are the Atlantic states and Europe, which is another reason for carrying the ore eastward.

In order that the ships which bring grain and ore from the west may have cargoes on their return voyages, the westward freight rate has been reduced until it is only about half as much as the eastward. This makes it worth while to carry millions of tons of soft coal to the Lake Superior region for use in smelting iron near the mines, and of hard coal from the eastern anthracite fields for house fuel through the Middle West. Yet in spite of the reduced rates, many of the westbound vessels go empty to the ports of the upper lakes where they get their grain and iron ore.

**Why the cost of transportation on the Great Lakes is low.** In order to get as much ore as possible into each vessel, special steamers are

Fig. 138. The ore boats, like the grain boats, are built especially to carry one kind of cargo, and are loaded by means of special loading devices that take the place of hundreds of laborers.

constructed. The engines are placed well aft and the pilot house and quarters for the crew well forward (Fig. 138). The chief expense in shipping by water is the cost of transshipping the cargo from cars to steamers, or back again. To reduce this expense at the ore ports of Duluth, Superior, Ashland, and elsewhere, the ore trains run out upon elevated docks where the ore is dumped from the cars directly into bins. From the bins it slides out through hatches into the hold of a steamer without any handling. A steamer can thus be loaded in less than an hour. At the end of the lake journey at such ports as Cleveland, Ashtabula, Erie, and Buffalo, huge self-filling grab-buckets, capable of lifting fifteen tons at a time, are let down into the hold, where they can scoop out an entire cargo of perhaps 14,000 tons in six hours.

So important is the commerce of these inland waters that it influences the cost of living not only among the millions of people who live near the lakes, but among those of the manufacturing regions of the North Atlantic states, England, and Germany. All these people consume goods carried on the lakes, and the goods are a trifle cheaper because of the low cost of transportation. Even the goods carried by the railroads are cheaper than they would be if there were not a cheap carrying service on the lakes, for the competition of the lake steamers keeps down the railway freight rates.

### BOATS ON RIVERS AND CANALS

Rivers and canals afford a cheap means of transportation far into the interior of the land, but their use requires a special kind of boat. Since most rivers are shallow in places, flat-bottomed boats have to be used. These boats do not sink into the water nearly so deep as do the round-bottomed ships that sail the oceans and lakes. The shallowness of the water also makes it necessary to use paddle wheels on the sides of the boats amidships, or in front, instead of propellers at the stern. Paddle boats are slower than those with propellers. The current also causes river navigation to be slow upstream.

Canals can be dug in almost any level plain, but at so great cost that it pays to build them only where there is sure to be a large amount of freight. Canal traffic is always slow; for if fast steamboats were used, the waves which they cause would soon wear away the banks and fill the canals. Often barges are used in great numbers, and are slowly drawn by tugboats, horses, donkeys, or even men. In densely populated plains like those of China, Japan, and Europe, even such slow transportation by inland waterways is important. If railroads are also present, as along the Vistula in Poland, the canals are used chiefly for bulky, non-perishable commodities such as ores, sand and gravel, cement, and lumber.

**Our most important inland waterways.** The map suggests that the Mississippi River should be the most important navigable waterway of North America aside from the Great Lakes. It is navigable for large steamers and barges at all seasons to St. Louis, 1256 miles from the mouth, and for smaller boats most of the year to St. Paul,

FIG. 139. Flat-bottomed boats that draw little water are used to haul barges in canals and shallow rivers.

Fig. 140. Locks at Waterford, the eastern terminus of the Erie Barge Canal. The old locks of the Erie Canal are seen at the right. Note the difference in size.

nearly 2000 miles from the mouth. Nevertheless, in commercial importance among our inland waterways it is exceeded not only by the Great Lakes but by the Erie Barge Canal and the Hudson and Ohio rivers.

One difficulty with the Mississippi River is that it flows in the wrong direction. If it flowed eastward from the heart of the United States to the Atlantic Ocean, it might be one of the busiest rivers in the world. As it is, it gives relatively little assistance to the interior states in marketing their products or in bringing manufactured goods from the northeastern United States and western Europe.

The work of connecting the central plains with the eastern part of the United States is largely done by railroads which cross the Appalachian Mountains. The railroads are assisted, however, by the Erie Barge Canal and the Hudson River, both of which run in the right direction for commerce. As far as Albany the Hudson River is an almost ideal waterway even for large boats, while the Erie Barge Canal is deep enough so that with the Hudson River it stands second to the Great Lakes among our inland waterways.

The Ohio River and its two tributaries, the Monongahela and the Allegheny, are also of some importance as waterways. Their importance springs chiefly from the presence of enormous deposits of coal near their banks and the great demand for this mineral in such river cities as Pittsburgh and Cincinnati.

**Why canals are numerous in Europe.** The American traveler in Europe is surprised at the number of canals. As he rides in a swiftly moving train with its load of passengers, mail, and express, he not infrequently may whiz past a line of slowly moving canal boats laden with heavy freight like coal, bricks, and cement. In Europe, railways and canals frequently run side by side, for wherever it is easy to locate a canal it is also easy to build railway tracks. Both means of transportation can prosper, since they carry different kinds of freight and compete with one another relatively little.

The canals and navigable rivers of Europe are so numerous that canal boats can take on loads at Marseilles, for instance, and deliver them a thousand miles away at Breslau. An intricate system of more than 150,000 miles of canals and navigable rivers covers the northern lowlands of Europe. From western France through Belgium, Holland, and Germany practically all the important rivers are connected by canals. There is even a limited canal connection between the principal rivers of Russia as far eastward as the Ural Mountains.

**Why the use of American canals has declined.** Nearly five thousand miles of canals have been constructed in the United States, but less than half of this mileage is now in use. This decline is due largely to the following causes:

(1) Canal transportation has proved too slow to meet the needs of the impatient American.

(2) The depth of water varies from canal to canal, which necessitates much transshipment, entailing great delay and expense; in a country as large as the United States, uninterrupted through traffic is very important.

(3) The winter suspension of traffic due to ice is particularly prolonged in the canals of the central and northeastern parts of the country.

(4) Canal traffic has often been forced to take roundabout routes because of the limited development of the canal system.

(5) By far the most important cause of the decline of canals, however, has been competition with the railroads. As railroads spread over the country, they were found to be largely free from the four drawbacks mentioned above; and this drove out of business the canals that were not particularly well located. About half the canals, however, especially the Erie Canal, were so well located that they survived.

**Our chief canals.** The Erie Barge Canal, the longest in the United States, replaces the old Erie Canal. With a depth of 12 feet and a bottom width of 75, it enables barges of 2000 tons capacity to go from Troy on the Hudson River to Lake Erie and Lake Ontario. A branch extends from Troy to Lake Champlain, and thence to the St. Lawrence

River. The tendency of the barge canal and its branches is to cheapen transportation from New York City to the Great Lakes and Canada.

The St. Mary's Canals, commonly called the "Soo"[1] Canals, allow ships to pass from Lake Superior to Lake Huron around St. Mary's Falls, which drop twenty feet in three fourths of a mile. A canal with one lock, built by Canada, lies north of the falls, while south of them are two American canals with four locks. The tonnage of freight passing through these canals is enormous. Each year nearly a hundred million tons of freight pass through the three canals. This is four times the tonnage passing through the Suez Canal and almost equals that handled by New York City. The value, however, is much less than at Suez or New York, for the merchandise consists principally of iron ore, lumber, and coal — bulky goods of low value.

**How the canals vary in their purposes.** Canals have various purposes. Some, like the Soo Canals, are cut to avoid rapids or falls. The Welland Canal in Canada between Lake Erie and Lake Ontario, avoiding Niagara Falls, is another example of this type.

Other canals shorten long or dangerous voyages. For example, the Suez Canal, which permits Europe to trade with the Orient and Australia without sending ships around the Cape of Good Hope, is a great carrier of the commerce of the oceans. The Kiel Canal, connecting the Baltic Sea with the North Sea, avoids the long route around the peninsula of Denmark. The Cape Cod Canal across the base of Cape Cod, Massachusetts, allows ships to save one hundred miles and avoid a dangerous part of the route between New York and Boston.

Still other canals allow inland cities to become seaports. The Manchester Ship Canal, in western England, permits ocean steamships to carry cotton thirty-five miles inland to Manchester. Another good illustration is in Texas, where Houston is trying to get part of Galveston's cotton shipping business. Houston has the advantage of being a railroad center and of lying nearer the cotton fields than does Galveston (Fig. 5). By building a canal and a "basin" in the level plain it gains also some of the advantages of being a seaport.

## The Panama Canal

**The difficulties of building the canal.** To many persons the most interesting of the world's artificial waterways is the Panama Canal. It was built by the United States at a cost of $400,000,000 and was the largest single piece of engineering ever undertaken by any govern-

---

[1] From the French name for the passage between the lakes — the Sault Ste. Marie.

ment. A channel 41 feet deep, 800 feet wide, and 50 miles in length had to be cut, largely in solid rock. Twelve pairs of locks had to be built so that the largest vessels could be lifted over a ridge from one

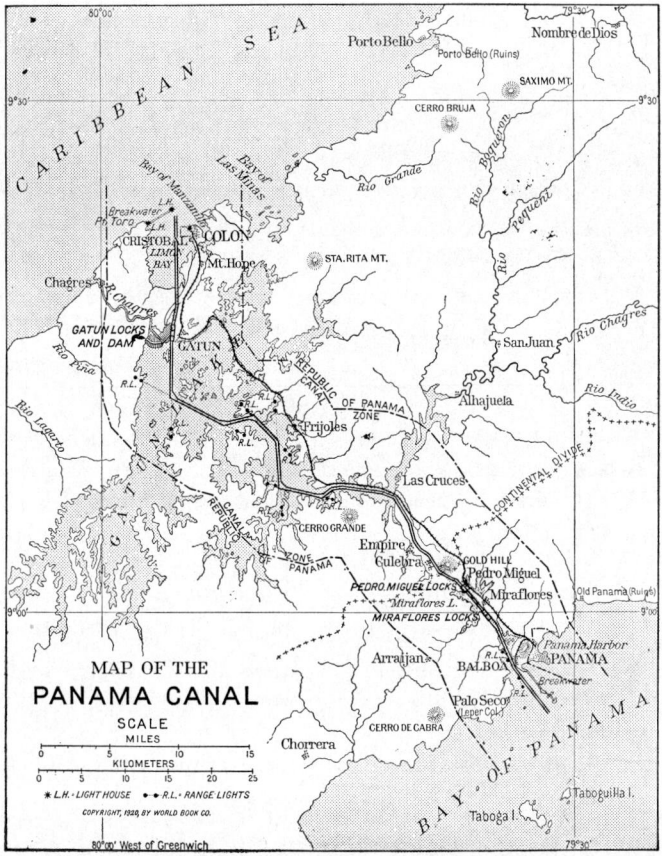

FIG. 141. The Panama Canal is about 50 miles long. The locks, which are at Gatun near the Atlantic and at Pedro Miguel and Miraflores near the Pacific, will accommodate the largest ships afloat. The canal took ten years to build. About the same tonnage now passes through it annually as goes through the Suez Canal.

ocean to the other. The ridge itself was cut down from 700 feet above sea level to 85 feet. A dam nearly a mile and a half long was constructed to control the floods of the torrential Chagres River and to turn its valley into a great lake, now used as part of the canal. Both the dam and the lake are the greatest of their kind ever made by man.

The engineering difficulties might have been overcome by the French when they attempted to build the canal, about thirty years before the United States undertook it. But at that time it was difficult for native laborers to live at Panama, and almost impossible for white

Fig. 142. Looking south over Miraflores Locks, in the Panama Canal.

men. The greatest achievement of the canal builders was the employment, for the first time, of modern knowledge of sanitation in connection with a great enterprise in the tropics. This made it possible for a large body of engineers and workmen to avoid the tropical diseases that usually attack the inhabitants of that region, and thus to live in good health.

**Where the ships at Panama come from.** Four chief routes traverse the canal and connect the following regions:

(1) The Atlantic and Pacific coasts of the United States.
(2) Europe and the Pacific coast of North America.
(3) The west coast of South America and the Atlantic coast of the United States and Europe.
(4) The Atlantic coast of the United States and the Far East, including Japan, China, the Philippines, Australia, and New Zealand.

**How the canal saves time, money, and distance.** On all these routes the canal saves greatly in both time and money. Take, for instance, an example from the first route. As soon as the canal was open, the liner *Arizonan* began to ply between the Atlantic and Pacific coasts of the United States. The canal route saves this ship 26.8 days on each voyage as compared with the route around South America.

Since it then cost about $450 a day to operate the vessel, the saving for 26.8 days amounted to $12,060. From this sum canal tolls of $7981.20 had to be subtracted, leaving a net saving of $4168.80 for each voyage. Today, since the cost of running the ship has increased, the saving has also increased.

One of the best indications of how the canal benefits seaborne trade may be seen in the following examples of the number of miles saved between ports on each of its four chief routes:

| Route | Miles Saved |
|---|---|
| (1) New York and San Francisco | 7873 |
| (2) San Francisco and Liverpool | 5666 |
| (3) Valparaiso and New York | 3717 |
| (4) New York and Yokohama | 3768 |

**How the Panama Canal benefits the people of the United States.** The great reason for building the Panama Canal was to secure the benefits which it confers upon the United States.

(1) *It keeps down prices.* As the cost of transportation is lowered, the prices of goods that come through the canal are also lowered. This does not mean that the prices are actually lower than formerly, but lower than they would presumably have been had not the canal been built. Thus the canal is believed to have prevented the prices of canned salmon and canned peaches, for instance, from rising as high as they otherwise would have risen in our eastern markets; while the price of coal on the Pacific coast has probably soared less than would otherwise have happened. The prices of nitrates for the southern farmers, and of bamboo and rattan for the furniture makers of the northeastern United States, have likewise been kept down. In the same way the canal tends to cheapen kerosene in China, wheat in England, and manufactured goods in western South America.

(2) *The canal has stimulated the trade of Gulf seaports and Mississippi waterways.* Gulf ports, such as New Orleans and Galveston, are growing in importance because of the traffic given them by the Panama Canal. These ports handle goods passing between the great Mississippi basin and the Pacific coast or the Orient — goods that were formerly handled by New York and Seattle. This traffic may in time lead to the improvement of the Mississippi River so that the cheap water route may continue even to Pittsburgh, Chicago, Minneapolis, and Omaha.

(3) *The canal brings North and South America together.* Since the canal was built, the Pacific coast of South America has been more easily within reach of the Atlantic cities of the United States than of the European cities which formerly supplied it

almost exclusively with their much needed manufactured goods. It is surprising to note on the map, or better on a globe, how nearly the Pacific coast of South America lies due south from the Atlantic coast of North America. Florida seems to point directly to the Panama Canal and the west coast of Colombia, Ecuador, Peru, and Chile.

(4) *The canal protects the United States in war.* If the United States should ever go to war again, the Panama Canal would enable the Atlantic and Pacific battleship fleets quickly to unite on either coast.

#### QUESTIONS, EXERCISES, AND PROBLEMS

A. **The ships of a great port.**

1. From the *New York Times* or some other newspaper that gives shipping news, clip the list of steamships arriving in New York. Indicate on an outline map the starting point of each ship. Compare the length of time of their voyages. Pick out three that you think are tramp steamers, and explain your choice.

2. What might reasonably be supposed to be the cargo of each of the ships arriving? Other geographies or an encyclopedia may help you to make reasonable suppositions. Make entries in your notebook in this way:

| Name of Ship | Port of Departure | Possible Cargo | Sailing Time |
| --- | --- | --- | --- |
| Columbia | Bristol, England | Coal; and steel manufactures | 18 days |

3. A steamship company must pay for the following expenses and equipment: (a) hulls and their fittings; (b) engines and other machinery; (c) fuel; (d) wages of crews; (e) wharves and docks; (f) agents, office expenses, and advertising. What corresponding items does a railroad pay for? What extra expenses must it meet that make transportation by rail more expensive than by steamship?

4. The North Atlantic liner route is mapped out on a double-track plan for eastbound and westbound vessels. What is the advantage of this? Both lanes are shifted southward at a certain season. When is this done, and why?

B. **The study of a harbor.**

1. A great deal is done to make harbors safe and convenient for shipping. Is this done by the United States, the local municipal government, or the state government? What are "port works"? Explain: buoy, lighthouse, jetty, breakwater, channel. Why must dredging and blasting be done in some harbors?

2. The Coast and Geodetic Survey, Washington, D. C., has maps of some ports. Let a member of the class write for a map of the port with

# The Use of Ships

which your city has the most direct communication, or take any of the great sea or lake ports of the country. Study the map and note the meaning of each of its symbols. Carry out a class exercise based on the map, appointing a committee to plan the exercise.

3. If you live near a port, visit the harbor and take notes concerning the kinds of vessels lying there. Visit the docks and note the cargoes that are being discharged and loaded. Ask the captain or other officer of one of the vessels about his ship and its cargo; take notes on the following points:

   (a) Name of vessel
   (b) Type of vessel
   (c) Home port
   (d) Length of voyage
   (e) Cargo discharging
   (f) Origin of cargo
   (g) Why such a cargo was available there
   (h) Why such a cargo is wanted in this port
   (i) Where the cargo is now to go
   (j) What cargo is to be taken on
   (k) Where this new cargo comes from
   (l) Where the vessel is to take it
   (m) Why such a cargo is needed at that port
   (n) How long the voyage is likely to be

4. Ships from foreign ports cannot slip in and out of the harbor at will. Certain regulations are enforced for the protection of the country to which the harbor belongs or in its interest. Let individuals or sections of the class make brief reports on the following topics:

   (a) Quarantine regulations
   (b) Immigrant inspection
   (c) The Public Health and Marine Hospital Service
   (d) The work of the Collector of the Port
   (e) The harbor
   (f) Clearance papers, and why a ship's captain must obtain them before sailing

## C. A voyage on a tramp steamer.

1. From the ten trips on the tramp steamer described on page 190, select the one which you would prefer to take and prepare to discuss it before the class according to the following plan:
   (a) What cargo was taken on at the port of departure
   (b) Why such a cargo was available at that port
   (c) The names and locations of the oceans, seas, gulfs, straits, and canals passed through during the trip
   (d) Why this cargo was needed at the port of arrival

2. Plan to take the tramp steamer *Bristol City* on a two-trip voyage. Decide the ports of departure, the cargoes, routes, ports of arrival, and dates. Bring your plan to the class and let the members discuss it to see if it is reasonable in all respects.

3. Who wants to organize a steamship company? Let several members of the class form a committee to organize a steamship company for trade with South America. The home port, the foreign port, and the ports of call must be selected carefully to insure success. In the report to the

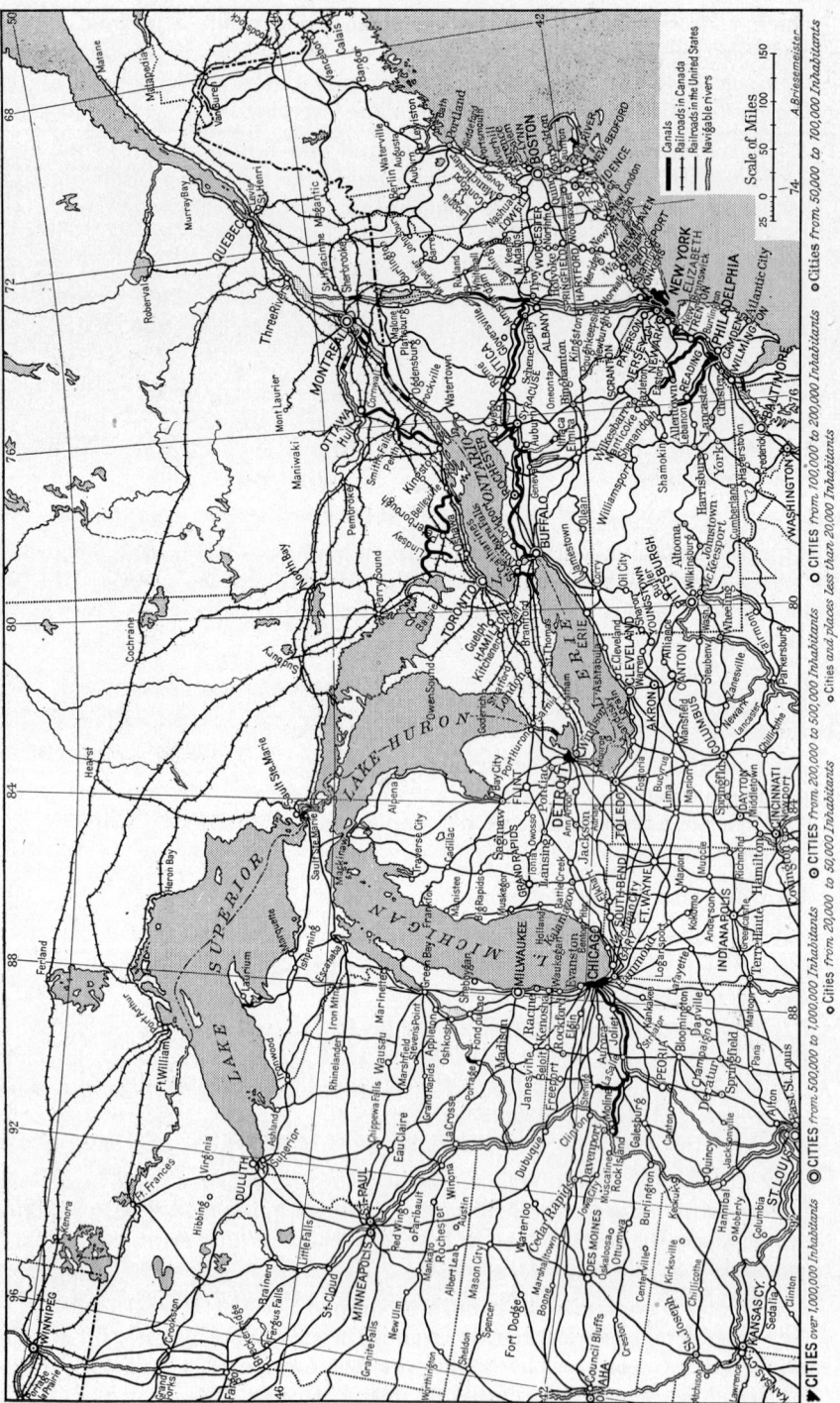

FIG. 143. Railways and waterways between the Atlantic seacoast and the middle west. Except where the cities are very closely crowded together, as in the suburbs of New York and Boston, all cities of 20,000 inhabitants or more are shown, and also a few others that are chiefly cities of importance as railroad junctions.

class, the committee will give the reasons for the selections and will tell the type of cargo that will be carried, so that the other members may be induced to invest in the company.

D. **Chief cargoes carried over routes through the Panama Canal.**

1. The leading commodities shipped through the canal, in the order of their tonnage, are mineral oils, lumber, wheat, ores, and nitrates. Why would you expect these commodities to lead in tonnage, rather than such goods as structural steel, canned goods, clothing, and straw matting?

2. Select one commodity shipped on each of the four routes listed below. Find out (*a*) the country that probably produced the commodity; (*b*) the probable port of shipment; (*c*) the country to which it is probably being shipped; (*d*) the probable importing port. In reporting to the class, use a map of the world or a large globe to show the full journey of the commodity. Explain your decisions, so that the class may judge of their reasonableness.

| Route | Eastbound | Westbound |
| --- | --- | --- |
| I. United States coastwise | Canned fruit, canned salmon, lumber, pineapples, sugar, petroleum | Coal, structural steel, machinery, a great variety of manufactured goods |
| II. Pacific coast of North America to Europe | Wheat, barley, canned fruit, canned salmon, lumber | Coal, structural steel, great variety of manufactured goods |
| III. West coast of South America to the United States and Europe | Nitrates, iron ore, petroleum, sugar, wool, lumber | Machinery, structural steel, clothing, great variety of manufactured goods |
| IV. Atlantic coast of the United States to the Far East | Straw matting, curios, rattan, bamboo, cinnamon, peanut oil, silk, tea, wool | Kerosene, raw cotton, machinery, great variety of manufactured goods |

3. The tonnage shipped through the canal from one coast of the United States to the other is nearly as great as the combined tonnage of the remaining routes. Why is this?

E. **The Great Lakes.**

1. Draw a map of the Great Lakes. First trace the outline a few times. Then locate a few points and sketch the outline from memory. Print on your map the names of the lake cities mentioned in the text. Indicate the Soo and Welland canals. Mark the position of the iron mines near Lake Superior.

2. The men who move the iron ore have this motto: " Up by steam and down by gravity." Explain how this applies (*a*) in the iron ranges; (*b*) at the Superior docks; (*c*) at Cleveland; (*d*) at Pittsburgh.

Fig. 144. The three lines represent the tonnage that passes through the Soo Canals, the Suez Canal, and the Panama Canal in an average year. If the lines represented the value of the cargoes that passed through, would the line for the Soo Canals be so much longer than the others?

3. On what part of a journey by water from New York to Duluth would there be fewest passengers? Why? At what cities would you change boats? Why? What freight would your boat be likely to pick up at each large city along the route?
4. Take a similar journey from Chicago to Quebec. Name at least seven bodies of water and six large cities that you would pass.
5. One commodity comprises 85 per cent of the westbound traffic through the Soo Canals. What commodity is it? Why is it shipped in such quantities?
6. Why do Duluth and Superior use Pennsylvania coal when Illinois and Indiana have plenty of coal not nearly so far away? Explain how the railroads running to Duluth and Superior benefit from the cheap Pennsylvania coal on the docks there, even when they do not carry it as freight.

F. **The effect of the Mississippi on transportation.**
1. By far the larger part of the traffic from St. Louis south to New Orleans goes by rail instead of by the Mississippi River. Yet the river is important to transportation because for bulky articles like coal and cement it serves as a " sword of Damocles " hanging over the heads of the railroads. Explain this statement. What canals have you studied that are a means of regulating railroad rates?
2. Water transport in the United States is unpopular because of the cost of transshipment. Show how the railroad is superior in this respect.

G. **The relation of governments to transportation by water.**
1. Explain how the government helps transportation by each of the following means: (a) the Rivers and Harbors Bill passed each year by Congress, usually carrying appropriations of about $50,000,000 or more; (b) the Panama Canal; (c) the charts of the United States Coast and Geodetic Survey; (d) the Weather Bureau; (e) the Lighthouse Bureau of the Department of Commerce; (f) the Coast Guard Service.
2. Find out what a ship subsidy is. In your notebook write a paragraph on " Advantages of Ship Subsidies," and another on " Disadvantages of Ship Subsidies."
3. According to the laws of the United States, all traffic between different ports of the United States must be carried in vessels flying the United States flag, which means those registered as belonging to this country. Does this encourage Japanese steamers to carry freight to Hawaii when on their way in either direction across the Pacific?

## CHAPTER SIXTEEN

### TRANSPORTATION AND THE LOCATION OF CITIES IN THE UNITED STATES

IMPORTANT commercial cities are usually located where main lines of transportation cross one another or where two different kinds of transportation meet. This is particularly the case where land routes meet water routes. At such places all the passengers who come by either land or water usually have to stop at least a few hours, and often stay some days before going on by the other means of transportation. More important still, all the freight that arrives by railroad and is to be shipped by water, for instance, not only must be unloaded but must usually be stored in warehouses until a ship is ready to proceed toward the proper destination. Moreover, the people who live in such a place do a great deal of business for those who live elsewhere. They import goods from across the water and sell them to the people who live along the various inland routes that diverge from the port. Or they purchase goods from customers along the inland routes and sell them abroad. Thus places where ocean routes meet land routes are the most favorable for the growth of great cities.

**The kind of harbor that attracts ocean traffic.** A distance of a few miles more or less makes little difference in the cost of transportation by water. Hence ships do not try to save expense by going to the nearest port of the country where they wish to leave their freight and passengers, but to the port from which they can most cheaply ship their loads to their destination.

The character of a harbor has a great influence upon the expense of shipment. The best kind of harbor has five characteristics:

(1) It is readily reached from the sea. Some harbors are especially easy to enter; for example, at Hongkong ships can sail almost up to the docks without a pilot and can easily enter the harbor either from the north or the south, for there is a clear, open channel safely protected between the mainland and the island. San Francisco and Brest are equally fortunate in this respect. At New Orleans, Calcutta, and Guayaquil, on the other hand, the windings and sandbars of the rivers make a pilot necessary for nearly a day before the port is reached.

(2) A good harbor also affords protection from wind and waves. In order to give great protection, breakwaters are often built to shut out the harbor from the open sea.

(3) A harbor ought also to have plenty of room and the right depth for anchorage. Since a good-sized steamship draws 30 feet or

more, mud or sand must often be dredged from the harbor floor. Dredgers are at work all the time at Philadelphia, New York, Boston, and many other ports. There must also be ample room for vessels to turn about and to swing at anchor. For this reason ledges in the midst of harbors are often blasted away, as at New York. Too deep a harbor, however, is bad, because it does not afford anchorage.

(4) Convenient space for docks, warehouses, and other buildings is likewise necessary. On the edge of the water there must be level land on which warehouses and other buildings can be erected. The harbor of Baltimore is fortunate in this respect. In such places as Boston, Buenos Aires, and Manila, where dredging has been carried on to make places for docks, the mud and sand dredged from the bottom have been used to fill up the shallow parts of the bay close to the land.

(5) A good harbor is free from ice. Since ships cannot move freely in the ice, harbors like those of Montreal and Riga must often be kept open by ice-breakers. No ports in the United States suffer much in this respect.

**How a prosperous hinterland helps a seaport to grow.** Even though a harbor is excellent and is the meeting place of many inland routes, a great city will grow up only if these routes penetrate a region which is prosperous. In that case the city collects abundant products of the fields, forests, mines, or factories of the interior and exchanges them for the goods of other regions. The region from which a city receives goods for exchange with other parts of the world is called its *hinterland;* Baltimore, for example, owes much of its growth and wealth to the fact that the land that lies behind (*hinter*) it is extensive and productive.

### THE SEAPORTS OF THE UNITED STATES

Transportation by water is so important that the majority of the world's great cities are located on waterways. In the United States more than one person out of every five lives in a port of some sort, either on the ocean, or on a lake or river. Of the people that live in cities with a population of more than 200,000, more than 15,000,000 live in the fourteen largest seaports, nearly 8,000,000 in seven lake ports, and about 4,000,000 in nine river ports. On the other hand, only 2,800,000 live in the eleven cities of more than 200,000 population which are not on waterways (page 330).

The ocean ports of the United States are all located where harbors make it possible for ships to come close to the land in safety, and where valleys or plains permit easy access to the interior. In practically all the ports, the harbors are bays or river mouths where

**Some of the reasons why New York has grown great.** New York, the "gateway of America," is a most impressive example of the way in which a great city grows up under the combined influence of a good harbor for ocean transportation, a rich hinterland full of energetic people, and easy routes of inland communication. The spacious and beautiful harbor is almost unexcelled in its natural advantages, but every year the national and city governments spend millions of dollars dredging deeper channels, and building new piers.

The hinterland includes the factory cities of the North Atlantic coast, the coal fields of Pennsylvania, the grain fields of the northern Mississippi basin, the cattle ranches of the Middle West, and even the

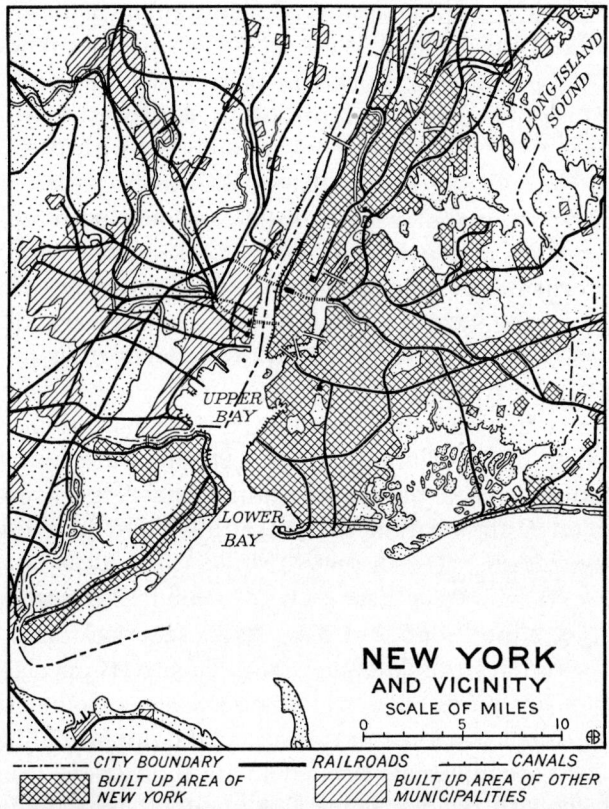

FIG. 145. New York harbor affords anchorage for sea-going vessels for fifteen miles from the mouth of the Hudson River. The city has the disadvantage of being on a long, narrow island, which makes it difficult for railroads to approach the center. Note the tunnel which affords through train service from New England to points west and south of New York. Another tunnel and the great George Washington Bridge enable vehicles to travel from one side of the Hudson to the other.

mines and orchards of the Far West. To and from these regions all kinds of products are easily transported.

**The routes that connect New York with its hinterland.** The chief route from New York runs northward up the Hudson and then westward along the Mohawk valley to the shores of the Great Lakes and beyond. This is much the easiest route across the Appalachian Mountains. It is followed by two railroads, the New York Central and the West Shore. The waterways of the navigable Hudson River and the Erie Barge Canal follow the same course. The Hudson-Mohawk route is so easy and important that it has been called the highway of the continent.

The other routes from New York westward are not so easy, for they cross the rugged regions of northern New Jersey, eastern Pennsylvania, and western New York. Nevertheless they are followed by three railroads: the Erie; the Delaware, Lackawanna, and Western; and the New York, Ontario, and Western. Two of the main routes by which products reach New York run parallel to the coast, one going northeast to New England and the other southwest to Philadelphia and Baltimore. Much of New York's commerce with the West passes via Philadelphia over the Pennsylvania Railroad.

It is not surprising that with so great and productive a hinterland and so many ways of reaching it, New York harbor carries on more than 50 per cent of the total foreign commerce of the United States. Nor is it surprising that such great cities as Newark, Jersey City, Paterson, and Yonkers have grown up as suburbs of New York, and share most of its advantages.

**Other great cities and their relation to transportation.** The other important ports of the United States well illustrate how cities grow up where routes from a productive hinterland reach a good harbor. In the order of their location the most important of these ports are Boston, Philadelphia, Baltimore, Norfolk, New Orleans, Galveston, Houston, Los Angeles, San Francisco, Portland, and Seattle.

**Why Boston is the " hub " of New England.** Boston is on a splendid harbor at the head of Massachusetts Bay. Its special hinterland includes nearly all parts of New England, except Connecticut. This whole region calls upon Boston to market its varied manufactures, or to furnish the raw materials needed in its industries. Since Boston has some trade with regions as far away as the Great Plains and Canada, it has a share in a hinterland far larger than New England; yet primarily Boston, once jokingly called the " Hub of the Universe," is merely the " hub " of New England.

In spite of its many railroads radiating outward like the spokes of a wheel, and its steamship lines radiating to all parts of the world, Boston cannot rival New York. When the Hoosac Tunnel was cut through Hoosac Mountain in the northwestern corner of Massachusetts in 1874, thus shortening the distance by rail between Boston and the Mohawk valley, it was thought that the grain and meat of the fertile Middle West would be brought to Boston on their way to the European market. Only small quantities of these products, however, are sent through Boston, although the route from Chicago to Europe is 180 miles shorter via Boston than via New York. The heavy railroad grades between Boston and the Hudson-Mohawk valley explain a part of Boston's disappointment, while the rest is largely due to New York's better harbor and to that city's location nearer to the food-producing plains of the West and South.

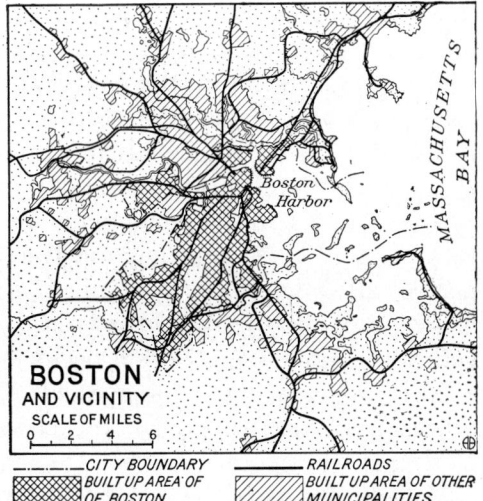

FIG. 146. Boston has an excellent harbor and is so situated that lines of communication can radiate from it. But it has no such river as the Hudson.

**Why Philadelphia is the third largest city in the United States.** Let us answer two questions in regard to Philadelphia: (1) Why has it grown to such great size? (2) Why is it not so large as New York?

One reason for Philadelphia's growth is its position on a good river harbor at the head of Delaware Bay. Another reason is that this harbor is the most convenient from which to ship the soft coal of western Pennsylvania to the manufacturing cities of the New England coast. The hard coal of the Scranton and Wilkes Barre region in eastern Pennsylvania can go to New York as easily as to Philadelphia, but the soft coal comes to Philadelphia, chiefly over the Pennsylvania Railroad, which crosses the Appalachian Mountains in the level valley of the Susquehanna. This Susquehanna route has more to do with Philadelphia's present prosperity than has the city's location at the junction of the Delaware and Schuylkill rivers.

Three geographical reasons have helped to prevent Philadelphia from becoming as large as New York. First, although the Susquehanna River provides a good route through the ridges of the Appalachians, it does not furnish a level path, like the Mohawk valley, through the Allegheny plateau. Hence west of Altoona the Pennsylvania Railroad must wind up the face of the escarpment over the Horseshoe Curve and then twist and turn for many miles in getting down to Pittsburgh. This is a disadvantage like that which the Berkshire hills in western Massachusetts impose on Boston. Another disadvantage is that the harbor of Philadelphia is not so deep or so easy to enter as that of New York, and has much less space for docks. Finally, the port of Philadelphia is 150 miles farther from Europe than is New York. No one of these disadvantages is perhaps great, but all together they give New York a decided advantage.

Nevertheless, Philadelphia stands second in size among the seaports of America, and among all the cities of the New World only New York and Chicago are larger.

**How Baltimore is helped by the water and hindered by the land.** The relation of Baltimore to Philadelphia is almost like that of Philadelphia to New York. Baltimore has a good harbor which has been much improved by dredging. Incidentally the harbor permits Baltimore to profit from a thriving oyster fishing business in Chesapeake Bay. The city is also helped by the Potomac River, which gives a nearly level route across part of the Appalachian Mountains. Here, just as at Philadelphia, the main railroad follows a river that enters a bay west of that which affords the city access to the ocean.

Baltimore's transportation facilities are hampered by the land. The peninsula of Delaware, east of the bay, obliges ships bound for Europe to go 160 miles south and then to sail an equal distance back toward the northeast before they reach a position as good as that of a ship starting from New York. On the inland side of Baltimore, the route up the Potomac is more difficult than that up the Susquehanna and cannot compare with the Hudson-Mohawk route. Thus Baltimore, although it has a fine hinterland in its immediate vicinity, does not draw extensively on the interior plains or the Great Lakes region. For shipping soft coal to the South and for southern trade in general it has a fine location, and this helps to make it one of the country's chief cities.

**The other end of Chesapeake Bay.** The trade of Chesapeake Bay is divided between the two ends. Philadelphia gets the most, but a good deal passes through Norfolk and the neighboring cities of Portsmouth and Newport News. By far the most important article of export here is coal from the mines of West Virginia, more than a million tons a month. Half of all the tobacco that we send abroad also goes from here, and many ships carry fresh vegetables to New York.

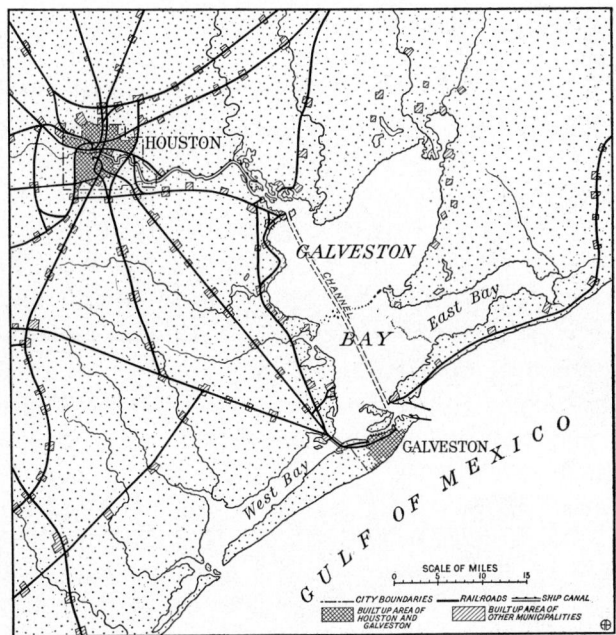

Fig. 147. Both Houston and Galveston show what can be done to improve a port. Houston could not be called a seaport if it were not for the ship canal which has been dredged out; and Galveston has made her harbor by building breakwaters and jetties.

**How New Orleans is favorably situated.** New Orleans is the meeting point of ocean lines, routes along the Mississippi valley both by water and by land, and railroads both from the East and the West. Its location on the broad Mississippi, a hundred miles from its mouth, gives it a good river harbor, while its commercial hinterland includes a large part of the cotton-growing region of the South. Although the Mississippi and a number of its tributaries are navigable, the cotton is collected almost exclusively by rail. With the increasing use of the Panama Canal, the hinterland of New Orleans is being extended to include portions of the northern Mississippi valley, and the city's importance is increasing correspondingly. New Orleans exports far more than it imports, for the limited wants of the cotton farmers are supplied largely by local and northern markets.

**The importance of Galveston as a port.** Galveston and Houston provide by far the most important outlet for American cotton. This is largely because Texas raises a fourth or even a third of the cotton of the United States. The hinterland of the two cities also furnishes exports of wheat, flour, and meat. The city shows what man can do in providing shipping facilities if the hinterland is sufficiently productive. Galveston was founded on a low, sandy island that separated

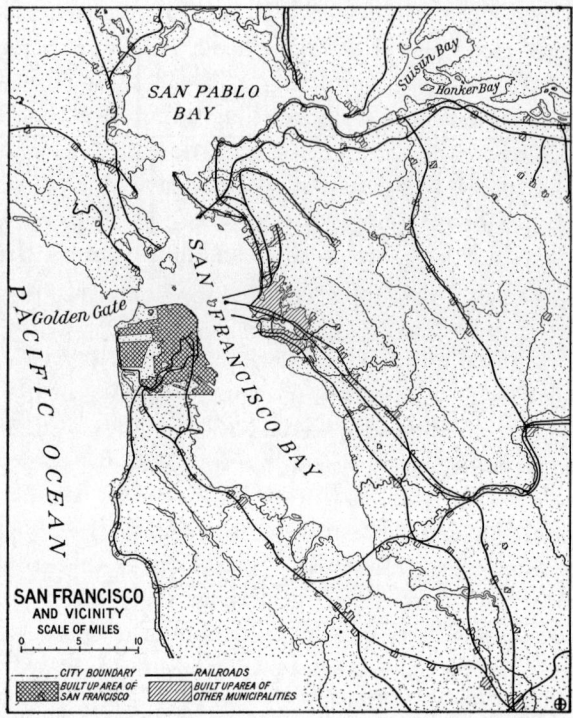

Fig. 148. San Francisco is built on a magnificent landlocked harbor. The transcontinental lines have their terminals at the ferry landings in Oakland, on the opposite side of the bay.

a shallow bay from the Gulf of Mexico. It has converted part of the bay into a deep harbor, well protected from the storms of the Gulf by great jetties. The wealth of the hinterland has made it profitable to dig a harbor at great expense, to build numerous railroads, and also to raise large parts of the city several feet in order to free them from the danger of being flooded by great waves during tropical hurricanes.

**Why some Pacific ports have grown great.** The Pacific coast has four chief ports. Two of these, San Francisco and Seattle, owe much of their growth to the fact that they lie on two of the world's best harbors. The other two, Los Angeles and Portland, have had to make for themselves good facilities as seaports.

Beginning with the most southerly, we find that Los Angeles was founded about 18 miles from the sea. When it grew so big (page 260) that it wanted a seaport, it reached out to San Pedro on the coast; there it has built a harbor that receives more ships each year than any other harbor in the country except New York. Oil from the great fields not far away is the chief export, while huge quantities of lumber from the north and rubber from the Far East are among the chief imports.

San Francisco is fortunate in being on the only good natural harbor from the Columbia River to San Diego, a distance of 950 miles. It is like the boy who has the only newspaper stand on a busy street; he gets all the trade because his competitors are far removed.

It is true that Oakland, just across the bay from San Francisco, has been helped by the same broad deep harbor to become a large city — nearly one half the size of its neighbor. But it is not so much a competitor as an aid to the larger city. In fact the two are really parts of one great center of population, just as are St. Paul and Minneapolis, New York and Newark, or Boston and Cambridge. Oakland is indeed indispensable to the continued growth of its larger neighbor. It receives many of the trains coming from the immediate hinterland, as well as those from the East. The passengers, fruits, grains, vegetables, oil, and lumber brought by the trains are ferried across to San Francisco. Only one railroad, the coast line from the south, has a branch to the end of the peninsula on which the main city lies between the bay and the Pacific.

The wharves at San Francisco show what the harbor means to the city. Here a Japanese steamship is unloading chests of tea, bales of silk, and bundles of straw matting. There a vessel is delivering raw sugar from Honolulu. Near by a British freighter is making fast to unload goods collected at Sydney in Australia, and at Hongkong and Manila. French freighters are bringing Belgian coke and pig iron and taking away California barley. Over there an American steamer is discharging manufactured goods, mainly of steel and iron, that she picked up at New York and Philadelphia and brought through the Panama Canal.

**Pacific cities on river and sound.** Portland in Oregon is like New Orleans in being located more than a hundred miles from the mouth of a great river. Its mountains and climate make its products very different, however. Instead of cotton, it exports lumber; and instead of cotton-seed oil and petroleum, it exports salmon, apples, wheat, and other kinds of food from the rich Willamette valley. Long breakwaters have been built at the mouth of the Columbia River so that ships may avoid the breaking waves of the great Pacific Ocean and easily enter the river.

Seattle, tucked safely away in Puget Sound, is like Portland in being a great meeting place of steamship lines and railroads. The steamships come from Australia, the Orient, and Alaska, from neighboring American ports, and through the Panama Canal from Atlantic ports. They bring goods needed by a bustling young city and a busy neighborhood that have not yet had time to manufacture enough goods even for their own needs, so occupied are they in getting lumber out of the forests and wheat and fruit out of the soil.

These steamers also bring from the Orient goods en route for New York. Sometimes, when the market is ready for a new supply, such goods as silk cannot wait to follow the slow water route via the canal to the New World metropolis. They are speedily transferred at

M. D. Boland

FIG. 149. Loading lumber at Seattle. Washington cuts more timber than any other state in the Union, and lumber is shipped from Seattle to ports all over the world, the largest amount going to the North Atlantic ports.

Seattle to express trains that have the right of way even over passenger trains for the three thousand miles across the continent.

So valuable has land become in Seattle and so troublesome are hills in the heart of a city, that the city cut off the top of one of its beautiful hills and washed the material down into the bay to fill up many acres of shallow water and make them into land.

**The work of our chief seaports.** Eleven cities — New York, Boston, Philadelphia, Baltimore, Norfolk, New Orleans, Galveston with Houston, Los Angeles, San Francisco, Portland, and Seattle — are the great seaports of the United States. They handle four fifths of all the foreign commerce and an even larger part of the coastwise commerce of the country. Like the great department stores located at busy corners in a large city, they hum with the business of buying and selling. There is ever an outpouring of goods purchased by their customers, and an inpouring of goods from distant parts. They have grown great largely because they can be readily reached.

### THE LAKE PORTS

Next to our seaports in importance come the ports of the Great Lakes. If goods collected on land are to be carried by lake, they are naturally taken to the nearest point on the lake, which means one of

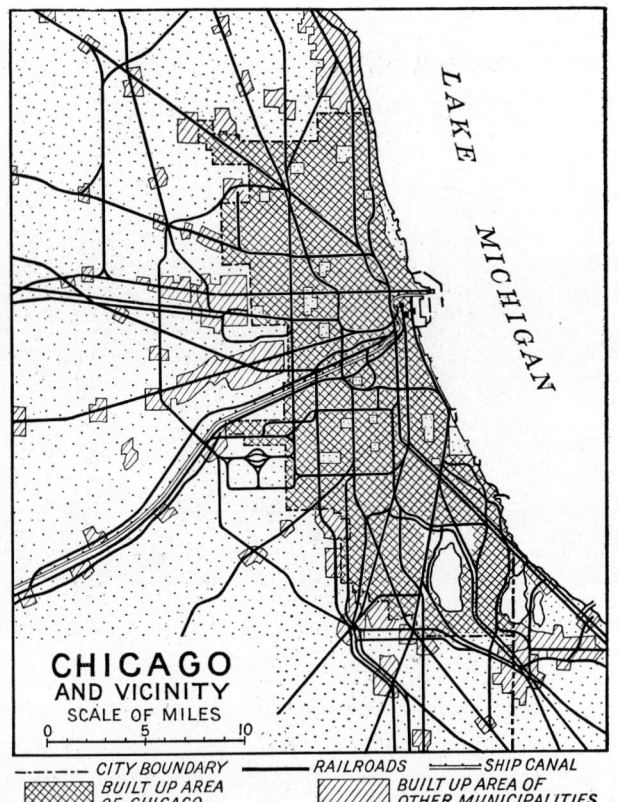

Fig. 150. Since practically the whole southern coast of Lake Michigan is without deep indentations, Chicago has had to make its own harbor by means of jetties. Note the number of railroad lines that run into the city.

the ends more frequently than any other point. Hence most of the important lake ports are near the ends of the various lakes.

**How lakes and railroads have helped Chicago.** The largest of the lake ports is Chicago, the world's most important railway center. The city owes much of this distinction to Lake Michigan, the southward extension of which obliges the railroads that connect the eastern states with much of the West and Northwest to swing around its end. Lake Michigan also causes railroads from the Southwest and South to converge near its southern end because it offers such an excellent and cheap water route to eastern markets, particularly New York. Although not quite at the southern end of the lake, Chicago lies at the nearest point where there is even a hint of a natural harbor, and has therefore become a great transportation center.

The routes centering at Chicago vibrate with activity. As you read these lines, freight and passenger trains are hurrying to Chicago

Fig. 151. Pittsburgh, the leading iron and steel city of the United States, has an advantageous location on the Ohio River, at the junction of the Allegheny and the Monongahela, within easy reach of great iron and coal fields.

along every one of the numerous railways that center in the city. Except when the Great Lakes are icebound, steamships of at least eighteen different companies are speeding to the city with their burden of goods and passengers from the fertile and well populated hinterland. At the same time, as many more trains and steamships are hurrying away from the city to distribute goods and passengers to the same great hinterland.

The most productive part of the hinterland is included in a circle with a radius of 425 miles, centering at Chicago. Such a circle contains about half a million square miles of plains whose productiveness is scarcely excelled by that of any similar area in any part of the earth. It includes an area as large as Great Britain, France, and Germany combined. It also contains most of the Great Lakes, which offer the best facilities for inland navigation in any part of the world.

Chicago illustrates the fact that where the convergence of land routes makes it necessary to have a harbor, man can build one even without help from nature. At the southern end of Lake Michigan there are no good harbors, and Chicago is located merely at the mouth of the little Chicago River. Improvements have constantly taken place, however, and when the present plans are completed the city will have an unsurpassed inland harbor.

**How transportation has helped the growth of Detroit.** Although Detroit lies on a river, it is essentially a lake port. Among the lake ports of the world it comes next to Chicago in size. It is nominally the fourth city in the United States, although metropolitan Boston is larger than metropolitan Detroit.

Detroit, like Chicago, lies near the end of a great lake. There a railway route between New York and Chicago meets a water route connecting the iron mines and the coal mines. Although the railway route is shorter than the one on the south side of Lake Erie, it is less important. This is partly because a portion of it passes through foreign (*i.e.*, Canadian) territory, and partly because it passes through few large cities. The iron-ore route helps Detroit relatively little because most of the ore goes past Detroit in order to reach a port as near the coal mines as possible. Thus in this case, even more than in others, transportation is only one of the factors in the extraordinary growth of the city. The fact that the automobile industry centers here is in many ways much more important.

The western end of Lake Erie and the southern end of Lake Huron form so important a center of communication that Toledo as well as Detroit has grown up here. It lies on the drowned mouth of the

Maumee River, which has been made into a good harbor. Here again, as in the case of almost every city, many factors besides transportation coöperate.

**Buffalo as a station on the route to Europe.** The extraordinary importance of the ends of the Great Lakes is evident from the location not only of Chicago, Detroit, and Toledo, but of Duluth and Toronto, and especially Buffalo.

Buffalo has the great advantages of (1) cheap iron ore from the Lake Superior region, (2) cheap grain from the same region, (3) cheap water power from Niagara, and (4) water transportation to New York through the Erie Barge Canal. In spite of the canal, however, the grain from the western lake ports is usually lifted out of the boats into elevators at Buffalo, and then transported to cars that carry it to the Jersey City water front of New York harbor (Fig. 145). There it is lightered to tramp steamers bound for Liverpool and Europe.

Strange as it may seem, the cost of unloading a bushel of wheat at Buffalo, plus the cost of the railway haul to Jersey City, plus the cost of reloading on the ocean-going steamer, is fully half the entire cost of transportation from Duluth to Liverpool. In normal times, for every bushel of wheat bound for Liverpool from six to eight cents is spent on costly railroad transportation. Yet when the wheat reaches Jersey City, it is farther from Liverpool than when it was on the dock at Buffalo. If Buffalo were a station on the route of ocean steamers instead of a terminal for lake steamers, the journey from the Middle West to Europe would be shortened almost a thousand miles, and five cents or more would be saved on every bushel of wheat bound for Europe from Manitoba, the Dakotas, and the neighboring wheat regions.

The waterways between the Great Lakes have been so much improved that all but the largest freight-carrying steamers could proceed from the Atlantic Ocean to Duluth or Chicago were it not for fifty miles of rapids in the upper St. Lawrence River above Montreal. It seems probable that if dams and large locks were built here, the cost of construction would be met by the water power that would be made available. It would then be possible to lift ocean steamers the entire 600 feet to the level of Lake Superior. Thus Buffalo and the other lake ports would, to all intents and purposes, become seaports.

**The transportation conditions that favor Cleveland and Milwaukee.** Cleveland and Milwaukee, unlike the other great cities on the lakes, are located at neither the head nor the foot of a body of water. Port Arthur, the wheat port of Manitoba, and Rochester, on a river a few miles from Lake Ontario, occupy similar positions. Cleveland owes its growth largely to the fact that it is the meeting place of two unusually important transportation routes: one, the chief railway between Chicago and New York; the other, the iron-ore route from Duluth to the western Pennsylvania coal mines. The cities, the iron mines, and the coal mines served by these routes all belong to the largest of their kind. Hence Cleveland has easy access to enormous markets and enormous sources of supplies, and has become not only a great transportation center, but a large iron-working town.

Milwaukee, in a similar position, has responded to the marked productiveness of southern Wisconsin and the plains to the west. From this hinterland railways converge upon the nearest natural harbor on Lake Michigan. There, at the common mouth of three improved and navigable rivers, Milwaukee has grown up. A train ferry to Grand Haven on the east shore of Lake Michigan now brings it some of the business that previously passed through Chicago.

**QUESTIONS, EXERCISES, AND PROBLEMS**

*A.* **How the hinterland determines the relative value of imports and exports.**

FOREIGN TRADE OF CHIEF PORTS OF UNITED STATES
(IN MILLIONS OF DOLLARS)

| Ports | Average of Two Years | | |
|---|---|---|---|
| | Imports | Exports | Total |
| New York | 1811 | 1644 | 3455 |
| Galveston | 26 | 485 | 511 |
| New Orleans | 173 | 329 | 502 |
| Detroit | 90 | 291 | 381 |
| San Francisco | 184 | 177 | 361 |
| Buffalo | 137 | 205 | 342 |
| Philadelphia | 204 | 113 | 317 |
| Seattle | 165 | 128 | 293 |
| Boston | 233 | 37 | 270 |
| Los Angeles | 57 | 156 | 213 |
| Norfolk | 32 | 159 | 191 |
| Baltimore | 110 | 69 | 179 |

1. Insert the names of these ports on an outline map. Underline the names of those which send out more goods than they receive. What occupations are most important in their hinterlands?
2. Why do people engaged in these occupations need to import less than people engaged in manufacturing? Name two classes of products which these people do not need to import, but which factory workers must import in order both to live and to work.
3. Frame a statement to show which section of the United States is most completely dependent upon transportation.

**B. What positions cause the greatest growth of cities.**

1. From Table 5 (page 330) make a list of the twenty-five largest cities of the United States. Check those that have been mentioned in this chapter as transportation centers. On an outline map put a small figure for each, to show its rank in population.
2. Classify the twenty-five cities as seaports, lake ports, or river ports. Frame a statement to show the sort of locations where transportation has most effect on the growth of cities.
3. Let each member choose the city in the United States that most interests him and report on it to the class. (See *Representative Cities*, by Caroline Hotchkiss.)

**C. Other ports on the Atlantic coast.**

1. Some of the seaports of second rank on the Atlantic coast are:

   (a) Portland, Maine   (d) New Haven   (g) Savannah
   (b) New Bedford      (e) Washington  (h) Miami
   (c) Providence       (f) Charleston  (i) Mobile

   Which of these are located (a) on harbors formed by submergence of the coast; (b) at the mouths of important rivers? Which are the terminals of railroads that run far inland without encountering rugged relief?
2. Decide which of these cities have been hampered by the following conditions: (a) small size of hinterland; (b) scanty population of hinterland; (c) limited production of hinterland; (d) slight depth of harbor; (e) competition with neighboring cities having better harbors or easier routes to the interior.
3. Find what each city is distinguished for and what are its chief exports and imports.

**D. Other ports on the Pacific coast.**

1. On the Pacific coast, what seaports not previously mentioned have a population of more than 75,000?
2. Explain how a city may start with an inland position but ultimately raise itself to great importance as a port. To what city on the Pacific coast does this apply? What has it done to make itself a great port?
3. Los Angeles ships from its harbor a huge *tonnage* of goods, — more than any other city in the United States except New York. Nevertheless, the *value* of its *foreign* trade is not much more than half that of Baltimore's. How do you reconcile these facts? (Pages 129, 131.)
4. What Pacific ports are especially important in the lumber and grain trades?

**E. River cities of the United States.**

1. Make a list of all the cities of more than 100,000 inhabitants that are located on navigable rivers in the United States. Check those already discussed in this chapter or in the exercises. Which ones are (a) at the mouths of rivers; (b) at the highest point to which ocean steamers can ascend; (c) at or near the junctions of navigable rivers?
2. How do the cities on the Mississippi and its branches compare with the other river cities in number and size?

Fig. 152. Ore docks at Chicago.

3. Look up the history and present transportation conditions of St. Louis. Describe how and when the growth of the city and of its transportation system has been connected with furs, cotton, railroad bridges, the Missouri River, and cattle ranches.
4. Compare Pittsburgh and Cincinnati with respect to (a) rivers; (b) through railway routes; (c) coal, iron, and other commodities for transportation.
5. Minneapolis, St. Paul, Kansas City, Omaha, and Louisville are all located on the Mississippi River system. What conditions of transportation or industry determined their position? Why is their river traffic of little importance?

**F. Summary of great cities in the United States.**

1. On an outline map indicate the location and name of each city mentioned in this chapter, including the exercises. Label the rivers, bays, or lakes mentioned either in the chapter or in reports on the exercises.
2. From Table 5, page 330, list the cities of the United States having a population of more than 300,000 and see if any have been omitted from this chapter and its exercises. If so, explain the reasons for their importance and the degree to which their position and growth depend on transportation.
3. Study the location of Indianapolis. If the capital of Indiana had been placed fifty miles in any direction from its present location, would the growth of the city have been different? Compare Indianapolis in this respect with any other great city with which you are familiar.
4. What important railway centers have a population of more than 200,000 and do not have any kind of transportation by water? How far does the position and growth of Denver depend on routes of transportation?

224  Modern Business Geography

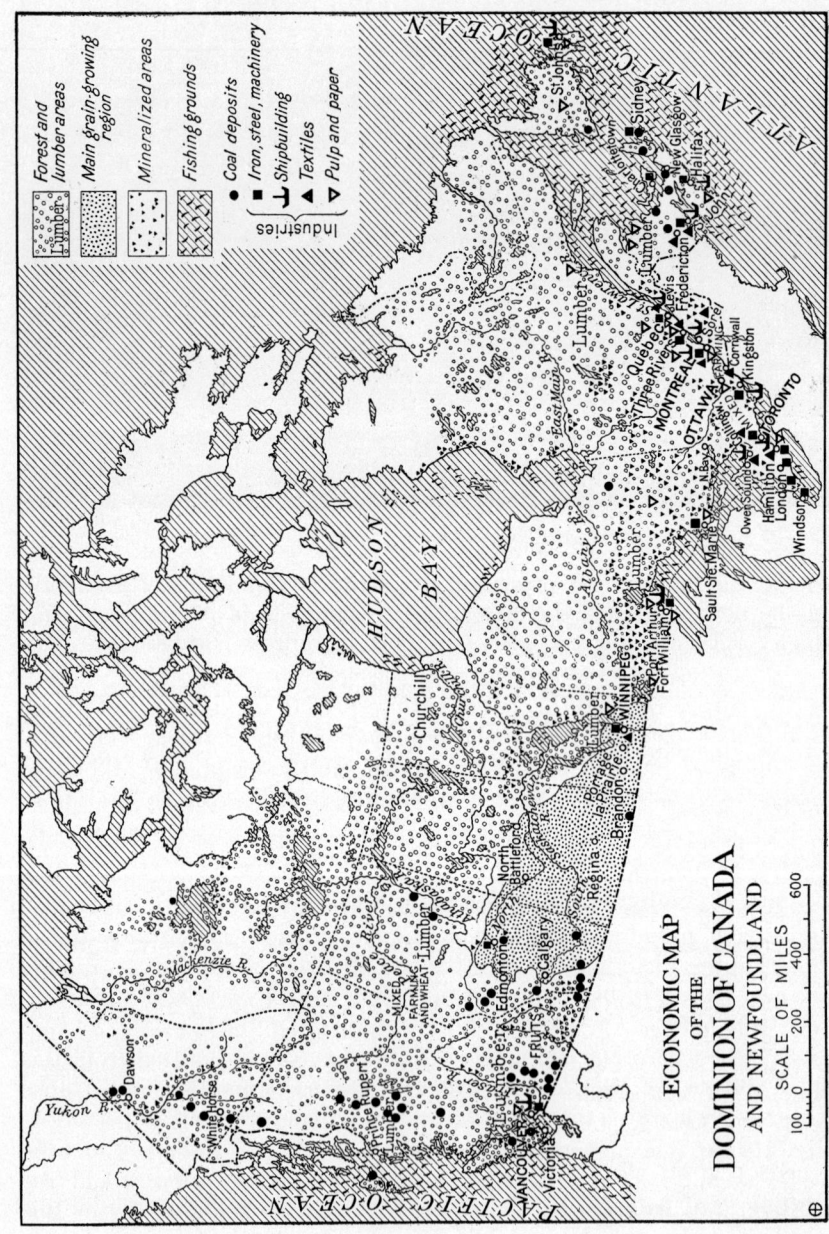

Fig. 153. Compare this map with Figures 28, 41, 55, 64, 67, 80 (pages 43, 56, 74, 84, 89, 101), showing some of the primary products in Canada. Compare it also with Figures 3 and 4 (pages 4, 5), showing range of temperatures.

# CHAPTER SEVENTEEN

## SPECIAL PROBLEMS IN TRANSPORTATION

(A) TRADE ROUTES AND CITIES OF BRITISH NORTH AMERICA

Fourteen cities in the Dominion of Canada have populations of more than fifty thousand. Because of the climate, these cities are crowded toward the southern border.

In the colony of Newfoundland (which includes Labrador) only the capital, St. John's, has a population of more than five thousand.

### LEADING CITIES AND THEIR POPULATIONS

| | | | | |
|---|---|---|---|---|
| Montreal | 810,295 | Edmonton | | 78,829 |
| Toronto | 627,582 | London | | 71,022 |
| Vancouver | 245,307 | Windsor | | 63,000 |
| Winnipeg | 217,587 | Halifax | | 58,939 |
| Hamilton | 154,307 | St. John | | 46,640 |
| Quebec | 129,103 | St. John's | | 41,757 |
| Ottawa | 124,988 | Victoria | | 38,411 |
| Calgary | 83,362 | Regina | | 53,209 |

1. What kinds of transportation connect the leading cities with one another and with the western plains?
2. Through what waterways does their inland commerce reach the ocean?
3. Divide the cities listed above into seaports, lake ports, river ports, and cities without water transportation. Which ports have good harbors?

**The eastern port of Canada.** The chief ports of Canada are Montreal and Vancouver. Montreal is almost as important as all the others combined. It is located as follows: (*a*) on the St. Lawrence-Great Lakes waterway; (*b*) at the head of navigation for ocean steamers; (*c*) a thousand miles from the open sea; (*d*) where the Champlain-Hudson valley gives an easy route to the south and the Ottawa valley an easy route to the west; and (*e*) nearer to Europe than is New York.

4. In what respects is the position of Montreal either superior or inferior to that of New York?

The cold climate does not permit agriculture in the regions north and northwest of Montreal. It causes the St. Lawrence to be frozen five months of the year.

5. What effect would you expect the foregoing facts to have on the commerce of Montreal?

6. To what three cities — one in Nova Scotia, one in New Brunswick, one in Maine — is its commerce transferred in winter? (Consult Figure 128 for railway connections.)

For a long time Quebec lost in commercial importance compared with Montreal, but now it is gaining.

7. Compare the two cities with respect to (a) position relative to Europe and to the densely populated parts of the United States; (b) ease of obtaining coal from Nova Scotia; (c) size and productivity of hinterland; (d) number of cities with more than 50,000 people within 800 miles; (e) climate.

The St. Lawrence has been deepened between Montreal and Quebec. The Grand Trunk Pacific Railroad has bridged the St. Lawrence near Quebec and built a line from Quebec to Prince Rupert on the northern part of the Pacific coast of Canada (Figs. 128, 153).

8. Which of these changes is more likely to have helped Quebec? Why?

**The main Pacific port of Canada.** Vancouver, the Pacific terminus of the Canadian Pacific Railroad, owes much of its growth to the rich mines and primeval forests of its hinterland, and to the need of western Europe for the speedy transportation of light, valuable goods, such as silk, from the Orient.

9. By what route can mail from London reach Yokohama most promptly?
10. Why is Vancouver, with a harbor as good as that of Seattle, only about one third as large as Seattle?

Although Vancouver is farther north than Quebec and Montreal, its port remains ice-free when the St. Lawrence is frozen.

11. Explain the fact stated above.
12. How does this fact explain an increase of eastbound Canadian traffic through the Panama Canal in winter?

**Minor ports.** Halifax and St. John are the leading secondary ports of Canada. Both are on good harbors, but have small hinterlands, except when the St. Lawrence freezes.

13. In what provinces are these cities located?
14. Why are their hinterlands small? What enlarges them in winter?

**Interior cities.** The important interior cities are Toronto, Winnipeg, and Ottawa. Toronto might almost be included among seaports, since from its good harbor near the head of Lake Ontario small ships may pass down the St. Lawrence to the sea. The Welland Canal also gives the city steamship connection with the Great Lakes. The region about the city, the rich Ontario peninsula, is often called the " garden of Canada."

15. What important railroads pass through Toronto?
16. Why is such a city a large importer of manufactured goods from the United States?

All the main east and west routes across Canada pass through the narrow belt separating Lake Winnipeg from the international boundary line, a region which is one of the world's richest wheat lands (Figs. 143, 153).

17. What city lies here, at the junction of the Red and Assiniboine rivers?
18. Why might this city be called "the Chicago of Canada"?

The importance of Ottawa is due almost entirely to the fact that it is the capital of the Dominion.

19. Compare Ottawa with Washington as to position and facilities for transportation.

The value of the combined commerce of all the Canadian ports is only about two thirds that of New York.

20. To what degree does this proportion depend on differences between Canada and the United States in (a) rainfall; (b) temperature; (c) relief; (d) coastline; (e) stage of development?
21. List according to size the Canadian cities mentioned in this section. In a parallel column, write beside each the name of a city in the United States having nearly the same population. Use Table 5, page 330.

*Ewing Galloway*

FIG. 154. A stock ranch in Alberta.

## (B) Trade Routes and Cities of Africa

Africa, like South America, makes its chief contribution to the world's commerce through primary production. The cities, therefore, serve as huge warehouses where raw materials are collected, rather than as manufacturing centers.

1. Make a table showing the approximate area of the following sections of Africa: (a) the deserts; (b) the great tropical forests; (c) the tropical grasslands; (d) the regions with a temperate climate.
2. Find some country in the temperate zone having an area somewhere near that of each of the four sections of Africa. How does the population of the four countries compare with that of Africa?

### Chief Cities of Africa and Their Approximate Populations

| City | Population | City | Population |
|---|---|---|---|
| Cairo | 1,065,000 | Casablanca | 107,000 |
| Alexandria | 573,000 | Port Said | 105,000 |
| Johannesburg | 325,000 | Constantine | 94,000 |
| Cape Town | 240,000 | Tanta | 90,000 |
| Algiers | 226,000 | Fez | 81,000 |
| Tunis | 186,000 | Omdurman | 79,000 |
| Durban (Port Natal) | 180,000 | Port Elizabeth | 65,000 |
| Oran | 150,000 | Mansura | 64,000 |
| Morocco (Marakesh) | 149,000 | Tripoli | 60,000 |
| Khartum | 124,000 | Tangier | 60,000 |

3. Divide the cities of Africa, as given in the table above, into two lists, — the seaports and the cities in the interior. Beside each city write the name of the country or colony in which it is situated.

**Location of the chief ports of Africa.** A comparison of the coast line of Africa with that of North America or Europe shows great differences. The characteristics of the African coastal regions account in part for the number, size, and stage of development of the seaports.

4. What portions of the continent have (a) a smooth, regular coast line; (b) swamps and dense forests; (c) mountains near the sea; (d) deserts; (e) deep rivers, navigable for many miles into the interior; (f) high temperature at all seasons; (g) a location near the commercial and industrial continents?
5. How does each of these conditions influence the development of seaports?
6. How many of the seaports in the table given above are along the Mediterranean coast?
7. How do they compare in size with the seaports on the north coast of the Mediterranean?

Fig. 155. A village on the Nile, built of sun-dried brick.

8. What and where are the other two chief African seaports? Give three general reasons for their location.
9. What difficulties do they have in reaching their hinterlands?

**The most important port of the continent.** Alexandria, besides being near the important route between Europe and Asia via the Suez Canal, includes in its hinterland an area, about half the size of Iowa, which produces two or three crops every year.

10. Why is this region so productive?
11. What fiber forms eighty per cent or more of the exports of Alexandria? What conditions favor its production, especially in the Nile delta?
12. What river gives Alexandria a water route far inland?
13. Find out how far boats can penetrate the interior. What obstacles to shipping are there, and how have they been overcome?
14. In how many ways is Alexandria like New Orleans?

The Egyptian railroad system is the most important in Africa and helps to make Alexandria the leading port. It extends from Alexandria to Assuan at the first cataract, and from the second cataract to

Khartum. A branch line has been built from Khartum to Port Sudan (Suakin) on the Red Sea.

15. What is the distance from Alexandria to Khartum in a straight line? Name a place about the same distance from your home.
16. Will the trade of Alexandria probably increase more or less rapidly because of the branch line to Port Sudan?
17. What goods are collected by Alexandria from Egypt? Where are they sent?
18. What goods are distributed by Alexandria to Egypt? Where do they come from?

Port Said lies at the entrance to the Suez Canal, and is a port of call for all the shipping that goes from the Mediterranean to the Red Sea. It also has rail connection, via Cairo, with the interior of Africa. Nevertheless, more than three fourths of the Egyptian imports and more than nine tenths of the exports pass through Alexandria.

19. What advantages in means of communication and in relation to the main export keep Alexandria so far ahead of Port Said?

Several fertile oases of the Sahara lie in the region for which Alexandria is the port.

20. What kinds of routes connect these oases with the outside world? Why are both oases and routes interesting rather than important in the world's commerce?

**Other northern ports of Africa.** The other northern ports, in order of size, are Algiers, Tunis, Oran, Casablanca, Tripoli, and Tangier. Since they are separated from the rest of Africa by the desert, they have much more commercial connection with southern Europe than with other ports of Africa. Wine is much the most valuable export, then cereals, sheep and wool, timber, and ores.

21. Answer the following questions concerning each of these ports:
    (a) On what body of water is it?
    (b) In what country or political division is it?
    (c) What European nation controls the country?
    (d) What large port of the controlling country is nearest it?
    (e) About how large is the hinterland of the port? how productive?
    (f) How far from the port does the railroad penetrate?
    (g) How are the oases reached?
22. How are the hinterlands of these ports adapted to the production of one or more of the chief exports mentioned above?
23. Why does the United States receive only a small share of the trade of North Africa? Give reasons based on (a) political conditions; (b) types of primary production; (c) transportation.

## Special Problems in Transportation

**South African ports.** Durban and Cape Town are the ports of the region that contains the Kimberley diamond mines and the gold mines about Johannesburg, both of which are the richest of their kind in the world. Nearly $50,000,000 worth of diamonds and $200,000,000 worth of gold are exported yearly.

24. If a ton of gold is worth $500,000, how many tons of freight would this yearly production make?

South Africa also produces for export wool which is sometimes worth over $80,000,000 per year; corn products, $15,000,000; hides and skins, $30,000,000; and coal, $10,000,000.

25. Arrange the chief South African products in the probable order of their value to the railroads and steamship companies as sources of revenue.
26. What four of these products reach the United States in good quantities? What two probably reach your own locality?
27. If the whole of South Africa were a desert, why would Cape Town still have some importance?
28. Would Cape Town and Alexandria be different from what they now are, if the Suez Canal had never been dug? In what respects?
29. What kind of machinery does the United States probably send to Durban and Cape Town?
30. In what respect has Cape Town the same advantage as Ottawa?

**The railroad penetration northward.** A railroad extends northward from Cape Town for more than two thousand miles, to the interior of Belgian Congo, near Lake Tanganyika. This is part of the Cape-to-Cairo railway which has been the desire of the British colonies in Africa for many years. It will have many branch lines running to ports on the east coast. Some day it will presumably carry plantation products, such as tea, coffee, sugar, cocoa, and palm oil; but now the interior of tropical Africa yields little except hides, ivory, gums, copper, and some gold and tin.

31. What ports are now reached by branches of the Cape-to-Cairo railway?
32. What great river has been bridged to carry the railroad north?
33. Through what political divisions may a Cape-to-Cairo railway run? Are these divisions independent, or are they under European control?
34. *Map exercise.* Practice making a sketch map of Africa, showing the location of every port with a population of more than 50,000. At first have a map before you as you sketch. After a few trials, try to do all the work from memory in five minutes.

**Interior centers of Africa.** Although Africa has several great rivers, there are few settlements of any size along them. Omdurman and

232  Modern Business Geography

Khartum form the only important centers on the upper Nile above the famous cataracts. The other great rivers are blocked by cataracts nearer the sea than those of the Nile, and consequently do not furnish routes of transportation of much importance.

35. Does this fact lead you to expect many or few large cities in the interior of Africa? Why?

36. Compare Africa with South America with respect to interior centers. How does the largest river of Africa compare with the largest river of South America as a means of transportation?

37. Where in Africa does the climate most favor the growth of cities?

38. How many of the interior cities in the table on page 228 are located outside of the tropics? How far from the coast are they?

Fig. 156. Taking clay pots down the Nile to market.

39. Which is the largest of the interior cities? How does it compare with the largest of the seaports?
40. Study the map of the Nile River to account for the location of Cairo. What three kinds of transportation routes meet at this point?
41. How does primary production combine with transportation to cause the growth of Cairo? Give another reason for its growth.
42. How does Khartum communicate with its hinterland and with the lower Nile?

Johannesburg, the great gold-mining center on the Witwatersrand in South Africa, is also a railroad center.

43. Is this chiefly because its products must be carried out to distant markets, or because machinery, laborers, food, and clothing must be brought to it? Explain.
44. If the great Witwaters gold deposits had been located in Central Africa, would the growth of a city have taken place more or less rapidly than at Johannesburg? Why?

Fez and Morocco, or Marakesh, like many other great overgrown villages near the borders of the Sahara, are the collecting points for wheat, barley, wool, hides, and other local products, and are meeting points of caravan routes from the desert. They also, in a primitive way, carry on manufacturing, such as tanning leather, making leather goods, and weaving cotton and woolen cloths.

Other centers, such as Kano and Ibadan in Nigeria, are even larger than Fez, but are not listed among the African cities because they are unimportant commercially. Their size is due not so much to transportation routes and primary products as to the desire of the natives to be within the protection of a powerful chief and behind the thick mud walls that surround the town. The houses are usually one story high and are made of sun-dried mud.

45. In developing communication between Algiers and interior towns, as Timbuktu, what are the advantages or disadvantages of employing (a) railways; (b) automobiles; (c) airplanes?
46. *Map exercise, continued.* Add to your map of African ports the important interior centers of population. Put in parentheses under each the name of the country in which it is, and the European nation that is in control.

   Under each of the names on your map write the approximate length of (a) the largest railroad running out of or through it, and (b) the internal waterway on which it is located.
47. Sum up your conclusions as to transportation and primary production in Africa compared with North America.

Fig. 157. Flour mills, railroad, and river at Minneapolis.

# PART THREE

## THE FIELD OF MANUFACTURE

### CHAPTER EIGHTEEN

#### THE GEOGRAPHICAL CONDITIONS OF MANUFACTURE

As students of industrial geography, our main problem in regard to manufacturing is to find out why factories are located in certain parts of the world.

There are at least eight conditions that favor the location of manufacturing industries.

(1) Energetic and inventive people
(2) Nearness to fuel or to abundant water power
(3) Nearness to raw materials
(4) Convenient transportation facilities
(5) Nearness to markets
(6) Large supply of efficient labor
(7) Abundant capital for investment
(8) The advantage of an early start

**Industries in relation to human ability.** In a broad way race and climate exert the most powerful influence on the general location of manufacturing industries. In almost every factory in our northern states men and women are working vigorously and rapidly, with their minds and muscles constantly alert. This kind of efficient work is rarely found except in places inhabited by a few energetic races and where the climate is invigorating. On a hot day in summer we seldom feel like doing our best work. From our feelings on such days we can readily see why tropical races have a reputation for laziness, and why it is difficult to secure efficient labor where the temperature is constantly high. In regions of excessive cold, efficient labor is again scarce; even in the northern parts of the United States factory operatives accomplish less in winter than in the spring and fall. In the southern states, on the other hand, the work falls off considerably during the hot summers.

The mind and body are most stimulated to efficient work and people enjoy the best health in the cooler portions of the temperate zone, particularly in those parts which have frequent changes of weather and frequent rainfall. Such regions are the home of the most active and inventive races, and include the chief industrial countries,—the United States, Great Britain, Germany, France, Belgium, Switzerland, and northern Italy.

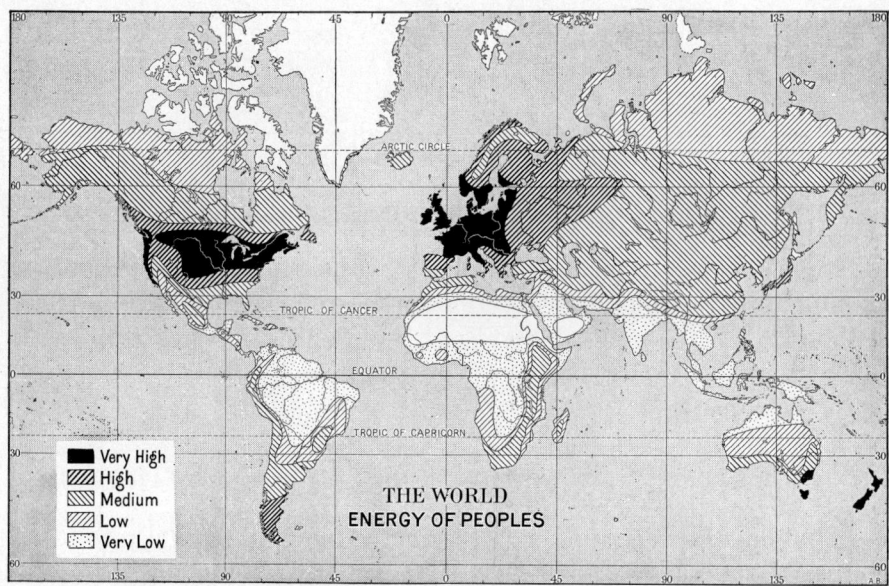

Fig. 158. This map shows the amount of energy that might be expected if people's energy depended solely on climate. What countries are most heavily shaded? What kind of countries are they? Compare the countries which have the second heaviest shading with those shaded most lightly. Compare this map with Figure 165, showing the distribution of manufacturing. What does this map indicate as to climate?

In Asia, the only country that is highly developed industrially is Japan, where the climate, unlike that of China, has frequent changes from day to day and is relatively stimulating. There the people are unusually active in both mind and body. In the southern hemisphere, parts of Argentina, Chile, and southeastern Australia are favored both in climate and in race, but they are so new in commercial development and so far from markets and from a large labor supply that they are not yet important industrially.

**How power determines the location of industries.** Those industries that consume great quantities of fuel are strongly influenced by the location of coal mines or other supplies of fuel, such as natural gas and petroleum.

*Fuel.* Pennsylvania well illustrates the effect of supplies of coal. Her preëminence in coal mining helps her to lead the states of the Union in the production of the following articles, which are among the heaviest consumers of fuel: coke; pig iron; pig steel; rolling mill products, such as rails and sheet iron; foundry and machine shop products, such as wrought iron and castings; railway cars, a large percentage of which are now made of steel; glass, which requires high temperatures and much fuel to melt the sand; cement, a mixture of pulverized limestone and clay heated to a high temperature. Pittsburgh in Pennsylvania, Birmingham in England, and Essen in Germany are examples of great cities which owe much of their growth to the fact that the presence of coal has favored the development of iron industries.

*Water power.* In many industries water power serves the same purpose as coal. The waterfalls of northern New York and New England turn the wheels of wood-pulp and paper mills that furnish much of the paper on which daily newspapers are printed. In the wheat region of the United States, falls determine the location of wheat-milling centers, as Minneapolis at St. Anthony's Falls on the Mississippi River. The falls along the lower course of the Merrimac River are one of the chief reasons why cotton mills developed there in great numbers at an early date.

More recently the water power of the piedmont belt at the foot of the mountains in the Carolinas and Georgia, together with the presence of abundant raw material, has brought about the location of many cotton mills at such cities as Greensboro and Charlotte, in North Carolina, and Columbia, in South Carolina (Fig. 12).

Advances in electrical engineering now make it possible for power from rivers to be conveyed long distances in the form of electricity, as in North Carolina, and at Niagara Falls. In the Pacific states several

FIG. 159. Mills on the Connecticut River, run by water power, with steam as auxiliary. Few of the great mills in New England now depend wholly on water power. When the rivers run low, if at no other time, steam is used; otherwise the mills would be forced to shut down.

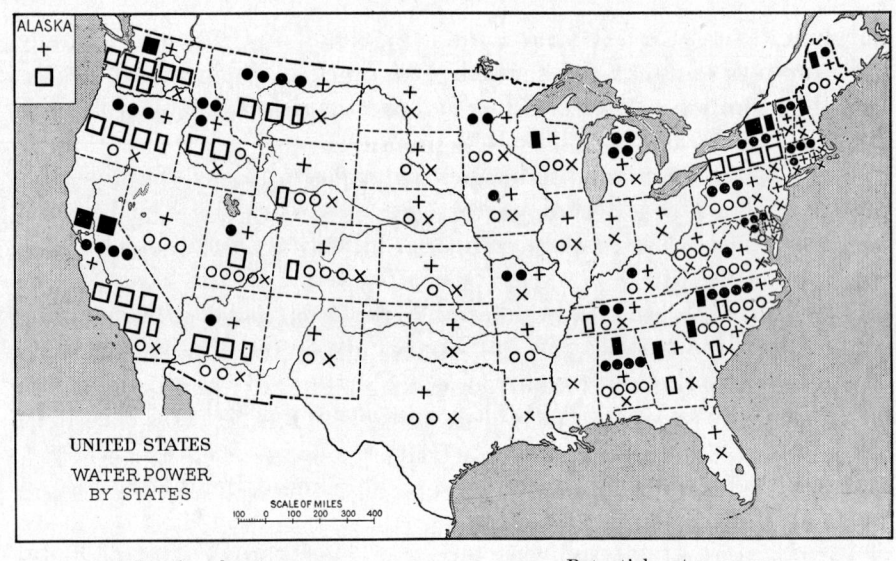

Fig. 160. Water power is found where the relief is rugged and the rainfall is at least moderate. Why is so little water power available in Ohio, Indiana, and Illinois? in the states from North Dakota to Texas? Why have the Pacific states so much? Why have Nevada and New Mexico together much less than California? Where is the available water power most nearly utilized?

lines bring the power two or even four hundred miles from the Sierras to the cities of the lowland where some of the other favorable conditions for manufacturing are found.

**Raw materials and the location of industries.** Many manufacturing industries are located near the source of their chief raw material. For instance, the industries of fruit canning and fruit drying are highly developed in California, where fruit grows in great abundance. For similar reasons Maryland cans many tomatoes, and the state of Washington many fish, while Wisconsin is a great state for butter, cheese, and condensed milk.

The raw materials for the products mentioned above are alike in being perishable, a condition which draws the industries to them. Where such materials are transported long distances in the fresh state, the cost of refrigeration makes the prices relatively much higher than for canned goods.

Other kinds of raw material that attract factories include the products of mines, quarries, and forests. Many metals, unlike the bulk of the American iron ore, are smelted near the mines. This accounts for the manufacturing carried on in mining centers like Butte, Montana, and Leadville, Colorado. At important quarries like those at Quincy in Massachusetts and Barre in Vermont, many men are engaged in chipping the huge rough blocks of granite and marble into symmetrical forms for buildings or monuments.

Near the forests one is likely to come upon sawmills, wood-pulp mills, and possibly woodworking and furniture factories. Near southern pine forests the turpentine industry and charcoal burning are usually found.

The raw materials from mines, quarries, and forests are almost all bulky. If rough blocks of granite, unsmelted zinc or lead ores, or undressed logs were shipped long distances, large sums would have to be paid for freight on worthless material which is thrown away in the processes of manufacturing. Hence bulky as well as perishable raw materials tend to cause manufacturing to be located close to their place of origin.

**How transportation facilities favor the location of manufacturing industries.** Aside from energetic people, transportation probably does more than any other one factor to determine the location of manufacturing industries. A great city like New York, Chicago, or London is the most inviting place for many industries, not only because the dense population furnishes a large market which can be reached with little transportation, but because there are good facilities for shipping to more distant points. Moreover, such facilities do much to determine how rapidly a city grows. For example, in 1790 New York with 33,000 people was only six times as large as New London, Connecticut, which had 5,150, and seven times as large as New Haven, which had 4,500. Today New London is only five times as populous as it was in 1790, New Haven has increased thirty-fold, and New York two hundred and ten fold. New London has a fairly good harbor, but its communications inland are poor because the country is hilly. New Haven has a poor, shallow harbor, but the valley leading northward has made the city an important railroad center. New York not only has a superb harbor, but lies at the end of a remarkable valley affording an outlet from the rich interior of a great country. When industries began to grow, New York attracted the manufacturer because there he could so easily obtain his raw materials and ship his products to other places. The establishment of each industry made the city more inviting for others, because the market and labor supply were correspondingly enlarged, and the facilities for transportation improved. Today the goods manufactured in New York and its immediate vicinity amount to an eighth of all the goods made in the United States.

**Manufacturing industries located at markets.** Just as perishable and bulky *raw materials* determine the location of some manufacturing industries at the source of supply, so perishable and bulky *finished products* determine the location of others at the market where they are consumed. The baking industry is usually located in the cities where its products are sold. Newspaper printing is carried on close to the market. Both bread and news grow stale if allowed to get old through transportation.

Farming machinery is an example of a finished product whose bulk causes it to be manufactured near its market. Huge, awkward machines like wheat harvesters or threshers occupy so much car space that there is a decided advantage in manufacturing them near the center of the market.

A third kind of manufacturing carried on at the market is a response to the particular needs of certain industries. Anchors, for instance, are made at Gloucester, Massachusetts, because the deep-sea fishermen require a special type in their work. A more important example is found in Detroit, where hundreds of factories turn out ball bearings, bolts, springs, axles, batteries, self-starters, fans, and other parts of automobiles in order to meet the special needs of the chief industry of the city.

**How the labor supply affects the location of manufacturing plants.** Manufacturing is possible only where there are plenty of laborers, both skilled and unskilled. This is one reason why cities attract manufacturing plants. The lack of skilled labor, on the other hand, is one of the chief causes of the scarcity of manufacturing plants outside the temperate zone.

Some industries, like the making of ready-to-wear clothing, require a great supply of cheap labor. Hence New York and Boston are especially prominent in such industries, because they have a constant supply of immigrants. Other cities depend more largely upon skilled labor. The shoe industry and the making of fine textiles are of this kind. Both maintain their firm position in the northeastern United States partly because of the presence of skilled workers.

Sometimes an industry flourishes in one place and not in another because of an unused labor supply. The silk industry is a striking illustration of this. In order to be profitable, it must have a large number of women who work for low wages; few men are required. Therefore silk weaving is located in places where large numbers of men are already employed in work like iron and cement making, which require cheap and heavy labor. Their wives and daughters, being

Fig. 161. An old-fashioned source of power for manufacturing and its modern substitute. Find out the difference between the old type of "water-wheel" and the new type of "turbine." How does each turn the machinery inside the "factory"?

without employment, and being poorly supported, are easily induced to become silk operatives at low wages. Paterson, New Jersey, Scranton, Pennsylvania, and Wilkes Barre, Pennsylvania, are thus important silk manufacturing centers.

**Manufacturing in relation to capital.** A great amount of money is required to build factories, equip them with machinery, buy raw materials, and pay the wages of workmen and superintendents before money comes in as a result of sales. Even after a factory is in good running order, more and more money may have to be invested to maintain it and to establish business relations. If a region lacks capital, it is hampered in building up manufacturing industries, for people are more willing to invest in local industries than in those of distant places not so well known to them. This is another reason why New York, the world's financial center, has so many industries.

**Relation of industries to an early start.** England was the first country to develop modern manufacturing. Long before most other countries had started, she had a body of skilled workers, numerous inventors of machinery, and a large capital derived from industrial activity. People all over the world had learned to look to England for manufactured goods, and had acquired confidence in English skill. Hence it was easier for new industries to begin in England than elsewhere. This advantage of an early start helps England even today.

What is true of England in Europe is true of New England in the United States. Being the first to start industries, she still maintains her supremacy in many lines, although other places are equally advantageous so far as other conditions are concerned. Manufactures of cotton, woolen, linen, and jute goods, brass ware, and boots and shoes are lines in which New England is still preëminent, and in many of which her cities have persistently maintained the lead; for example, Lynn and Brockton in the shoe industry; Lawrence in the woolen industry; Fall River, New Bedford, and Lowell in the cotton industry; and Waterbury in brass ware.

**The coöperation of many factors in manufacturing.** The location of most manufacturing industries is influenced by nearly all the eight conditions described in this chapter. When the silk industry of Paterson, for instance, is used to illustrate the influence of a cheap labor supply, it is merely because that condition exerts the greatest influence. Paterson is not far from the coal mines, it has excellent transportation facilities, it is near the great New York market, and it is able to avail itself of abundant capital. But so far as the silk industry is concerned, the labor factor is the most important.

When a business man establishes a manufacturing plant, he must take into account the ability and energy of the people, the climate, the supply of fuel or water power, the nature of the raw material, the transportation facilities, the location and character of his market, the labor supply, and the possibility of obtaining capital. Many men avoid the necessity of thinking about all these conditions by starting business or factories where a given line of business has already been successful; but they run the risk of failing, for conditions keep changing.

### THE GREAT MANUFACTURING REGIONS OF THE WORLD

The conditions described in the preceding pages have much to do with the distribution of manufacturing, as shown in Figure 162. Areas of highly intensive manufacturing, where nearly half the workers and more than a fifth of all the inhabitants are engaged in industrial work, are limited to a small area in northwestern Europe near the North Sea, and a still smaller area in the United States. Areas where more than five per cent of the total population are engaged in manufacturing, the lightly shaded areas in Figure 162, are found only around the more intensive areas, and in the Pacific states, Japan, southeastern Australia, and Argentina. When we remember that practically everyone uses manufactured goods, and that iron for machinery, coal for fuel,

# Geographical Conditions of Manufacture

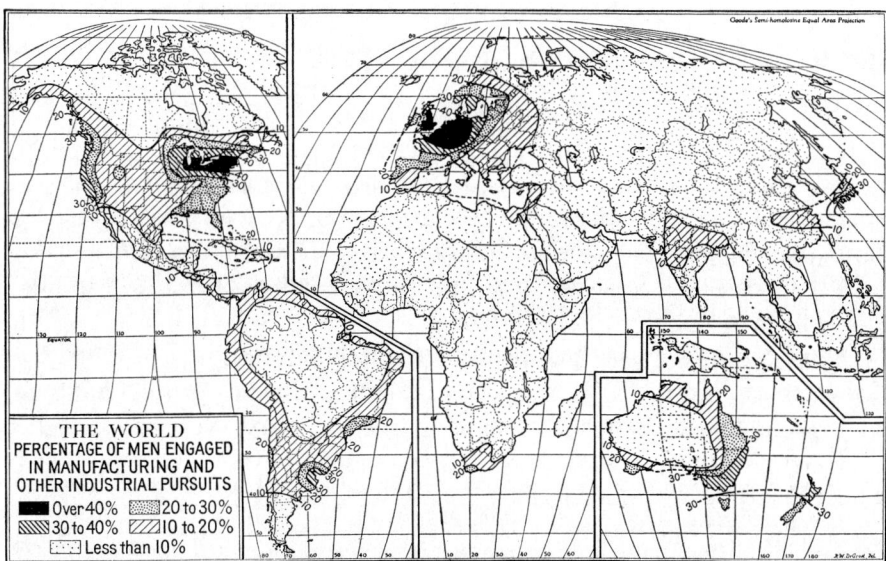

Fig. 162. Compare this map with Figure 158 (page 236). What are the two areas of most intensive manufacturing? What is the only Asiatic country that has more than 5 per cent of its population engaged in manufacturing? Locate the two areas south of the equator where manufacturing is carried on. Make two lists: (1) the countries that are wholly or partly in the group having 15 per cent or more of the population in manufacturing; (2) those wholly or partly in the group having from 5 to 15 per cent.

and raw materials of many sorts are found in many countries, we are surprised that manufacturing is carried on extensively in so few places.

**The decisive factor in the distribution of manufacturing.** The most important quality which all six of the shaded areas in Figure 162 have in common is that all are inhabited by energetic and progressive people. This is partly a matter of race and training and partly of climate and health. Only in a few regions outside the six manufacturing sections do the people show such a combination of inventiveness and determination, or have their ancestors developed such good methods of work, that a high development of manufacturing is possible. Elsewhere, it is likewise hard to find a climate which combines so many favorable qualities, both for man and for agriculture. In general, it appears that the primary factor in the distribution of manufacturing is the character of the people, their energy, progressiveness, and skill; next to this in importance come supplies of coal and other sources of power; while raw materials occupy third place in determining which parts of the world shall carry on manufacturing. Transportation facilities, markets, labor, capital, and an early start all play a great part, but often these factors depend largely on the energy, ability, and training of the people. (See page 32.)

## QUESTIONS, EXERCISES, AND PROBLEMS

**A. Making a diagram of a manufacturing industry.**

1. Visit a local manufacturing plant and take notes from which you can prepare a large diagram similar to the one for the tanning industry, shown on page 245. Read about the industry in books, magazines, and papers, and ask questions of your parents and friends. Illustrate your diagram by pictures, maps, drawings, and specimens wherever it is possible to do so.

2. Prepare a statement showing how far each of the eight conditions listed at the beginning of this chapter is important in determining the location of your factory or workshop.

**B. Other centers of your chosen manufacturing industry.**

1. From this book or from other books find out what other localities are especially good for the manufacturing industry that you have studied in Exercise A. What are the special advantages of these locations? Does some other region seem to be a better location for the industry than your own region? Why, or why not?

2. On an outline map show how much of the world is called upon to contribute to this industry, and on another show how much of the world depends upon its finished product.

**C. A study of local industries in general.**

1. Make a list of the chief local manufacturing industries. The local Chamber of Commerce probably has a full list. Let each pupil report on the industry for which he has made a diagram, and let the class then decide which industries are best suited to your locality.

2. Make a simple sketch map of your town or city. On it locate as many industrial plants as you can. Explain why they are located where they are in the town. Are the newer industries in the suburbs or the center? Why?

3. What is a "zoning ordinance"? If your local government has made one, indicate the zones on your sketch map.

4. Write an answer to a manufacturer who has written to the Chamber of Commerce to ask whether your community is a good place in which to locate a factory. Choose for yourself the industry which he wishes to establish.

**D. The relative rank of different countries in manufacturing.**

1. From Figure 162 estimate the relative importance of the six manufacturing areas, and arrange the regions in their probable order of importance. Take into consideration the following points: (a) area where manufacturing is important; (b) density of population of the manufacturing area; (c) percentage of population engaged in manufacturing; (d) distance from large markets.

2. Give reasons for the leadership of the two regions that stand first.

3. Pick out ten countries that show little sign of becoming leaders in industry, and give reasons for your choice.

## Geographical Conditions of Manufacture

### The Tanning Industry

| Raw Materials | Processes | By-Products | Products | Uses |
|---|---|---|---|---|
| 1. HIDES AND SKINS | | | | |
| *a* Cattle hides | | | | |
| *b* Horse hides | | | | |
| *c* Goat skins | | | | |
| *d* Calf skins | | | | |
| *e* Colt skins | | | | |
| *f* Sheep skins | | | | |
| *g* Pig skins | | | | |
| 2. Water | 1. Washing | | | |
| 3. Lime | 2. Liming | | | |
| | 3. Hairing | 1. Hair | | Plaster, mattresses, felt |
| | 4. Fleshing | 2. Flesh | | Glue, fertilizer |
| | 5. De-liming | 3. Ammonia | | Chemical works, household uses |
| 4. Bark | 6. Tanning | | | |
| *a* Hemlock | | | | |
| *b* Oak | | | | |
| *c* Sumac | | | | |
| *d* Mangrove | | | | |
| *e* Cutch | | | | |
| 5. Salt | 7. Washing | | 1. Leather: | 1. Shoes |
| | 8. Drying | | *a* Sole leather | 2. Bookbinding |
| 6. Dyes | 9. Dyeing | | *b* Morocco | 3. Traveling bags |
| | 10. Finishing | | *c* Calfskin | 4. Pocket-books |
| | | | *d* Russian | 5. Gloves |
| | | | *e* Patent | 6. Automobiles |
| | | | *f* Crown | 7. Furniture |
| | | | *g* Seal | 8. Harness |
| | | | *h* Buckskin | 9. Saddles |
| | | | *i* Grain, etc. | 10. Belts |
| | | | | 11. Hose, etc. |

This diagram was made by a boy from the notes taken at a tanning factory. With the help of commercial geographies and an encyclopedia, he then traced each of the raw materials to its source, and under two new headings at the left of the diagram wrote the country of origin and the source of the product. He found, for example, that goat skins usually come from semi-arid countries where the grass is too meager or too coarse for sheep or cattle. Hence in the two additional columns, opposite the words "Goat skins," he made these entries:

| Country of Origin | Source of Product |
|---|---|
| Semi-arid and often poverty-stricken countries, like India, Mexico, Turkey, and Algeria | Goats — hardy animals that can live on coarse and meager food |

The boy found that the leather tanned at this factory is mostly sold to shoe factories and automobile factories in Massachusetts and Michigan. Hence, after the list of finished products he added another column at the right, headed "Distribution," in which he wrote this information.

E. **The relation of governments to manufacturing.**

1. Look up the labor laws of your state as to (a) minimum wage; (b) overtime work; (c) labor disputes and arbitration; (d) safety appliances. Decide what parts of your state are especially influenced by these laws. Why?

2. What technical or vocational schools are there in your vicinity? In what parts of the United States are such schools likely to be most highly developed? Why? If you were the owner or manager of a large factory, would you or would you not favor the establishment of technical schools?

3. Explain how a tariff may benefit or injure manufacturing industries. Why do the dye and silk industries in the United States assert that they need protection by a tariff? Why are the southern cotton mills, which make coarse cloth, less insistent on a protective tariff than the northern mills that make fine woolen goods?

4. Ask some business men how their industries were affected when the latest tariff went into operation. When did this occur? Was the tariff intended to increase or decrease the amount of protection to home industries?

5. Get a list of articles upon which duties are charged when imported into the United States. The World Almanac gives such a list. From this, decide which of your local industries are protected from foreign competition.

6. What parts of the United States are most strongly in favor of protection and free trade respectively? Explain.

F. **What a consul does for manufacturers.**

1. Imagine yourself a United States consul in a large foreign city. Prepare for publication in the Commerce Reports of the United States Department of Commerce a statement of the foreign trade opportunities of the city where you are stationed. Include a description of (a) the kind of American manufactured goods that will interest buyers in your city; (b) the kind of goods that the city wishes to sell to the United States; (c) the best trade routes for American exporters to use from New York to your city; (d) a summary of the transportation facilities, so that American exporters may pack their goods intelligently; (e) advice in regard to systems of measurement, coinage, and language.

G. **Manufacturers and foreign trade.**

1. Great Britain, which is a great manufacturing country, obtained control of the Suez Canal and negotiated with the United States for the building of the Panama Canal. Explain the connection between Great Britain's rank in manufacturing and its interest in these two canals.

2. Compare the resources of Sweden and of Spain in coal and iron. Sweden manufactures much of her ore into high-grade steel and exports it in that form, while Spain exports most of her iron as ore. What geographic conditions help to explain these facts?

Fig. 163. Locomotive mills at Milwaukee. Are these mills conveniently situated with respect to supplies of iron and steel for raw material and coal for power? The metal industries cannot make much use of water power; they must have fuel. Why is this so?

## CHAPTER NINETEEN

### MANUFACTURING REGIONS OF THE UNITED STATES

The distribution of manufacturing in the United States is illustrated in Figure 165, which shows the percentage of the gainfully employed population engaged in manufacturing and mechanical industries. Notice the very heavily shaded area on the North Atlantic coast, the heavy shading in a large part of the northeastern quarter of the country, the two fairly heavy areas in the West, the fairly heavy tongue extending into the South, and the light shading elsewhere.

**Industries commonly found in all modern cities.** In the areas that are more lightly shaded in Figure 165, a large part of the manufacturing consists of kinds that are almost essential to every civilized region. These include printing plants, foundries and machine shops, sawmills, grist mills, bakeries, and plants for supplying gas and power.

Printing is necessary in every modern city that has a newspaper, and even small towns of a few thousand inhabitants often have printing establishments. Foundries and machine shops, or at least black-

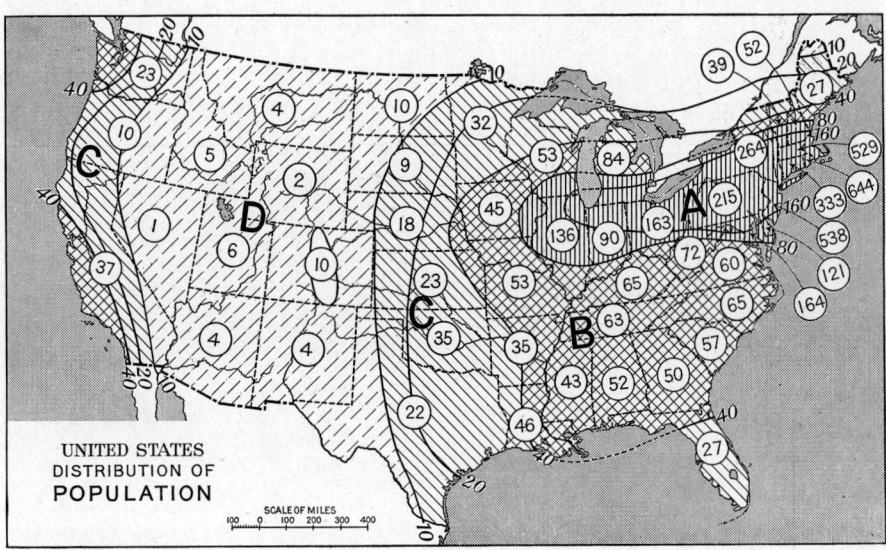

Fig. 164. The region marked A has a population of 80 or more to the square mile; B, between 80 and 40 to the square mile; C, 40 and 10; D, below 10. The circles give the number to the square mile in the different states. Which state has the highest figure? the lowest? What two regions are marked C? From this map and the map on the opposite page, where should you expect the railway network to be closest? Verify your answer by reference to Figure 128, page 176. Are the states of the wheat belt and the corn belt among the most populous?

smith shops and repair shops, are needed even in farming regions to keep all kinds of machinery and tools in repair. Sawmills are needed to supply building material, and gristmills to grind the grain which is grown almost everywhere. Each city must also have bakeries, for people demand fresh bread and pastry. Gas for lighting and heating is usually produced locally, because the coal from which it is made can be transported and stored more cheaply than can the gas, which requires special pipes and tanks. All modern cities and many small towns also have electric light plants to provide power both for lighting and for trolley lines, and for use in small shops and homes. These universal manufacturing industries, as we may call them, form a large part of the manufacturing in the more lightly shaded areas of Figure 165, and are of great importance in the heavily shaded areas where other types of manufacturing are also prominent.

## MANUFACTURING IN NORTHEASTERN UNITED STATES

The northeastern quarter of the United States adds to these universal industries many others, which differ greatly from place to place. More than 30 per cent of all the gainfully employed workers in the states from Maine and Maryland westward to the Mississippi River

# Manufacturing Regions of the United States

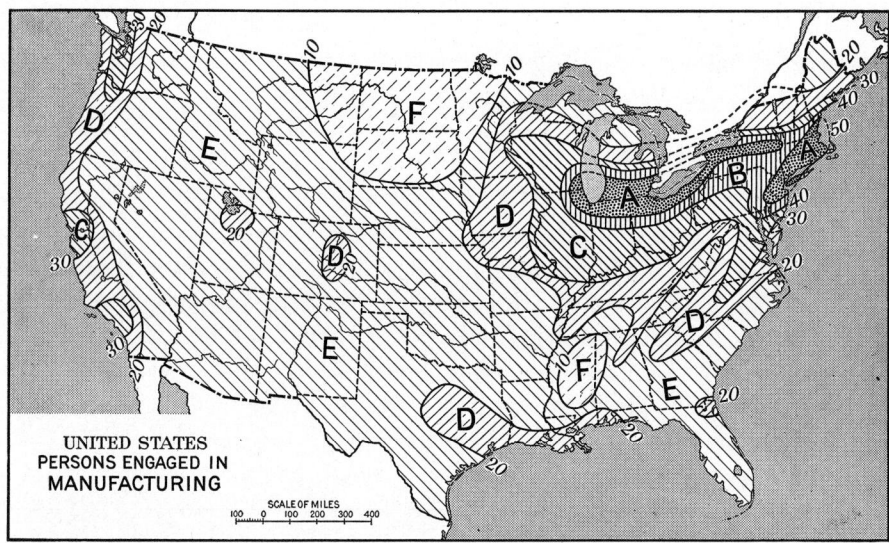

Fig. 165. In the region marked A on this map, 50 per cent of the workers or more are engaged in manufacturing; in that marked B, between 50 and 40 per cent; C, between 40 and 30 per cent; D, between 30 and 20 per cent; E, between 20 and 10 per cent; F, less than 10 per cent. What states are wholly or partly in the most intensive manufacturing area? the least intensive? Look at the primary production maps in Part One to discover whether any of the chief areas for primary production coincide with the manufacturing areas.

and north of the Ohio are engaged in manufacturing. Some of the chief reasons for the great development of manufacturing in this region are as follows:

(1) The northeastern quarter of the United States has a climate that gives a healthy person pleasure in active work.
(2) It has access to two important bodies of water, the Atlantic Ocean and the Great Lakes.
(3) It contains the greatest coal mines in the world; it has abundant water power; and the world's greatest iron mines are within easy reach by water.
(4) The climate and, in large areas, the soil and relief are admirably adapted to produce large supplies of food and raw materials.
(5) On the east this section faces Europe, a fact which not only favors trade now, but has given the region a stream of energetic settlers bringing with them a high civilization and furnishing a splendid supply of labor.
(6) The parts of the United States west and south of the manufacturing section supply abundant food and raw materials, including wheat, corn, hides, wool, and cotton.

Within the northeastern section three manufacturing districts stand out as especially important: (1) the North Atlantic district; (2) the Central New York district; and (3) the Great Lakes-Ohio River, or

Middle-West, district. In these districts manufacturing is carried on *intensively*, that is, the cities are closely grouped and manufacturing is the chief business.

### The North Atlantic Manufacturing District

The North Atlantic manufacturing district extends from Portland, Maine, to Baltimore. Although its area is small, as shown by the heaviest shading in Figure 165, it contains more than a third of the cities of the United States that have more than 75,000 inhabitants.

**The type of manufacturing.** In addition to the universal industries, the chief manufactures are such goods as shoes, watches, and cloth; that is, goods that are expensive in proportion to their size and weight and that require skilled labor and complicated machinery. The making of such goods is called *complex manufacturing*. Goods like these are rarely manufactured where their raw materials are produced, since the raw materials are not heavy enough to make the cost of transportation a main factor. Skilled labor and cheap power, however, are absolutely necessary, and of both these the North Atlantic district has an abundance.

**Manufacturing industries of the North Atlantic ports.** The important ports of the North Atlantic manufacturing district have many factories that use raw materials brought from distant points by water. Thus Boston, Providence, New York, Jersey City, Newark, Philadelphia, and Baltimore prepare such products as spices, coffee, cocoa, and chocolate. They also refine sugar and oil, make confectionery, cut cork, manufacture rattan ware, and spin and weave cotton. Most of them, too, tan imported hides, weave imported wool, and make the cloth into clothing or carpets.

New York and Philadelphia, being the greatest manufacturing centers, require special mention.

**New York as a manufacturing city.** New York is the leading manufacturing center of North America. Its varied and abundant goods are sold not only in the city and its vicinity, but in nearly all parts of the country. Wherever you live, it is probable that most of the women's suits and dresses, artificial flowers and feathers, millinery, lace goods, and furs used in your town were made in New York. The same is true of the clothing for men and the pipes they smoke. Probably the ink used in printing your books and newspapers, and the pens you write with, were made in New York. The nearer we live to this metropolitan city the more we use the articles that it manufactures; but some of its goods go all over the country.

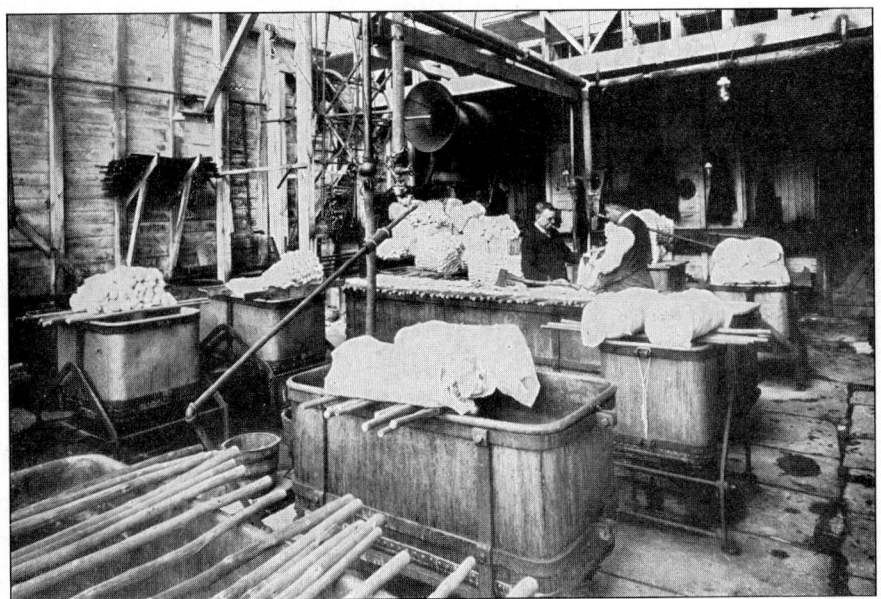

Fig. 166. Dyeing room in a silk mill at Paterson, New Jersey. Where does the mill obtain the raw silk? What kinds of power can silk mills use?

The leading industry of New York is the manufacture of men's and women's clothing. Since this city is the center for style throughout the country, not only the buyers for stores but people in general think that the clothing made in New York must be of the latest style, and therefore prefer to buy New York clothing. Slaughtering and meat packing and the making of iron and steel goods are also important industries.

As might be expected in so great a city, the printing and publishing trades are highly developed. New York is also the musical, dramatic, and artistic center of the country.

**The manufactures of Philadelphia.** Philadelphia stands next to New York and Chicago not only in population, but in manufacturing. The great resources of Pennsylvania, the excellent communication with the West by means of the Pennsylvania Railroad, and the good quality of the harbor make it easy to get raw materials and fuel and to ship manufactured goods all over the world. Yet the fact that New York has greater advantages, as explained in a previous chapter (page 211), prevents Philadelphia from equaling the great metropolis. Nevertheless, even though New York and Chicago are greater, Philadelphia is noteworthy for its vast machine shops, locomotive factories, and shipyards. At one of the most famous plants an average of seven locomotives can be completed per day. During the World War the shipyards became temporarily the most enormous in the whole world. Philadelphia is also a great center for textiles, such as rugs, carpets, underwear, stockings, and cotton and woolen goods.

### The Central New York Manufacturing District

The Central New York district of intensive manufacturing owes its location chiefly to the busy trade route from Albany to Buffalo. Although the district is nearly as long as the North Atlantic district, its width is limited, for it is scarcely more than a single string of cities.

**The industries of the cities.** The cities of this district fall into three groups whose location, like that of most cities, depends largely on conditions of transportation.

At the eastern end Albany, Schenectady, Troy, Gloversville, and Johnstown form a peculiarly specialized little group. Troy is engaged mainly in making collars and cuffs, simply because that business happened to get started there. Gloversville and Johnstown are devoted almost exclusively to glove-making because some Scotch glove-makers settled there more than a century ago. They made such good gloves and were so progressive in adopting the sewing machine and the factory system that these two small cities still make more than half the gloves produced in the whole country. Schenectady is not quite so specialized, but is known chiefly for its great electrical factory and locomotive works.

A little farther west, Utica has important cotton and woolen mills, while Syracuse specializes in automobiles and typewriters. These two cities and their smaller neighbors form a group in which transportation by water is of no importance.

Still farther west the third group of the Central New York district comprises the lake cities of Rochester and Buffalo, together with Niagara Falls. Rochester has made a great reputation for its cameras, photographic materials, optical instruments, and thermometers. It is a city where a large part of the work is of an unusually skilled type. Buffalo has taken advantage of the great quantities of raw materials which come to it because it is the eastern terminus of a large part of the Great Lakes transportation. Hence it converts wheat and meat into finished products, and is a great center for the larger kinds of iron and steel work. The splendid supply of hydroelectric power from Niagara Falls is a wonderful advantage to Buffalo and to the city of Niagara Falls, which has the same kind of industries as Buffalo.

## The Great Lakes-Ohio River Manufacturing District

The third of the intensive manufacturing districts is fan-shaped, with Pittsburgh, Cincinnati, and Milwaukee at the angles. One sixth of the country's cities of more than 75,000 people are in this district.

**The kind of manufacturing carried on.** This district may well be called the coal and iron district, because it is covered with cities whose chief raw materials are coal and iron. These two minerals naturally meet here, for much of the surface is underlain by coal deposits and the best of iron ore is brought at low cost from the western end of Lake Superior.

In scores of cities coal and iron are the rough sources of all sorts of wonderful machines and articles of steel. These articles are chiefly automobiles at Detroit, ships at Cleveland, cars at Chicago, rails at Pittsburgh, machinery at Milwaukee, building frames at Youngstown, and cash registers at Dayton. The exact kind of product in each city is often determined by the striking success of one company in a pioneer industry. For instance, after one company had made Detroit famous for automobiles, other companies were formed to take advantage not only of the fame of the city in this line, but of the skilled labor which had gathered there.

**Other important manufacturing industries.** Although the Great Lakes-Ohio River district is best known for steel products, it is important in many other respects also. No other region, for instance, is so prominent in the slaughtering and meat-packing industry. This is partly because there is an abundant supply of corn, hay, and alfalfa for fattening cattle and pigs, and partly because the region lies midway between the western grazing lands and the eastern markets. Chicago alone carries on about one seventh of the country's slaughtering and meat packing.

The location of this district in the eastern part of the grain region, and its dense population, make it important in milling flour and grinding corn. Nearly every town, large or small, has its own flour mills. Some convert corn, wheat, and oats into many kinds of cereal foods. Battle Creek, Michigan, is well known for such foods.

Still another important industry is the manufacture of wooden articles, such as furniture, refrigerators, carriages, boxes, and barrels. Most of the lumber for these comes from the forests of Michigan, Wisconsin, and Minnesota. Chicago makes more wooden articles of all kinds than any other place in the country, while Grand Rapids is more especially devoted to furniture making.

Fig. 167. Some of the foundries at Homestead, a typical "steel city." Here many thousands of iron, or in the steel plants where the smelted iron is made into steel, or in the

**The great manufacturing cities of the Middle West.** Four cities of this third manufacturing district — namely, Chicago, Cleveland, Pittsburgh, and Detroit — rank among the world's greatest industrial centers. Their advantages in the matter of transportation have already been discussed (pages 217 to 221).

Chicago, with two thirds of the factory workers of Illinois, stands first among the cities of the United States not only in wooden products, but in slaughtering and meat packing, in foundry and machine-shop work, and in making and repairing railroad cars. Almost everyone knows of the Pullman cars, which are made in a Chicago suburb.

Cleveland, by reason of its favorable position on Lake Erie, finds that it pays to bring coal from near Pittsburgh to meet the iron ore that comes from the Lake Superior region. Its specialties range from small articles like nails, wire, bolts, and hardware, to bulky ships and bridges, — practically all of them products that use large amounts of iron.

Pittsburgh is the center of a cluster of great iron-working communities, including McKeesport, South Bethlehem, Braddock, and Homestead. The growth of this cluster in just this area depends largely on the fact that the meeting point of the Allegheny and Ohio rivers happens to lie near a great seam of coal sixteen feet thick. The cities stretch along the rivers more than twenty miles. Their growth is helped by enormous quantities of petroleum and natural gas, which supplement the coal in the steel industries. In early days the necessary iron ore also was mined in the neighborhood, but this is now displaced by ore from Lake Superior.

Detroit is an interesting response to a new industry. The location of the city, as we have seen, is favorable; but in 1900 twelve cities exceeded it in size and it was about the same size as Milwaukee. Then

men, of all nationalities, work at the great blast furnaces where iron ore is smelted to make pig mills where the steel is rolled out into rods and plates for further use in industry.

the automobile began to be important, and the industry naturally came to have a center. Detroit was no better adapted to be such a center than several other cities; but when once it had become the automobile city, it grew so fast that it is more than twice as large as Milwaukee, and is one of the world's greatest cities.

In the southern part of the middle-western manufacturing district, Cincinnati is the largest of a group of cities which includes Indianapolis, Columbus, and Dayton. These cities lie some distance from the iron-ore route of the Great Lakes, but are supplied with cheap coal either by way of the Ohio River or from local coal fields. Consequently they do not engage largely in the manufacture of the heavier kinds of iron goods, such as steel rails and steel cars, but specialize in articles like typewriters, cash registers, and automobile ignition apparatus, articles in which the amount of iron is small in proportion to the work put into the product. Slaughtering, meat packing, and the accompanying occupations, such as soap making, are also important, because many animals are raised on the surrounding farms; but the bulk of the animals produced farther west go to Chicago and St. Louis.

### Manufacturing in the Northeastern Section outside of the Three Districts

There is a large part of the northeastern section of the United States that is in marked contrast to the area of concentrated manufacturing.

**Where manufacturing is extensive and simple.** In the North Atlantic district, the Central New York district, and the Middle West district, manufacturing is *intensive;* that is, the region is well covered with manufacturing cities. Many of them are large, and their industrial plants are on a great scale. The type of manufacturing is also *complex* in that it requires much skilled labor and complicated machinery, and the raw materials are greatly changed before they become finished products. In the northeastern section outside of these three districts, on the other hand, although manufacturing is important it is generally *extensive*. That is, the distances between manufacturing cities are relatively great and the cities and plants are commonly small. In fact, much of the manufacturing is carried on in villages. The type of manufacturing in these outside regions is also likely to be *simple*. The raw materials are usually found close at hand; they pass through only a few processes, and complicated machinery is rarely used. Logs, for example, are cut into lumber, turned into wooden ware, or ground into wood pulp for paper; milk is made into butter, cheese, and condensed milk; fruit and vegetables are canned; and rocks like granite and marble are chiseled into blocks and slabs.

**Why parts of the northeastern section have only simple manufacturing.** In the northeastern section of the United States the industries outside the three districts of intensive, complex manufacturing are relatively undeveloped for three reasons: (1) Some regions, such as the Appalachians, are too rugged for manufacturing, and transportation costs too much. (2) Other regions, such as the peninsulas of Maryland and Cape Cod, are located at a distance from important trade routes. (3) Some regions are still young, industrially. The iron region of Minnesota is a good example.

**Cities of the northeastern manufacturing section outside the most intensive areas.** Important manufacturing cities may be located in regions which are not as a whole characterized by intensive manufacturing. Such regions within or on the edges of the northeastern manufacturing section contain the cities of St. Louis, Minneapolis, St. Paul, Scranton, and Duluth.

St. Louis resembles Chicago in its great meat-packing industries, but being off the routes on which iron ore is cheaply transported, and near places where hides and tobacco are produced, it specializes in shoemaking and tobacco products. When the nearness of St. Louis to a great supply of hides convinced eastern companies of the advantages of St. Louis for shoemaking, skilled labor and complicated machinery were moved bodily from the East to start the industry.

Minneapolis and St. Paul, commonly called the Twin Cities, find unusually favorable conditions for milling wheat at the Falls of St. Anthony on the Mississippi River, where 50,000 horse power are

# Manufacturing Regions of the United States

Fig. 168. Rolling steel plate.

developed. The best part of the wheat belt lies just to the northwest, and the flour market lies farther east.

Scranton is a little Pittsburgh, for its chief industries are founded on coal, — anthracite in this case, — and it is the head of a cluster of steel towns.

Duluth is the main outlet on the Great Lakes for the Superior iron ore. It now receives quantities of coal from Pittsburgh, so that it carries on iron and steel manufacturing to help satisfy the market of its hinterland to the west.

### SIMPLE MANUFACTURING IN OTHER PARTS OF THE UNITED STATES

Outside of the northeastern section, the manufacturing industries of the United States are generally simple. Because of their simplicity, many of them do not require a large body of skilled workers and are therefore often scattered widely at small centers where they can get a local supply of the chief raw material.

### The Southern States

In the southern states the presence of cotton fields has led to the establishment of many small factories that make oil and " cake " from the seeds (page 23). Likewise the southern forests supply the pine wood from which turpentine and rosin are manufactured.

**Industries fostered by cotton growing.** Cotton growing has also built up the cotton spinning and weaving industry of the piedmont belt in North and South Carolina, Georgia, and Alabama. This industry requires more skilled labor than the other simple industries mentioned in this section, but much less than the cotton manufacturing of the New England states, where finer thread is spun and finer cloth is woven. The chief reasons for its interesting growth are: (1) the local supply of raw cotton; (2) the falls and rapids where the rivers flow from the hard rocks of the old land to the loose soil of the coastal plain; (3) a labor supply cheaper than that of the northeastern section, and (4) a local southern market for cotton goods.

No large city has yet developed as a result of the southern cotton industry. The two chief cities in this region are not devoted chiefly to cotton. Birmingham, because of its proximity to mines of both coal and iron, is a center for crude iron and steel. In Atlanta printing and publishing rank first, since the city is a state capital and the seat of many educational institutions.

**The industrial center of the far South.** Farther to the southwest, New Orleans is by far the greatest of the southern industrial centers. Its industries depend largely on local raw materials furnished by forests, rice fields, and sugar and cotton plantations. Hence wooden goods, especially shingles, and tanks for sugar, are important products. Sugar refining and the making of confectionery hold a high place. Each year the city makes many million dollars' worth of burlap bags for use in handling cotton seed, cottonseed meal, rice, and fertilizer. Naturally much cottonseed oil is prepared; and New Orleans is the chief center for the cleaning and polishing of rice. Because of the warm climate, the city likewise makes an unusually large amount of ice.

The difference between the industries of a southern city like New Orleans, which depends largely on plantation products, and a northern city like Cleveland, which depends largely on the products of mines, is most interesting.

### Cities of the Western Plains

**The meat-packing cities.** Westward from the main manufacturing section of the United States the work of St. Louis is continued in a group of meat-packing cities. Kansas City, St. Joseph, Des Moines, and Omaha are in part a response to the refrigerator car and the other methods that have made it possible to preserve meat a long time and transport it long distances. They have the advantages of being located (1) in the corn belt, (2) near the edge of the grazing lands, and (3) on main routes from the grazing lands to the great markets. Some of these advantages are shared in a less degree by a more southerly group of meat-packing cities, including Oklahoma City, Fort Worth, San Antonio, Dallas, and Houston; but there the cotton-ginning and cottonseed oil industries also become important.

**In the mountain section.** Farther west, the only large city in or near the Rocky Mountains is Denver. It lies just east of a great mining region and west of the country's largest grazing region. Hence its manufacturing takes the two-fold form of (1) animal industries, including some dairying as well as slaughtering and meat packing, and (2) mining industries in the form of great smelters, the sulphur by-products of which are used for sulphuric acid.

## The Pacific Manufacturing Centers

**The type of industries.** Although many signs point to the future development of a Pacific manufacturing section resembling the intensive eastern section, most of the Pacific industries are still of the simple type. The splendid forests furnish lumber, which at places like Seattle, Tacoma, and Portland is sawed and planed or made into boxes for the vast amount of fruit raised in the Pacific lowlands. Extensive grazing ranges produce not only meat but some milk for butter and cheese. Flour mills are needed because of the great wheat fields. In Washington the streams and bays support the important salmon-canning industry; while in California the climate is so favorable for the growth of fruits in great variety that vast quantities of canned peaches, dried prunes, and other preserved fruits are prepared for sale in the eastern and foreign markets.

**The possible use of water power.** The industrial development of the Pacific coast was at first hampered by the scarcity and costliness of coal. At present the extensive use of water power, the production of petroleum in southern California, and some coal mining in Washington much lessen this handicap. So great are the possibilities of developing water power in Oregon and Washington that many people expect the Willamette Valley and Puget Sound region to become one of the world's greatest manufacturing districts, with Seattle as its metropolis and Portland and Tacoma as two other great cities. The unexcelled forests in the neighboring mountains, and the great wheat fields farther east, with Spokane as their center, are important factors in promoting such development. An added advantage is the peculiarly healthful climate.

**The two leading California cities.** The industries of San Francisco are chiefly those that satisfy the local needs of a large city, such as printing and publishing, slaughtering, iron and steel works, and baking. Another type consists of the manufacture of imported raw materials, such as sugar, spices, coffee, and silk goods. Oakland is especially important for lumber products from lumber cut in the Sierra Nevada Mountains on the east or brought from Washington and Oregon by boat.

Aside from the universal industries and the canning factories, Los Angeles has two great industries. One is the refining of oil, the supply of which comes from the California oil fields, shown in figure 102 (page 129). The other is unique, because Los Angeles is by far the greatest center of the motion picture industry. Scenes pictured there are shown daily to audiences in almost every country of the world. Several geographical factors combine to produce this result. (1) First comes the climate, with its clear sunny skies at all seasons, and its absence of extremes of either heat or cold. (2) The mountains furnish splendid scenery close to the great city. (3) Not far away the ocean with its fine surf and picturesque islands supplies the scenery for plays of another type. (4) And lastly the vegetation varies greatly. Tracts of desert bushes occupy the low, dry plains, wonderful orchards of oranges and other fruits interspersed with rich gardens and grain fields are found in the irrigated areas; while open forests of live oak cover the lower slopes of the mountains and denser pine forests abound higher up. To the stranger who has the privilege of seeing how motion pictures are made, Los Angeles seems like a city in wonderland, but to the players it is a place where a great industry has its home.

### CANADIAN SECTION OF THE NORTH AMERICAN MANUFACTURING AREA

The manufacturing region of southeastern Canada is practically a continuation of that of the eastern United States. Toronto, as may be seen in Figure 162, lies almost in the area of intensive manufacturing, while Montreal is an outlier like Minneapolis and St. Paul. These places draw coal, iron, raw cotton, rubber, sugar, and wool from a distance, and convert them into manufactured goods that are sold all over Canada. Other cities, such as Quebec, Winnipeg, and Vancouver, supply local demands.

Nevertheless, most of the manufacturing of Canada consists of relatively simple operations, such as sawing boards and shingles, making wood pulp, canning fish, and making butter and cheese. Like such states as Maine, Minnesota, Tennessee, and Arizona, most of Canada relies on the northeastern United States and England for a large part of its more complex manufactured goods, and devotes its energies chiefly to taking care of its natural resources.

# Manufacturing Regions of the United States

## QUESTIONS, EXERCISES, AND PROBLEMS

**A. Manufacturing in your own state.**

1. For detailed information on your own state, consult the Supplement to the last Census of the United States. Write for a copy to your congressman, or to the Director, Bureau of the Census, Department of Commerce and Labor, Washington, D. C.

    (a) What is the population of your state?
    (b) How many persons in the state have occupations?
    (c) How many out of every hundred?
    (d) How many are engaged in farming? mining? manufacturing? transportation?
    (e) How many out of every hundred in the state are in each of these occupations?
    (f) What occupation predominates in your state? Why?
    (g) What are the occupations of most of the people whom you know?
    (h) What occupation would you like to follow? Why?
    (i) Of what type is the manufacturing carried on in your state — complex and intensive, or simple?

**B. The relative position of manufacturing in various parts of the United States.**

1. In spite of their lack of coal, southern New England and New York are two of our most advanced industrial regions. Explain this condition.

2. Why is the South less advanced in manufacture than the North?

3. Explain why manufacturing has developed more rapidly:

    (a) along the Great Lakes than along the Mississippi.
    (b) along the Ohio than along the Missouri.
    (c) along the Merrimac than along the Columbia.
    (d) along the shore of Lake Erie than along the shore of Lake Ontario.

4. Which parts of the United States have a climate best suited for the energetic work required in manufacturing?

5. In which parts do the conditions of climate, soil, and relief make it difficult to produce the abundant food supply required by a large manufacturing population? Are any such areas prominent in manufacturing? Explain.

**C. Where to locate a manufacturing industry.**

1. Suppose that you have charge of locating a factory somewhere in the United States. Convince the rest of the class that you have chosen the best location for a factory of one of the following kinds:

    (a) Steel making
    (b) Meat packing
    (c) Making coarse cotton cloth
    (d) Making shoes
    (e) Refining beet sugar
    (f) Making paper

2. Give reasons why you think it wise or unwise to attempt to manufacture the following products on a large scale in the states mentioned:
   - (a) Cane sugar in Illinois
   - (b) Lard in Ohio
   - (c) Paper in Nebraska
   - (d) Shoes in Florida
   - (e) Cotton goods in Washington
   - (f) Woolen carpets in Montana
   - (g) Farming implements in Pennsylvania
   - (h) Steel cars in Arizona
3. Compare the general advantages for manufacturing in (a) Connecticut and Mississippi, (b) Ohio and New Mexico, (c) West Virginia and Utah.
4. The United States has about 3000 flour mills widely distributed throughout the country, but there are only about 20 sugar refineries and these are located at comparatively few places. Give reasons for these conditions.
5. Why are most of the cane-sugar refineries situated near the northern Atlantic coast, although cane sugar is raised only near the southern coast, where there are some 200 mills producing crude sugar?

D. **The manufacturing industries of a state.**

1. Let each pupil select a state or small group of states and study its manufacturing industries. Use an encyclopedia, *The Statesman's Year-Book*, and the reports on manufacturing by states, issued by the Bureau of the Census, Washington, D. C. Often the secretaries of the Chambers of Commerce in large cities are willing to send pamphlets telling about manufacturing as well as various other activities. After all the available information has been gathered, put it into a booklet containing these items:
   - (a) A map showing the position of the chosen state or group of states.
   - (b) A map of the state or group, as large as the page will allow, showing centers of manufacturing, rivers that may be used for power or transportation, coal deposits, petroleum or natural gas supplies.
   - (c) A list of raw materials produced in large quantities.
   - (d) A description of the advantages for manufacturing.
   - (e) A description of the disadvantages.
   - (f) A list of the chief kinds of manufacturing, with the reasons for occurrence in the region.
   - (g) An estimate of the probable rate at which the state or group of states will increase its manufacturing in the next ten years.

E. **A review of manufacturing in the northeastern United States.**

1. (Do as much of the work of this problem from memory as you can.) Draw a map of the states included in the northeastern manufacturing section. Label the states, the important rivers, the Great Lakes, and the Erie Barge Canal. Print the name of each city mentioned in this chapter, and in parentheses beneath the name print its chief manufactures. From Table 3, page 327, find the rank of each of the northeastern states in the value of manufactures per person. After the name of each state on the map, put a figure to indicate its rank.
2. Compare the amount of manufacturing done by the three northern and the three southern New England states. What advantages have the three southern states?

3. What advantages has New York over Pennsylvania? Pennsylvania over New York? What effect has each set of advantages on the type of manufacturing? Why?
4. New Jersey has neither water power nor mineral resources, yet stands high as a manufacturing state. Explain why she specializes in (a) oil refining; (b) sugar refining; (c) silk weaving; (d) steel manufacturing.

F. **Niagara Falls as a source of power.**
1. How does it happen that the United States and Canada share the power obtained at Niagara? How do they use this power?
2. Let some member of the class who is interested in machinery make a brief report on the means by which the power is conveyed to the factories, illustrating with drawings, if possible.
3. Canada lacks abundant supplies of coal. Canada has utilized most of her share in the power from the falls. Explain the connection between these two facts.
4. Many persons object to unrestricted use of the falls for manufacturing purposes. What are their reasons? Do you agree or disagree?
5. Locate Muscle Shoals, and find out how the potential water power compares with that at Niagara.

FIG. 169. These falls in northern India are an undeveloped source of water power. Until recently such falls have been likely to remain unused, since they are far distant from towns and villages; but now that electricity is making it possible to carry water power long distances, cities in the lowlands are able to utilize it.

*Brown Brothers*

Fig. 170. The Bank of England, to the left. For two centuries "the Old Lady of Threadneedle Street" has been the center of the commercial and financial world. The London Stock Exchange is shown to the right.

## CHAPTER TWENTY

### MANUFACTURING OUTSIDE THE UNITED STATES

MODERN manufacturing had its beginnings in Europe, and there it is supreme today. The continent not only cares for its own needs almost entirely, but supplies most of the rest of the world with vast quantities of manufactured articles. Not all of Europe, however, engages intensively in manufacturing. The manufacturing section is found in western Europe and includes Great Britain, France, Germany, and the small adjoining countries, — Belgium, Holland, and Switzerland. Detached manufacturing areas flourish in northern Italy, southern Sweden, and northeastern Spain; Czechoslovakia carries some special industries to a high point of excellence; and small industrial areas and local industries are scattered elsewhere in Europe. Nevertheless, the bulk of the manufacturing, especially of the great staples of industry, is done in the six countries first mentioned.

**Why western Europe carries on most of the manufacturing of the continent.** Western Europe holds the same relation to the rest of Europe that our northeastern section holds to the rest of the United States. It occupies only one seventh of Europe, yet it produces more than three fourths of the manufactures.

Here are some of the chief reasons for these striking conditions:

(1) Western Europe, more than any other part, is inhabited by vigorous and inventive peoples, and enjoys a climate that encourages active work.
(2) Its position near the center of the land hemisphere gives it an advantage over an out-of-the-way region like New Zealand, for instance.
(3) The European manufacturing section faces the North Atlantic, and is traversed by navigable rivers leading to the Baltic, North, and Mediterranean seas. No part is more than three hundred miles from an arm of the sea.
(4) The many fine harbors allow raw materials to be readily imported and the finished products to be exported.
(5) Western Europe contains excellent coal and iron mines.
(6) The relief, soil, and climate are almost ideal for many of the chief crops that supply raw materials for factories and food for workers.
(7) Within the section, or only a few hundred miles outside it, live about two hundred million highly civilized people who constitute a compact market which normally has great purchasing power.

GREAT BRITAIN — THE LEADER IN TEXTILES AND SHIPBUILDING

Great Britain is second only to the United States in the production of manufactured goods. It makes more cotton and woolen goods than any other country. Half the value of the exports consists of cotton and woolen textiles.

**The British textile industry.** Though Great Britain produces such fine cotton and woolen goods, it gets most of its raw cotton from the United States and imports a large part of its wool. How, then, do we explain its leadership in the textile industry? One reason is the advantage of an early start. Others are the supplies of fuel and the climate. Lancaster County (Lancashire), which is the leading cotton manufacturing district, not only has the advantage of coal fields, but faces the Irish Sea, whence the prevailing west wind brings moist air that favors the spinning of cotton. Manchester, the chief cotton center, is so famous that everywhere in the commercial world the term "Manchester goods" means "cotton goods." Farther east the cities of Bradford and Leeds, near a sheep-raising district with coal deposits beneath, are the centers of the woolen industry.

**British iron and steel centers.** Great Britain normally stands next to the United States and Germany in the production of iron and steel goods. Near Birmingham, midway between Liverpool and London,

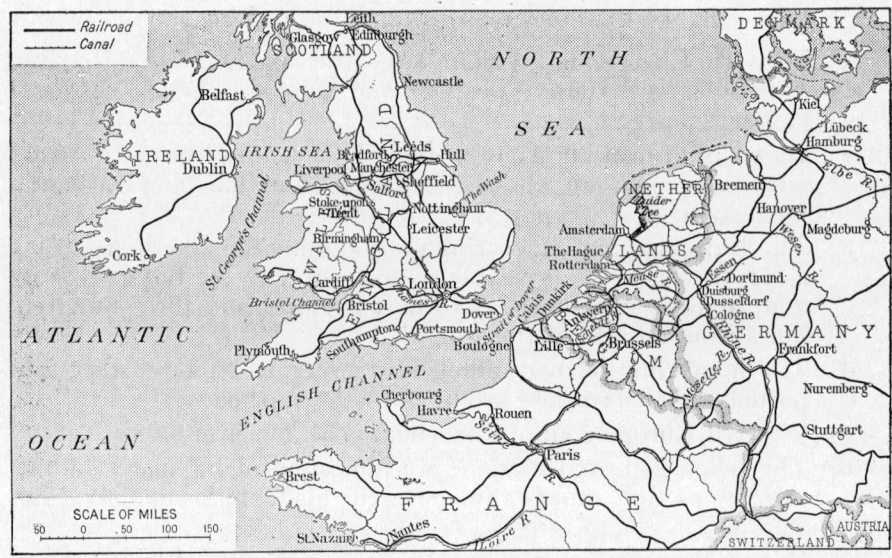

Fig. 171. Western Europe is one of the world's two great factory regions. What is the other? On this map, only the main rivers and canals, and a small fraction of the many railway lines are given; the units of the transportation system are too numerous and too close together for all of them to be shown on a map of this size. Note how railway lines radiate from London, Paris, and Brussels. Observe the number of ports with which Paris is connected. In northwestern Europe, the lower courses of many rivers are so broad and deep that ocean vessels can go a considerable distance up stream, as at London. Why is this an advantage to manufacturing?

a vast forest of tall factory chimneys sends so much smoke into the air that this region has long been called " the Black Country." The presence of coal and iron mines close by explains why the chief center of the British steel and iron industry is located here.

Two large districts in the British Isles resound continually with the hammering of steel as it is framed into ships. Along the River Clyde the greatest shipbuilding district in the world centers at Glasgow; while the Newcastle district on the River Tyne adds to Britain's prestige as the greatest shipbuilding country. Both districts have plenty of iron and coal in their immediate vicinity. Sheffield, long famed as the home of the finest cutlery, has also turned its skill to guns, projectiles, and steel armor plates for warships.

There is hardly a city in Great Britain that cannot boast of its manufactures. London, like New York, is a great clothing center and also manufactures an enormous variety of other goods. So does Liverpool, but that city specializes in the milling of American wheat, just as Dundee specializes in spinning and weaving jute from Calcutta, and Cardiff in smelting Spanish iron at its coal mines.

### FRANCE — THE COUNTRY OF ARTISTIC MANUFACTURE

France is noted for producing goods of unusually fine quality. The people of France have been artistic for centuries; the government and other organizations have encouraged art. This artistic taste shows itself in delicate and elegant manufactured products, such as expensive silks and velvets, fine cottons with original designs, exquisite laces, fine porcelain ware, beautiful gowns and robes, costly hats and dainty gloves.

Paris is especially noted for the articles of luxury that are in demand in cities of great wealth. These articles include fancy clothing, jewelry, perfumes, costly furniture, and artificial flowers and feathers. In spite of the efforts of rival cities like New York, Paris gowns and Paris styles are still the favorites. As a great railroad center the city has large establishments for repairing cars and engines. The chief advantage of industrial Paris is its location in the center of a great plain, which allows railroads and canals to be built in almost every direction. The Seine has been canalized so that Paris is now a port for small vessels. But we must not think of Paris chiefly as an industrial center; it is far more noted as a center of art, society, politics, and education.

Marseilles, on a fine Mediterranean harbor near the mouth of the Rhone, may be compared with New Orleans, since its southern location causes its raw materials to be largely vegetable products other than the staple cereals and cottons. It refines the oil pressed from the olives grown not far away, and from great quantities of peanuts, coconuts, and other oil-seeds brought from the Orient. Soap is made from some of the oil, and macaroni from wheat imported from Italy.

Lyons is the chief silk manufacturing city in the world. The early introduction of mulberry trees and silkworms in the Rhone valley started the silk industry at Lyons. Its location in the upper Rhone valley, near coal mines, has favored its growth.

In addition to Paris, Marseilles, and Lyons, France has many minor manufacturing centers in all parts of the country. In the northeast the presence of coal and iron have made Nancy and Verdun great steel centers; Lille and Roubaix in the north long ago got a start as woolen cities because of the sheep in the surrounding country; while Rouen on the Seine is naturally the leading cotton center because of its position in relation to America and to moist winds from the ocean.

For marketing her manufactures, France has the great advantage of both Atlantic and Mediterranean ports.

### GERMANY'S SPECIAL MANUFACTURES

Germany manufactures great quantities of iron and steel products, cotton, woolen, and silk goods, chemicals, and beet sugar. The iron and steel products are made near the coal mines that stretch across south central Germany from west to east. Essen on the Ruhr, near the Rhine, is the center of a great iron and steel district. It is the home of the vast Krupp steel works, which make all kinds of steel products for railroads, ships, engines, and mills, and were formerly famed as the greatest munitions plant in the world.

This same district supplies coal for leading textile centers — for making silk at Crefeld, woolen goods at Aachen (Aix-la-Chapelle), woolen, cotton, and linen goods at Elberfeld and Barmen. Steel ships are built at the ports of Stettin and Kiel on the Baltic, and at Hamburg on the River Elbe.

**Why Germany developed her chemical manufactures.** Germany is famous for her skill in applying the science learned in schools and universities to the work of manufacturing. Before the World War, Germany was far ahead of any other country in the chemical industries. This happened partly because numerous chemists who had been trained in the universities were employed to discover methods of cheaply producing the chemicals needed for such things as dyes, fertilizers, drugs, perfumes, and artificial camphor. For instance, German chemists have produced dyes of hundreds of hues out of tar that was formerly wasted. This same tar supplies carbolic acid and many drugs.

The chemical plants are located chiefly at Stassfurt in central Germany, which lies over a bed of "potash salts." Elberfeld and Barmen, near the western coal mines, and Frankfurt and Mannheim, in the upper Rhine valley, are also great chemical centers.

One of the greatest advantages that Germany has derived from her chemists is the ability to extract sugar from beets at low cost. Her scientific farmer has done his part by developing sugar beets that contain twice the amount of sugar formerly obtained from the vegetable. As a result, Germany before the war manufactured more sugar than any other country. Beet sugar is manufactured in hundreds of factories scattered over northern Germany, where the soil and climate permit sugar beets to grow profitably. After harvesting the beets, many farmers become workers in the factories. Germany supplies all the sugar that she needs herself and has great quantities of sugar for export.

*Swiss Aviation Service*

Fig. 172. Berne, photographed from an airplane. Switzerland has no large industrial cities, such as Sheffield and Lille. Her products are the kind that require small amounts of raw material and highly skilled workmanship, and are made in small factories and home workshops.

Throughout the mountains of southern Germany many handmade goods, such as toys, wooden clocks, and harmonicas, are manufactured in homes, often from wood taken from the surrounding forests.

### HOLLAND, BELGIUM, AND SWITZERLAND

The three small countries of Holland, Belgium, and Switzerland are much like their larger neighbors in being regions of relatively intensive manufacturing. They differ a good deal from one another, however, because Belgium has local supplies of coal, Holland has remarkable advantages in transportation, and Switzerland has no special advantage except the character of its people.

**Holland as a manufacturing country.** Holland is included in the manufacturing section of Europe because it is surrounded by industrial countries and helps many of them by the lively commerce which its position on the delta of the Rhine helps it to maintain. Commerce is the leading occupation, farming is second, and manufacturing third. In its favorable position and lack of resources Holland is much like the state of New Jersey.

With two excellent seaports, Amsterdam and Rotterdam, and its great interest in commerce, Holland builds many ships of all sizes, in spite of the fact that coal and iron must be imported. Many centers manufacture cotton, woolen, linen, and jute goods. Chocolate, cocoa, quinine, and cigars are manufactured in large quantities because their raw materials are grown extensively in the Dutch East Indies. Amsterdam is especially known as a place where great numbers of diamonds are cut.

**The advantages of Belgium in manufacturing.** Its position, its coal fields, and its iron mines, with the excellent harbor of Antwerp, make Belgium a great manufacturing country in proportion to its size. Liége, because of its coal fields, is a great steel center like Birmingham and Pittsburgh. Belgium leads the world in glass-making, with the main center at Charleroi. Ghent, in the center of a flax-growing district, is famous for linen, Verviers in a sheep-grazing district is noted for woolen goods, and Brussels for carpets. In no other country are intensive manufacturing and intensive agriculture more intimately combined.

**Why Switzerland is a manufacturing country.** Although Switzerland is an independent country, it is only three fifths the size of West Virginia, and is far more rugged. Since coal as well as iron must be imported from Germany or elsewhere, the streams flowing down steep mountain slopes have been made to do most of the work that is usually done by coal. Thus the industrial workers of Switzerland are as numerous as the farmers. In spite of the disadvantages of a mountainous relief and no seacoast, the earnest, careful, intelligent work of the Swiss people has made Switzerland thrive in manufacturing. It specializes chiefly in products for which raw materials can be easily imported and which take up little room in proportion to their value, so that their transportation to distant markets is cheap; for instance, watches, jewelry, silks, and embroideries.

Zurich, a large railroad center at the foot of the Lake of Zurich, makes jewelry and is the trading center for watches, which it collects from western Switzerland, the watch manufacturing district. St. Gallen near the Lake of Constance is famous for embroideries on cotton. The United States often imports more than $10,000,000 worth of embroideries from Switzerland in a year.

The mountainous parts of Switzerland support so many cattle that great quantities of milk are available for cheese, butter, condensed milk, and milk chocolate. The United States imports several million dollars' worth of Swiss cheese each year, and Neufchâtel cheese is a well known food product in most parts of America.

### MANUFACTURING IN OTHER EUROPEAN COUNTRIES

In the areas outside the six countries already described in this chapter, Europe carries on considerable manufacturing when compared with any other parts of the world except its own manufacturing section and the United States. Northern Italy with its silk and other factories; Sweden with its steel works, wood pulp, paper, and match factories; Denmark with its butter and cheese factories; and several other countries, all deserve notice in any complete study of manufacturing. In the same way Barcelona, Prague, Warsaw, Budapest, and Moscow are examples of cities where manufacturing is more advanced and active than almost anywhere else except western Europe, the United States, and parts of Japan. Nevertheless, the manufactures of Europe outside the main industrial district near the North Sea are relatively slight.

### MANUFACTURING OUTSIDE THE UNITED STATES AND EUROPE

Outside the United States and Europe, all the rest of the world makes far less cotton cloth than the one small British county of Lancaster, and less chemical products than one small valley in western Germany. It refines less petroleum than the single city of Bayonne; and manufactures fewer leather shoes than the small city of Brockton, less woolen cloth than a single company in Massachusetts, and less iron than a single company in Pennsylvania. Nevertheless, certain regions show many signs of rapid development.

**Japan.** Foremost among these stands Japan. The energy of the people, their artistic ability, and the large supply of labor are rapidly making great industrial centers of Osaka, Kobe, Nagoya, and Tokio. Even in the manufacture of ordinary cotton goods the Japanese love of beauty displays itself, while the Japanese silks, lacquered ware, floor matting, earthenware, and paper, even when machine made, often have a distinctive quality that finds them a market all over the world.

**The promise of industrial development in the Commonwealth of Australia.** Southeastern Australia and New Zealand resemble the Pacific coast of the United States in their relation to manufacturing, as in many other ways. Because they are new regions with splendid natural resources, the energy of the people is still largely devoted to producing food and raw materials; but the people are wide awake and energetic and are far both from markets for their products and from the sources of supply of manufactured goods. Hence they not only find it necessary to carry on the kinds of manufacturing that prepare their goods for market, — for example, meat packing, cheese making, flour milling, and smelting, — but are also beginning to produce more complex manufactured goods, such as farm machinery, which they have hitherto taken in considerable quantities from the United States. If the number of people were greater, Australia and New Zealand might soon become important manufacturing regions.

**South American industries.** In the temperate parts of South America, the countries of Argentina, Chile, and Uruguay display conditions somewhat like those of Australia, but are not quite so advanced industrially. Argentina and Uruguay thus far have done little manufacturing except in preparing cereals and meat for the market. Chile, with coal, iron, and copper within easy reach, has established steel works at Corral and chemical works to produce iodine and borate of lime from the famous Chilean nitrates.

**India and China.** The two most populous regions of Asia, India and China, are in a much more backward stage of manufacturing than are the countries hitherto discussed. In India a good deal is said about the cotton and jute factories, which employ about a quarter of a million people apiece. But the goods made there are practically all of the coarsest kind, while the total number of persons engaged in manufacturing among the entire 340,000,000 people of India is less than among the 10,000,000 of Pennsylvania.

Since manufacturing in China has not been fostered by a progressive government such as that of the British in India, it is even less developed than in India. Nevertheless, enormous deposits of coal and iron, a vast and marvellously hardworking population, and a huge home market, even though the people are poor, are conditions highly favorable to manufacturing. The great question is whether the Chinese have the initiative and inventiveness to carry on the complicated business of manufacturing without depending on foreigners.

**Why oriental countries excel in handmade goods.** Thus far we have been considering only the kinds of manufactures made by machines. But handmade goods, such as the beautiful oriental rugs of Turkey and Persia, also enter into the world's commerce. Their quantity is indeed very small compared with the others, but their beauty often gives them unusual importance. They are produced largely in oriental countries, partly because those countries, through long centuries of development, have acquired great skill in certain lines, and partly because western nations rarely have the patience to work long and painstakingly on articles which might be made almost as well by machines and which rarely bring a price proportional to the work spent on them.

Fig. 173. Raw silk is produced only (1) where the mulberry tree will flourish, (2) where there are many patient workers with deft fingers, and (3) where labor is cheap. Japan produces almost 60 per cent of the world supply of raw silk; China about 26 per cent of it; and Italy a little more than 10 per cent. The small remainder comes chiefly from southern France and Spain. In Japan factories have been established for unwinding the cocoons and spinning the thread; but a great deal of the spinning is still done by hand, as shown here.

The handmade articles of China take the form of beautiful woven silks and other textiles, delicate carvings in wood and ivory, and also of commoner articles such as bamboo goods, straw matting, and the fire crackers which almost every American boy and girl formerly set off on the Fourth of July. With the exception of ivory, the raw materials of most of these handmade goods are easily produced close to the home of the workers, and the finished products are so small or so light that they can be transported long distances with little expense.

World commerce draws from India such handmade goods as cashmere shawls, print cloths, metal ware like Benares brass, and carvings in ivory and wood. Especially interesting are the elephants carved in ivory, some as small as one's finger nail, yet so delicately carved as to show every feature and wrinkle.

Japan, like China, still furnishes handmade cloths, mattings, and carvings. Its strong, thin, handmade paper is used in place of leather, oil-cloth, and glass; and its handmade porcelain and lacquered and enameled goods find a large market because their grace and elegance give them among handmade products much the same position that French goods hold among manufactured products.

QUESTIONS, EXERCISES, AND PROBLEMS

A. **The industrial map of Europe.**

1. On an outline map of Europe, place a heavy line around the countries that form the group of manufacturing countries of western Europe. Label each large river, and indicate the main canals (Fig. 171). Insert the name of each city mentioned in the text. Put under it in parentheses the name of a manufactured specialty.

2. List the countries of Europe that are outside the manufacturing area. What is their type of industry? What is their type of agriculture? What kind of farming machinery would you expect them to use?

3. What types of manufacturing and of agriculture are usually found in the same regions? Why? Is this true of Great Britain? France? the United States? Russia? China?

B. **Where the industrial countries of Europe obtain their raw materials.**

1. List the industrial countries of Europe. Which of them have colonies or dependencies in other parts of the world? Which can obtain from their own colonies the products of both temperate and tropical regions? Which can get only tropical products?

2. To great industrial countries coal and iron are essentials; without them the factories must stand idle. By reference to the maps of coal and iron production of the world (Figs. 86, 99), form an opinion on these questions:

   (a) Why have France and Germany struggled for possession of the iron-ore district of Lorraine and the coal district in the Saar valley to the north of Lorraine?
   (b) Does Great Britain have iron or coal in excess of her own needs?
   (c) Which of the industrial countries have enough iron for themselves? enough coal?
   (d) Which must import some of their iron ore? their coal?
   (e) Which are almost wholly dependent on outside supplies of iron? of coal?
   (f) Which countries have iron to export? Which have coal?

3. Of the copper used in Great Britain yearly, only 25 per cent can be obtained from parts of the British Empire (Australia and Canada). What country supplies most of the remaining 75 per cent? (Fig. 91.)

4. From her own scanty stock, Great Britain can draw only a small part of the lumber that she needs. What countries near her have lumber to export? What waterways can she use to keep down the cost of transportation on this bulky commodity?

5. The bulk of the world's supply of the following raw materials is produced in the regions named below. Tell which of the industrial countries of Europe would have an advantage in obtaining supplies of each kind because of nearness, ease of transportation, or political relationship.

| | |
|---|---|
| Cotton | United States, India, Egypt |
| Wool | Argentina, Russia, Australia, United States, Great Britain |
| Raw silk | Japan, China, Italy |
| Hides | India, United States, Russia, Argentina, Brazil |
| Rubber | Brazil, Belgian Congo, Indo-China, East Indies, Mexico |
| Lead | United States, Spain, Germany |
| Zinc | United States, Germany |
| Tin | Malay Peninsula, Spain, East Indies |

**C. How the great industrial countries obtain food supplies for their crowded populations.**

1. Great Britain produces only about 20 per cent of the wheat it consumes. Of the rest about one half comes from India, Australia, and Canada. The other half must be imported from regions not a part of the British Empire. From what regions does Figure 38 suggest that Great Britain may import wheat? Find out which of these countries are likely to take some of Britain's surplus coal in exchange (Fig. 99). Why is it an advantage to British shipping to have this product to exchange for the foreign wheat?

2. In England, about 7 per cent of the workers are engaged in farming, and 40 per cent in manufacturing. In France, 42 per cent of the workers are engaged in farming, and 28 per cent in industries. Which country is more nearly self-supporting? Which could better endure a blockade of her coasts? Which is more dependent on a strong merchant marine? Which would suffer less if supplies of raw materials for manufacturing were cut off?

3. Denmark, which is about half the size of Maine and has four times the population, produces a surplus of dairy products and beet sugar. She has no coal or iron. What neighboring industrial countries are likely to be her customers, and what kind of goods will she take in exchange?

4. Little Holland may be said to run a great shop for selling sugar, coffee, hemp, vegetable oils, and rubber to more industrial countries. Where does she obtain the stock for her shop? How does it happen that she can specialize as a trader in tropical raw materials?

5. Hungary consists mainly of a great grain-producing plain, one of the most fertile in the world. She has great milling establishments, but must import most of her manufactured goods. With what countries is she likely to exchange products? Refer to the transportation map of Europe, as well as to the manufacturing map.

6. Czechoslovakia has both farming and manufacturing sections, but does not produce all the cereals and meat needed by the industrial centers. Which three of her neighbors are grain-producing countries? What other

great grain-producer is not far away? Note the rivers that touch her territory, and consider why her manufacturers are especially interested in the international agreement whereby inland nations are allowed free transport of goods along their natural outlets, even through foreign territory.

D. **The manufacture of textiles in Europe.**

1. At the largest dry goods store in your locality, ask to see the finest cotton cloth and inquire where it was manufactured. If the clerk does not know, the label or stamp will probably tell. Inquire likewise of a tailor about his best woolen cloth.

2. Let some of the girls in the class make out a list of the names of cotton, woolen, and silk goods, such as gingham, velour, crêpe de chîne, and collect samples of these fabrics. With the help of your teacher, check the names that are French. Compare those checked with those not checked, in number, quality, and design. What do you conclude in regard to the character of French textile manufactures?

3. *Cotton.* During our Civil War, British manufacturers became interested in the establishment of cotton growing on a large scale in Egypt and India. What had the Civil War to do with their action? Why did they select these regions for experiment (page 7)?

4. *Woolen goods.* In large parts of Great Britain, sheep raising can be carried on successfully; yet the woolen industry imports great quantities of wool, chiefly from Australia and Argentina. What conditions make it profitable to bring wool so great a distance for use in manufacture?

5. *Silk.* The mulberry tree can be grown as far north as southern England and southern New England. From Figures 17 and 18, decide which countries in Europe might produce silk if they wished. Have all these countries a supply of cheap labor to carry on silkworm culture? Could France maintain the production of silk textiles on the present scale and become independent of the Italian raw silk?

6. How has the building of the Swiss tunnels helped to give Germany an advantage in the manufacture of silk? Is this industry important?

7. *Jute.* What is jute? For what is it used? Where is it raised? The United States buys a good deal from Mexico. From what countries does Great Britain find it most economical to purchase her supplies?

8. In the textile industry, Great Britain finds the competition of other countries increasingly keen. Her markets for woolen cloth are being supplied by an increasing amount of French goods; her silk, jute, and linen manufacturers find themselves competing with makers of the same goods in the United States; and her cheap cotton cloths are being replaced by those made by the newly established Asian manufacturers. What cities in France manufacture the woolens? Which Asiatic nations are learning to supply themselves and their neighbors with cheap cottons? Give two reasons why they can manufacture these cottons cheaper than England can.

9. Although England's exports of textiles are relatively declining, her exports of machinery are increasing. Is there any connection between these two facts?

*E.* **Japan's progress in manufacturing.**

1. What countries will be especially affected by further growth of competition from Japan in the manufacture of artistic textiles? of fine earthenware? of paper? of matches?
2. Why do the Japanese pack goods in rice-matting wrappers instead of in heavy paper, as we do?
3. High-priced labor and inventive skill are usually found together. Explain their relation. Do you expect that the Japanese will be as quick to invent labor-saving devices as the Americans have been? Justify your answer.

*F.* **Manufacturing in remote regions.**

1. In appearance and climate New Zealand, in the southern hemisphere, is somewhat like New England in the northern. Examine New Zealand's statistics in an encyclopedia or in *The Statesman's Year Book* to see if the two regions are similar in industry. Explain why they are or are not.
2. In the United States, although the government is encouraging the manufacture of iodine, we still import a great deal produced in Chile. Some of our iodine we get from a peculiar source. You will find this worth looking for in the *Encyclopedia Britannica* under *Iodine*.
3. Several meat-packing concerns of the United States have established branch houses in Argentina. What does this suggest as to the manufacturing industries in Argentina? What other kinds of companies might profitably do the same?
4. For an example of isolated manufacturing, study Formosa's camphor industry as described in *The National Geographic Magazine* for March, 1912; or Turkey's rug manufacture as explained in Ross's *Russia in Revolution*.

*G.* **Hand manufactures.**

1. During one week keep a list of all the handmade things you can see in your own homes, the homes of your friends, or the stores of your town, particularly the oriental store, if there is one. Take notes as follows:
   (*a*) Brief description of the article.
   (*b*) Where it came from.
   (*c*) Materials of which it is made.
   (*d*) Where the raw materials were produced.
   (*e*) Whether it indicates great skill in the maker.
   (*f*) In what respects it seems to you artistic.

## CHAPTER TWENTY-ONE

### WHAT EUROPE DOES FOR A LIVING

(A) AN EXERCISE IN PRIMARY PRODUCTION, MANUFACTURING, AND TRANSPORTATION

THE chief ways of getting a living are by (1) raising food, (2) raising raw materials, (3) producing minerals, (4) engaging in manufacturing, and (5) engaging in commerce. In this exercise we shall try to find out in which of these ways the people of Europe get their living. The more backward parts of the continent are engaged almost exclusively in one of these occupations, while in the most advanced parts all five are highly developed.

**The parts of Europe that raise food.** This book contains maps of the following great food products:

Wheat (Fig. 38)   Rice (Fig. 35)      Cattle (Fig. 68)   Rye (Fig. 43)
Corn (Fig. 39)    Potatoes (Fig. 48)  Sheep (Fig. 71)    Barley (Fig. 45)
Oats (Fig. 40)    Sugar (Fig. 54)     Swine (Fig. 72)    Grapes (Fig. 61)

1. Make an alphabetical list of the countries of Europe arranged vertically, and to the right arrange twelve columns headed Wheat, Corn, Oats, etc., according to the list of products given above. Turn now to Figure 38, and after each country write something to indicate how much wheat is produced in proportion to the country's size, and also in what part of the country it is produced, provided there are great differences from part to part; then how much corn, oats, rice, etc. Your table will be something like this:

FOOD PRODUCTS OF EUROPE

| COUNTRY | WHEAT | CORN | OATS |
|---|---|---|---|
| Austria | little | none | little |
| Belgium | much | none | much |
| Bulgaria | much | much | little |
| Czechoslovakia | some | none | much |
| Denmark | little | none | much |
| Great Britain | some in southeast | none | some |
| Russia | much in south | little in south | much in center |

Fill out each of the other columns in the same way.

2. Give each country credit for the amount of food which it raises by counting "much" as equal to 3, "some" as equal to 2, "little" as 1, and "none" as 0. Add up the figures for each country and insert them on a

map of Europe. What parts of the country produce a large and varied supply of food in proportion to their area? Shade heavily the six or seven countries having the largest food supply in proportion to their area, shade lightly the next six or seven countries or parts of countries, and leave the rest unshaded. Remember that if the population is dense and the standard of living high, a country may produce a great amount in proportion to its area, but only a little in proportion to its needs.

**The parts of Europe that raise raw materials.** In this book the cotton map, Figure 7, is the only map of a raw material that is raised as a crop. The other chief vegetable or animal raw materials are:

*Wood*, which can be raised abundantly in all parts of Europe except the three southern peninsulas and southern Russia. But it is relatively scarce in the densely populated parts of Europe, where the land is used for other purposes, and very abundant in the northern parts, where the population is scanty (Fig. 176).

*Wool*, the distribution of which is shown by the map of sheep (Fig. 71).

*Hides*, which come chiefly from cattle (Fig. 68).

*Rubber*, which is a purely tropical product.

*Raw silk*, produced abundantly in Italy; somewhat in southern France and Greece; and a little in Spain, Austria, Hungary, Bulgaria, Yugoslavia, and Rumania.

*Flax*, produced abundantly in Ireland, Belgium, and especially northern Russia; somewhat in France, the Netherlands, Czechoslovakia, Rumania, Poland, and the remainder of Russia; a little in Spain, Italy, Austria, Hungary, and Serbia; and not enough to mention in other countries.

3. On the basis of these facts, prepare a table like that for food on the preceding page, and a map.
4. As a producer of raw materials, how does Europe compare with itself as a producer of food? What parts are most productive?

The products that enter chiefly into the commerce of western Europe are foodstuffs and raw materials.

5. Is this due to scanty production of these products at home? If it is due to some other cause, explain.

**The parts that produce minerals.** The production of minerals in Europe is shown by the following maps in this book:

| | |
|---|---|
| Iron (Fig. 86) | Gold and silver (Fig. 92) |
| Coal (Fig. 99) | Petroleum (Fig. 103) |
| Zinc (Fig. 95) | Lead (Fig. 94) |
| Tin (Fig. 93) | Copper (Fig. 91) |

Fig. 174. Bremgarten, in Switzerland, photographed from an airplane. What kind of farming is indicated by the many small farms? What accounts for the evident fertility of the soil, in a region that has been farmed for many centuries?

6. On the basis of these figures, prepare a table and map like those of the preceding exercises.
7. Explain how Europe ranks as a producer of minerals, and how different parts of the continent compare with one another.
8. From what regions may Europe import the copper needed in all electrical work?
9. What advantage has Great Britain in manufactures that make use of tin?

**The parts that engage in manufacturing.** On the basis of manufacturing, the countries of Europe may be divided into three groups (Fig. 162):

(a) Those having areas where more than 15 per cent of all the people are engaged in manufacturing (the heaviest shading).
(b) Other countries where at least 5 per cent of the population are engaged in manufacturing.
(c) Countries that have very little manufacturing throughout most of their area.

10. Compare the European part of Figure 162 with Figure 176, and draw conclusions as to the relation between manufacturing and density of population.

**The parts that engage in commerce.** The following figures show the total foreign commerce per capita of countries of Europe:

FOREIGN COMMERCE PER CAPITA IN A TYPICAL YEAR

| | | | |
|---|---|---|---|
| Austria | $105 | Netherlands | $234 |
| Belgium | 188 | Norway | 155 |
| Bulgaria | 17 | Poland | 21 |
| Czechoslovakia | 78 | Portugal | 25 |
| Denmark | 249 | Rumania | 24 |
| Finland | 90 | Russia | 5 |
| France | 104 | Spain | 33 |
| Germany | 93 | Sweden | 141 |
| Greece | 40 | Switzerland | 205 |
| Hungary | 40 | United Kingdom | 219 |
| Italy | 46 | Yugoslavia | 18 |
| Latvia | 48 | | |

11. Insert these figures on an outline map of Europe. Shade heavily the countries where the foreign commerce amounts to more than $50 per capita, and lightly those where it amounts to from $30 to $50. Why do Denmark, the Netherlands, and the United Kingdom rank so high?

12. How does this map compare with the map of manufacturing (Fig. 162) and with that showing density of population (Fig. 176)? Do you see in it any resemblance to your own maps showing where food, raw materials, and minerals are produced most abundantly?

13. Rearrange the list of countries given above, placing them in the order of the amounts. Which countries stand highest, those that produce food, raw materials, or manufactured goods?

**Europe's transportation facilities.** In some parts of Europe a highly complex system of transportation has developed. Natural waterways are utilized, canals and railroads have been built, and fine roads have been constructed.

14. Compare the maps showing density of population (Fig. 176), energy of peoples (Fig. 158), and percentage of population engaged in manufacturing (Fig. 162). What part of Europe is most heavily shaded on the three maps? Now look at the map showing the main shipping routes of the world (Fig. 117). In what part of Europe would you expect to find the closest railway network? Why?

15. Select the areas where transportation (a) by land, (b) by water, is best developed. How are these two areas related to each other? to the areas of most intense primary production and manufacturing? Explain what you find.

Fig. 175. A view of Moscow, the leading commercial city of Russia.

**The distribution of cities in Europe.** We must remember, in considering the location of cities in Europe, that many of them were great centers of trade and industry thousands of years before there was a single mile of railway in the world. And we must remember also that until modern times there was no advance in road building beyond what the Romans had done; indeed, in most parts of Europe roads were poorer than when the Roman Empire was at its height. Up to the nineteenth century, then, cities would naturally tend to be located where there was easy communication by water, and we may expect to find that they grew up along main routes of trade by sea and river. When railroads were first built, they branched out to connect near-by towns with the great centers, which thus became railroad cities as well as ports. Later, industries began to be established in districts where coal and iron could be mined; for the work could be done cheaper where these two basic materials were at hand, and the products could be shipped out by rail from districts lacking in waterways.

Thus we find in Europe two kinds of large cities; (1) historic cities with good communication by water; and (2) new industrial cities dependent chiefly on railways.

16. On an outline map of Europe insert all the European cities mentioned in Table 5 B (page 330). In what region are the cities most numerous? Why?
17. Divide the cities into the following groups:

    *Seaports* on (a) the English Channel and the North Sea; (b) the Atlantic Ocean; (c) the Baltic Sea; (d) the Mediterranean Sea; (e) other bodies of water which you will name.
    *River cities* with good transportation by inland waterways.
    *Inland cities* without important transportation by water.
    Compare the various groups in number and size, and explain your results.
18. Arrange the European cities of Table 5 B according to size. Among the first twenty, place as many stars as necessary before the names of those located in areas that excel in the following respects: (a) food production; (b) production of raw materials; (c) production of minerals; (d) manufacturing; (e) foreign commerce; (f) transportation.
19. Locate on the map of Europe a city that you think may be important as an exporter of each of the products mentioned in this chapter. Do the same for cities that may be importers. Consult the encyclopedia to see if you are right.

### (B) A Study of a European Country

Let each member of the class select a country of Europe upon which to report to the whole class. Follow this plan for preparing the report:

(1) First study the conditions of the country as shown in the tables and maps of the preceding exercises.
(2) Then look up the country in reference books.
(3) Write a report telling on what occupations the people mainly depend for a living. Explain what kinds of business are most important. Tell what products are produced in sufficient quantities to provide important exports; what ones are imported, and why. Find out how imports and exports come into the country and go out.

284                    *Modern Business Geography*

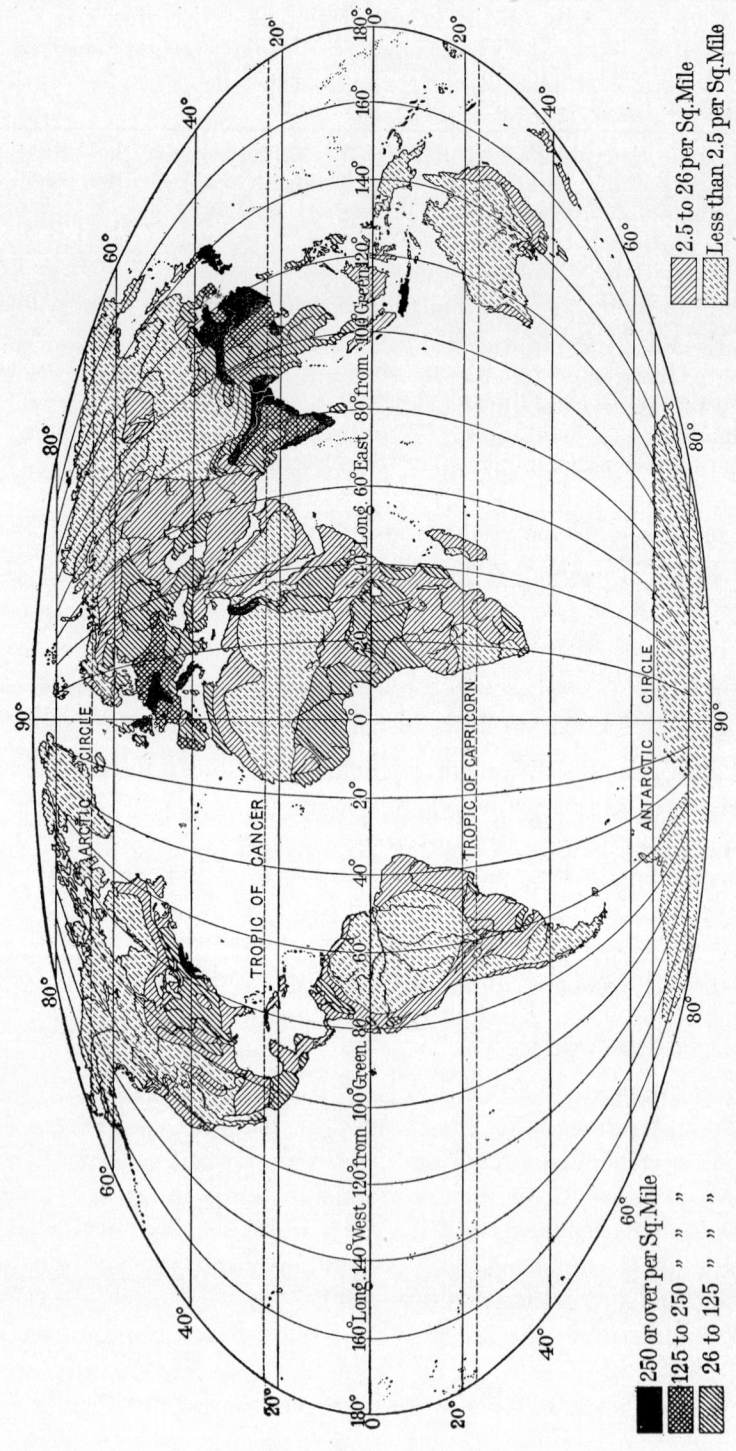

Fig. 176. This map shows the density of population in the different parts of the world. The regions of greatest density are not certain to have the highest purchasing power. Compare this map with Figure 162 (page 243). How does the eastern part of the United States stand on that map and on this? western Europe? India? China? Japan? Which is a larger world market, and which is more densely populated, the Pacific states of the United States or Java? Egypt or southeastern Australia? Is central Brazil a good market or a poor one, and why? northern Canada? South Africa? the Netherlands?

# PART FOUR

## The Field of Consumption

### CHAPTER TWENTY-TWO

#### THE UNITED STATES AS A MARKET

The object of all kinds of industry and commerce is to provide consumers with the right kinds of goods. The word " consume " sometimes means simply " eat"; but it may also mean " use in any way." In this sense every one of us is a consumer. Every day of our lives we consume food, shoe-leather, clothing, furniture, pencils, knives, and a hundred other things. Whenever we travel we consume a little share of a train, trolley car, steamboat, or automobile. When we go to a picture show we are among the consumers for whom the theater, the films, and the musical instruments were made. In fact, consumption is by far the most universal of the four fields of industrial and commercial geography. Vast numbers of people do not engage in either primary production or manufacturing, and many have little to do with any transportation except that in which they themselves supply the power. But no one can live without being a consumer. It is for the sake of ourselves as consumers that we engage in primary production, in transportation, and in manufacturing.

**How the character of the consumers influences the market.** In the ordinary language of business, the consumers are spoken of as " the market." The wholesale market consists of the people who buy goods with the purpose of selling them again; the retail market consists of the people who buy goods for their own use, or at least with no purpose of selling them. Every business man needs to understand exactly what sort of market his goods will find. The farmers, for instance, raise wheat because there is a good market for it; but if they should all raise three times as much as now, the market would be destroyed. There would be so much wheat that the price would drop so low that the wheat farmers could scarcely make a living. Suppose a merchant wishes to sell textiles in the Amazon valley. Since the people there are few in number and poor, and live in a warm climate, he may be able to sell a small amount of thin cotton clothing; but he finds no market at all for heavy, expensive woolens.

As a rule, backward peoples provide only a small market, while progressive peoples supply a large market. In the same way city people provide a larger market in proportion to their numbers than

Fig. 177. Isolated groups of people living in primitive conditions furnish the smallest markets, as this family of Ladakhis, a shepherd people of central Asia. They are clad in sheepskins and their food also comes mainly from their flocks. They use almost nothing which they must purchase, except an occasional weapon or tool made of iron.

country people; for the country people usually raise part of their own food; they may also supply part of their own firewood by cutting it in the forest; they generally wear tougher and more durable clothing than the city people; and they do not have so much in the way of luxuries and amusements. The greatest of all consumers are rich city people in the most progressive parts of the world. Such people buy everything that they consume, for they produce nothing that can be consumed by themselves or others, even when they do the most valuable work with their brains. Moreover, some of them consume huge amounts of very expensive goods. A man may have several automobiles; a woman may have twenty or thirty dresses a year; they may live in a huge house, entertain many guests, have a steam yacht, and go to the highest-priced theaters. Clearly the differences in these respects from place to place are enormous, and must be fully understood by anyone who wishes to have a useful knowledge of commercial and industrial geography. Such differences, together with differences in the kinds of products, are the basis of the foreign commerce which is so important in all progressive countries.

## The United States as a Market

**Why the United States is the greatest of the world's markets.** No other country furnishes so large a market as the United States. Both India and China are several times more populous, but both are more backward and much poorer than the United States. Russia also has more people than this country, but is less progressive and prosperous.

Aside from the United States, the countries of Great Britain, France, and Germany are the largest consumers of goods from other regions. But Great Britain and Germany together have not so many people as this country; while the French are only one third as numerous as the people of the United States. The World War drained these three countries of so much wealth and killed so many of their best men that their value as markets has been greatly decreased.

Even before the World War the average wealth and buying power per person were greater in the United States than in the leading nations of Europe. This does not necessarily mean that our people are more industrious or skillful than those of Europe, but merely that we have been gaining wealth rapidly from a great new country. We have been skimming off the cream of the land in the form of primeval forests, virgin soil, and the best of mineral deposits. With such wealth it is no wonder that the people of the United States are great consumers.

Fig. 178. Bathing in the sacred Ganges is a religious rite for a large part of India's 315,000,000 people. In spite of the enormous total population, India does not represent the largest kind of market, for the individual purchasing power is low.

Brown Brothers

Fig. 179. The city of Paris represents the largest kind of market. The total population is large, and the purchasing power of the average individual is high. Both domestic and foreign goods and products of high cost are in general use.

Our natural wealth, however, like that of Europe, is being used up rapidly. The country must carefully plan for a future when its buying power, and hence its value as a market, will depend more upon the efforts of the people than upon vast natural riches.

**Why the United States supplies most of its own needs.** One of the most noteworthy differences between the United States and the other populous and highly progressive countries is that the United States has a far larger area than any of the others and hence a much greater variety of products. China rivals the United States in resources and in the variety of its climate, but its people are not progressive. Russia is even more extensive, but is largely undeveloped. Great Britain rivals the United States in progressiveness, but its resources are relatively limited and its climate almost the same in all parts. Because of the great variety of the climate and resources of the United States, this country is capable of supplying practically all its own needs. For example, the northern part of the Mississippi valley is a great grain region; the Pacific states supply fruit, the southern states cotton, the Rocky Mountain states live stock, wool, and many metals; the Lake Superior region provides iron; Texas furnishes petroleum; Pennsylvania and other states have coal; and the northeastern states have all sorts of manufactured goods. Every state supplies something, and the facilities for communication are so good that products can easily be carried from one state to another. In fact, this exchange of goods is so extensive that the value of the *domestic* trade of the United States alone is estimated to be equal to the entire *foreign* trade of all countries.

**Imports from Foreign Countries.** In spite of the fact that the domestic trade of the United States has a value of perhaps forty or fifty billion dollars a year, this country imports three or four billion dollars' worth of goods each year, and exports a still larger amount.

There are at least five chief reasons why the country imports goods instead of producing them:

(1) The United States lacks a suitable climate for some products.
(2) It lacks certain mineral deposits.
(3) Our labor costs are high.
(4) We lack the skill necessary to produce certain goods abundantly and cheaply.
(5) The home supply of some goods is not great enough to meet the home demand.

### HOW OUR CLIMATIC CONDITIONS EXPLAIN CERTAIN IMPORTS

Since the United States does not extend into tropical regions, it has to import all products that require a continuously warm climate. Hence coffee, rubber, Manila hemp (abacá), sisal, cacao, and tropical fruits and nuts are brought into the country in great quantities. Southern Brazil sends most of our coffee; the Amazon basin, considerable rubber; the Philippines send Manila hemp; Yucatán, the sisal; Ecuador and the Amazon basin, most of the cacao; and the West Indies and Central America, the tropical fruits and nuts. Thus, with the exception of hemp, most of our chief needs for tropical products are supplied by fairly near neighbors. But if we were to trace back to its source every tropical product consumed in the United States, we should be taken into every land within the torrid zone.

### HOW THE LACK OF CERTAIN MINERAL DEPOSITS ACCOUNTS FOR OTHER IMPORTS

Nature has been generous in endowing the United States with great quantities of many kinds of minerals. A few of the less important ones, however, are lacking. The chief of these are tin, precious stones, nitrate of soda, and potash.

**Where tin is obtained.** Tin is imported to coat our pans, cans, and many other iron articles to keep them from rusting. Part of our supply comes from Bolivia, but the greater part comes from the Malay Peninsula.

**Precious stones.** The great value of the precious stones purchased each year ($76,000,000 in some years) shows how rich our market is. No other market takes so many. Nearly all of the world's diamonds are mined in South Africa and the majority are cut in Amsterdam.

**Our chief imports from Chile.** Nitrate of soda is brought in shiploads from the desert ports of northern Chile. Chile has long supplied the world with this important fertilizer, which furnishes nitrogen for fields, but now Norway and other countries are taking nitrogen out of the air by electricity. Before the Chilean nitrate deposits become exhausted, our country should supply its own market.

**Potash.** Most of the potash, or potassium chloride, is taken from the famous deposits of Stassfurt in central Germany. We consume it chiefly in fertilizers, but also in making gunpowder, matches, fireworks, and many kinds of chemicals. It is likely that some of the dried-up western lakes or similar beds in the old rocks of Texas and the great kelp beds of the Pacific coast will sometime yield enough potash to make us independent of Germany.

### WHY WE IMPORT GOODS REQUIRING MUCH HAND LABOR

Each year we import several hundred million dollars' worth of handmade goods that would be unduly expensive if manufactured at home. They include chiefly raw silk, tea, toys, and hand embroideries. Practically all of these could be produced at home, but not with profit; for wages are higher in the United States than in any other great manufacturing country. Some of the imported goods, such as embroideries from Switzerland, Japan, China, and Madeira, and laces from Ireland and France, have been imitated on American machines, but not with great success.

**Why the United States does not supply its market for raw silk.** Although the white mulberry tree on which the silkworm thrives grows well in large parts of the United States, silk is not produced, because it requires a great amount of very cheap labor for a few weeks in the spring, when the eggs are hatching and the silkworms have to be carefully fed and tended. In China, Japan, Italy, and even parts of France, women and children do this work for a few cents a day. If labor-saving machines could be devised to gather the mulberry leaves, feed the worms, and clean the trays, the United States might perhaps raise some raw silk, at least enough so that it would not have to import from these countries.

**Why the United States does not supply its own market for tea.** Americans consume annually about $20,000,000 worth of tea, or about a pound per person. The case is like that of raw silk. Cheap hand labor is needed not only to prune the tea bushes to a height of five feet or less, so that the leaves can be easily picked, but especially to pick the leaves and cure them over fires and in the sun. Hence the tea industry is confined to such places as India, China, Ceylon, and Japan, which not only have abundant moisture during long warm summers, but are long-settled regions of dense population.

### GOODS REQUIRING MORE SKILL THAN THE UNITED STATES HAS DEVELOPED

The goods which the United States might make if sufficient skill were employed include many chemicals, drugs, dyes, and medicines bought from Germany before the World War. They also include beautiful silks from France, and fine woolens and cottons from England.

**The problem of chemicals.** Germany's advantage in the chemical industries, as we have seen, arose largely from her attention to chemical education. It also depends partly on the fact that when a country once gets a good start, it is hard for others to overtake it. Notwithstanding the advantage which the World War gave to our industries, it is difficult to keep German goods from ousting the American product even in our own market.

**Why we import textiles.** The fact that Americans who can afford them purchase silks from France and broadcloths and lawns from England does not arise from superior technical schools such as those which give Germany such an advantage in the chemical industries, but from skill developed in the school of experience. For centuries both France and England have devoted great energy to improving their machinery and their methods of treating textiles. The United States has been so busy in making its production as large as possible that it has paid relatively less attention to making the quality as high as possible. Nevertheless, the quality of our goods is improving. For instance, our manufactures of silk were six times as valuable in 1914 as in 1879, while our imports had increased scarcely 50 per cent. In the same period our manufactures of wool doubled in value, while the imports of woolen cloth diminished. Since the World War there have been still further changes of the same kind. In other words, we are learning to supply our own needs, even in the finer grades of cloth.

RAW MATERIAL IMPORTED BECAUSE THE HOME SUPPLY,
THOUGH LARGE, IS NOT SUFFICIENT

The United States produces great quantities of raw sugar, hides, wool, and other raw materials, but the demands of the country are so large that still more is needed.

**Why we import raw sugar.** The use of sugar has increased faster in the United States than in any other country except Great Britain. Here is the average consumption per person in the United States for certain years:

| | | | |
|---|---|---|---|
| 1870 . . . 33 pounds | 1890 . . . 51 pounds | 1910 . . . 80 pounds |
| 1880 . . . 39 pounds | 1900 . . . 59 pounds | 1920 . . . 91 pounds |

With about one sixteenth of the world's inhabitants, we consume one fourth of all the sugar. This fact shows how enormous is our buying power. It also shows how much we spend for luxuries, for a large part of the sugar is used in candy and confectionery.

The sugar-cane plantations of Louisiana and Texas, and the sugar-beet farms of Colorado, Utah, California, Michigan, and other states, yield only about a fifth of the raw sugar needed by our refineries; the Hawaiian Islands, Puerto Rico, and the Philippine Islands yield nearly a third. The rest must be imported from foreign countries, chiefly Cuba, which lies at our very door. The home production of sugar beets can be greatly increased, but whether this pays or not depends on whether our tariff and the consequent price of sugar are high enough to keep out the sugar of India, Germany, Cuba, Russia, and the other great producers.

**Why hides and skins are imported and where they come from.** An enormous quantity of leather, in such forms as shoes, gloves, belts, suitcases, coats, and the upholstery of chairs and automobiles, is consumed in the most progressive countries. Our country probably consumes more per person than any other. Each year we make more than a billion dollars' worth of leather and leather goods. It is no wonder, then, that the hides supplied by our cattle, cows, and horses, and the skins from our sheep and goats, are insufficient to supply the needs of American tanneries.

Every year foreign countries supply the American market with one or two hundred million dollars' worth of hides and skins. Nearly every country in the world sends at least a few tons. Poor and backward countries with scanty pasturage, such as India and Mexico, send great quantities of goat skins, for the goat thrives under conditions that

## (I) Leading Imports into the United States during a Typical Year

| Articles | Values (in Millions of Dollars) | | |
|---|---|---|---|
| | Total | Raw or unmanufactured | Manufactured |
| Silk | 441 | 399 | 42 |
| Rubber | 349 | 347 | 2 |
| Coffee | 264 | 264 | — |
| Paper | 263 | 114 | 149 |
| Sugar | 260 | 258 | 2 |
| Wood | 191 | 54 | 137 |
| Wool | 182 | 83 | 79 |
| Hides and skins | 172 | 113 | 59 |
| Furs | 136 | 124 | 12 |
| Petroleum | 113 | 79 | 34 |
| Cotton | 110 | 46 | 66 |
| Tin | 101 | 101 | — |
| Vegetable oils | 94 | 27 | 67 |
| Fibers (except cotton) | 93 | 18 | 75 |
| Copper | 88 | 85 | 3 |
| Tobacco | 83 | 75 | 8 |
| Precious stones | 69 | 20 | 49 |
| Chemicals | 58 | — | 58 |
| Iron and steel | 58 | 22 | 36 |
| Cocoa | 58 | 57 | 1 |
| Fruits | 54 | 52 | 2 |
| Flaxseed (linseed) | 38 | 38 | — |
| Gums | 33 | 33 | — |
| Nuts | 31 | 31 | — |
| Sodium nitrate | 30 | 30 | — |
| Tea | 28 | 28 | — |
| Breadstuffs | 24 | 22 | 2 |

would kill most domestic animals. Hides of cattle come from grasslands, like those of our own western plains, Argentina, and Canada. The importation of hides and skins is increasing rapidly because our domestic production does not keep pace with our market.

**Our imports of wool.** The reasons why we import wool for home consumption are nearly the same as for hides and skins. Our standard of living and our location in the temperate climate call for woolen wearing apparel. Our farmers find it profitable to use most of their lands for raising crops rather than sheep. Moreover, the sheep raised

(II) MERCHANDISE IMPORTED ANNUALLY INTO THE UNITED STATES

(A) WHAT OUR IMPORTS ARE

| CLASS OF GOODS | 1879–1883 | | RECENTLY | | CHANGE IN PERCENTAGES |
|---|---|---|---|---|---|
| | Value (in millions of dollars) | Per cent of total | Value (in millions of dollars) | Per cent of total | |
| Raw materials for use in manufacturing | 117 | 18 | 1601 | 38 | + 20 |
| Foodstuffs, crude | 97 | 15 | 505 | 12 | − 3 |
| Foodstuffs, manufactured | 125 | 19 | 451 | 11 | − 8 |
| Manufactures for further use in manufacturing | 89 | 14 | 750 | 18 | + 4 |
| Manufactures ready for consumption | 202 | 32 | 878 | 21 | − 9 |

(B) WHERE OUR IMPORTS COME FROM

| CONTINENT | AVERAGE OF 1879–1883 (in millions of dollars) | RECENTLY (in millions of dollars) | GROWTH (in millions of dollars) | GROWTH IN PER CENT |
|---|---|---|---|---|
| Europe | 346 | 1276 | 930 | 268 |
| North America | 136 | 986 | 850 | 625 |
| South America | 76 | 518 | 442 | 580 |
| Asia | 60 | 1257 | 1197 | 1999 |
| Africa | 12 | 93 | 81 | 675 |
| Australia and Oceania | 10 | 55 | 45 | 450 |

in our pastures do not supply all the different kinds of wool that are consumed in our industries. For instance, the best wool for making fine cloth comes chiefly from Australia, Argentina, and Uruguay. Our supply of coarse wool for making carpets comes from backward countries where the flocks are given little care, such as China, Russia, and Turkey.

The importation of wool, as of other goods, varies greatly according to the tariff. If our woolen industries are protected by a high tariff, they use much more wool than is produced at home; but if they are

(III) MERCHANDISE EXPORTED ANNUALLY FROM THE UNITED STATES

(A) WHAT OUR EXPORTS ARE

| CLASS OF GOODS | 1879–1883 | | RECENTLY | | CHANGE IN PERCENTAGES |
|---|---|---|---|---|---|
| | Value (in millions of dollars) | Per cent of total | Value (in millions of dollars) | Per cent of total | |
| Raw materials for manufacturing | 247 | 31 | 1193 | 25 | − 6 |
| Foodstuffs, crude | 202 | 26 | 421 | 9 | − 17 |
| Foodstuffs, manufactured | 192 | 24 | 463 | 10 | − 14 |
| Manufactures for further use in manufacture | 33 | 4 | 700 | 15 | + 11 |
| Manufactures ready for consumption | 109 | 14 | 1981 | 42 | + 28 |

(B) WHERE OUR EXPORTS GO

| CONTINENT | AVERAGE OF 1879–1883 (in millions of dollars) | RECENTLY (in millions of dollars) | GROWTH (in millions of dollars) | GROWTH IN PER CENT |
|---|---|---|---|---|
| Europe | 628 | 2314 | 1686 | 269 |
| North America | 80 | 1235 | 1173 | 1468 |
| South America | 26 | 438 | 412 | 1580 |
| Asia | 14 | 560 | 546 | 3910 |
| Australia and Oceania | 10 | 194 | 184 | 1840 |
| Africa | 5 | 107 | 102 | 2140 |

only slightly protected, manufacturing decreases and the imports of wool diminish correspondingly. In that event the wool comes into the country, but in the form of cloth manufactured in Europe rather than as raw material.

QUESTIONS, EXERCISES, AND PROBLEMS

A. The leading imports of the United States.

1. Table I, on page 293, gives the leading imports of the United States. Classify these imports as:

   (a) Foodstuffs
   (b) Vegetable raw materials
   (c) Animal raw materials
   (d) Mineral raw materials

In making your table, divide each class into (*i*) raw or unmanufactured products, and (*ii*) manufactured. Compare the eight groups in number of articles and in value. In what kind of climates are the two most valuable classes chiefly produced?

2. In your table, place a star before articles that the United States cannot easily produce. Which of your groups contains the largest number of such articles?

3. In Table I (page 293), pick out five commodities not elsewhere mentioned in this chapter. Decide why each is imported instead of being produced here. Which ones are not produced at all in this country? How many have you used in the condition in which they were imported? Which have you used after they were made into other products?

**B. The volume of imports of the United States from particular countries.**

1. In Table IV, on page 308, the countries are listed alphabetically. Rearrange the list according to the value of the goods sent to the United States.

2. Among the nations shown in Table IV, why does Great Britain lead in total commerce? What sort of goods does she send us? Name some goods imported from Great Britain and tell why we purchase them.

3. Why does Germany, in normal times, stand high among countries from which we receive imports? Name some of the goods included among the imports and tell why we buy them from Germany.

4. Why does Canada send us more imports than France does? What raw materials does Canada produce that we require? Explain how the value of our imports from Canada would differ if Canada were in Siberia.

5. Name some of the goods included in imports from France. Why do we not make these goods ourselves instead of importing them?

6. How does it happen that Cuba stands so high in the table on page 308?

7. What two commodities comprise practically all our imports from Brazil?

8. Name at least one product among the imports from each of the remaining countries listed in Table IV, and account for the importation.

**C. The change in the kind of goods imported by the United States.**

1. In Tables II and III (pages 294, 295), pick out the percentages that indicate a change in the manufacturing of the United States. By what percentage has each class of imports increased or decreased? Explain the reason for these changes.

2. If the United States is developing its own natural resources, why does it import an increasing amount of raw materials for manufacture?

3. Give an illustration of a commodity that would be classified under each one of the headings in Table II, A (page 294).

4. Frame a general rule to be a guide in deciding how the industrial growth of the United States is affecting the kind of goods that the country imports.

D. Account for the change in the sources of goods imported by the United States.

1. According to the figures given in Table II, B, from which continent do we make the heaviest purchases? the lightest?
2. Compare the rates at which imports from the various continents have increased. With what regions has our import trade been increasing most?
3. Name an important commodity included in the imports from each continent.
4. Under which headings in Table I, A would you place the main imports from each continent? Which classes of goods show most tendency to increase or decrease among our imports?
5. Frame a general rule as to how the relative value of imports from different sources is influenced by the industrial growth of the United States.

E. **The balance of trade.**

1. If the exports of a country amount to more than its imports, its balance of trade is said to be favorable. Can you explain why? The United States has unfavorable balances with Brazil and India. Explain what this means and why it is so.
2. Divide the countries listed in Table IV (page 308) into two groups: (*a*) those with which the United States has a favorable balance of trade; (*b*) those with which the balance of trade is unfavorable to us.

Fig. 180. A shipload of sugar from American refineries being unloaded by lighters at a modern pier in Naples.

## CHAPTER TWENTY-THREE

### FOREIGN COUNTRIES AND WORLD MARKETS

ENTERPRISING nations and enterprising individuals seek to extend their markets. Both the government and the business men work to this end. With greater sales not only is the total profit greater, but the profit on each piece of goods increases. For instance, if a Chicago firm can manufacture 500,000 cakes of soap at four cents apiece, it may be able to make 5,000,000 cakes at two cents apiece. In that case the company would make more by selling the second lot for two and a half cents a cake than by selling the first lot at five cents.

So it is in the manufacture of steel rails, shoes, automobiles, pencils, and other articles. Manufacturers therefore strive to increase their output, and to extend their market even if this takes them into foreign countries. Those who do this have had to find out through years of endeavor which countries want their goods, and which offer them no market.

## THE EUROPEAN MARKET

We have already seen that because of the high civilization of Europe the inhabitants are large consumers. With 400,000,000 inhabitants and with more people living in cities than is the case in any other continent, Europe is the greatest of the world's markets. One might think that in a continent where manufacturing is so active few manufactured goods would be imported from abroad. Nevertheless, in normal times, the United States sells almost as many manufactured goods to Europe as to the rest of the world combined. On the whole, however, Europe is a market for the foodstuffs and raw materials of other countries rather than for their manufactured articles.

**What the United States contributes to the European market.** Almost every part of the earth sends food and raw materials to Europe. The United States is one of the chief contributors, for about half of our exports usually go to European countries. As foodstuffs, we send great quantities of wheat, corn, flour, hams, bacon, lard, and beef. As industrial raw materials, we send cotton, copper, tobacco, and leather. Cotton is the most important item of the list. No less than half a billion dollars' worth goes to Europe annually.

**American labor-saving machinery in the European market.** Among the manufactured products of the United States, labor-saving machinery finds an especially ready market in Europe. American cash registers, typewriters, and automatic weighing machines are found in European stores and offices; American sewing machines in European homes; and ingenious shoe machines, screw machines, and many others in European factories; while many European fields are harvested by machines made in America.

The American machines, however, are soon copied by European manufacturers, and the market is lost unless improvements are made constantly. Thus far Americans have to a large degree been able to make such improvements, for the power of invention seems to be more highly developed in America than in any other country. This is partly because wages in the United States are so high that employers are eager to adopt every possible invention that will save labor.

**Advantage of exporting manufactured goods instead of raw materials.** The United States need not take satisfaction in sending to Europe great quantities of foodstuffs and raw materials. Many people think that this country would be far better off if we manufactured all our surplus cotton, copper, and other raw materials into finished products for foreign markets. We should then make not only a primary producers' profit on the raw materials, but a manufacturers' profit on the finished products. This plan would require the United States either to win from Europe the markets that Europeans now supply with goods made from our surplus raw materials, or to develop new markets. Both are difficult to do. Europe, through long experience, understands many foreign markets better than we do and has a great supply of skilled labor that is willing to work for lower wages than our own workmen. Moreover, Europe excels the United States in training her boys and girls for commerce and industry. On the other hand, it is very difficult to arouse a people like the Chinese so that they will provide a new market, even though this would be to their advantage. Nevertheless, a larger percentage of our population is turning to manufacturing, and our exports of foodstuffs are relatively declining. Soon our industries will use a large part of the raw materials which we produce, and Europe will have to look elsewhere for her supply.

**Great Britain as a market.** Among individual European countries, Great Britain is by far the greatest market of the United States. Each year our total trade with her amounts to much more than one billion dollars. Great Britain takes a fifth or a sixth of our exports and supplies us with a twelfth of our imports. This enormous trade is handled by the largest and swiftest steamers of the world's most important transportation lines. No other pair of nations except Canada and the United States are such important customers of one another.

The cotton manufacturing industry of Great Britain — her greatest industry — is based upon our raw cotton, for we supply about half of all that the country consumes, and used to supply still more. This is the greatest single item in our whole export trade.

Our exports of foodstuffs to Great Britain are gradually dropping off, because while our needs are increasing at home, Great Britain is able to procure an increasing supply from her colonies — especially Canada, Australia, and New Zealand — and from Argentina. It is likely that our exports of cotton to Great Britain will diminish similarly, but more gradually; for India, Egypt, and British East Africa are increasing their supply for the mother country.

**Germany as a market.** Aside from Great Britain and Canada, Germany stands highest as a consumer of our goods. On an average not far from a twelfth of our total exports go to Germany and about one sixteenth of our imports come from that country. The goods we send to Germany are about the same as those we send to Great Britain — foodstuffs and raw materials for industries, especially cotton and copper.

Our trade with Germany increased rapidly from the time when she began her manufacturing career, a few decades ago, but it has been of the kind that benefits that country more than this. We send her raw materials or goods like bacon, lard, and sheet copper, that have been only a little changed, and upon which we make only a slight profit. She sends back dyes, drugs, and chemicals, — highly manufactured goods upon which she makes a large profit.

### PROMISING MARKETS FOR THE UNITED STATES

Although the trade of the United States with Europe is likely always to remain our most important commerce, the opportunities for a rapid broadening of the market for our manufactured goods are great elsewhere. Such opportunities are found in four groups of countries where manufacturing is carried on and where we have some advantage over Europe:

(1) Countries in which we have the advantage of nearness. This group includes Canada, Mexico, Central America, and the Pacific countries of South America.

(2) Regions in which we have tariff advantages. This group includes only our own detached units; namely, the Philippines, Puerto Rico, Alaska, the Hawaiian Islands, and some smaller islands.

(3) Countries that require goods made from raw materials which we produce in far greater abundance than Europe. This group includes certain markets in various countries. For instance, we raise so large a part of the world's cotton crop that we ought to furnish cotton goods to such countries as China. We mine so much copper that we should supply the market with electrical goods in countries like India and Argentina. Such a flood of petroleum comes from American wells that we supply much of the world's market with kerosene.

(4) Regions like South Africa, Australia, and Argentina, that are in about the same stage of industrial development as the western United States. Hence the agricultural and mining machinery that we make in great quantities for our own use is just what they require.

### CHINA AS A MARKET

China's enormous population of about 325,000,000, or nearly a fifth of the human race, ought to make it a huge market. But these millions are not advanced and prosperous enough to desire what the outside world has to offer them or to be willing and able to pay for it. Instead of demanding the manufactured leather shoe of the West, they are content to go barefooted or to wear a simple straw sandal.

The conditions in China, however, are gradually changing. Increasing exports of tea, silk, beans, and raw cotton enlarge China's power to buy from the outside world. Missionaries, merchants, and Chinese students who have studied abroad are teaching the Chinese new standards of living, and are creating new desires. Hence imports into China are increasing in both quantity and variety. Among the imports, cotton goods are the most important, but metal goods, rice, fish, coal, and cigarettes also find a market.

The imports of today, however, are generally supposed to be merely a promise of the great volume that may be wanted in the not distant future. Therefore all the great commercial countries are much interested in China. Nevertheless, in spite of our position just across the Pacific from China, we have only one sixth of the country's foreign trade while the British Empire and Japan each have more than a quarter.

In southeastern China, Great Britain controls the island of Hongkong and the opposite mainland. She has loaned money to China, established banks, built railroads, secured mining concessions, assisted in the collection of customs, and in various other ways has strengthened her position.

Japan has lagged only a little behind Great Britain in attention to Chinese trade. The Japanese are trying in every possible way to develop a Chinese market for their rapidly increasing manufactures, and they have been eager to secure railroad, mining, police, and banking rights, especially in the part of China near Chosen, and in Shantung.

The United States has always stood for the equal rights of all nations in the Chinese market, and for fair play to the Chinese. This " open door " policy has been subscribed to by all the principal nations. It will not, however, create American trade unless alert business men are ready to supply just the goods that the Chinese want, at prices they can afford to pay, and of as good quality as those offered by other countries.

SOUTH AMERICA AS A MARKET

The continent of South America buys great quantities of manufactured goods, especially textiles, farming implements and machinery, railroad equipment, and other iron and steel goods. It pays for these by exporting rubber, coffee, foodstuffs, wool, hides, and minerals like nitrate of soda. The whole continent of ten republics and

*Ellsworth Huntington*

FIG. 181. This market in western China represents the earliest kind of market place, which is merely an open space where goods for sale may be set out on the ground or on low benches. Most of the venders sell what they themselves have produced or have helped to produce.

the Guianas constitutes a region where practically all the manufactured goods must be imported from other continents. Nevertheless, although there are fine modern cities like Buenos Aires and Rio de Janeiro with hundreds of thousands of highly civilized people, the majority of the 81,000,000 South Americans are small consumers.

The best South American market is in the temperate regions of the south where Spaniards, Portuguese, Italians, and other Europeans make up most of the population, and where the natives themselves are more energetic than elsewhere in the continent.

**The United States and the South American market.** One would think that the United States, being advanced in manufacturing and near South America, would almost entirely supply the markets of that continent. In recent years, however, we have generally supplied only about one fourth of the nearly two billion dollars' worth of goods imported by all the South American countries. This was not much more than half as much as we sent to Great Britain alone. Nevertheless, it was a great improvement over 1907, when we supplied only one tenth of the imports of the countries of South America. During the

World War the United States took a rapidly increasing share of the South American trade, because western Europe was so busy with war that it had little opportunity to care for the regular trade; but since the war we have dropped back to almost our old relative position.

**Advantages of western Europe in the South American market.** Four conditions make it easy for western Europe, especially Germany and Great Britain, to regain most of their trade in South America:

(1) *European residents.* There are many European business houses and millions of European immigrants in South America, whereas there are only a few Americans. Therefore the inhabitants much prefer European goods.

(2) *Price competition.* Europe is very eager for foreign trade to help pay her war debts. Therefore she is willing to sell at a small margin of profit. This is particularly true of Germany, which almost completely lost its great overseas trade during the war.

(3) *Ignorance of needs of market.* Many American business firms have not yet learned how to get and keep South American trade. They sometimes send catalogues printed in English, forward goods in great boxes for places where only pack animals are used, or put up goods in packages so frail that many are spoiled before they reach their destination. They seem to expect that an agent at Rio de Janeiro, for instance, where Portuguese is spoken, can take care of buyers at Buenos Aires, fourteen hundred miles away, and at Valparaiso, twenty-two hundred miles away, where the language is Spanish, — even when the agent knows neither Spanish nor Portuguese! Such conditions, however, are passing away, and many South American centers now have American banks and American agents well trained in South American languages and customs.

(4) *Distance from American centers.* Another reason why the United States finds it difficult to hold the trade of some of the South American countries is the great distance. By actual measurement on a globe, it will be seen that ports south of Cape San Roque are nearer to some seaports of western Europe than they are to the important ports of the United States. The Panama Canal, to be sure, puts the manufacturing region of the United States within easy reach of the Pacific countries of South America; but the Pacific countries import only one fourth as much as the rest of South America. From southern Brazil, Uruguay, and Argentina, where commercial possibilities are greatest, the distance to western Europe and to the United States is so nearly equal that Europe's other advantages are likely to cause her to hold much of the South American trade.

Fig. 182. The main street of a town in Guatemala illustrates a more advanced kind of marketing than the open market place. Here the shops are in the front part of the houses. The vender has become a shopkeeper, a middleman who buys what other people produce and sells it to the consumer.

## CANADA AS A MARKET

Canada is an important market for foreign manufactured goods, for the Canadians are largely engaged in primary production, and are extremely prosperous and progressive. These nine million competent people want strong, high-grade woolen clothing, to withstand the low winter temperatures, and to last under the hard wear of rough outdoor work. The farmers require elaborate machinery ranging from traction plows to great harvesters. A variety of mining machinery is needed in Canada, because many different minerals and metals are mined. Railroad equipment is constantly required, not only to meet the growing needs of the existing lines, but to build and operate new ones.

Since the United States is separated from Canada neither by geographical barriers nor by those of race and language, it is in an excellent position to supply the Canadian market. Hence this country furnishes two thirds of the Canadian imports. Each year, in spite of a heavy tariff and the fact that American manufactures are taxed much more heavily than British, Canada consumes almost a billion dollars' worth of our goods, or nearly the same amount as Great Britain.

Table IV (page 308) shows that the balance of trade with Canada is in our favor.

## MEXICO AS A MARKET

Although Mexico contains twice as many people as Canada, its value to us as a market in many years has been only one tenth as great. This is partly because people living under a mild climate like that of Mexico are not so ambitious and energetic as the Canadians. Another reason is that among the Mexican people about two fifths are Indians, two fifths mixed Indian and white, and only one fifth white. Again, the adjoining portions of the United States and Mexico are arid and thinly populated. Although the two countries are connected by both railroads and steamship lines, there is not a close enough relation to overcome the barriers of race and language. Misunderstandings due to these barriers have often led to serious disagreements that have hindered trade for long periods. Moreover, the Spaniards, the merchants of Mexico, seem to prefer to trade with Europeans rather than with Americans. With proper planning, however, we might sell to Mexico almost everything she wants. At present only three fourths of her imports come from the United States.

## THE PHILIPPINE ISLANDS AS A MARKET

When the Philippine Islands were acquired by the United States in 1898, many people predicted that they would become a large market for our products. These persons did not realize that nearly a million of the twelve million Filipinos are primitive people who use almost nothing from outside their forest homes, and that the wants of most of the remainder are few and simple.

During the thirty years and more of American occupation of the Philippines, the process of educating the inhabitants has gone on constantly, principally through an efficient system of public schools. Every step in advance has meant a higher standard of living, greater home production, and a greater market for foreign imported goods. Now the Philippine imports have risen above ten dollars a person. This is small compared with the Canadian figure of one hundred dollars or more, but it is many times larger than it was before the United States was in control.

Up to 1909, imports from the United States to the Philippines had to compete on equal terms with those from other countries, and consequently our trade made only slow headway. The manufacturing countries of western Europe had the advantage of being nearer to the islands than those of the northeastern United States. In 1909, however, free trade, with slight limitations, was established between

Fig. 183. In the modern city, the market place has become a whole district of streets with large shops, like this street in Chicago, where goods from all over the world are sold.

the Philippines and the United States. Then American trade increased rapidly. It was further favored by the opening of the Panama Canal in 1918. About three fifths of all the Philippine imports come from the United States and Hawaii.

The best way for our country to increase trade not only in the Philippines but everywhere else is to play fair, make the best kind of goods at the lowest reasonable prices, be content with moderate profits, and remember that even the most backward people will buy more if treated with honesty and respect.

## QUESTIONS, EXERCISES, AND PROBLEMS

A. **Trade of the United States with its neighbors.**

1. The United States supplies two thirds of the Canadian imports, whereas only one eighth of Australia's imports are from the United States. How do you explain this difference?
2. Compare Hawaii, Puerto Rico, and Cuba as markets for American goods. Consider these points: (a) the number of people; (b) their stage of progress; (c) their governmental relations; (d) the products they can offer in exchange; (e) their position.
3. Compare these three with Alaska. Why should Alaska rather than any of the others be called "a market of the future"?
4. Give examples of commodities that each one of these regions needs and can purchase from the United States.

## (IV) Foreign Commerce of Leading Countries

(All countries or colonies having a total foreign trade of more than $100,000,000 are included. Figures are for 1927, or for latest date available in Statistical Abstract of the United States for 1928.)

| Country | Imports (in millions of dollars) | | Exports (in millions of dollars) | |
|---|---|---|---|---|
| | Total | From United States | Total | To United States |
| Algeria | 190 | 7 | 138 | 5 |
| Argentina | 825 | 163 | 972 | 97 |
| Australia | 783 | 159 | 684 | 39 |
| Austria | 428 | 4 | 278 | 11 |
| Belgium | 807 | 116 | 739 | 72 |
| Brazil | 388 | 89 | 432 | 203 |
| Canada | 1087 | 837 | 1239 | 475 |
| Ceylon | 148 | 3 | 174 | 41 |
| Chile | 134 | 38 | 211 | 62 |
| China | 714 | 107 | 648 | 169 |
| Chosen | 182 | — | 170 | — |
| Colombia | 119 | — | 122 | — |
| Cuba | 257 | 155 | 323 | 257 |
| Czechoslovakia | 531 | 7 | 596 | 32 |
| Denmark | 443 | 59 | 425 | 4 |
| Dutch East Indies | 221 | 24 | 324 | 52 |
| Egypt | 243 | 11 | 248 | 33 |
| Finland | 161 | 16 | 159 | 9 |
| France | 2072 | 229 | 2165 | 168 |
| French Indo-China | 104 | 1 | 112 | — |
| Germany | 3360 | 482 | 2428 | 201 |
| Greece | 166 | 15 | 80 | 30 |
| Hungary | 200 | 2 | 140 | 1 |
| India | 896 | 63 | 1186 | 131 |
| Irish Free State | 296 | 11 | 218 | 2 |
| Italy | 1051 | 132 | 806 | 109 |
| Japan | 1033 | 258 | 945 | 402 |
| Malaya | 563 | 14 | 596 | 278 |
| Mexico | 164 | 109 | 295 | 138 |
| Morocco (French) | 70 | 3 | 33 | 1 |
| Netherlands | 1022 | 148 | 762 | 87 |
| New Zealand | 218 | 33 | 232 | 13 |
| Nigeria | 60 | — | 76 | — |
| Norway | 256 | 23 | 178 | 22 |
| Persia | 77 | 2 | 108 | 8 |
| Peru | 69 | 25 | 109 | 20 |
| Philippines | 116 | 70 | 156 | 116 |
| Poland | 325 | 9 | 282 | 5 |

# Foreign Countries and World Markets

| Country | Imports (in millions of dollars) | | Exports (in millions of dollars) | |
|---|---|---|---|---|
| | Total | From United States | Total | To United States |
| Portugal | 111 | 11 | 36 | 5 |
| Puerto Rico | 92 | 80 | 104 | 97 |
| Rumania | 202 | 5 | 228 | 1 |
| Russia | 367 | 65 | 397 | 13 |
| Siam | 74 | 2 | 88 | 1 |
| Spain | 458 | 74 | 369 | 34 |
| Sweden | 425 | 45 | 433 | 48 |
| Switzerland | 383 | 10 | 386 | 46 |
| Turkey | 123 | 4 | 98 | 20 |
| Union of South Africa | 343 | — | 249 | — |
| United Kingdom | 5927 | 840 | 4045 | 358 |
| United States | 4185 | — | 4865 | — |
| Uruguay | 85 | 25 | 98 | 11 |
| Venezuela | 94 | 35 | 81 | 29 |
| Yugoslavia | 128 | 1 | 113 | 1 |

B. **The change in the kind of goods exported by the United States.**

(Compare this problem with Problem D, page 297. Use Figure 117.)

1. Supply the figures for the last column of Table III, A (page 295), by finding the percentage by which each class of exports has increased or decreased. Why have some classes changed more than others?
2. In 1880 about 23 per cent of the population of the United States lived in cities of more than 8000, while now the percentage is 50. What has this to do with the change in our exports of (a) foodstuffs? (b) manufactures?
3. Name four of the foodstuffs that are exported most largely from the United States. From what part of the country do they chiefly come?
4. How has the increase in our city population prevented our decrease in exports of foods from causing a lowering of prices in the United States?
5. Name three countries that are gradually taking our place in supplying the world's market with foods. What geographical conditions make it possible for them to do this?
6. Name three nations that call on us to help feed them. Describe the geographical conditions that lead them to do this.
7. Compare the changes in the percentages of foodstuffs and of manufactures exported by the United States (Table III, A).
8. What parts of the world do we endeavor to supply with manufactured products?
9. With what nations do we compete for these sales? What are the conditions that enable them to compete with us?

10. The proportion of raw materials for manufacturing among our exports (Table III) has not decreased; this is because of the great quantities of raw cotton that we send abroad. How have the southern farmers been able to supply both the European markets and our own increasing number of cotton mills? How is the boll weevil changing this state of affairs?

11. Write a paragraph as to the way in which the industrial growth of our country is affecting the character of our exports.

C. **The change in the destination of goods exported by the United States.**

1. Turn back to Problem *D*, page 297. Compare the headings of that problem and this. Try to change the wording of that problem so that it will apply to Table III instead of Table II. Find out whether your statement of the present problem is clear, by giving the questions that you have framed to one of your classmates.

2. Why have our exports to Europe increased relatively little?

3. What figures in Table III answer the question:—Why have we introduced Spanish courses in many high schools and courses in commercial Chinese in our colleges?

D. **How the United States can keep pace with the manufacturing exporters of Europe.**

1. About 80 per cent of the total exports of Great Britain, Germany, France, Belgium, and the Netherlands are manufactured products. These countries preserve their commercial leadership by following as many as possible of the policies mentioned below:

   (*a*) Maintaining merchant marines.
   (*b*) Encouraging foreign investments and banks.
   (*c*) Establishing commercial schools.
   (*d*) Granting subsidies to shipping concerns.
   (*e*) Holding foreign colonies.

   Explain how each of those policies helps in obtaining customers for manufactures.

E. **How the United States government helps in foreign commerce.**

1. Find out in what ways American consuls assist American business firms in foreign commerce. How many American consular offices are there? In what continent are they most numerous?

2. Find out the purpose of the Pan-American Union. Why is our Bureau of Foreign and Domestic Commerce interested in its success?

# CHAPTER TWENTY-FOUR

## THE CONTRAST BETWEEN ASIA AND AUSTRALIA

### An Exercise in Business Geography

Asia and Australia present a notable contrast. Asia is the oldest of the continents so far as human history is concerned; Australia is the youngest. Asia is five times as large as Australia, and has more than a hundred times as many people as Australia and New Zealand combined. Asia contains vast supplies of coal, iron, and probably other mineral wealth, and its agricultural possibilities are almost unlimited. Australia has little coal and iron; its other mineral wealth is probably much less than that of Asia, although more developed; and agriculture is not possible on any such scale as in Asia. Nevertheless the people of Asia are far less prosperous than those of Australia and New Zealand. This is due partly to the density of the population in Asia, partly to historical causes, and partly to lack of initiative among most of the people of Asia in contrast with great energy and initiative among the Australians. The contrast illustrates the fact that in commerce and industry the most important of all factors is the character of the people.

### PRODUCTION

**What Asia and Australia produce.** Table V, on pages 312 and 313, lists the fifty primary products most important in the world as a whole. It shows what percentage of each is produced in Asia and in Australia, as well as the part of Asia where production is most active.

1. *Map exercise.* On an outline map of Asia draw a map of Australia, using the same scale, to show how the two continents compare in size.
2. Explain why the figures for Asia in Table V are generally much larger than for Australia. How is this possible when the average wealth per inhabitant is estimated to be ten or twelve times as great in Australia as in Asia?
3. From Table V select the seven products of which Asia produces the largest percentage of the world's total. Then select the seven in which Australia and New Zealand rank highest. Draw a diagram to illustrate your selection.
4. Make a list of products produced in Asia to the extent of at least twenty per cent of the world's total, but not produced in Australia to any

## (V) The Primary Production of Asia and Australia[1]

| World's Chief Primary Products (in approximate order of total value) | Percentage Produced in Asia | Percentage Produced in Australia and New Zealand | Parts of Asia in which Chiefly Produced |
|---|---|---|---|
| Dairy products | (4) | (3.0) | See Fig. 68 (Siberia) |
| Rice | 98 | 0.0 | See Fig. 35 |
| Cattle (excluding hides) | 25 | 2.0 | See Fig. 68 |
| Coal | 4 | 1.2 | Japan, India, China |
| Hay | (2) | (0.5) | Western Siberia |
| Wood | (10) | (0.5) | Northern Asia, S. E. Asia |
| Poultry and eggs | (5) | (1.0) | Widely distributed |
| Wheat | 20 | 2.6 | See Fig. 38 |
| Potatoes | 2 | 0.4 | Siberia, Japan |
| Vegetables | (40) | (1.0) | China, Japan |
| Swine | (5) | 0.6 | See Fig. 72 |
| Millet | (75) | 0.0 | S. E. Asia, wherever rice is not raised |
| Grapes | (5) | (0.4) | Turkey, Persia, etc. |
| Corn | 3 | 0.3 | See Fig. 39 |
| Sugar | 25 | 1.2 | See Fig. 54 |
| Cotton | 25 | 0.0 | See Fig. 7 |
| Petroleum | 22 | 0.0 | Transcaucasia, East Indies, India |
| Iron | 1 | 0.0 | Japan |
| Horses, asses, and mules | 20 | 2.6 | Siberia, Turkestan |
| Sheep and goats | 25 | 14.0 | See Fig. 71 |
| Beans | 80 | 0.2 | China, Japan, India |
| Oats | 4 | 0.7 | See Fig. 40 |
| Orchard fruits (not apples) | (5) | (0.6) | Western Asia |
| Fish | (25) | 0.6 | Japan, China |
| Rye | 2 | 0.0 | Siberia |
| Sweet potatoes and yams | (5) | 0.0 | East Indies, Indo-China, India, China |
| Olives | (5) | 0.0 | Syria |
| Wool | (20) | (15.0) | See Fig. 71 |
| Apples | (2) | (0.4) | Western Asia |
| Barley | 15 | 0.3 | India, Japan, W. Asia |
| Tobacco | 45 | 0.0 | India, China, Turkey, Philippines, Dutch E. Indies |
| Hides | (20) | (5.0) | See Figs. 68, 71, 72 |
| Peas, gram, etc. | (20) | 0.80 | China, Japan |

[1] Figures for Australia include New Zealand. Parentheses indicate that exact statistics are not available, and the figure given is an estimate.

## (V) The Primary Production of Asia and Australia (Continued)

| World's Chief Primary Products (in approximate order of total value) | Percentage Produced in Asia | Percentage Produced in Australia and New Zealand | Parts of Asia in which Chiefly Produced |
|---|---|---|---|
| Copper | 7 | 4.7 | Japan, India |
| Citrus fruits | (25) | 1.4 | — |
| Cement | (2) | (0.4) | India and Japan |
| Gold | 6 | 11.4 | Widely distributed |
| Bananas | (20) | 0.1 | India to S. China |
| Berries | (2) | (0.4) | W. and N. Asia |
| Tea | 99 | 0.0 | N. E. India, Ceylon, S. E. China, Japan, Java |
| Cottonseed | 25 | 0.0 | Dutch E. Indies, India |
| Stone | (5) | (0.4) | Widely distributed |
| Peanuts | (25) | 0.0 | S. E. Asia |
| Clay and brick | (5) | (0.6) | W. Asia, China, India |
| Raw silk | 80 | 0.0 | Japan, China (center and southeast) |
| Rubber | 97 | 0.0 | Ceylon, East Indies, Malay Peninsula |
| Flaxseed (linseed) | 30 | 0.0 | India (Ganges valley) |
| Coffee | 5 | 0.0 | East Indies, India |
| Water for power | 5 | 0.6 | Japan |
| Flax fiber | 5 | 0.0 | Western Siberia |
| Coconuts | (20) | 0.0 | S. E. Asia |
| Lead | 1 | 9.7 | India, Japan |
| Silver | 2 | 8.7 | Japan |
| Tin | 85 | 4.8 | Malay Peninsula |
| Zinc | 0 | 0.4 | — |
| Jute | 90 | 0.0 | Bengal |

appreciable extent, and hence marked 0.0 in Table V. What kinds of products are they — food fibers, metals, fuels, other raw materials?

List articles in which the production of Australia exceeds that of Asia. What kinds of products are they?

**Dependence of people of Asia upon local products.** Americans consume many goods brought from a distance, and they often fail to realize that far more than half the people of the world consume little except the products of their own immediate locality. In China and India the average consumption of imported products per capita among hundreds of millions of people amounts to less than fifty cents' worth per year. Those same people rarely consume more than two or three dollars' worth of domestic goods other than those produced within a few score miles of their homes. The high cost of primitive transportation, as well as their own poverty, makes the people unable to pay for goods from a distance. Among the majority of the Chinese and Indians, eighty per cent of a family's entire income is often represented by the rice, millet, beans, and other food products on which they live.

5. *Map exercise.* On an outline map of Asia, insert in their proper places in each country the names of all products which are produced there abundantly and of which Asia produces at least 20 per cent of the world's total. Use Table V. What parts of Asia have the greatest variety of products?

6. Judging from Table V and your map, state the kinds of foods that you would expect to be most common in the following regions:

    (a) West central Siberia   (c) Southern Japan   (f) Java
    (b) Manchuria              (d) Northern India   (g) Turkey
                               (e) Central India

    Verify your answers from reference books.

7. What indications do you see in Table V that most of the people of Asia live on a vegetable diet? What products are most widely eaten? What ones take the place of meat?

In India, where the Asiatic cattle are most abundant, and to a less extent in neighboring countries, cattle are used largely as draft animals and beasts of burden.

8. What effect does this have on people's diet? How do the figures for dairy products in Table V bear out your conclusion? What is the effect of the use of cattle as draft animals upon the number of hides available from a given number of animals?

**Effect of climatic and physical conditions on production in Asia and Australia.** Climatically Asia and Australia are alike in having a vast central area too dry for extensive human occupation, and in having the chief agricultural areas along the east coast and in the peninsulas that project equatorward. There heavy summer rains of the monsoon type permit a dense population to find a living. Both continents also have a western region more than 30° from the equator, where winter rains permit a moderately dense population to support itself by agriculture in spite of summer droughts. On the side away from the equator Asia projects into latitudes so high that agriculture is impossible in a large Siberian region, but Australia has nothing corresponding to this. Its southeastern corner, however, together with Tasmania and New Zealand, is like the best or western part of Siberia in being traversed by cyclonic storms, at least in winter, so that it has a fair amount of rain in winter as well as in summer.

# The Contrast between Asia and Australia

Fig. 184. On an Australian sheep farm. The landscape is typical of the southeastern states, Victoria and New South Wales.

The two continents are quite unlike in their relief. Asia's main mountains and plateaus are in the center with projections extending in many directions toward the sea. The Australian mountains lie parallel to the seacoast, while the interior assumes the form of a great desert basin.

9. *Map exercise.* On an outline map of Asia shade these parts: (*a*) where the July temperature (Fig. 18) is less than 52°; (*b*) where the rainfall (Fig. 1) is less than 10 inches; (*c*) where the mountains are high and rugged. What areas are left unshaded in your map? Compare this map with your other map (Exercise 5) and see what products are characteristic of each unshaded area. Compare the production in these areas with that in the shaded portions.

10. *Map exercise.* Make a similar map of Australia. What resemblances do you see between this map and that of Asia? What differences? Explain.

**The productive southeastern areas of Asia and Australia.** One of the most noteworthy features of both Asia and Australia is the concentration of population and of production in the southeastern sections.

11. Write a paragraph proving the statement made above, and explaining the physical conditions which make it possible.

Fig. 185. Calcutta, on the Hooghly River, is the leading port of India. It is a city of almost as many people as Philadelphia, but the average purchasing power of its inhabitants is much lower. What details in this illustration indicate a state of community development that means low purchasing power?

**Why the Siberian wheat region plays so small a part in commerce.** On the map made in Exercise 9, the center of the northern unshaded area is the Siberian wheat and cattle region. This extends about five hundred miles from north to south and two thousand miles from east to west, and is a third as large as the United States. It is less productive than would be expected from its extent.

12. What handicap to the Siberian wheat region is shown by the map of average temperatures in January (Fig. 17)?
13. What is the effect of the direction in which the rivers flow?
14. Discuss the position of the Siberian wheat region in relation to the progressive countries of Europe and America that furnish the chief markets for food and raw materials.
15. Why is it advisable for the Siberian farmers to specialize in butter and cheese, which have a small bulk compared with their value?
16. What can you find out about railroad development in this region?
17. Find two American cities that resemble Irkutsk and Omsk, the two largest cities of Siberia, in population and in the kind of business that they transact.

## The Contrast between Asia and Australia

### TRANSPORTATION

**Transportation in Asia compared with that of Australia and the United States.** The following figures illustrate the degree to which transportation has been developed in certain countries.

| Country | Total Railway Mileage | Miles of Railroad per 10,000 Inhabitants | Miles of Railroad per 1000 Square Miles | Motor Vehicles per 1000 Inhabitants |
|---|---|---|---|---|
| China | 6,836 | 0.2 | 1.6 | 0.07 |
| India | 36,616 | 1.2 | 20.3 | 0.41 |
| Turkey | 3,842 | 1.8 | 5.6 | 1.10 |
| Japan | 7,834 | 1.4 | 53.0 | 1.26 |
| Australia | 25,657 | 49.9 | 8.6 | 82.00 |
| New Zealand | 3,009 | 25.1 | 29.0 | 107.00 |
| United States | 264,233 | 24.8 | 88.8 | 200.00 |

18. How do the Asiatic countries compare with the others in (a) miles of railroad in proportion to population; (b) miles of railroad in proportion to area; (c) number of motor vehicles compared with the number of people?

19. Which of the Asiatic countries here given appears to you to have the best system of transportation? Why? How do its transportation facilities compare with those of each of the three non-Asiatic countries in the table? Why does it stand higher than the other Asiatic countries?

**The distribution of railroads in Asia.** The following conditions have played an important part in determining the location and extent of the railways of Asia: (a) the height and extent of the mountains and plateaus; (b) climatic conditions, including low temperature, lack of rain, summer floods, and dense vegetation; (c) density of the population; (d) poverty; (e) degree of progressiveness; (f) kind of government; (g) famines, which have led a great European country to build many miles of railway in one of its chief possessions in order to transport food from regions of abundance to those where food is scarce; (h) valuable products wanted by Europeans.

20. Explain how each of these conditions influences railroad building.

21. On an outline map of Asia write in each country a series of letters to indicate which of the conditions given above have had an important effect. Underline the letters indicating conditions that have stimulated railroad building.

**The historical lands of western Asia.** From the historical standpoint Palestine, Syria, Mesopotamia, Turkey, and Persia are especially important parts of Asia. Lack of rain in summer causes their population to be far less dense than that of India, China, and Japan. Nevertheless, their nearness to Europe and their historical connection have caused them to have more dealings with the western world than have the countries of southeastern Asia.

22. From a topographical map of Asia find out what mountain barrier has made it difficult to construct a railway connecting Constantinople with the Euphrates valley.

23. Work out two routes of travel from London to Bagdad and decide which would be the quicker.

24. Locate the following regions: (a) Transcaucasia; (b) Russian Turkestan; (c) Asia Minor; (d) Palestine. For each of these four regions, answer the following questions:

   (a) Why are railroads fairly numerous?
   (b) How important is irrigation?
   (c) What crops are planted in the autumn and reaped in the spring, thus making agriculture possible in spite of the long, rainless summer?
   (d) What cities are the most important?
   (e) What are the reasons for their importance and their location?

**The location of Asiatic cities.** Although Asia has a great number of large cities, the number is small in comparison with the population. For example, while Europe has nearly seventy cities with a population of more than 300,000, Asia with twice as many inhabitants has only about twenty-six. Most of the large Asiatic cities are in India, China, and Japan. The majority have hitherto been important chiefly as centers of trade for the surrounding regions or as capitals, but are now becoming great centers of foreign commerce.

25. From Table 5, B (page 330), make a list of all the Asiatic cities with more than 200,000 people. Locate them on the map made in Exercise 8.

26. Describe the relation of each of these cities to (a) density of population; (b) waterways; (c) railroads; (d) the more important primary products.

### MANUFACTURING

**Asia's position in manufacturing.** Aside from small quantities of handmade goods which often have a high artistic value, the chief manufactured goods of Asia are these:

   (a) India: coarse cotton cloth; jute bagging; linseed oil.
   (b) China: silk floss or partly spun thread; relatively little cotton, woolen, and silk cloth.

Fig. 186. Owing to the scarcity of grazing land in Japan, and the poor quality of the grass and of the rice straw, there are few draft animals. The Japanese make use of man power and of boats on their narrow rivers and deeply indented coasts to supplement railway transportation.

(c) Japan: a considerable variety of goods, especially silk, cotton, and woolen textiles (the cotton being eight times as valuable as the wool and twice as valuable as the silk); paper, matches; earthenware; oil.

Elsewhere in Asia there is almost no manufacturing except of a very simple or even primitive type. In fact, except in Japan there is not a single manufacturing city in our sense of the word. Even in Japan, although there are more than half as many people as in the United States, the number engaged in manufacturing is only one third as great as here.

27. How far does Table V indicate that Asiatic industries use raw materials imported from other continents?
28. Which of the raw materials used in the industries mentioned above are produced in Asia to the extent of at least 30 per cent of the world's total?
29. What does Figure 7 show as to the cotton production of Japan? Why does Japan import raw cotton from the United States?
30. Why are Japan's exports of cotton and silk cloth worth ten to twenty times as much as her exports of iron goods and machinery?

Fig. 187. In Jaipur, as in many other cities of India, the open space of the main street is the public market.

## CONSUMPTION

**What primary products are available for export from Asia.** The importance of an article in world trade depends partly on whether it is produced in amounts larger than are needed for immediate consumption. For instance, the Indian peninsula produces an enormous amount of millet, but as practically all of it is used as food, locally, it is far less important in world trade than the lead of Australia, even though its actual value is greater. Moreover, millet is not a kind of food that is desired in large quantities in progressive countries, and the demand for it is therefore small.

31. Is this true of any of the important products of the United States? Have we a large export trade in corn? sugar? lumber? Consult the *Year Book* of the Department of Agriculture.

If each of the continents consumed goods in proportion to the number of its people, Asia would need about 50 per cent of each of the products shown in Table V. China alone has as many people as Europe, and about four times the number of people in the United States.

32. Take the list made for Exercise 4, of the primary products which Asia produces to the extent of at least 20 per cent of the world's total. Arrange the products according to the size of the percentages in Table V,

## The Contrast between Asia and Australia

and write after each product your estimate of how much is consumed locally and how much is available for export. Your table may begin like this:

| Product | Percentage Produced in Asia | Local Consumption | Amount Available for Export |
|---|---|---|---|
| Tea | 99 | Large | Much |
| Rice | 98 | Very large | Some |
| Jute | 90 | Moderate | Much, because the commerce and industry of Asia are relatively inactive. |
| Tin | 85 | Very slight | Practically all, because Asia does little manufacturing of iron goods. |

33. Divide the products of your list into the following classes, and decide which classes contain the most products available for export: (a) foods, (b) fibers, (c) metals, (d) fuels, (e) other raw materials.
34. Compare your list with Table IV (page 308) to see which of these products the United States imports in appreciable amounts.

**The products that Asia exports.** The chief exports from Asiatic countries and their approximate annual values are as follows:

| Product | Value (Approximate) | Product | Value (Approximate) |
|---|---|---|---|
| Raw Rubber | Over $250,000,000 each | Jute | $150,000,000 each |
| Raw Cotton | | Tin | |
| Raw Silk | | Sugar | |
| | | Rice | |
| Manufactured Jute | 200,000,000 to 250,000,000 each | Hides and Furs | 100,000,000 each |
| Manufactured Cotton | | Manufactured Silk | |
| Oil (chiefly coconut) | | Tobacco | |
| Tea | | Beans | |
| | | Petroleum | |

35. How does this list compare with the list which you made in Exercise 32?
36. What countries are commercially important to the rest of the world because they furnish the exports listed above?
37. Why is Asia more important as a source of raw materials than of food?
38. Why does it furnish less food for other countries than do regions like southern South America and Canada, where the number of people engaged in raising food is not a tenth as great as in Asia?

**The character of primary production in Australia.** Among the primary products of Australia, metals are important because Australia is a dry country with many rugged regions, which an energetic people is rapidly exploiting. Wool is important for the same reasons and because Australia still has enormous areas which are not yet thickly settled.

39. From Table V make a list of the commodities whose production in Australia is at least as great as Australia's percentage of the world's population; that is, 0.4 per cent of the world's total.

40. How far does this list indicate that Australia supplies its own needs for primary products? What kinds of products are most conspicuously lacking? Does Australia supply anything that can easily take their place?

**The exports of Australia.** So far as the rest of the world is concerned, the important products of Australia are those that are produced to the extent of more than two per cent of the world's total.

41. Make a list of such products, divided into foods, fibers, metals, fuels, and other raw materials. Which group is the most numerous and most important, as indicated by the percentages?

42. How does this list compare with the similar list for Asia?

43. What do these products suggest as to the main occupations in Australia and New Zealand, compared with Asia?

**The great activity of Australia.** Remember that Australia and New Zealand together have only as many people as Illinois; that is, they have only one person where Asia has more than a hundred. Their foreign commerce is normally about a fourth as much as that of Asia.

44. Considering these facts, how does Australia compare with Asia in (a) mileage of railroads (page 317); (b) number of great cities (page 330); (c) foreign commerce?

45. Observe the location of cities in Australia and tell where you would expect to find the railway net closest.

46. On an outline map of Australia insert the cities of more than 200,000 people.

47. Find out something about each city. What does each export?

Australia and New Zealand are progressing in manufacturing much faster than any part of Asia, unless it be Japan.

48. Will the progress in manufacturing tend to increase or decrease the importance of Asia as a source of raw materials for the United States?

Fig. 188. Loading coal at Newcastle, in New South Wales. The derrick picks up the body of the coal car on the track, swings it over to the ship, and empties it into the hold. Sydney and Newcastle are the ports from which Australian coal is shipped throughout the South Pacific region.

**Position of Asia and Australia in production and commerce.** The trade of the United States with Australia and Asia is increasing faster than with any other parts of the world (pages 294, 295). Both continents are relatively undeveloped, Australia because it is new and sparsely settled, Asia because its people, as a rule, have not made much progress in modern methods of industry, commerce, and government. Both continents offer enormous possibilities: Asia because it contains a vast number of industrious inhabitants whose activities in both production and consumption can be greatly stimulated; Australia because it contains some of the world's most competent and progressive people, who are determined that newcomers to their continent shall be of the same kind.

Asia and Australia stand in an intermediate group among the continents. Europe and North America are highly developed and carry on much manufacturing. They are coming more and more to consume the food and the raw materials that they produce, and to call for more from other regions. In Africa and South America commerce and industry are limited because in large areas, although by no means everywhere, the people have the tropical inertia which hinders them from being either large producers or large consumers. Those continents are to a large degree the sources of food products, among which the most characteristic types come from plantations. Asia and Australia are great sources of raw materials. Their importance in this respect is likely to increase for a long time. Asia supplies relatively little food to other continents because her own dense population requires so much, but as a source of raw materials for manufacturing her importance is rapidly growing.

49. Suppose that a man in Sydney, Australia, decides to invest his money in manufacturing. Would you advise him to start a factory for manufacturing cotton cloth? Why, or why not? Where would he get his raw materials? Where would he get his machinery? For what kind of cotton goods would he find a strong local demand? With what foreign manufacturers would he find himself in competition? Would he need skilled or unskilled labor? Could he obtain labor easily?

50. Would he find it more profitable, or less, to start a shoe factory? Where would he get his materials? his machinery? What kind of labor would he employ?

51. Suppose that a Chinese company is formed to engage in the mining of iron in northern China. Where would the company order its machinery? Could any of it be manufactured in China? What transportation problems would be met? What labor could be obtained?

52. Suppose that the manager of a cotton factory in Kobe finds his supply of raw cotton running short. To what cities may he cable to see if he can procure a large quantity at a satisfactory price?

# APPENDIX

TABLE 1 — UNITED STATES: TOTAL PRODUCTION OF CHIEF MINERALS IN THE CHIEF MINERAL PRODUCING STATES AND ALASKA

(Figures in thousands)

| STATE | COAL (Short Tons) | IRON[1] (Long Tons) | PETRO-LEUM (Barrels) | COPPER[2] (Pounds Fine) | LEAD (Short Tons) | ZINC (Short Tons) | GOLD (Troy Oz.) | SILVER (Troy Oz.) |
|---|---|---|---|---|---|---|---|---|
| Alabama | 18,400 | 6,508 | — | — | — | — | — | — |
| Alaska | 87 | — | 8 | 56,489 | 1 | — | 286 | 606 |
| Arizona | — | — | — | 681,168 | 12 | — | 203 | 6,601 |
| Arkansas | 2,079 | — | 40,179 | — | — | 26 | — | — |
| California | 20 | — | 230,752 | 25,803 | 4 | — | 565 | 1,558 |
| Colorado | 9,693 | 32 | 2,787 | 8,007 | 34 | — | 259 | 3,941 |
| Georgia | 60 | 50 | — | — | — | — | — | — |
| Idaho | — | — | — | 1,811 | 136 | — | 15 | 8,929 |
| Illinois | 45,408 | — | 7,024 | — | 1 | 103 | — | 2 |
| Indiana | 17,699 | — | 852 | — | — | — | — | — |
| Iowa | 2,526 | — | — | — | — | — | — | — |
| Kansas | 2,517 | — | 40,740 | — | 28 | 33 | — | — |
| Kentucky | 72,626 | — | 6,733 | — | — | — | — | — |
| Louisiana | — | — | 21,061 | — | — | — | — | — |
| Maryland | 2,890 | — | — | — | — | — | — | — |
| Michigan | 749 | 14,533 | 435 | 195,135 | — | — | — | 52 |
| Minnesota | — | 35,563 | — | — | — | — | — | — |
| Missouri | 2,741 | 77 | — | 5 | 207 | — | — | 87 |
| Montana | 3,205 | 3 | 5,048 | 225,209 | 21 | — | 56 | 11,810 |
| Nevada | — | — | — | 118,298 | 11 | — | 149 | 5,373 |
| New Jersey | — | 203 | — | — | — | — | — | — |
| New Mexico | 2,998 | 215 | 1,203 | 79,761 | 3 | — | 26 | 755 |
| New York | — | 937 | 2,239 | — | — | — | — | — |
| North Carolina | 58 | 33 | — | 5,362 | — | — | — | — |
| North Dakota | 1,485 | — | — | — | — | — | — | — |
| Ohio | 14,668 | — | 7,529 | — | — | — | — | — |
| Oklahoma | 3,125 | — | 277,274 | — | 70 | 121 | — | — |
| Oregon | — | — | — | 485 | — | — | 14 | 42 |
| Pennsylvania | 211,659 | 1,125 | 9,596 | 2,149 | — | 106 | — | 2 |
| South Dakota | 14 | — | — | — | — | — | 323 | 95 |
| Tennessee | 5,256 | 121 | 60 | 14,499 | 2 | — | — | 82 |
| Texas | 1,134 | — | 213,768 | 25 | — | — | — | 943 |
| Utah | 4,869 | 223 | 1 | 267,706 | 148 | — | 200 | 19,354 |
| Virginia | 13,366 | 67 | — | — | — | — | — | — |
| Washington | 2,381 | 1 | — | 1,767 | 2 | — | 19 | 162 |
| West Virginia | 151,680 | — | 6,009 | — | — | — | — | — |
| Wisconsin | — | 938 | — | — | 2 | — | — | — |
| Wyoming | 7,085 | 603 | 21,146 | — | — | — | — | — |

[1] Ore shipped from mine. [2] Smelter output.

TABLE 2 — AREA AND POPULATION OF THE UNITED STATES, 1930

| GROUP | STATE, TERRITORY, OR POSSESSION | LAND AREA SQ. MI. | POPULATION | POPULATION PER SQ. MI. |
|---|---|---|---|---|
| NEW ENGLAND | Maine | 29,895 | 797,423 | 26.7 |
| | New Hampshire | 9,031 | 465,293 | 51.5 |
| | Vermont | 9,124 | 359,611 | 39.4 |
| | Massachusetts | 8,039 | 4,249,614 | 528.7 |
| | Rhode Island | 1,067 | 687,497 | 644.3 |
| | Connecticut | 4,820 | 1,606,903 | 333.4 |
| MIDDLE ATLANTIC | New York | 47,654 | 12,588,066 | 264.2 |
| | New Jersey | 7,514 | 4,041,334 | 537.8 |
| | Pennsylvania | 44,832 | 9,631,350 | 214.8 |
| EAST NORTH CENTRAL | Ohio | 40,740 | 6,646,697 | 163.1 |
| | Indiana | 36,045 | 3,238,503 | 89.8 |
| | Illinois | 56,043 | 7,630,654 | 136.2 |
| | Michigan | 57,480 | 4,842,325 | 84.2 |
| | Wisconsin | 55,256 | 2,939,006 | 53.2 |
| WEST NORTH CENTRAL | Minnesota | 80,858 | 2,563,953 | 31.7 |
| | Iowa | 55,586 | 2,470,939 | 44.5 |
| | Missouri | 68,727 | 3,629,367 | 52.8 |
| | North Dakota | 70,183 | 680,845 | 9.7 |
| | South Dakota | 76,868 | 692,849 | 9.0 |
| | Nebraska | 76,808 | 1,377,963 | 17.9 |
| | Kansas | 81,774 | 1,880,999 | 23.0 |
| SOUTH ATLANTIC | Delaware | 1,965 | 238,380 | 121.3 |
| | Maryland | 9,941 | 1,631,526 | 164.1 |
| | Virginia | 40,262 | 2,421,851 | 60.2 |
| | West Virginia | 24,022 | 1,729,205 | 72.0 |
| | North Carolina | 48,740 | 3,170,276 | 65.0 |
| | South Carolina | 30,495 | 1,738,765 | 57.0 |
| | Georgia | 58,725 | 2,908,506 | 49.5 |
| | Florida | 54,861 | 1,468,211 | 26.8 |
| EAST SOUTH CENTRAL | Kentucky | 40,181 | 2,614,589 | 65.0 |
| | Tennessee | 41,687 | 2,616,556 | 62.8 |
| | Alabama | 51,279 | 2,646,248 | 51.6 |
| | Mississippi | 46,362 | 2,009,821 | 43.4 |
| WEST SOUTH CENTRAL | Arkansas | 52,525 | 1,854,482 | 35.3 |
| | Louisiana | 45,409 | 2,101,593 | 46.3 |
| | Oklahoma | 69,414 | 2,396,040 | 34.5 |
| | Texas | 262,398 | 5,824,715 | 22.2 |
| MOUNTAIN | Montana | 146,131 | 537,606 | 3.7 |
| | Idaho | 83,354 | 445,032 | 5.3 |
| | Wyoming | 97,548 | 225,565 | 2.3 |
| | Colorado | 103,658 | 1,035,791 | 10.0 |
| | New Mexico | 122,503 | 423,317 | 3.5 |
| | Arizona | 113,810 | 435,573 | 3.8 |
| | Utah | 82,184 | 507,847 | 6.2 |
| | Nevada | 109,821 | 91,058 | 0.8 |
| PACIFIC | Washington | 66,836 | 1,563,396 | 23.4 |
| | Oregon | 95,607 | 953,786 | 10.0 |
| | California | 155,652 | 5,677,251 | 36.5 |
| | Alaska | 590,884 | 59,278 | .1 |
| INSULAR | Puerto Rico | 3,435 | 1,543,913 | 449.4 |
| | Virgin Islands | 133 | 22,012 | 165.5 |
| | Hawaiian Islands | 6,400 | 368,336 | 57.4 |
| | Philippine Islands | 114,400 | 12,604,100 | 111.7 |

District of Columbia, Canal Zone, American Samoa, Guam, Wake Island, and Midway Islands are not included in this table.

TABLE 3 — MANUFACTURING IN THE UNITED STATES

| STATE | TOTAL VALUE OF MANUFACTURES (Millions of Dollars) | VALUE PER PERSON | VALUE ADDED BY MANUFACTURING PER PERSON |
|---|---|---|---|
| New York | $8969 | $803 | $382 |
| Pennsylvania | 6902 | 731 | 319 |
| Ohio | 5348 | 825 | 357 |
| Illinois | 5322 | 751 | 338 |
| Michigan | 4373 | 1023 | 445 |
| New Jersey | 3539 | 1005 | 411 |
| Massachusetts | 3427 | 828 | 395 |
| California | 2442 | 584 | 231 |
| Indiana | 2125 | 688 | 284 |
| Wisconsin | 1859 | 653 | 272 |
| Missouri | 1607 | 461 | 180 |
| Connecticut | 1275 | 810 | 422 |
| Minnesota | 1102 | 423 | 127 |
| Texas | 1050 | 238 | 77 |
| North Carolina | 1050 | 373 | 178 |
| Maryland | 926 | 600 | 232 |
| Iowa | 758 | 313 | 107 |
| Louisiana | 710 | 374 | 129 |
| Kansas | 706 | 389 | 92 |
| Washington | 659 | 436 | 190 |
| Georgia | 649 | 209 | 80 |
| Rhode Island | 622 | 916 | 407 |
| Tennessee | 601 | 245 | 100 |
| Virginia | 590 | 241 | 112 |
| Alabama | 553 | 221 | 91 |
| West Virginia | 471 | 293 | 131 |
| Kentucky | 454 | 180 | 79 |
| Nebraska | 443 | 326 | 70 |
| Oklahoma | 403 | 180 | 44 |
| South Carolina | 373 | 207 | 74 |
| Maine | 372 | 474 | 211 |
| Oregon | 353 | 409 | 184 |
| New Hampshire | 327 | 723 | 286 |
| Colorado | 279 | 268 | 104 |
| Florida | 267 | 211 | 121 |
| Montana | 205 | 306 | 81 |
| Mississippi | 200 | 112 | 54 |
| Arkansas | 195 | 104 | 45 |
| Utah | 177 | 351 | 100 |
| Arizona | 139 | 324 | 96 |
| Vermont | 138 | 392 | 182 |
| Delaware | 125 | 531 | 244 |
| Wyoming | 108 | 472 | 140 |
| Idaho | 97 | 191 | 87 |
| South Dakota | 63 | 94 | 25 |
| North Dakota | 45 | 70 | 19 |
| Nevada | 22 | 281 | 125 |
| New Mexico | 19 | 51 | 23 |

TABLE 4 — AREA AND POPULATION OF CHIEF COUNTRIES AND COLONIES

(Based on figures for nearest available date. An asterisk (*) indicates an estimate.)

| CONTINENT AND COUNTRY | AREA (In thousands of square miles) | POPULATION (In thousands) | CONTINENT AND COUNTRY | AREA (In thousands of square miles) | POPULATION (In thousands) | CONTINENT AND COUNTRY | AREA (In thousands of square miles) | POPULATION (In thousands) |
|---|---|---|---|---|---|---|---|---|
| **Africa** | *11,000. | *140,000 | Chinese Republic | *4,283. | *490,000 | **Australasia & Pacific Is.** | *3,300. | *9,500 |
| Algeria | 848. | 6,063 | China (Proper) | *1,534. | *459,000 | Australia | 2,974.6 | 6,439 |
| Anglo-Egypt. Sudan | 1,008.1 | 5,580 | Manchuria | *363.6 | 23,800 | New South Wales | 309.4 | 2,485 |
| Angola | 486.1 | 2,522 | Mongolia | *1,370. | *2,500 | Northern Territory | 523.6 | *25 |
| Belgian Congo | *938. | *10,000 | Sinkiang | *550. | *2,688 | Queensland | 670.5 | 942 |
| British East Africa | *694. | *11,400 | Tibet | *465. | *1,500 | South Australia | 330.1 | 581 |
| Egypt | *383. | 14,217 | Cyprus | 3.6 | 311 | Tasmania | 26.2 | 216 |
| Ethiopia | *350. | *5,009 | Hongkong | .4 | 1,144 | Victoria | 87.9 | 1,784 |
| French Equat. Africa | *1,142. | *14,505 | India | 1,408. | 340,500 | Western Australia | *975.9 | 419 |
| French West Africa | *1,469. | *2,000 | Indo-China | 285. | 20,700 | New Zealand | 103.7 | 1,490 |
| Liberia | *43. | *720 | Iraq (Mesopotamia) | *177.1 | *3,300 | Borneo (British) | 83.6 | 884 |
| Libya | *634. | 3,621 | Japanese Empire | 265.1 | 90,395 | Dutch East Indies | 733.7 | 52,825 |
| Madagascar | 241.1 | *5,000 | Japan (Proper) | 152.4 | 64,448 | Philippine Islands | 114.4 | 12,204 |
| Morocco | *218. | 3,515 | Chōsen (Korea) | 84.9 | 21,058 | Hawaiian Islands | 6.4 | 368 |
| Mozambique | 287.8 | *19,409 | Karafuto | 13.9 | 295 | | | |
| Nigeria | *335.7 | *1,308 | Taiwan (Formosa) | 13.8 | 4,594 | **Antarctica** | *5,000. | 0 |
| Northern Rhodesia | *287.9 | *1,092 | Lebanon | *4. | 863 | | | |
| Southern Rhodesia | *149. | *260 | Malay Peninsula | 56.6 | 3,920 | **Europe** | *3,690. | *483,000 |
| Southwest Africa | *322.8 | 2,160 | Nejd and Hedjaz | *373. | *4,000 | Albania | 10.6 | 1,003 |
| Tunisia | 48.3 | 7,659 | Nepal | *54. | *5,600 | Andorra | .2 | 5 |
| Union of South Africa | 471.9 | | Oman | *82. | *500 | Austria | 32.4 | 6,704 |
| | | | Palestine | *10. | 946 | Belgium | 11.8 | 8,060 |
| **Asia** | *16,900. | *1,100,000 | Persia | 628. | *10,000 | Bulgaria | 39.8 | 5,597 |
| Afghanistan | 245. | *11,000 | Russia in Asia | 6,632.7 | 38,677 | Czechoslovakia | 54.2 | 14,608 |
| Aden | 9. | 55 | Siam | 200.1 | 11,506 | Denmark | 16.6 | 3,542 |
| Baluchistan | 134.6 | 800 | Syria | Unsettled | *1,697 | Estonia | 18.4 | 1,115 |
| Bhutan | 18. | 300 | Trans-Jordan | *60. | *260 | Finland | 151. | 3,634 |
| Burma | 262.7 | 13,212 | Turkey in Asia | 273.8 | 12,477 | | | |
| Ceylon | 25.3 | 5,479 | Yemen | *75. | *2,500 | | | |

TABLE 4 — AREA AND POPULATION OF CHIEF COUNTRIES AND COLONIES — Continued

| CONTINENT AND COUNTRY | AREA (In thousands of square miles) | POPULATION (In thousands) | CONTINENT AND COUNTRY | AREA (In thousands of square miles) | POPULATION (In thousands) | CONTINENT AND COUNTRY | AREA (In thousands of square miles) | POPULATION (In thousands) |
|---|---|---|---|---|---|---|---|---|
| France | 212.7 | 41,835 | **North America** | *9,355. | 166,900 | United States | 3,026.8 | 122,775 |
| Germany | 181. | 64,036 | Alaska | 586.4 | 59 | West Indies | 91.1 | 11,381 |
| Grt. Britain & N. Ire. | 94.6 | 45,938 | Bermuda Islands | .02 | 32 | Bahama Islands | 4.4 | 61 |
| England | 50.9 | 37,355 | Canada | 3,684.7 | 10,354 | Cuba | 44.2 | 3,608 |
| Northern Ireland | 5.2 | 1,244 | Alberta | 255.3 | 727 | Dominican Repub. | 19.3 | 1,200 |
| Scotland | 30.4 | 4,843 | British Columbia | 355.9 | 689 | Haiti | 10.2 | 2,550 |
| Wales | 7.5 | 2,593 | Manitoba | 251.8 | 700 | Jamaica | 4.7 | 994 |
| Greece | 49.9 | 6,205 | New Brunswick | 28. | 408 | Lesser Antilles | 4.8 | 1,402 |
| Hungary | 35.9 | 8,684 | Nova Scotia | 21.4 | 512 | Puerto Rico | 3.4 | 1,544 |
| Iceland | 39.7 | 106 | Ontario | 412.6 | 3,426 | Virgin Islands | .133 | 22 |
| Irish Free State | 27. | 2,972 | Prince Edward Isl. | 2.2 | 89 | | | |
| Italy | 119.7 | 42,875 | Quebec | 594.4 | 2,870 | | | |
| Latvia | 25.4 | 1,900 | Saskatchewan | 251.7 | 921 | | | |
| Lithuania | *21.5 | *2,340 | Northwest Terr. | 1,309.7 | 7 | | | |
| Luxembourg | 1. | 222 | Yukon | 207.1 | 4 | **South America** | *7,242. | *81,420 |
| Monaco | .008 | 25 | **Central America** | 215. | 6,539 | Argentina | 1,153. | 11,193 |
| The Netherlands | 13.2 | 7,832 | British Honduras | 8.6 | 51 | Bolivia | *547. | *3,000 |
| Norway | 125.1 | 2,890 | Costa Rica | 23. | 472 | Brazil | 3,286. | 40,273 |
| Poland | *150. | 31,928 | Guatemala | 42.4 | 2,177 | British Guiana | 89.5 | 310 |
| Portugal | 35.8 | 6,440 | Honduras | 46.3 | 860 | Chile | 290.1 | 4,265 |
| Rumania | 122.3 | 18,172 | Nicaragua | 49.5 | 750 | Colombia | *497.3 | *7,993 |
| Russia(U.S.S.R.)Eur. | 1,607.8 | 108,336 | Panama | 32.4 | 467 | Ecuador | *110. | *2,000 |
| Spain | 196.6 | 22,760 | Panama Canal Z. | .55 | 39 | French Guiana | 34.8 | 47 |
| Sweden | 173.1 | 6,120 | El Salvador | 13.2 | 1,723 | Paraguay | *176. | *843 |
| Switzerland | 15.9 | 4,067 | Greenland | 827.3 | 16 | Peru | *532. | *6,187 |
| Turkey in Europe | 9. | 1,203 | Mexico | 760.3 | 16,404 | Surinam (Dutch G.) | 54.3 | 151 |
| Vatican City | 108.7 acres | .639 | Newfoundland | 42.7 | 266 | Uruguay | 72.2 | 2,037 |
| Yugoslavia | 96.1 | 13,290 | Labrador | 120. | 4 | Venezuela | 394. | 3,116 |

TABLE 5 — COMMERCIAL CITIES OF THE WORLD

In this table are given first the cities of 200,000 population and more, (A) in the United States, (B) in the rest of the world. Next (C) come important cities of less than 200,000 population, in the United States. The figures in the columns for population are given in thousands; that is, 215 means 215,000; 324 means 324,000, etc.

(A) CITIES IN THE UNITED STATES
Population of 200,000 or more (1930 Census)

| CITY | POPULATION | STATE | CITY | POPULATION | STATE |
|---|---|---|---|---|---|
| SEAPORTS [1] | | | RIVER PORTS | | |
| Baltimore | 804 | Md. | Cincinnati | 451 | Ohio |
| Boston | 781 | Mass. | Kansas City | 399 | Mo. |
| Houston | 292 | Tex. | Louisville | 307 | Ky. |
| Jersey City | 316 | N. J. | Memphis | 253 | Tenn. |
| Los Angeles | 1,238 | Calif. | Minneapolis | 464 | Minn. |
| Newark | 442 | N. J. | Pittsburgh | 669 | Pa. |
| New Orleans [2] | 458 | La. | St. Louis | 821 | Mo. |
| New York | 6,930 | N. Y. | St. Paul | 271 | Minn. |
| Oakland | 284 | Calif. | Washington | 486 | D. C. |
| Philadelphia [2] | 1,950 | Pa. | | | |
| Portland [2] | 301 | Ore. | INLAND CITIES | | |
| Providence | 252 | R. I. | Akron | 255 | Ohio |
| San Francisco | 634 | Calif. | Atlanta | 270 | Ga. |
| Seattle | 365 | Wash. | Birmingham | 259 | Ala. |
| | | | Columbus | 290 | Ohio |
| LAKE PORTS | | | Dallas | 260 | Tex. |
| Buffalo | 573 | N. Y. | Dayton | 200 | Ohio |
| Chicago | 3,376 | Ill. | Denver | 287 | Colo. |
| Cleveland | 900 | Ohio | Indianapolis | 364 | Ind. |
| Detroit | 1,568 | Mich. | Omaha | 214 | Neb. |
| Milwaukee | 578 | Wis. | San Antonio | 231 | Tex. |
| Rochester | 328 | N. Y. | Syracuse | 209 | N. Y. |
| Toledo | 290 | Ohio | | | |

(B) CITIES OUTSIDE THE UNITED STATES
Population of 200,000 or more

| CITY | POPULATION | CENSUS YEAR | COUNTRY | CITY | POPULATION | CENSUS YEAR | COUNTRY |
|---|---|---|---|---|---|---|---|
| | | | | Belfast | 415 | '31 | N. Ireland |
| SEAPORTS | | | | Bombay | 1,176 | '21 | India |
| Adelaide | 325 | '29 | Australia | Bordeaux | 256 | '26 | France |
| Alexandria | 573 | '27 | Egypt | Bremen | 295 | '25 | Germany |
| Algiers | 226 | '26 | Algeria | Brisbane | 319 | '29 | Australia |
| Amoy | 400 | '30 | China | Bristol | 397 | '31 | England |
| Amsterdam | 752 | '30 | Netherlands | Brussels | 839 | '30 | Belgium |
| Antwerp | 424 | '30 | Belgium | Buenos Aires [2] | 2,163 | '30 | Argentina |
| Athens and Piræus | 700[3] | '28 | Greece | Calcutta [2] | 1,328 | '31 | India |
| Auckland | 210 | '29 | New Zealand | Canton | 1,368[3] | '30 | China |
| Bahia | 330 | '30 | Brazil | Cape Town | 265 | '30 | South Africa |
| Bangkok | 667 | '20 | Siam | Cardiff | 224 | '31 | England |
| Barcelona | 775 | '29 | Spain | Catania | 384 | '30 | Sicily |
| Batavia | 437 | '30 | Java | Colombo | 268 | '29 | Ceylon |

[1] That is, ports reached by ocean vessels.  [2] Might also be called a river port.  [3] Estimated.

TABLE 5 — *Continued*

(B) CITIES OUTSIDE THE UNITED STATES — *Continued*

Population of 200,000 or more

| City | Population (In thousands) | Census Year | Country | City | Population (In thousands) | Census Year | Country |
|---|---|---|---|---|---|---|---|
| SEAPORTS — *Cont.* | | | | Nagoya | 907 | '30 | Japan |
| Constantinople | 673 | '27 | Turkey | Nanking [2] | 902[3] | '30 | China |
| Copenhagen | 771 | '30 | Denmark | Naples | 991 | '30 | Italy |
| Dairen | 250 | '30 | China | Newcastle | 283 | '31 | England |
| Danzig | 390 | '28 | Free City | Ningpo | 212[3] | '27 | China |
| Dublin | 419 | '26 | Ireland | Odessa | 421 | '26 | Russia |
| Edinburgh and Leith | 439 | '31 | Scotland | Oporto | 227 | '30 | Portugal |
| Foochow [1] | 388[3] | '29 | China | Osaka | 2,454 | '30 | Japan |
| Genoa | 632 | '30 | Italy | Oslo | 249 | '30 | Norway |
| Glasgow | 1,088 | '31 | Scotland | Palermo | 465 | '30 | Italy |
| Göteborg | 243 | '30 | Sweden | Pará (Belem) | 279 | '30 | Brazil |
| Hamburg | 1,079 | '25 | Germany | Penang | 333 | '27 | Straits Settlements |
| Hangchow [2] | 730[3] | '30 | China | | | | |
| Havana | 589 | '30 | Cuba | Pernambuco (Recife) | 341 | '30 | Brazil |
| Helsinki | 235 | '30 | Finland | Porto Alegre | 273 | '30 | Brazil |
| Hongkong | 853 | '30 | China | Portsmouth | 249 | '31 | England |
| Karachi | 217 | '21 | India | Rangoon | 342 | '21 | Burma |
| Kiel | 214 | '29 | Germany | Riga | 377 | '30 | Russia |
| Kingston-upon-Hull | 313 | '31 | England | Rio de Janeiro | 1,469 | '30 | Brazil |
| Kobe | 788 | '30 | Japan | Rotterdam | 581 | '30 | Netherlands |
| Königsberg | 287 | '25 | Germany | Saloniki | 237 | '28 | Greece |
| Leningrad | 1,614 | '26 | Russia | Shanghai | 1,713 | '30 | China |
| Lima and Callao | 375 | '30 | Peru | Singapore | 559 | '28 | Straits Settlements |
| Lisbon | 587 | '30 | Portugal | Soerabaya | 337[3] | '30 | Java |
| Liverpool | 856 | '31 | England | Stettin | 254 | '25 | Germany |
| London | 4,397 | '31 | England | Stockholm | 502 | '30 | Sweden |
| Madras | 527 | '21 | India | Sydney | 1,238 | '29 | Australia |
| Manchester | 766 | '31 | England | Tientsin | 1,000[3] | '30 | China |
| Manila [2] | 337 | '28 | Philippines | Trieste | 255 | '30 | Italy |
| Marseilles | 652 | '26 | France | Tsingtao | 318[3] | '27 | China |
| Melbourne | 1,018 | '29 | Australia | Valencia | 272 | '30 | Spain |
| Messina | 203 | '30 | Italy | Vancouver | 245 | '31 | Canada |
| Montevideo | 600 | '30 | Uruguay | Venice | 260 | '30 | Italy |
| Montreal [2] | 810 | '31 | Canada | Yokohama | 620 | '30 | Japan |

[1] Many Chinese cities have extensive rural districts, which, if counted in, give a large population figure. For the purposes of this table, only the population of the main part of the city, the commercial city, is given.

[2] Might also be called a river port.

[3] Estimated.

TABLE 5 — *Continued*

(*B*) CITIES OUTSIDE THE UNITED STATES — *Continued*

Population of 200,000 or more

| City | Population (In thousands) | Census Year | Country | River, Canal, or Lake |
|---|---|---|---|---|
| RIVER, CANAL, AND LAKE PORTS | | | | |
| Baghdad | 300 | 1928 | Irak | Tigris |
| Baku | 453 | 1926 | Caucasia | Caspian Sea |
| Belgrade | 242 | 1931 | Yugoslavia | Danube |
| Benares | 200 | 1927 | India | Ganges |
| Berlin | 4,346 | 1929 | Germany | Spree |
| Bradford | 298 | 1931 | England | Canal |
| Breslau | 600 | 1929 | Germany | Oder |
| Budapest | 1,005 | 1930 | Hungary | Danube |
| Cairo | 1,065 | 1927 | Egypt | Nile |
| Changsha | 550 [1] | 1930 | China | Siung |
| Chungking | 625 [1] | 1930 | China | Yangtsekiang |
| Cologne | 700 | 1925 | Germany | Rhine |
| Dnepropetrovsk | 233 | 1926 | Russia | Dnieper |
| Dortmund | 526 | 1929 | Germany | Canal |
| Dresden | 619 | 1925 | Germany | Elbe |
| Duisburg | 421 | 1929 | Germany | Canal |
| Düsseldorf | 465 | 1929 | Germany | Rhine |
| Frankfurt | 540 | 1929 | Germany | Main |
| Gelsenkirchen | 330 | 1929 | Germany | Ems Canal |
| Hankow | 819 [1] | 1928 | China | Yangtsekiang |
| Hannover | 425 | 1929 | Germany | Leine |
| Kiev | 514 | 1926 | Russia | Dnieper |
| Leicester | 239 | 1931 | England | Canal |
| Lucknow | 241 | 1921 | India | Guma |
| Lyons | 571 | 1926 | France | Rhone |
| Magdeburg | 297 | 1929 | Germany | Elbe |
| Mannheim | 247 | 1925 | Germany | Rhine |
| Nottingham | 269 | 1931 | England | Canal |
| Nürnberg | 393 | 1925 | Germany | Canal |
| Paris | 2,871 | 1926 | France | Seine |
| Prague | 848 | 1930 | Czechoslovakia | Elbe |
| Rosario | 470 | 1930 | Argentina | La Plata |
| Rostov-on-Don | 308 | 1926 | Russia | Don |
| Salford | 223 | 1931 | England | Canal |
| Saratov | 215 | 1926 | Russia | Volga |
| Seville | 217 | 1929 | Spain | Guadalquivir |
| Stoke-upon-Trent | 277 | 1931 | England | Trent |
| Suchow | 350 [1] | 1930 | China | Grand Canal |
| Toronto | 628 | 1931 | Canada | Ontario |
| Vienna | 1,843 | 1929 | Austria | Danube |
| Warsaw | 1,109 | 1930 | Poland | Vistula |
| West Ham | 294 | 1931 | England | Thames |
| Zurich | 249 | 1930 | Switzerland | Zurich |

[1] Estimated.

## Table 5 — Continued

### (B) Cities Outside the United States — Continued
### Population of 200,000 or more

| City | Population (In thousands) | Census Year | Country |
|---|---|---|---|
| **Inland Cities** [1] | | | |
| Ahmedabad | 274 | 1921 | India |
| Bangalore | 237 | 1921 | India |
| Birmingham | 1,002 | 1931 | England |
| Bochum | 313 | 1929 | Germany |
| Bogotá | 241 | 1928 | Colombia |
| Bologna | 248 | 1930 | Italy |
| Brno | 264 | 1930 | Czechoslovakia |
| Bucarest | 890 | 1928 | Rumania |
| Cawnpore | 216 | 1921 | India |
| Changchow | 600 [2] | 1920 | China |
| Chemnitz | 336 | 1925 | Germany |
| Croydon | 233 | 1931 | England |
| Delhi | 304 | 1921 | India |
| Essen | 471 | 1925 | Germany |
| Fatshan | 450 [2] | 1931 | China |
| Florence | 319 | 1930 | Italy |
| Hague, The | 436 | 1930 | Netherlands |
| Hyderabad | 404 | 1921 | India |
| Johannesburg | 331 | 1930 | South Africa |
| Keijo (Seoul) | 315 | 1926 | Chosen |
| Kharkov | 417 | 1926 | Russia |
| Kyoto | 765 | 1930 | Japan |
| Lahore | 282 | 1921 | India |
| Leeds | 483 | 1931 | England |
| Leipzig | 679 | 1925 | Germany |
| Lemberg | 240 | 1930 | Poland |
| Lille | 202 | 1926 | France |
| Lodz | 607 | 1930 | Poland |
| Madrid | 825 | 1929 | Spain |
| Mexico | 960 | 1930 | Mexico |
| Milan | 981 | 1930 | Italy |
| Moscow | 2,026 | 1926 | Russia |
| Munich | 681 | 1925 | Germany |
| Peiping (Peking) | 1,298 [2] | 1926 | China |
| Poona | 215 | 1921 | India |
| Rome | 1,004 | 1930 | Italy |
| Santiago | 696 | 1930 | Chile |
| São Paulo | 880 | 1930 | Brazil |
| Sheffield | 512 | 1931 | England |
| Sofia | 213 | 1926 | Bulgaria |
| Stuttgart | 343 | 1925 | Germany |
| Tashkent | 324 | 1926 | Turkestan |
| Tehran | 335 [2] | 1931 | Persia |
| Tiflis | 293 | 1926 | Georgia |
| Tokyo | 2,071 | 1930 | Japan |
| Torino | 651 | 1930 | Italy |
| Tsinanfu | 621 [2] | 1931 | China |

[1] Some of these cities are on small rivers or canals, but can scarcely be called "ports."
[2] Estimated.

334                     *Modern Business Geography*

TABLE 5 — *Continued*

(C) COMMERCIAL CITIES OF THE UNITED STATES

Population less than 200,000 (1930 Census)

All the cities of the United States that are mentioned in this book are given below, unless listed in Section A of this table. Some comparatively small cities are included because of their importance as commercial centers.

| City | Population (In thousands) | State or Territory | City | Population (In thousands) | State or Territory |
|---|---|---|---|---|---|
| Albany | 127 | N. Y. | Honolulu | 137 | H. T. |
| Albuquerque | 26 | N. M. | Jacksonville | 129 | Fla. |
| Allentown | 92 | Pa. | Johnstown | 10 | N. Y. |
| Altoona | 82 | Pa. | Johnstown | 66 | Pa. |
| Ashland | 11 | Ohio | Joliet | 42 | Ill. |
| Ashtabula | 23 | Ohio | Kansas City | 121 | Kan. |
| Barre | 11 | Vt. | Knoxville | 105 | Tenn. |
| Battle Creek | 43 | Mich. | Lawrence | 85 | Mass. |
| Bayonne | 88 | N. J. | Leadville | 3 | Colo. |
| Bellingham | 30 | Wash. | Lincoln | 75 | Neb. |
| Bethlehem | 57 | Pa. | Little Rock | 81 | Ark. |
| Binghamton | 76 | N. Y. | Long Beach | 142 | Calif. |
| Boise | 21 | Idaho | Lowell | 100 | Mass. |
| Braddock | 19 | Pa. | Lynn | 102 | Mass. |
| Bridgeport | 46 | Conn. | Manchester | 76 | N. H. |
| Brockton | 63 | Mass. | McKeesport | 54 | Pa. |
| Burlington | 24 | Vt. | Miami | 110 | Fla. |
| Butte | 39 | Mont. | Mobile | 68 | Ala. |
| Cambridge | 113 | Mass. | Nashua | 31 | N. H. |
| Camden | 118 | N. J. | Nashville | 153 | Tenn. |
| Canton | 104 | Ohio | New Bedford | 112 | Mass. |
| Charleston | 62 | S. C. | New Haven | 162 | Conn. |
| Charlotte | 82 | N. C. | New London | 29 | Conn. |
| Cheyenne | 17 | Wyo. | Newport News | 34 | Va. |
| Columbia | 51 | S. C. | Niagara Falls | 75 | N. Y. |
| Des Moines | 142 | Iowa | Norfolk | 129 | Va. |
| Duluth | 101 | Minn. | Olympia | 11 | Wash. |
| El Paso | 102 | Texas | Oklahoma City | 185 | Okla. |
| Elizabeth | 114 | N. J. | Passaic | 62 | N. J. |
| Erie | 115 | Pa. | Paterson | 138 | N. J. |
| Everett | 30 | Wash. | Pawtucket | 77 | R. I. |
| Fall River | 115 | Mass. | Pensacola | 31 | Fla. |
| Fargo | 28 | N. Dak. | Peoria | 104 | Ill. |
| Flint | 156 | Mich. | Phoenix | 48 | Ariz. |
| Fort Wayne | 114 | Ind. | Ponce | 75 | P. R. |
| Fort Worth | 163 | Texas | Portland | 70 | Maine |
| Galveston | 52 | Texas | Portsmouth | 45 | Va. |
| Gary | 100 | Ind. | Quincy | 71 | Mass. |
| Gloucester | 24 | Mass. | Racine | 67 | Wis. |
| Gloversville | 23 | N. Y. | Reading | 111 | Pa. |
| Grand Rapids | 168 | Mich. | Richmond | 182 | Va. |
| Harrisburg | 80 | Pa. | Roanoke | 69 | Va. |
| Hartford | 164 | Conn. | Sacramento | 93 | Calif. |
| Haverhill | 48 | Mass. | Salem | 43 | Mass. |
| Hoboken | 59 | N. J. | Salt Lake City | 140 | Utah |
| Homestead | 20 | Pa. | San Diego | 147 | Calif. |

## Appendix

### Table 5 — *Continued*
#### (C) Commercial Cities of the United States — *Continued*
#### Population less than 200,000

| City | Population (In thousands) | State or Territory | City | Population (In thousands) | State or Territory |
|---|---|---|---|---|---|
| San Juan | 114 | P. R. | Trenton | 123 | N. J. |
| Savannah | 85 | Ga. | Troy | 72 | N. Y. |
| Schenectady | 95 | N. Y. | Tulsa | 141 | Okla. |
| Scranton | 143 | Pa. | Utica | 101 | N. Y. |
| Shreveport | 76 | La. | Vicksburg | 22 | Miss. |
| Sioux City | 79 | Iowa | Waterbury | 99 | Conn. |
| Sioux Falls | 33 | S. Dak. | Wichita | 111 | Kan. |
| South Bend | 104 | Ind. | Wheeling | 61 | W. Va. |
| Spokane | 115 | Wash. | Wilkes Barre | 86 | Pa. |
| Springfield | 149 | Mass. | Wilmington | 106 | Del. |
| St. Joseph | 80 | Mo. | Winston-Salem | 75 | N. C. |
| Superior | 36 | Wis. | Woonsocket | 49 | R. I. |
| Tacoma | 106 | Wash. | Worcester | 195 | Mass. |
| Tampa | 101 | Fla. | Yonkers | 134 | N. Y. |
| Terre Haute | 62 | Ind. | Youngstown | 170 | Ohio |

### Table 6 — Chief Cities of South America

| City | Population (In thousands) | Country | Census Year |
|---|---|---|---|
| Antofagasta | 53 | Chile | 1930 |
| Arequipa | 70 | Peru | 1930 |
| Asunción | 142 | Paraguay | 1928 |
| Bahia (São Salvador) | 330 | Brazil | 1930 |
| Bahía Blanca | 121 | Argentina | 1930 |
| Barranquilla | 139 | Colombia | 1928 |
| Bello Horizonte | 109 | Brazil | 1930 |
| Bogotá | 241 | Colombia | 1928 |
| **Buenos Aires** | **2,116** | Argentina | 1930 |
| Cali | 122 | Colombia | 1928 |
| Callao | 75 | Peru | 1930 |
| Caracas | 135 | Venezuela | 1926 |
| Cartagena | 92 | Colombia | 1928 |
| Cayenne | 14 | French Guiana | 1926 |
| Cochabamba | 36 | Bolivia | 1930 |
| Córdoba | 228 | Argentina | 1930 |
| Cuzco | 40 | Peru | 1930 |
| Fortaleza | 99 | Brazil | 1930 |
| Georgetown | 57 | British Guiana | 1929 |
| Guayaquil | 100 | Ecuador | 1929 |
| Iquique | 46 | Chile | 1930 |
| La Paz | 149 | Bolivia | 1930 |
| La Plata | 169 | Argentina | 1930 |
| Lima | 375 | Peru | 1930 |
| Maceió | 104 | Brazil | 1930 |
| Manaos | 84 | Brazil | 1930 |
| Manizales | 81 | Colombia | 1928 |

TABLE 6 — CHIEF CITIES OF SOUTH AMERICA — *Continued*

| CITY | POPULATION (In thousands) | COUNTRY | CENSUS YEAR |
|---|---|---|---|
| Maracaibo | 75 | Venezuela | 1926 |
| Medellin | 120 | Colombia | 1928 |
| Montevideo | 600 | Uruguay | 1930 |
| Nictheroy | 108 | Brazil | 1930 |
| Oruro | 41 | Bolivia | 1930 |
| Parahyba | 74 | Brazil | 1930 |
| Pará (Belem) | 279 | Brazil | 1930 |
| Paramaribo | 46 | Dutch Guiana | 1929 |
| Pernambuco (Recife) | 341 | Brazil | 1930 |
| Porto Alegre | 273 | Brazil | 1930 |
| Quito | 100 | Ecuador | 1929 |
| **Rio de Janeiro** | **1,469** | Brazil | 1930 |
| Rosario | 470 | Argentina | 1930 |
| Santiago | 696 | Chile | 1930 |
| Santos | 102 | Brazil | 1930 (est.) |
| São Paulo | 880 | Brazil | 1930 |
| Sucre | 35 | Bolivia | 1930 |
| Tucumán | 116 | Argentina | 1930 |
| Valencia | 37 | Venezuela | 1926 |
| Valparaiso | 193 | Chile | 1930 |

TABLE 7 — SOUTH AMERICAN EXPORTS

This table lists all the articles usually exported from South America to a value of more than $1,000,000 a year. They are arranged in order of value. The countries that contribute $500,000 or more are listed in order according to the usual proportion of their contribution.

| PRODUCT | COUNTRIES |
|---|---|
| 1. Coffee | Brazil  Colombia  Venezuela  Ecuador |
| 2. Animal products[1] | Argentina  Uruguay  Brazil  Colombia  Paraguay  Peru |
| 3. Cereals | Argentina  Uruguay  Brazil |
| 4. Rubber | Brazil  Bolivia  Peru  Colombia  Ecuador  Uruguay |
| 5. Nitrate | Chile  Ecuador  Colombia |
| 6. Tin | Bolivia |
| 7. Cacao | Ecuador  Brazil  Venezuela |
| 8. Copper | Peru  Chile  Bolivia |
| 9. Sugar | Peru  British Guiana  Dutch Guiana |
| 10. Cotton | Brazil  Peru |
| 11. Gold | Colombia  Brazil  British Guiana  Venezuela  Dutch Guiana |
| 12. Mate | Brazil |
| 13. Quebracho | Argentina |
| 14. Tobacco | Brazil |
| 15. Hats, straw | Peru  Ecuador  Colombia |
| 16. Wax, carnauba | Brazil  Venezuela |
| 17. Silver | Bolivia  Chile |
| 18. Nuts[2] | Brazil |
| 19. Bananas | Colombia |
| 20. Balata | Dutch Guiana |
| 21. Guano | Peru |
| 22. Manganese | Brazil |

[1] Wools, hides, skins, meat, hair, bones.   [2] Both edible and ivory.

# INDEX

A star (*) after a page number indicates that an illustration will be found on that page.

Aachen (Germany) 267
Abyssinia 175, 328
Adriatic Sea, fisheries of 103
Africa, rice 50; sugar 71; raisin grapes 81; tin 120, 231; trade with United States 230, 294, 295; transportation backward 159; few horses 165; trade routes and cities 228–233; raw materials 228; railways 229–231; area and population 328
Agriculture. See Farming
Airplane transportation 159, 167,* 168, 169*
Aix la Chapelle (Germany) 267
Akron (Ohio) 168, 330
Alabama, mining 116, 117, 126, 325; lumber 141; value of manufacturing 257; area and population 326
Alaska, average temperature 36*; fisheries 105, 107; fur-seals 106; fish hatcheries 108; value of purchase 111; copper 118*; gold 120; forests 138, 141; as market 301; mineral production 325; area and population 326, 329
Albany (New York) 196, 252, 334
Alberta, farm in 227*
Alexandria (Egypt) 228, 229, 330
Alfalfa 73, 88, 101*
Algeria, wheat harvest in 53; citrus fruits 78; goatskins exported 245; foreign commerce 308; area and population 328
Algiers (Algeria) 165, 228, 230, 233
Allegheny River 196, 218
Altoona (Pennsylvania) 212, 334
Aluminum 112
Amazon River 151, 289
Amsterdam (Holland) 269, 290, 330
Andes Mountains, effect on climate 146, 150
Animal products 83–101,* 149,* 152,* 336
Animal power, used in farming 26,* 33, 44, 46, 51*; in mines 113; in lumbering 133; in transportation 9,* 10, 159, 162,* 163,* 164,* 165,* 166, 171, 174, 179,* 195
Annapolis valley, apple growing 75
Anthracite coal 113, 124, 125, 126
Appalachian Mountains, apple growing district 75; coal fields 124; national forest 139; routes through 210, 211, 212

Apples 74–76,* 313
Area, of United States, and western Europe 29*; of United States, by states 326; of chief countries and colonies 328–329
Argentina, farming methods 33; wheat 43, 53, 55; corn 49; sugar cane 71; grapes 81; cattle 89, 90; sheep 93; exports of beef 97; mining 122; railways 167, 183; need for shipping 191; industrial development 236, 242, 272; wool 275, 276, 294; hides 293; market for manufactured goods 301; foreign commerce 304, 308; area and population 329; exports 336
Arizona, cotton 5; sugar beets 70*; citrus fruits 77; mining 118,* 325; railway mileage 187; manufactures 327; area 326
*Arizonan*, voyage of 200
Arkansas, cotton 5; rice 49*; apples 75; lumber 141; mining 325; area and population 326; manufacturing 327
Arkwright, Richard 14
Aroostook County (Maine), potatoes 62
Ashland (Ohio) 194, 333
Ashtabula (Ohio) 194, 333
Asia, transportation 159, 160, 161,* 162,* 163,* 164,* 165,* 317, 318; tin 120; manufacturing 272, 276, 318, 319; living conditions in central 286*; trade with United States 294, 295; contrasted with Australia 311–324*; countries of western 318; cities 318; consumption of products 320; exports 321; as source of raw materials 323; area and population 328
Asiatic Russia 165, 329
Assiniboine River 227
Assuan (Egypt) 8, 229
Asunción (Paraguay) 147, 335
Atlanta (Georgia) 258, 330
Atlantic Ocean, fisheries in 103, 105; steamship routes 158, 202, 212, 220, 225
Australia, farming in 33, 315; wheat 53, 55, 275, 300; cattle 90; sheep 92, 93, 316*; copper 119, 274; gold 120; tin 120; railway mileage 183; shipping 191; industrial development 236, 242, 271, 322; wool 275, 276, 294; trade with Great Britain 300; as market 301; foreign

Australia — *Continued*
  commerce 308; production 311–316,* 322; climatic conditions 314; transportation 317; position among continents 323; coal ports 323*; area and population 328
Austria, apple orchards in western, 76; copper 119; improved roads 170; railways 183; cereals 278; raw silk 279; flax 279; foreign commerce 281; area and population 329
Austria-Hungary, foreign commerce 308
Automobiles, usefulness and cost 164, 167, 174; manufacture of 219, 252, 253, 255. *See also* Motor transportation

Baghdad (Iraq) 165, 332
Bahia (Brazil) 150, 330
Bahía Blanca (Argentina) 152
Balata 336
Balkan countries, wheat cultivation in 53
Baltic Sea, fishing in 103
Baltimore (Maryland) 72, 208, 212, 216, 221, 222, 250, 330
Bamboo 140, 273
Bananas 78, 79,* 82, 336
Bank of England 264*
Barcelona (Spain) 271, 330
Bark, for tanning 245
Barley, in northern Europe 41; in United States and Europe 59,* 60; as feed 100; in Syria 160; in Asia and Australia 312
Barmen (Germany) 268
Barre (Vermont) 239, 334
Battle Creek (Michigan) 253, 334
Bayonne (New Jersey) 271, 334
Beans 312, 321
Beets. *See* Sugar beets
Belgian Congo 119, 231, 275, 328
Belgium, size of 29*; time of wheat harvest 53; potatoes 63; zinc 121; transportation 183, 197; manufacturing 235, 264, 270, 310; cereals 278; flax 279; commerce 281, 308, 310; area and population 329
Bengal 313
Benzine 128
Berne (Switzerland) 269*
Berries 313
Birmingham (Alabama) 117, 126, 334
Birmingham (England) 126, 237, 258, 333
Bogotá (Colombia) 153, 335
Bohemia 70. *See also* Czechoslovakia
Bolivia, wheat 53; tin 112, 120, 290; copper 119; climatic conditions 144; area and population 329; exports 336
Boll weevil 2, 310
Boston (Massachusetts) 25, 72, 78, 102, 104, 178, 208, 210, 211,* 212, 215, 216, 221, 240, 250, 330
Braddock (Pennsylvania) 254, 334

Brass 242, 272
Brazil, cotton in 7, 8; rice 50; sugar cane 71; cattle 89,* 149*; iron deposits 114; as mining country 122; coffee 146, 148, 289; cocoa 150; hides 275; rubber 275, 289; balance of trade with United States 267; area and population 329; exports 336
Breadstuffs. *See* Cereals
Breslau (Germany) 197, 332
Brest (France) 207
Brick 312
British Columbia 139. *See also* Canada
British East Africa 300, 328
British Guiana 150, 303, 329, 336
Brockton (Massachusetts) 161, 242, 271, 334
Brussels (Belgium) 266,* 270, 333
Buckwheat 73
Budapest (Austria) 271, 332
Buenos Aires (Argentina) 147, 148, 149, 151, 190, 191, 208, 304, 330, 335
Buffalo (New York) 193, 194, 220, 221, 252, 330
Bulgaria, cereals 278; raw silk 279; foreign commerce 281; area and population 329
Burma, wheat harvest in 53; junk 166*
Butte (Montana) 238, 334
Butter 256, 259, 260, 270, 271

Cacao 150, 289, 293, 336
Cairo (Egypt) 228, 230, 332
Calcutta (India) 166, 207, 315,* 330
Calgary (Alberta) 225
California, cotton production 5*; rice 49; wheat 53; barley 60; vegetables 62, 64; sugar beets 70, 292; fruits 75, 77,* 80*; mining 120, 325; petroleum 128,* 259; timber 135; lumber 141; railways 179, 187; water power 238, 259; fruit canning and drying 238, 259; area and population 326; manufacturing 327
Callao (Peru) 149, 335
Cambridge (Massachusetts) 215, 334
Camels 86,* 87, 163,* 164, 165
Camphor 268, 277
Canada, average temperature 4,* 5*; farming methods 33, 47; wheat 43,* 53, 55, 224*, 275*; corn 49*; oats 56*; maple sugar 69; apples 74,* 75; cattle 84,* 88*; milk 87; cheese 95; hay and forage 101*; protection of fur-seal 106; fisheries 107; copper 119, 276; gold 120; forests 138, 139, 143; transportation 183, 186,* 192,* 198, 204,* 226; economic map 224*; cities 225–227*; manufacturing 260; use of Niagara Falls 263; hides 295; trade, foreign 296, 301, 305, 308; with Great Britain 300; area and population 329
Canadian Pacific Railroad 226

Canals, Liverpool to Manchester 20; Suez 191, 198, 199, 229, 230, 246; in America 192, 196,* 197, 198, 204*; transportation by 194, 195*; in Europe 196, 197; Panama Canal 198, 199,* 200,* 201, 202, 205, 206, 246; in France 267
Canary Islands 79
Cane, sugar. *See* Sugar cane
Canning, fruits 238, 259; fish 259, 260
Canton (China) 178, 330
Cape Cod Canal 198
Cape Town (South Africa) 228, 231
Cape Verde Islands 79
Capital, required for railroad building 178; and establishment of industries 241, 243
Caracas (Venezuela) 153, 335
Carbolic acid 268
Cardiff (Wales) 267, 331
Carpets 270. *See also* Textiles
Carrara (Italy) 122*
Carvings 273
Casablanca (Morocco) 228, 230
Caspian Sea, fisheries 103
Cataracts, of the Nile 232
Cattle, dairy 84,* 85,* 86, 87, 95, 96, 259, 275; in United States 87–89,* 96,* 97*; world production 89*; Europe 90, 95*; feeding 98; in South America 149,* 152*; in Asia 312, 314, 316, 319; in Australia 312, 316*
Cement 112, 113, 236, 313
Census, Bureau of the 261, 262
Central America 41, 78, 154–156, 289, 301
Cereals, farming 40–60*; consumption of 57; from South America 152, 336; from North Africa 230; cereal foods 253
Ceylon 291, 308, 313, 328
Chagres River 199
Champlain, Lake 225
Charcoal 239
Charleroi (Belgium) 270
Charleston (South Carolina) 9, 222, 334
Charlotte (North Carolina) 237, 334
Cheese 84, 86, 94, 95; in United States 256, 259; in Canada 260; in Switzerland 270; in Denmark 271; in Australia 271
Chemicals, manufactured in Germany 268, 271, 291; in Chile 272; in United States 290; United States imports of 293
Chesapeake Bay, oyster fishing 105, 212
Chiaravalle (Italy) 38
Chicago (Illinois), as market for citrus fruits 78; meat packing 88; stockyards 96*; number of horses 100; transshipment point 161; railway center 178; as a great lake port 193, 217,* 219, 220; population 212, 330; ore docks 223*; manufacturing 253, 254; street in 307*
Chicago River, improvements in 219

Chile, wheat harvest in 53; copper 112, 119; position as mining country 122; coast region 146; nitrate of soda 150, 290; railway mileage 183; industrial development 236, 272; foreign commerce 308; area and population 329; exports 336
China, cotton 7, 19, 23; percentage of farmers 27; intensive farming 29; rice and millet 41, 50, 52; wheat 53; vegetables 61, 65, 67; swine 94; fishing 103; tin 120; mining 122; coal 123, 127; transportation 159, 160,* 165, 195, 317; railway mileage 175, 183, 317; climatic conditions and industry 236; manufacturing 272, 273, 290, 318; silk 273, 275, 290; population and purchasing power 287, 288, 320; cheap labor 290, 291; market for foreign goods 300, 301, 302, 303, 313; foreign commerce 308; primary production 312–313; area and population 328
Chinese sugar. *See* Sorghum cane
Chocolate 150, 250, 269, 270
Chosen 107, 302, 308, 328
Cincinnati (Ohio) 196, 253, 255, 330
Cities, of South America 145–153,* 335; of northeastern North America 204*; of United States 207–223,* 250–260,* 309, 330, 334; of Canada 224–226, 260; of Europe 265–270,* 282; Asiatic 318, 319; chief commercial, of world 330–333
Clay 112, 236, 312
Cleveland (Ohio) 194, 220, 253, 254, 330
Climate, and cotton industry 17; and farming, in United States 30–32; conditions of, for wheat 42–45; for corn 49; for rice 50, 60; oats 56; rye 58; barley 59, 60; potatoes 62; vegetables 64; sugar beets 69, 70; sugar cane 69, 71; sorghum cane 72; apples 75, 76; citrus fruits 76, 77; bananas 78; peaches 80; cattle 85, 87, 95; sheep 91, 92, 93; fisheries 102, 103, 107; of South America 145, 146, 148, 150, 151, 153; effect of, on use of horses 165; on location of Canadian cities 225; influence on manufacturing 235, 236,* 243; in United States 249, 259, 260; in Europe 265; of New Zealand 277; in Mexico 306; in Asia and Australia 314
Clothing industry, in United States 240, 250, 251, 252; London 266; France 267
Clyde River, shipbuilding along 266
Coal, as source of power 15; importance of 111, 117; uses 112, 123; value in United States 113; ventilation of mines 113; use in smelting 115; conservation of 115, 127, 128; mining in United States 123, 124,* 125, 126, 325; deposits in United States 124,* 196, 254; production in Pennsylvania 124; coal cities 125, 126; world

Coal — *Continued*
production 125\*; consumption in United States 127; culm 128; coke 128; in Great Lakes region 193, 206; price of, on Pacific coast, affected by Panama Canal 196; from Philadelphia 211; from New York 211; from Baltimore 212; from Norfolk 212; from South Africa 231; and industries 236, 253; in western Europe 265, 266, 267, 268, 269, 270; in Asia 311, 312; in Australia 311, 312, 323\*

Coal tar 15

Coast and Geodetic Survey, maps 202

Cobalt 112

Cocoa 150, 250, 269

Cod fishing 103, 104

Coffee 148, 151,\* 154, 250, 260, 289, 293, 302, 312, 336

Coke 128

Colombia, climate 144, 145; cacao 150; area and population 329; commerce 308, 336

Colonies 310, 328, 329

Colorado, sugar beets 72, 92; apples 75; mineral production 325; area and population 326; value of manufacturing 327

Columbia (South Carolina) 237, 331

Columbus (Ohio) 255, 330

Commerce, world, in wheat 55; of Buenos Aires 147; shipping routes of world 158\*; internal, of United States 183, 289; foreign, of United States 210, 216, 249, 300, 302, 322; of Canadian ports 227; of Africa 230, 231, 233; in Holland 269; of Europe 281; of Great Britain with United States 300; of China 302; of Japan 302; of South America 302, 304; of leading countries 308; of Australia 322; in the different continents 323

Confectionery 250, 258

Connecticut, corn 55; railways 187; area and population 326; manufacturing 327

Conservation, of fur-seals 106; of fish 109; of coal 127, 128; of petroleum 129; of forests 134, 138, 139, 142, 143

Constantine (Algeria) 2

Consumption, field of 2, 285–324\*; definition of 285; where greatest 286, 287, 288\*; in United States 287, 291; in South America 303; of foreign goods in Philippines 306; in Asia 313, 320, 321

Copper, mining 110,\* 112; production in United States 112, 113, 118,\* 301, 325; in world 112, 119\*; in Alaska 118\*; where Great Britain obtains 274; imports into United States 293; in Asia and Australia 312; from South America 336

Córdoba (Argentina) 153, 335

Corn, a grass 40; as staple food 41; in United States 47,\* 48,\* 49, 55, 56; in other countries 49, 278, 312; world production 54\*; glucose 73; for feed 83, 88, 100; exports from South America 152

Corn Clubs, Boys', yield of 48,\* 55

Corral (Chile) 272

Cost, of different types of transportation 166, 167, 168, 171, 174; of railways 180, 181; of land and water routes 189; of freight, Great Lakes 193, 194; of Panama tolls 201, 206; of steamships 202; of shipping wheat 220

Costa Rica 79, 329

Cotton, primary production of 1–8\*; transportation of, 8–11,\* 24; manufacturing of 11–20,\* 25; United States tariff on 20; consumption of 21–24; by-products of 23, 96; under irrigation 35; honey from 73; export ports for 213; industries of southern states 257, 258, 259; of Great Britain 265, 271, 300; at Rouen 267; in Germany 268; in Holland 269; in India 272, 318; United States imports of 293; exports of 299, 300; production in Asia and Australia 312; manufacture in Japan 319; exports from Asia 321; from South America 336

Cotton flea 2

Cotton gin 3, 4

Cottonseed, oil 23, 257, 258, 259; cake 23, 96; production in Asia and Australia 313

Countries, area and population 328–329

Crefeld (Germany) 268

Cuba, sugar production 69, 71, 73, 292; iron 114, 117; copper 119; foreign commerce 308; area and population 329

Culm 128

Cultivation, intensive and extensive 29

Czechoslovakia, potatoes 67; sugar beets 70; railways 183; manufacturing 264; cereals, 275, 278; flax 279; commerce 281, 308; area and population 329

Dairying 84,\* 85,\* 86, 87, 95, 96, 259, 275

Dallas (Texas) 259, 334

Damascus (Syria) 165, 178, 333

Dates 159, 166

Dayton (Ohio) 169, 253, 334

Delaware, sweet potatoes 63; railway mileage 187; area and population 326; value of manufacturing 327

Delaware, Lackawanna, and Western Railroad 210

Denmark, size of 29,\* 275; dairy products 96, 271, 275; population 275, 329; beet sugar 275; cereals 278; foreign commerce 281, 308; area 329

Denver (Colorado) 223, 259, 330

Department of Agriculture, work of 34, 38, 41; *Year Book* 67, 277

Des Moines (Iowa) 258, 334

Desert, of South America 146; railroad building in 181; of the Sahara 230, 233
Detroit (Michigan) 78, 168, 219, 221, 240, 253, 254, 330
Detroit River 193
Diamonds 231, 270, 290
Dogs, and sheep-killing 100
Donkeys, used in transportation 163, 165
Drugs, chemicals for 268
Duluth (Minnesota) 180, 181,* 193, 194, 206, 220, 256, 257, 334
Dundee (Scotland) 267
Durban (Natal) 228, 231
Dutch East Indies, commerce 270, 308; primary products 312, 313; area and population 328. *See also* East Indies
Dutch Guiana 303, 329, 336
Dyeing, of cotton 14; of silk 251*
Dyes, manufacture of 15, 268

Earthenware 271
East Indies, rice and millet 41; tin 120, 275; petroleum 130*; exports to Holland 270; rubber 275; primary products 312, 313
Ecuador, climate 144, 145; cacao 150, 289; area and population 329; exports 336
Edmonton (Alberta) 225
Egypt, cotton 7,* 8, 275, 300; corn 41; rice 50*; wheat harvest 53; sugar cane 71; railway mileage 183; foreign commerce 308; area and population 328
Elberfeld (Germany) 268
Electric railways 184
Electrical industries 252
Elephants 162,* 163
Embroideries 270, 290
England, invention of spinning and weaving machinery 14; cotton manufacturing 17, 20; wheat harvest in 53; consumption of cereals and meat 56; potatoes 63; apples 76; smelting of iron ore 117; coal 123, 127; roads 170; merchant marine 191; manufacturing 241; area and population 329. *See also* Great Britain
Erie Barge Canal 193, 196,* 197, 220
Erie Canal 196,* 197
Erie (Pennsylvania) 194, 334
Erie Railroad 210
Essen (Germany) 126, 237, 268, 333
Europe, intensive cultivation in 29; size 29*; wheat 43, 53, 54*; corn 49; oats 54*; rye 58*; barley 59*; vegetables 61; potatoes 62, 67; sugar beets 70; fruits 76, 78, 79, 80, 81*; dairy products 87, 95; cattle 89,* 90, 91, 95*; swine 93; zinc 112, 121; iron 114; tin 120; forest conservation 139, 140, 143; lumber 140, 143; animal transportation 164, 165; steamships 166; motor vehicles 167; roads, in southeastern part 170; railways 183, 266*; steamship lines from 191; use of rivers and canals 195, 196, 197, 266*; manufacturing 264–271*; transportation facilities 266,* 281; problem: what Europe does for a living 278–283*; food products 278; raw materials 279; minerals 279; foreign commerce 281; cities 282, 318; value of exports to United States 294; imports 295, 323; as market 299–301; trade with South America 304; area and population of chief countries and colonies 329
Explosives, use of nitrates for 150
Exports, from United States, of wheat 55; of petroleum 129; value of, at principal ports of United States 221; from Africa 230, 231; from Germany, of beet sugar 268; from United States, of farm machinery for Australia 272; from Great Britain, of textiles and farm machinery 277; from United States 295; to Germany 300; from leading countries to United States 308; from western Europe 310; from South America 336

Factories, cotton 17*; man power in 161; for airplanes 169. *See also* Manufacturing
Fairfield (Ohio) 169*
Falkland Islands 93
Fall River (Massachusetts) 10, 15, 17, 18, 242, 334
Farming, of cotton 2–8*; in United States 27–39*; methods 26,* 45,* 46,* 51,* 57*; importance 27; where possible 30,* 31*; kinds of 31, 61, 280*; farming population 32, 33; soil 33; government aid 34, 38, 41; in Alaska 36*; in Italy 38*; in Ohio 38; cereals 40–60*; vegetables 61–67*; sugar 68–73*; fruit 74–82*; animal 83–101*; use of man power in 160; of horses 164; in Canada 225, 227*; in Holland 269
Farms, number in the United States 47
Faeroe Islands 107
Feed, cotton-seed products used for 23, 96; sugar beet pulp 70; hay, corn, oats 83; and swine raising 100; forage crops 101*
Fernandina (Florida) 136
Fertilizers, nitrates 150, 289, 290; chemical 268
Fez (Morocco) 228, 233
Fibers, imports of, into United States 293. *See also* Cotton, Flax, Silk, Sisal, Wool
Finland 281, 308, 329
Fire, protection of forests from 142
Fire-pots, in fruit orchards 77
Fireworks, potash used for 290

Fisheries, of United States 102–109*; of the world 103*; of countries outside United States 106,* 107, 108,* 224*
Fishing, as occupation 27, 102
Flax 270, 279, 313
Flaxseed 293, 313
Florida, watermelons 64; citrus fruits 77,* 78; mangoes 82; forest 136; area and population 326; manufacturing 327
Foochow (China) 162, 331
Foods, foodstuffs, production of, in Europe 278; imports and exports of, United States 294, 295, 299. See also Cereals, Vegetables, Fruits, Meat, Fisheries
Forest Service 138, 139
Forestry, scientific 140, 143
Forests, of the United States 134–138*; cutting in 134, 142, 143; National Forests 138*; Canadian 139, 224*; Mexican 139; conservation of European 139; protection from fire 142; rate of consumption 143; rate of growth 143; South American 145, 146, 151; industries attached to 239, 259
Formosa 277, 328
Fort Worth (Texas) 259, 334
France, cotton manufacturing 19; size 29*; wheat 41, 43, 53, 55; consumption of cereals and meat 56; potatoes 67; sugar beets 70, 73; apples 76; peaches 80; grapes 81; export of cheese to United States 95; iron 114, 274; coal 125, 274; water power 125; forest conservation 139, 143; roads 170; transportation 183, 197; industries 235, 264, 267; silk 273, 279, 290, 291; occupations 275; competition with Great Britain 276; flax 279; foreign commerce 281, 290, 308, 310; as market 287; population 287, 329; area 329
Frankfurt (Germany) 268, 332
Free trade, with Philippines, effect of 307
Freight, cost of 43, 166, 167, 193, 194, 201, 220, 239; by steamship 166, 190, 191; by railroad 167; on Great Lakes 193, 194*; rivers and canals 195, 197, 198, 205, 206
French Guiana 303, 329
French Indo-China, foreign commerce 308
Frost, and fruits 75, 76, 77, 80
Fruit, cultivation and marketing 74–82*; apples 74–76,* 82; citrus fruits 76, 77,* 78; bananas 78, 79,* 82; coconuts 79*; transportation 76, 78, 79, 82; grapes 79, 80, 81*; peaches 80*; mangoes 82*; canning and drying 238; imports of 289, 293; in Asia and Australia 313
Fuels, kinds and uses 112, 247; in United States 113; coal 123–126,* 127–128*; petroleum 126, 128–132*; natural gas 131; and location of industries 236, 243
Furniture 136, 239, 253, 267

Furs, imports of into United States 293
Fur-seals 106

Galveston (Texas) 9, 136, 198, 201, 213,* 216, 221, 334
Ganges River 287*
Gasoline 128
Gatun Locks 199
Genoa (Italy) 106,* 331
Georgetown (British Guiana) 150
Georgia, cotton 6, 237, 257, 258; peach crop 80; lumber 141; minerals 325; area and population 326; value of manufacturing 327
Germany, dyes 15; cotton 19*; size 29*; rye 41; millet 52; wheat 53, 55; meat and cereals 56; potatoes 63, 67; beet sugar 70, 292; apples 76; meat 97; fisheries 107; copper 119; zinc 121; coal 124, 274; interest in petroleum fields 130; forest conservation 139, 143; improved roads 170; railways 174, 183; need for shipping 190; canals and rivers 197, 198; as industrial country 235, 264; manufactures 268, 310; lead and zinc 275; silk 276; commerce 281, 287, 291, 296, 300, 304, 308, 310; area and population 329
Ghent (Belgium) 270
Glaciation, as source of water power 15, 16
Glasgow (Scotland) 126, 165, 190, 266, 331
Glass 236, 270
Gloucester (Massachusetts) 102,* 104, 240, 334
Gloversville (New York) 252, 334
Goats 87, 245, 292, 312
Gold, one of chief metals 112; production in United States 113, 325; world production 120*; in Africa 231; in Asia and Australia 313; from South America 336
Government, aid to farming 34, 38, 41; inspection of milk 87; of meat 97*; protection of fur-seal 106; fish hatcheries 108; conservation of oysters and lobsters 109; National Forests 138*; protection of forests 139
Grain, how loaded at lake ports 191*; chief cargo through Panama Canal 205; cost of transportation to Europe 220; grown in Canada 224.* See also Cereals, Wheat
Grand Banks 103, 107
Grand Haven (Michigan) 221
Grand Rapids (Michigan) 136, 252, 334
Grand Trunk Pacific Railroad 226
Grapes 74, 79, 80, 81,* 313
Gravel 112
Great Britain, cotton manufacturing 19,* 20; size 29*; wheat 40, 53, 55, 275, 278; potatoes 67; fisheries 107; iron 114; tin 120; coal 124; leadership in commerce and industry 125, 235–264, 310; forest con-

Great Britain — *Continued*
servation, in colonies 140; consumption of timber 143; railways 175, 183; control of Suez Canal 246; and Panama Canal 246; textiles 265, 276, 291; iron and steel 265; shipbuilding 266; cities 266; sources of supply for copper 274; wool 275, 276; lumber 275; coal 275; percentage of workers in farming and industry 275; exports of machinery 277; as market 287, 288; population 287; commerce 281, 296, 300, 301, 302, 309, 310. *See also* England, Ireland, Scotland
Great Lakes 106, 116, 166, 192–194,* 195, 204,* 205, 216, 219, 220, 225, 226
Great Plains, wheat growing 42, 43,* 224*; cattle raising 83,* 88
Greece 53, 279, 281, 308, 329
Greensboro (North Carolina) 237
Guadalajara (Mexico) 155
Guano 336
Guatemala 78, 162, 305,* 329
Guayaquil (Ecuador) 150, 207, 335
Gums 231, 293, 336
Gunpowder 290

Halifax (Nova Scotia) 225, 226
Hamburg (Germany) 190, 268, 331
Hamilton (Ontario) 225
Harbors, satisfactory 207; of United States 208–217,* 219*; of northwestern Europe 266
Hats, exported from South America 336
Hawaii, sugar 71, 292; citrus fruits 77; commerce 301; area and population 326, 329
Hay 83, 101,* 312
Hemp, Manila 289, 329
Henequen 154*
Hessian fly 44
Hides 147, 148, 152, 231, 245, 275, 292, 293, 312, 321
Himalaya Mountains, carriers in 159
Hinterland 208. *See also* Seaports
Hoang Ho, cotton in valley of 7
Holland. *See* Netherlands
Homestead (Pennsylvania) 254,* 334
Honduras 79, 329
Honey 68, 73
Hongkong 207, 302, 328, 331
Honolulu (Hawaii) 215, 334
Hoosac Tunnel 211
Horses, in United States 100,* 101; used in transportation 162, 163,* 164, 167, 168, 174; in Asia and Australia 312
Houston (Texas) 198, 213,* 216, 259, 334
Hudson River 193, 196
Hulls, of cotton seed 23
Hungary, percentage of farmers 27; wheat 43; corn 49; cattle 90; copper 119; railways 183; manufactures 275; silk 279; flax 279; commerce 281, 308; area and population 329
Hunting, as occupation 27
Hydroelectric power 237, 263
Hydroplanes 169

Ibadan (Nigeria) 233
Ice, in harbors 208, 219, 225, 226; artificial, manufactured in New Orleans 258
Iceland, fisheries 103, 107
Idaho, sugar beets 70; minerals 325; area and population 326; manufacturing 327
Illinois, corn 47; wheat 53; apples 75; coal fields 124; forests 135; railways 187; roads 173; electric railways 185; factory workers in Chicago 254; minerals 325; area and population 326; manufacturing 327
Imports, of cotton into United States 20; into India 22; into China 23; of wheat in leading countries 55; value of, at principal ports of United States 221; of cotton into Great Britain 265; of wool into Great Britain 265, 276; into Holland from Dutch East Indies 270; from Switzerland into United States 270; of wheat into Great Britain 275; into United States 289–293, 294, 296, 308; from Great Britain, into United States 300; into China 302; into Mexico, from United States 306; rise in value of, into Philippine Islands 306; into Canada and Australia from United States 307; into outlying possessions from United States 310; of raw cotton, into Japan 319
India, cotton 7, 13,* 19,* 275, 276, 300; population 22, 328; percentage of farmers 27; size of crops 30; rice and millet 41, 50, 52, 320; wheat 53, 55, 275; vegetables 61; sugar cane 71, 292; cattle raising 89*; gold 120; forest conservation 140; transportation 159, 167, 183, 317; goatskins 245, 292; water power 263*; industrial development 272; hides 275; purchasing power 287; tea 291; foreign commerce 297, 300, 301, 308; percentage of production of chief primary products 312–313; cattle as draft animals 314; Calcutta, port 315*; goods manufactured 318; area 328
Indiana, corn 47; wheat 47; forests 135; electric railways 185; minerals 325; area and population 326; manufacturing 327
Indianapolis (Indiana) 223, 255, 330
Industries, basis of modern 117, 125; and water power 125; location of 125, 235; of cities 247; districts of, in United States 249–263*; in the different continents 323

Insects, and transportation 159, 164
Iodine 272, 277
Iowa, wheat 53; beef cattle 96; coal 125, 325; in central forest region 135; automobiles 168; railway mileage 187; area and population 326; manufacturing 327
Iquique (Chile) 150, 335
Ireland, cotton 19; potatoes 63; fisheries 107; mining 122; flax 279; lace 290
Iridium 112
Irish Free State 308, 329. *See also* Ireland
Irkutsk (Siberia) 316
Iron, one of chief metals 112; mining, in United States 113, 115, 116,* 117; world production 114*; smelting 114, 115; consumption 115, 117; movements of ore 117, 193, 194,* 205; use in manufacture, in United States 221, 236, 247,* 249, 251, 252, 253-255,* 257, 258, 259, 271; in Europe 265, 266, 267, 268, 269, 271, 274; in Chile 272; imports into United States 293; supplies in Asia and Australia 311, 312; production, in United States 325
Irrigation, for cotton growing 5, 6*; in United States 31, 32,* 35,* 36; in Italy 38*; in California, for rice 49; for sugar beets 70*; for fruit 75, 77; for alfalfa 88; on west coast of South America 146
Italy, cotton manufacturing 19; irrigated fields in 38*; rice 50; millet 52; wheat 53, 55; fruits 78, 80, 81; exports of cheese to United States 95; copper 119; marble 122*; mining 125; coal and water power 125; roads 170; railways 174, 183; manufactures 235, 264; silk 271, 273, 275, 279, 290; flax 279; commerce 281, 308; area and population 329
Ivory 159, 231, 273

Jacquard loom 25
Jaipur (India) 320*
Jamaica 78, 329
Japan, cotton 19*; intensive cultivation 29; rice and millet 41, 50, 52; wheat 53, 55; vegetables 61, 65, 67; fisheries 107, 108*; whale meat 109; copper 119; gold 120; zinc 121; mining 122; transportation 167, 174, 175, 183, 195, 317, 319*; climate and industry 236; manufacturing 242, 271, 273, 277, 290, 319; silk 273,* 275, 290; tea 291; foreign commerce 302, 308, 319; chief primary products 312, 313; area and population 328
Java, sugar cane 71*; railways 167; primary products 313
Jersey City (New Jersey) 175,* 210, 220, 250, 330
Jewelry 267, 270
Jinrikisha 160,* 162

Johannesburg (South Africa) 228, 231, 233, 333
Johnstown (New York) 252, 334
Jugo-Slavia. *See* Yugoslavia
Junk, Burmese 166*
Jute, manufacture of 266, 269, 272, 318, 321; production of 276, 313, 321

Kano (Nigeria) 233
Kansas, wheat 42, 43, 53; meat packing 88, 258; automobiles 168; railways 187; minerals 325; area and population 326; manufacturing 327
Kansas City (Kansas) 88, 223, 258, 330
Kelp 290
Kentucky, coal 125; minerals 325; area and population 326; manufacturing 327
Kerosene 128
Khartum (Egypt) 228, 230, 231
Kiel (Germany) 268, 330
Kiel Canal 198
Kimberley mines 231
Kobe (Japan) 271, 331
Korea. *See* Chosen
Krupp steel works 268

Labor, in New England 18; oriental 60, 272, 273; for sugar beet industry 69, 70; Hindu, in British Guiana 150; in transportation 160,* 161; and climatic conditions 235; and location of industries 240, 243; skilled, in England 241; legislation 246; in northeastern United States 249; in complex manufacturing 250; in Europe 268, 269, 270, 275; Japanese 271; in Australia 271; for silk 273, 290; and inventive skill 277, 299; for tea 291
Labrador, fisheries 105
Laces 290
Lacquered ware 271, 273
La Guaira (Venezuela) 150, 335
Lancaster County (England) 271
La Paz (Bolivia) 153, 335
La Plata (Argentina) 147, 335
La Plata River 147, 151
Latvia 281
Lawrence (Massachusetts) 242, 334
Lead, one of chief metals 112; production in United States 113, 325; world production 121,* 275; in Asia and Australia 313
Leadville (Colorado) 239, 334
Leather 245. *See also* Hides, Tanning
Leeds (England) 178, 333
Liége (Belgium) 126, 270
Lille (France) 267, 269, 333
Lima (Peru) 153, 335
Linen 268, 269, 276. *See also* Flax
Linseed oil 318
Liverpool (England) 20, 201, 220, 266, 331

Llamas 163
Lobsters 109
London (England) 225, 264,* 266,* 331
London Stock Exchange 264*
Long Island Sound 105
Lorraine, iron-ore district 274
Los Angeles (California) 214, 216, 221, 222, 260, 330
Louisiana, rice 60; sugar cane 69,* 292; lumber 141; petroleum 325; area and population 326; manufacturing 327
Louisville (Kentucky) 223, 330
Lowell (Massachusetts) 12, 15, 242, 334
Lumber, leading states in 141, 259; at Panama Canal 205; at Seattle 216*
Lumbering, how carried on 132,* 133, 134,* 137, 160; log-boom 137*; need of conservation in 139, 140, 142; in tropics 140
Lynn (Massachusetts) 161, 242, 334
Lyons (France) 267, 332

McKeesport (Pennsylvania) 254, 334
Macaroni 267
Machinery, use of, in farming 26,* 33, 42, 45,* 46, 47, 60; in mining 113, 114, 115, 125,* 128; to supplement man power 161; manufacturing of, in the United States 240, 251, 253, 254, 255; in Australia 272; markets for American 299, 301, 305
Madagascar 50, 328
Madeira 79, 290
Madras (India) 162, 331
Mahogany 140
Maine, potatoes 62; apples 75; forests 135; railways 178, 179, 187; area and population 326; value of manufacturing 327
Maize. *See* Corn
Malaria 145
Malay Peninsula 112, 120, 275, 290, 313
Malaya 308
Man power 159, 160,* 161,* 162, 166, 170, 195
Manaos (Brazil) 151, 335
Manchester (England) 20, 126, 190, 331
Manchester (New Hampshire) 15, 334
Manchester Ship Canal 198
Manchuria 67, 164, 328
Manganese 336
Mangoes 82*
Manila (Philippine Islands) 208
Manitoba, wheat 193
Mannheim (Germany) 268
Mansura (Egypt) 228
Manufacturing, of cotton 11-20*; in South America 145, 272; of automobiles 168; in Canada 224,* 261; in African cities 233; field of 235-284*; conditions affecting 235-246*; regions of 241, 242, 243*; in United States 247-263,* 291, 299, 326; types of 250, 255, 256, 264; use of power from Niagara Falls in 263; in Europe 264-271,* 274-277,* 280, 282, 299; in Asia 271, 272, 273,* 274, 318; in Australia 271, 322; and markets 298
Maple sugar 68, 69
Marakesh. *See* Morocco
Marco Polo, and coal in China 123
Markets, for cotton 9, 10; wheat 43; vegetables 62, 64; sugar beets 70; sugar cane 71; fruits 75, 76, 77, 78, 79, 81; cattle 87; sheep, 93; iron 117; and manufactures 240-243; of western Europe 265; United States 285-297; and purchasing power 285, 286,* 287,* 288*; European 299-301; promising, for United States goods 301; China 301; South America 302; Canada 305; Mexico 306; Philippines 307; types of 303,* 305,* 307,* 320*
Marseilles (France) 197, 267, 331
Maryland, sweet potatoes 63; tomatoes 64, 238; railways 187; minerals 325; area and population 326; manufacturing 327
Massachusetts, good roads 173; railway mileage 187; glass making 245; area and population 326; value of manufacturing 327
Matches 271, 290
Mate 336
Matting 271, 273
Maumee River 220
Mauritius 71
Meat, consumption of 57, 97, 98; substitutes for 65, 107, 108; beef 87, 90; slaughtering and packing 88, 90, 251, 253, 254, 255, 258, 270, 277; cost 90; mutton 91, 92; pork 94; exports, from United States and Argentina 97, 147; whale meat 109
Mediterranean Sea 103, 166
Merrimac River 237
Mesaba Range 115
Mesopotamia 130, 318, 328
Mexico, cotton 7; corn 41, 49; wheat 53; silver 112, 120; copper 119; gold 120; lead 121; as mining country 122; petroleum 130*; forests 139; henequen (sisal) 154,* 289; problem in production 154-156; transportation 162, 183, 186*; goatskins 245, 292; rubber 275; jute 276; commerce 301, 306, 308; area and population 329
Miami (Florida) 222
Michigan, potatoes 62; sugar beets 70, 292; apples 75; sheep 91; minerals 116, 117, 118, 325; lumber 136, 253; railway mileage 187; shoe factories 245; area and population 326; manufacturing 327
Milk 85, 86, 87, 94,* 100, 256, 259, 270
Millet 40, 52,* 312, 314, 320
Milling 234, 253, 256, 259, 262, 266, 272
Milwaukee (Wisconsin) 220, 247,* 253, 255, 330

Minerals, location of 111; metals 112–122*; value in United States 113; in South America 149, 150; from North Africa 230; imported by United States 289, 290, 293; in Asia and Australia 311
Mining, industry 110–131,* 259; and railways 179, 180*; and manufacturing 238; concessions in China 302
Minneapolis (Minnesota) 215, 223, 234,* 237, 256, 330
Minnesota, wheat 42, 43, 53, 193; barley 60; potatoes 62; iron 111, 114, 115, 116, 117, 325; logging 132*; in northeastern forest region 135; railways 187; lumber 253; area and population 326; manufacturing 327
Miraflores Locks 199, 200*
Mississippi, cotton 5; lumber 141; roads 173; area and population 326; manufacturing 327
Mississippi River 195, 196, 201, 206, 213
Missouri, minerals 119, 325; railway mileage 187; area and population 326; value of manufacturing 327
Mobile (Alabama) 222, 334
Mohawk-Hudson valley 193
Monongahela River 196, 218
Montana, minerals 118, 325; area and population 326; value of manufacturing 327
Montevideo (Uruguay) 147, 151, 331, 335
Montreal (Quebec) 151, 208, 225, 226, 260, 331
Morocco 53, 162, 228, 233, 308, 328
Moscow (Russia) 165, 271, 282,* 333
Motion picture industry 260
Motor transportation 9*, 10, 11, 100, 129, 168
Mulberry tree, where grown 276, 290
Mules 9, 10, 163
Munitions 268

Nagoya (Japan) 271, 333
Nancy (France) 267
Naphtha 128
Naples (Italy) 189,* 331
Napoleon I 73
National Forests 137, 138*
*National Geographic Magazine* 39, 107, 277
Natural gas 112, 131; in United States 113; waste of 131; use of 254
Naval stores 136
Nebraska, wheat 42, 43, 53; corn 47; area and population 326; manufacturing 327
Netherlands, size 29*; wheat harvest 53; exports of cheese 95; fisheries 107; waterways 197; manufacturing 264, 269; tropical trade 275; flax 279; commerce 281, 308, 310; area and population 329
Neufchâtel (Switzerland) 270
Nevada, lumber 141; minerals 325; area and population 326; manufacturing 327
New Bedford (Massachusetts) 222, 242, 334

New Brunswick 225
New England, cotton mills 15–18, 19, 242, 277; sheep 100; water power 237
New Hampshire, railway mileage 187; area and population 326; manufacturing 327
New Haven (Connecticut) 222, 229, 334
New Jersey, sweet potatoes 63; milk supply 94*; oil pipe lines 130; railway mileage 175, 187; manufacturing 263, 269, 327; minerals 325; area and population 326
New London (Connecticut) 239, 334
New Mexico, cotton 5; minerals 325; area and population 326; manufacturing 327
New Orleans (Louisiana) 9, 10, 72, 201, 207, 213, 216, 221, 258, 267, 330
New South Wales 53, 316*
New York (City) 72, 78, 81, 96,* 100, 161, 171, 190, 191, 193, 201, 208, 209,* 210, 211, 212, 214, 216, 221, 239, 240, 250, 330
New York (State), wheat 43; truck farming 61*; potatoes 62; other vegetables 64; apples 75; milk supply 94*; minerals 117, 325; railways 187; water power 237; area and population 326; manufacturing 327
New York Central Railroad 193, 210
New York, Ontario, and Western Railroad 210
New Zealand, wheat 53; apples 76; sheep 92; manufacturing 265, 272, 277, 322; exports to Great Britain 300; commerce 308, 322; primary products 312; transportation 317; area and population 328
Newark (New Jersey) 210, 215, 250, 330
Newcastle (Australia) 323
Newcastle (England) 126, 266, 331
Newfoundland 103, 107, 114, 225, 329
Newport News (Virginia) 212, 334
Niagara Falls 192, 198, 220, 237, 263
Niagara Falls (New York) 252, 334
Nickel 112
Nigeria 120, 233, 308
Nile River 8, 229,* 232*
Nitrate of soda 150, 205, 272, 289, 290, 293, 336
Nitrogen 290
Norfolk (Virginia) 136, 210, 212, 216, 221, 334
North America, oats 56*; fishing areas 103; lack of tin 120; animal transportation in mountainous parts 164; steamships 167; railways 176,* 184, 186*; transportation in northeast 192–204*; canals 197–202*; trade of United States with other parts of 294, 295; increasing home consumption 323; area and population 329
North Carolina, apples 75; forests and lumber 136, 141; water power 237; cotton industries 237, 257, 258; iron 325; area and population 326; manufacturing 327
North Dakota, wheat 33, 42, 43, 53; barley 60; coal 325; area and population 326;

North Dakota — *Continued*
  value of manufacturing 327
North Sea 103, 107
Norway, barley 41; wheat 53; oats 57; fisheries 102, 103*; copper 119; mining 122; forests 140; foreign commerce 281, 308; nitrogen 290; area and population 329
Nova Scotia 75, 225, 226
Nuts 289, 293, 336

Oakland (California) 214,* 215, 260, 330
Oats, chief cereal 40, 41*; in Scotland 41, 57; world production 54*; in North America 56,* 57,* 58; for feed 83; in Europe 278; in Asia and Australia 312
Oceania 329
Ohio, corn 47; wheat 53; sheep 91, 93; in central forest region 135; electric railways 185; railway mileage 187; minerals 193, 325; area and population 326; manufacturing 327
Ohio River 196, 218*
Oil. *See* Petroleum
Oil cake 23
Oils, vegetable 267, 293, 321
Oklahoma, petroleum 129, 325; coal 325; area and population 326; manufacturing 327
Oklahoma City (Oklahoma) 259, 334
Omaha (Nebraska) 88, 223, 258, 334
Omdurman (Egypt) 228, 231
Omsk (Siberia) 316
Ontario 75
Optical goods 252
Oran (Algeria) 228, 230
Oranges. *See* Fruits
Orchards. *See* Fruits
Oregon, wheat 42, 46, 53; apples 75; forests and lumber 135,* 138, 141; minerals 325; area and population 326; manufacturing 327
Orient, farming in 26,* 32, 44,* 51,* 61, 64, 67; labor 60, 272, 273; exports to United States 214, 215
Osaka (Japan) 271
Ottawa (Ontario) 225, 226, 227
Oxen 163,* 166
Oyster fishing 105, 109, 212
Ozark Mountains 75

Pacific Ocean, fisheries, 105; fur-seal 106
Pacific states, manufacturing 242
Packing, of fruit 76; of Japanese goods 277; of goods for South American market 304
Palestine 41, 318, 328
Panama 79, 145, 329
Panama Canal, and Zone 138, 198, 199,* 200,* 201, 202, 205, 206, 215, 246, 329
Paper 27, 132, 138, 139, 140, 237, 241, 271, 273, 293
Pará (Brazil) 151, 331, 335

Paraguay, cattle 89; railways 175; area and population 329; exports 336
Paris (France) 266, 267, 288,* 332
Paraffin 128
Paterson (New Jersey) 210, 241, 242, 334
Pawtucket (Rhode Island) 15, 334
Peaches 74, 80*
Peas 313
Pennsylvania, wheat 43; potatoes 62; milk supply 94*; iron ore 117; coal 124,* 125, 127, 193; railways 187; coal routes 211; iron and steel industries 236, 271; workers engaged in manufacturing 272; mineral production 325; area and population 326; value of manufacturing 327
Pennsylvania Railroad 210, 212
Perfumes 267, 268
Pernambuco (Brazil) 150, 331, 335
Persia, cotton 7; rice 50; wheat 50; petroleum 130*; transportation 165,* 175; commerce 308; primary products 313; and western world 318; area and population 328
Peru, cotton 7, 8, 25; wheat 53; potatoes 63; copper 119; climate 144; transportation 162; commerce 308; area and population 329; exports 336
Petroleum, control of 111; a mineral product 112; production in United States 113, 120,* 126, 129, 301, 325; consumption in United States 126, 128; uses 126, 129, 130, 254; pipe lines, tank cars, etc. 127, 130, 131*; oil well 128*; conservation of supply 129; world production 130*; through Panama Canal 205; refineries 250, 263, 271; imports into United States 293; in Asia and Australia 312; from Asia 321
Philadelphia (Pennsylvania) 72, 78, 94, 161, 190, 210, 211, 212, 215, 216, 221, 251, 330
Philippine Islands, rice 51,* 52; sugar cane 71, 292; fruits 77, 78; coconuts and copra 79*; water power 263; abacá (Manila hemp) 289; as market for United States goods 301, 306, 308; foreign commerce 306, 308; primary products 312; area and population 326, 328
Photographic goods 252
Pikes Peak 180
Pipe lines 127, 130, 131*
Pitch 136
Pittsburgh (Pennsylvania) 125, 218,* 236, 253, 254, 330
Platinum 112
Poland, potatoes 67; zinc 121; transportation 195; flax 279; area and population 329
Population, farming, in United States 32; in Orient 33; concentration of 54; relation to potato growing 67; to sheep 97; to swine 98; of South America 146, 153, 303, 304; and railways 178, 179; percen-

Population — *Continued*
  tage in ports of United States 208; of Canadian cities 225; of African cities 228; in manufacturing centers 235, 243, 265; percentage of workers engaged in industries 243, 247, 248, 249,* 319; distribution of, in United States 248,* 309; of European countries 265, 269, 270, 275, 287, 299; of Australia 272; world density of 284*; and importance of markets 285–288; of India 287; of China 301, 320; of Canada 305; of Mexico 306; of Philippine Islands 306; of Asia and Australia 311, 315, 318, 319, 322; of United States, by states 327; of chief countries and colonies 328; of commercial cities of United States 330, 334; of cities outside United States 330, 335
Porcelain 267, 273
Port Arthur (Manitoba) 220
Port Elizabeth (South Africa) 228
Port Natal (South Africa) 228, 231
Port Said (Egypt) 228, 230
Port Sudan (Anglo-Egyptian Sudan) 230
Port works 207, 209, 212, 214, 219, 220
Portland (Maine) 222, 334
Portland (Oregon) 138, 210, 214, 215, 216, 259, 330
Portsmouth (Virginia) 212
Portugal, fruits 78; fisheries 103, 107; commerce 281, 309; area and population 329
Potash 268, 289, 290
Potassium chloride. *See* Potash
Potatoes 62, 63,* 67, 74, 100, 312
Poultry 99,* 101
Power, and industries 235, 236, 237,* 238,* 243. *See also* Coal, Fuels, Water power
Prague (Czechoslovakia) 271, 332
Precious stones 168, 289, 290, 293
Pribilof Islands 106
Prince Rupert (British Columbia) 226
Printing 247, 251, 258, 259
Production, primary 1, 8; of cotton 2–8*; field of 27–157*; in Africa 228; of Asia and Australia 312, 313
Products, world's chief primary 312, 313
Providence (Rhode Island) 222, 250, 330
Prussia 41
Puebla (Mexico) 155
Puerto Rico, sugar 69, 73, 292; citrus fruits 77; as market 301; area and population 326, 329
Puget Sound 215, 259
Punta Arenas (Chile) 152, 335
Purchasing power, of United States and Europe 287; of Paris 288; of Asiatic peoples 313, 314, 315*

Quarrying 112, 117–122,* 239
Quebec (Quebec) 139, 225, 226, 260
Quebracho wood 140, 148, 336
Quincy (Massachusetts) 239, 334
Quinine 270
Quito (Ecuador) 153, 336

Railroads, in Central America 79; and cattle raising 87; and mining 124; of South America 148, 167, 177,* 184,* 302; government ownership of 174; in progressive countries 175; of North America 176,* 184,* 186*; under local management 178; conditions affecting development of 178, 179, 186*; cost of 180–183; of world 183, 184*; of United States 183, 186,* 187, 192,* 193, 204*; of Canada 186,* 192,* 204,* 226, 227; of Europe 197, 266,* 267; cities of United States as centers of 209, 210, 211, 214, 217, 219; routes across Appalachians 210, 211, 212; of Africa 229, 230, 231, 233; of Asia and Australia 317
Rainfall, of world xii; in United States 6,* 30; methods used to offset unfavorable 31; and wheat 42, 43; and corn 47, 49; and rice 50, 60; and sugar beets 70; and sugar cane 71; and apples 75; and bananas 78, 79; and coconuts 79; and sheep raising 92; and forests 134; on west coast of South America 146; and water power 238; in Asia and Australia 314, 318
Raisins 81
Rangoon (Burma) 162, 331
Raw materials, kinds shipped by tramp steamers 191; Africa as producer of 228; and location of industries 238, 243, 250; production of, in Australia 271, 312, 313, 321; Holland as dealer in tropical 275; production of, in Europe 279; United States imports and exports of 294, 295; Europe as market for 299; from South America 302; from Asia and Australia 312, 313, 321
Rayon 21
Reclamation Service, U. S. 35,* 36
Red Sea 230
Refrigeration, for fruit 76; for milk 86; for meat 90, 97; for fish 105; cost of 238
Regina (Saskatchewan) 225
Reindeer 87
Relief, and wheat farming 42, 43, 47; and corn 49; and rice 50, 51; and apples 75; and mineral deposits 112, 119; and lumbering 132; of South America 145, 146, 148, 149, 153; and air transportation 169; and railways 179, 180, 186*; and water power 238*; and industries in Switzerland 270; of Asia and Australia 315
Resin 136
Rhode Island, railway mileage 187; area and population 326; manufacturing 327

Rhodesia, gold in 120
Rice, staple food in Orient 40, 41; acreage in United States 49*; production 50–52*; culture 51,* 52; at New Orleans 258; in Asia 312, 314, 321; from Asia 321
Riga (Latvia) 208, 331
Rio de Janeiro (Brazil) 147,* 148, 151, 304, 331, 336
Rivers, transportation on 194, 195,* 319; ports on 330, 332
Rivers and Harbors Bill 206
Roads, advantages of good 9,* 10; as factor in transportation 168, 169; roadmaking 170; and geographic conditions 173
Rochester (New York) 220, 252, 330
Rocky Mountains, sheep raising in 91, 92; forest regions of 134, 136–137
Rosario (Argentina) 147, 153, 332, 336
Rosin 257
Rotterdam (Netherlands) 269, 332
Roubaix (France) 267
Rouen (France) 267
Routes, shipping, of world 158*; principal, for liners 191, 202; for wheat 220; from Montreal 225; through Panama Canal 200, 201, 205; railway, from New York 210; United States to Europe 211, 212
Rubber, South America 147, 151, 336; where world's supply produced 275; United States supply imported 289; production in Asia and Australia 313; from Asia 321
Rugs 272, 277
Rumania, corn 41, 49; wheat 55; petroleum 130*; raw silk 279; flax 279; foreign commerce 281, 309; area and population 329
Russia, cotton 7,* 8, 19; rye 41, 58; wheat 43, 53, 55; potatoes 63, 67; sugar beets 70, 292; cattle 90, 95; sale of Alaska 105; protection of fur seals 106; copper 119; gold 120; petroleum 130*; forests 140, 143; roads 170; railway mileage 183; wool and hides 275, 294; cereals 278; wood 279; flax 279; commerce 281, 309; industries 288; area and population 329
Russian Turkestan. See Turkestan
Rye, stalk of 40*; in Europe 41, 58*; production in Asia and Australia 312

St. Anthony's Falls 237
St. Gallen (Switzerland) 270
St. John (New Brunswick) 225, 226
St. John's (Newfoundland) 225
St. Joseph (Missouri) 258, 335
St. Lawrence River 193, 220, 225, 226
St. Louis (Missouri) 78, 161, 195. 223, 256, 330
St. Mary's Falls 192, 198
St. Mary's Canals 198, 206
St. Paul (Minnesota) 195, 215, 223, 256, 330
Saar valley 274

Sahara, desert of 230, 233
Salt River valley 35, 70*
San Antonio (Texas) 259
San Diego (California) 214
San Francisco (California) 62, 72, 138, 201, 207, 214,* 215, 216, 221, 259, 330
San Pedro (California) 214
Sand 112, 113, 117
Santiago (Chile) 153, 333, 336
Santos (Brazil) 147, 148, 151, 190, 336
São Paulo (Brazil) 153, 332, 336
Sault Ste. Marie 198
Savannah (Georgia) 9, 136, 222, 335
Schenectady (New York) 252, 335
Scotland, oats 41, 57*; wheat 53; sheep 93; fishing 107, 108; area and population 327
Scranton (Pennsylvania) 125, 211, 241, 256, 257, 335
Seaports, of South America 145–153*; of United States 201, 208–216,* 222, 330; of Canada 225, 226; of Africa 228–231; of Europe 266,* 267, 268, 269, 283; chief, of world 330–332
Seattle (Washington) 138, 161, 190, 214, 215, 216,* 221, 226, 259, 330
Seine River 267
Shanghai 160,* 332
Shantung 302
Sheep, and wool 91–93,* 97, 99, 100; and milk 87; in United States 90,* 91*; in tropics 91; in world 92–93*; meat production 98; exports of, from North Africa 230; in France 267; in Belgium 270; in Asia 312; in Australia 312, 316*
Sheffield (England) 266, 268, 333
Shepherd, life of 90,* 93
Shipbuilding, at Philadelphia 251, 252; in Great Britain 266; in Germany 268; in Holland 269
Ships, for cattle 87; oil-burning 129; ownership of 125; on La Plata 147; world routes for 158*; as means of transportation 160, 166,* 171, 172, 189, 206*; ocean traffic of 189–191; on Great Lakes 192–194,* 219; on rivers and canals 194–202*
Shoe industry 161, 242, 250, 256, 271
Siam 120, 175, 309, 328
Siberia, forests 140; railways 175, 181; primary products 312, 313; wheat 316; area and population 328
Silk, transportation of 168, 216; industry 240, 242, 260, 263, 267, 268, 270, 291; raw, where produced 271, 273,* 275, 276, 290, 313, 318, 319; imports into United States 290, 291, 293; exports of, from Asia 321
Silver, world production 112, 120*; in United States 113, 325; in Asia and Australia 313; from South America 336
Sisal 154,* 289

Skins. *See* Hides
Slaughtering and meat packing 90, 97,* 99, 251, 253, 255, 256, 258, 259, 277
Smelting, iron 114, 115, 116, 117, 125, 266; copper 118, 121
Soap 255, 267
Sodium nitrate. *See* Nitrate of soda
Soil, improvement of 41; for corn 47, 49; for rye 58; for barley 60; for potatoes 62; for sweet potatoes 63; for sugar beets 69; for sugar cane 72; for apples 75
Soo Canals. *See* St. Mary's Canals
Sorghum cane 68, 69, 72, 73
South Africa, wheat 53; cattle 90; sheep 93; copper 119; gold 120, 231; tin 120; railways 183, 233; products 191; ports 231; foreign commerce 231, 309; diamonds 231, 290; as market 301; area and population 328
South America, swine 93; gold 120; tin 120; a study of 144–153*; railways 177*; effect on trade, of Panama Canal 201; industrial development 272; foreign trade 294, 295, 302, 303, 304; area and population 329; cities 335; value of principal exports 336
South Bethlehem (Pennsylvania) 254
South Carolina, sea-island cotton 6; in southern forest region 136; water power 237; cotton industries 237, 257, 258; area and population 326; manufacturing 327
South Dakota, wheat 33, 42, 43, 53; barley 60; minerals 119, 325; railways 178; area and population 326; manufacturing 327
Soy beans 65, 67
Spain, rice 50; wheat harvest 53; citrus fruits 78; sheep 93; iron ore shipped to England 117, 246; copper 119; tin 120, 275; lead 121, 275; position as mining country 122; coal and water power 125; railway mileage 183; industries 264; raw silk 273, 279; flax 279; commerce 281, 309; area and population 329
Spices 250, 260
Spokane (Washington) 259, 335
Stassfurt (Germany) 268, 290
Steamships. *See* Ships
Steel. *See* Iron
Stettin (Germany) 268, 332
Stone 112, 113, 117, 140, 313
Subsidies, to shipping 310
Suakin. *See* Port Sudan
Suez Canal 198, 199, 206, 229, 230, 246
Sugar, production of 68–73,* 292, 312; consumption of, in United States 69, 73, 292; refineries 250, 258, 260, 262, 263, 268; imports of, into United States 292, 293; from Asia 321; from South America 336
Sugar beets 69–71,* 73, 268, 275, 292

Sugar cane 68,* 69,* 71–73,* 150, 292
Superior (Wisconsin) 206, 335
Susquehanna River, and valley 211
Swamp lands 36, 37, 181
Sweden, rye 41; wheat 53; oats 57; iron and steel 114, 117, 246, 271; copper 119; mining 122; coal and water power 125; forests 140; railways 178, 183; manufacturing 264, 271; commerce 281, 309; area and population 329
Sweet potatoes 63, 312
Swine, world production 92,* 93; in United States 98, 100; in Asia and Australia 312
Switzerland, cotton manufacturing 19; size 29*; apples 76; sheep 92; exports of cheese to United States 95; minerals 122; roads 173; railways 183; industries 235–264, 270, 290; farming 280*; commerce 281, 309; area and population 329
Sydney (Australia) 90, 190, 215, 332
Syracuse (New York) 252, 335
Syria 318, 328

Tacoma (Washington) 138, 259, 335
Taft, William H. 129
Tanganyika, Lake 231
Tangier (Morocco) 228, 230
Tanning 244, 245, 250
Tanta (Egypt) 228
Tar 268
Tariff, United States, on textiles 20, 25, 246; on sugar 292; on woolen industries 294; effect of, on United States trade with possessions 307
Tashkent (Russia-in-Asia) 165, 333
Tasmania 176, 328
Tea 159, 162, 290, 291, 293, 313, 321
Temperature, United States and Canada 4,* 5,* 30; world 30,* 31*; for wheat 42, 43*; for corn 47, 49; for rice 49, 50; for rye 58; for sugar plants 69, 70, 71; for apples 75; for citrus fruits 76, 77, 78; for peaches 80; relation to efficiency 235
Tennessee, cotton 5; time of wheat harvest 53; minerals 117, 325; area and population 326; value of manufacturing 327
Texas, rice 49*; time of wheat harvest 53; watermelons 64; coal 125; forests and lumber 36, 141; railways 187; cotton 213; potash 290; sugar cane 292; minerals 325; area and population 326; manufacturing 327
Textiles, in United States 250, 251,* 252, 257, 258, 265, 266, 267, 268, 269, 270, 273,* 291; of India 273, 318; Great Britain's competition in 276; imports of, by United States 291; by South America 302. *See also* Cotton, Flax, Silk, Wool

## Index

Tin, world production 112, 120,* 275; in Africa 231; imported by United States 289, 290, 293; in Asia 313, 321; in Australia 313; from South America 336
Tobacco 212, 270, 293, 312, 321, 336
Tokio (Japan) 271, 333
Toledo (Ohio) 219, 330
Toronto (Ontario) 220, 225, 226, 260
Toys 290
Tractors 168
Trade, balance of 297, 305
Transcaspia 181, 328
Transcaucasia 8, 130, 312
Transportation 1–8; good vs. poor roads 9,* 168, 169, 170, 174; of cotton 9, 10, 24; and farming 34; of fruits 76,* 78, 79, 81, 82; of cattle 87, 100; of petroleum 127, 130, 131*; of logs 132*; backward in South America 145; field of 158–233*; by water 158*; means of 159–173*; problems in 171–174; by railroad 175–188*; use of ships 189–206*; on the Great Lakes 192–194*; by canal 196–201*; and location of cities in United States 207–223*; trade routes of British North America 225–227*; of Africa 228–233; and location of industries, in United States 239, 243, 252, 254; in Europe 265, 266,* 267, 269, 276, 281; cost of, in Asia, 314, 317
Transshipment 161, 194, 207, 220
Transvaal, gold 120
Tripoli (Italian Africa) 228, 230
Tropics, vegetable growing 64; fruits 76, 78, 79,* 82*; woods 140
Troy (New York) 252, 335
Truck gardening 61*
Tunis 228, 230, 328, 331
Turkestan 8, 44,* 312, 328
Turkey, rice 50; wheat 53; sheep and wool 92, 294; transportation 165,* 317; goat skins 245; rugs 272; foreign commerce 309, 318; primary products 312–313; area and population 328, 329
Turpentine 136, 239, 257
Tyne River 266
Typewriters 252

United Kingdom. See Great Britain
United States, cotton 3, 5,* 7,* 9, 15, 17,* 19*; temperature 4,* 5,* 36*; rainfall 6, 30; range of climate 32; farming population 27, 32; conditions affecting farming 28–36*; area 28–29,* 326, 329; advantage of new soil 33; transportation facilities 34; government aid to farming 34, 38; irrigation 35,* 36; public works 35; value of farm lands 36; arid and swamp lands 37*; average value of crops 37; wheat 40, 42, 43,* 55; corn 47,* 48,* 56; rice 49,* 60; consumption of cereals and meat 57; oats 57*; barley 60*; vegetables 61–67*; sugar 68–73*; fruits 74–78,* 80–82*; animal farming 83–101,* 165; dairy products 94, 95; hay and forage 100*; fisheries 102–109*; minerals and mining industry 110–122*; coal 123–126,* 127; petroleum and natural gas 126, 128–131*; forests and lumbering 132–139,* 141–143*; imports of rubber and coffee 151; primary production 156; railway transportation 167, 175, 183, 185, 186,* 204,* 206, 207, 209,* 210, 211,* 214,* 216, 217,* 218,* 219, 220, 317; motor transportation 167, 317; improved roads 170; canals 197; Panama Canal 198, 199–202*; location of cities 207; seaports 208–216*; lake ports 216–221*; value of imports and exports at principal ports 221; climatic conditions and industrial development 235; manufacturing 247–263,* 277, 327; census 261; production of cotton, wool, hides, lead, zinc 275; jute from Mexico 276; competition in textiles 276; as market 287–297*; purchasing power 287; how far self-sufficient 289; value of domestic trade 289; imports 289–295, 296, 297; exports 295, 299–301; balance of trade with Brazil 297; with India 297; foreign trade 299–310*; population 326, 329
Uruguay, cattle 83, 89, 90; industrial development 272; commerce 304, 309, 336; area and population 329; exports 336
Utah, sugar beets 70, 292; minerals 118, 120, 125, 325; railways 187; area and population 326; manufacturing 327
Utica (New York) 252, 335

Valparaiso (Chile) 146, 147, 149, 201, 304, 331, 336
Vancouver (British Columbia) 190, 225, 226, 260
Vaselin 128
Vegetables 61–67,* 238, 312, 313
Vehicles 160,* 161,* 162, 163, 164,* 165,* 167, 168
Venezuela, petroleum 130*; cacao 150; commerce 308; area and population 329; exports 336
Verdun (France) 267
Vermont, railway mileage 187; area and population 326; manufacturing 327
Verviers (Belgium) 270
Vetarrabia Canal 38*
Victoria (Australia) 315
Victoria (British Columbia) 225
Virgin Islands 327, 329
Virginia, wheat 53; minerals 117, 325; area and population 326; manufacturing 327

Vistula River 195

Wales, area and population 329
Warsaw (Poland) 271
Washington, wheat in, 42, 46, 53; dairy cattle 85*; sheep 90*; fisheries 105, 108; forests and lumber 135, 138, 141, 216; fish canning 238, 259; coal and industries 259; minerals 325; area and population 326; value of manufacturing 327
Washington, Mt. 180
Watches 250, 270
Water buffalo 51, 87
Water power, in New England 15; utilized for industries 125, 237, 247, 249, 252, 259, 263*; and location of industries 235, 237,* 238,* 243; in United States 238*; in Asia and Australia 312
Water transportation, on Great Lakes 116, 217, 219, 220; shipping routes of world 158*; compared with railway transportation 166, 206; less used in United States than in Europe 183; use of ships 189–206*; of northeastern United States 249; of western Europe 265, 266; in Japan 319*
Waterbury (Connecticut) 242, 335
Waterford (New York) 186
Wax 336
Weaving 12,* 13, 14
Welland Canal 198, 226
West Indies, sugar cane 71; bananas 78, 79; problem in primary production of 154–156; tropical fruits and nuts 289. See also Cuba
West Shore Railroad 193, 210
West Virginia, coal 124, 212; size 270; minerals 325; area and population 326; manufacturing 327
Whale meat 109
Wheat, in Dakotas 33, 34; varieties 40,* 42, 43; where the staple food 40; improved through cultivation 41; production of 42–47*; in the United States 42, 43,* 53, 193; elsewhere in world 43, 54*; harvesting 44,* 45,* 53, 154, 160; world's imports and exports 55; yield per acre 55; exported from South America 148, 149, 152; storage 191*; transportation 192, 193, 205, 220, 227; in Canada 224,* 227; milling 234, 253, 256, 259, 262, 266, 272; in Europe 267, 278; in Great Britain 275; in Hungary 275; in Asia and Australia 312; in Siberia 316
White Mountains 139
White Sea 103
Whitney, Eli 3
Wilkes Barre (Pennsylvania) 211, 241, 335
Willamette Valley 215, 259
Windsor (Ontario) 225

Wine 79, 81, 230
Winnipeg (Manitoba) 225, 226, 227, 260
Winnipeg, Lake 227
Wisconsin, barley 60; potatoes 62; apples 75; dairying 94, 238; lumber 253; railway mileage 187; minerals 325; area and population 326; manufacturing 327
Witwatersrand (South Africa) 233
Wood, uses of 132, 135, 136, 137, 140, 141; from forests of North America 135–137; in Europe 140, 279; tropical 140; conservation by chemicals 143; imports into United States 293; in Asia and Australia 312
Wood alcohol 129
Wood pulp 27. See also Paper
Wool 91, 92, 93; exported from South America 148, 152; from Africa 230, 231; where produced 275; imported into United States 293, 294; fine and coarse, 294; in Asia and Australia 312. See also Sheep
Woolen industry, in United States 242, 250, 252, 271, 291, 294; in Great Britain 265; in France 267; in Germany 268; in Belgium 270; in China 318; in Japan 319
World, rainfall xii; cotton production of 7*; average temperature 30,* 31*; wheat 43, 54,* 55; rice 50*; corn 54*; oats 54*; potatoes 63*; sugar 71*; cattle 89*; sheep 92*; swine 92*; fishing grounds 103*; production of iron 114*; copper 119*; gold and silver 120*; tin 120*; lead 121*; zinc 121*; coal 125*; petroleum 130*; shipping routes 158*; railway mileage 183, 184,* 185; energy of peoples 236*; manufacturing 243*; density of population 284*; area and population of chief countries and colonies 328, 329
World War 5, 42, 152, 268, 287
Wright Flying Field 169*
Wyoming, sheep and wool 93, 179*; area 175; railway mileage 175, 187; minerals 325; area and population 326; value of manufacturing 327

Yak 163
Yams 64
Yokohama (Japan) 162, 201, 332
Yonkers (New York) 210, 335
Youngstown (Ohio) 253, 335
Yucatán, sisal from 289
Yugoslavia, copper 119; raw silk 279; foreign commerce 281, 309; area and population 329

Zinc, world production 112, 121*; in United States 113, 275, 325; in Poland 121; in Germany 275; production in Asia and Australia 313
Zurich (Switzerland) 167,* 270